Jihadi Culture

Thomas Hegghammer is senior research fellow at the Norwegian Defence Research Establishment (FFI) and adjunct professor in the Department of Political Science at the University of Oslo. Trained in Middle East Studies at the University of Oxford and at Sciences-Po, Paris, he has held fellowships at Harvard, Princeton, New York, and Stanford Universities and at the Institute for Advanced Study in Princeton. He is the author of the prize-winning *Jihad in Saudi Arabia* (Cambridge, 2010) and many other books and articles on jihadism. He has conducted extensive field-work in the Middle East, including interviews with former militants, and he has testified on jihadism in the U.S. Congress and the British Parliament.

Jihadi Culture

The Art and Social Practices
of Militant Islamists

THOMAS HEGGHAMMER
Norwegian Defence Research Establishment (FFI)

CAMBRIDGE
UNIVERSITY PRESS

CAMBRIDGE
UNIVERSITY PRESS

University Printing House, Cambridge CB2 8BS, United Kingdom

One Liberty Plaza, 20th Floor, New York, NY 10006, USA

477 Williamstown Road, Port Melbourne, VIC 3207, Australia

4843/24, 2nd Floor, Ansari Road, Daryaganj, Delhi – 110002, India

79 Anson Road, #06–04/06, Singapore 079906

Cambridge University Press is part of the University of Cambridge.

It furthers the University's mission by disseminating knowledge in the pursuit of education, learning, and research at the highest international levels of excellence.

www.cambridge.org
Information on this title: www.cambridge.org/9781107017955
DOI: 10.1017/9781139086141

© Cambridge University Press 2017

First published 2017
Reprinted 2017

Printed in the United Kingdom by TJ International Ltd. Padstow Cornwall

A catalogue record for this publication is available from the British Library.

Library of Congress Cataloging-in-Publication Data
Names: Hegghammer, Thomas, editor.
Title: Jihadi culture : the art and social practices of militant Islamists / [edited by] Thomas Hegghammer.
Description: Cambridge, United Kingdom : Cambridge University Press, 2017. | Includes bibliographical references and index.
Identifiers: LCCN 2016054366| ISBN 9781107017955 (Hardback : alk. paper) | ISBN 9781107614567 (pbk. : alk. paper)
Subjects: LCSH: Jihad. | Jihad in literature. | Islamic music–History and criticism. | Islamic countries–Civilization.
Classification: LCC BP182 .J54155 2017 | DDC 297.7/2–dc23 LC record available at https://lccn.loc.gov/2016054366

ISBN 978-1-107-01795-5 Hardback
ISBN 978-1-107-61456-7 Paperback

To the memory of Patricia Crone

Contents

Illustrations	*page* ix	
Tables	x	
Acknowledgments	xi	
About the Contributors	xiii	
	Introduction: What Is Jihadi Culture and Why Should We Study It? *Thomas Hegghammer*	1
1	Poetry in Jihadi Culture *Robyn Creswell and Bernard Haykel*	22
2	A Cappella Songs (*anashid*) in Jihadi Culture *Nelly Lahoud*	42
3	A Musicological Perspective on Jihadi *anashid* *Jonathan Pieslak*	63
4	The Visual Culture of Jihad *Afshon Ostovar*	82
5	A History of Jihadi Cinematography *Anne Stenersen*	108
6	The Islamic Dream Tradition and Jihadi Militancy *Iain R. Edgar and Gwynned de Looijer*	128
7	Contemporary Martyrdom: Ideology and Material Culture *David B. Cook*	151
8	Non-military Practices in Jihadi Groups *Thomas Hegghammer*	171

Bibliography   202
Notes   221
Index   264

Illustrations

2.1 Distribution by topic of *anashid* in sample collection   *page* 56

4.1 Flag of the Tamil Tigers and the emblem of al-Shabab   85

4.2 Emblems of (left to right) Iranian Revolutionary Guards, Lebanese Hezbollah, and Kata'ib Hezbollah   86

4.3 Emblems of (left to right) Jamaat-ud-Dawa, Jaysh-e Muhammad, and Sipah-e Sahaba   86

4.4 The flag of Islamic State   89

4.5 Flags of al-Qaida and associated jihadi groups   92

4.6 Minbar al-Tawhid wa'l-Jihad (c. 2011), Kuwait jihad (c. 2005)   94

4.7 Nusra Front, "Day of the Infiltration" (2012)   95

4.8 Jundallah poster (c. 2010) and Global Islamic Media Front advertisement (c. 2005)   96

4.9 Mujahid as superhero (left) and Marvel's The Punisher (right)   98

4.10 "Khattab, Lion of Chechnya ..." (c. 2005)   99

4.11 "Lion of Tawhid: Abu Umar al-Maqdisi" (2012)   100

4.12 "O Martyr, You Have Illuminated!" (2010)   101

4.13 "Calls" to Paradise Jama' (c. 2005) and AQAP (c. 2011)   102

4.14 Iranian Baluch martyrs (c. 2010) and Usama bin Ladin in Paradise (2010)   103

4.15 Ansar al-Mujahidin Internet forum art competition submissions   106

Tables

8.1 Key primary source documents   *page* 175

Acknowledgments

This book owes its existence to many extraordinary people and institutions. As the editor, I thank the Institute for Advanced Study in Princeton for hosting me as a William D. Loughlin fellow in 2009–2010, when I had the idea for the book. The Institute's quiet surroundings, Princeton's stimulating intellectual environment, and Patricia Crone's enthusiastic encouragement helped nurture the project in its crucial early stages. Moreover, the Institute hosted me again as a summer visitor in 2015, enabling me to undertake the final editorial work. In the meantime, I had enjoyed the generous support of Stanford University's Centre for International Security and Cooperation (CISAC), which gave me a Zuckerman Fellowship in 2012–2013 to work on jihadi culture, among other things. At Stanford, CISAC's research director Lynn Eden was a particularly strong supporter of the project and a very useful discussion partner.

I am extremely grateful to the Norwegian Defence Research Establishment (FFI) for supporting the project throughout the six years it took to complete. In an age where research is increasingly expected to offer short-term policy relevance, Espen Skjelland and Espen Berg-Knutsen let me spend considerable time on the seemingly esoteric topic of jihadi culture. FFI also funded two workshops at which the contributors got together to discuss early drafts of their chapters. One workshop was held in Oslo in July 2011, the other in Washington, DC, in December 2011. For the Washington meeting, Odd-Inge Kvalheim and Olav Heian-Engdahl at the Norwegian Embassy kindly helped with advice on logistics.

The book has also benefited from stimulating discussions at seminars on jihadi culture held at University of California–Berkeley, the University of Exeter, University of Oxford, University of St Andrews, the U.S. State Department, and the Oslo Student Society. I am also extremely grateful to the many people who have contributed ideas and source material for the book, including Christopher Anzalone, J. M.

Berger, Michael Cook, Martha Crenshaw, Manni Crone, Alexander De la Paz, James Fearon, Diego Gambetta, Amir Goldberg, Ron Hassner, Ann-Sophie Hemmingsen, Elisabeth Kendall, Stéphane Lacroix, Brynjar Lia, Will McCants, Flagg Miller, Petter Nesser, Joanna Paraszczuk, Behnam Said, Alex Strick van Linschoten, Jeremy Weinstein, Elisabeth Wood, and Aaron Zelin. The list is undoubtedly incomplete, and I apologize to all whose name escaped me as I wrote this note.

I am also grateful to the editors at Cambridge University Press, in particular Marigold Acland and her successor, Maria Marsh. Both enthusiastically supported the project throughout and displayed exceptional patience as we missed deadline after deadline. Last, but not least, I want to thank Juan Masullo, whose meticulous copyediting improved both the content and the form of the manuscript.

The names I have mentioned here are only those that I, the book's editor, relied on. The nine other authors no doubt have additional people to thank. We are all acutely aware that we stand on the shoulders of an entire community of writers. We hope that the same community will appreciate this humble contribution to the literature and forgive its errors.

About the Contributors

David B. Cook is associate professor of religion at Rice University.

Robyn Creswell is assistant professor of comparative literature at Yale University and poetry editor of *The Paris Review*.

Gwynned de Looijer is honorary research fellow in anthropology at Durham University.

Iain R. Edgar is emeritus reader in anthropology at Durham University.

Bernard Haykel is professor of Near Eastern studies at Princeton University.

Thomas Hegghammer is senior research fellow at the Norwegian Defence Research Establishment (FFI) and adjunct professor of political science at the University of Oslo.

Nelly Lahoud is senior fellow for political Islamism at the International Institute for Strategic Studies–Middle East.

Afshon Ostovar is assistant professor of National Security Affairs at the Naval Postgraduate School.

Jonathan Pieslak is professor of music at the City College of New York.

Anne Stenersen is director of terrorism studies at the Norwegian Defence Research Establishment (FFI).

Introduction: What Is Jihadi Culture and Why Should We Study It?

THOMAS HEGGHAMMER

This book is the first in-depth exploration of the cultural dimension of jihadism. We wrote it because so many others cover the operational stuff. There is no shortage of works on the operations, structures, and resources of radical groups, and many studies of jihadi ideology focus on political objectives, strategic thinking, or views on tactics. But militancy is about more than bombs and doctrines. It is also about rituals, customs, and dress codes. It is about music, films, and story-telling. It is about sports, jokes, and food. Look inside any radical group – or conventional army for that matter – and you will see daily life inside it filled with a range of artistic products and social practices that serve no obvious strategic purpose: Think of the songs of leftist revolutionaries, the tattoos of neo-Nazis, or the cadence calls of the U.S. Marines. This soft dimension of military life tends to get much less attention than the guns and the blaze, no doubt because it is seen as less consequential. After all, who cares what warriors do in their spare time?

This book does, and it will show that jihadis have a rich aesthetic culture that is essential for understanding their mindset and worldview. Readers who have not studied or frequented radical Islamists will find parts of this subculture surprising. We will see, for example, that jihadis love poetry, that they talk regularly about dreams, and that they weep – a lot. We will also see that jihadism has fostered an entire music industry, as well as a massive body of film productions. Jihadis may have a reputation as ruthless macho men – and there is some truth to that – but they also value personal humility, artistic sensitivity, and displays of emotion.

Aside from being inherently interesting, the cultural practices of rebel groups pose a social scientific puzzle in that they defy expectations of utility-maximizing behavior. Jihadis are usually hunted men; they are sought by their enemies and dispose of limited time and resources. We should expect them to spend all their time honing their bomb-making skills, raising funds, or studying the enemy's weak-nesses. Yet they "waste" time on poetry recitation, hymn singing, and other activities that serve no apparent strategic purpose. And it is not just that they do it – they do it *a lot*, which suggests it is significant to their whole enterprise. Non-military products and practices fill a surprisingly large proportion of life in the jihadi underground. This is especially true of groups operating in high-repression environments, like Western cities, where outdoor military training is impossible and operations rare. But even in war zones and training camps we see jihadis spend hours each day praying, listening to hymns, telling stories, watching jihadi videos, and interpreting dreams. Moreover, these products and practices feature prominently at the earliest stages of the recruits' induction into jihadi groups. Many new recruits seem to indulge in jihadi music and videos long before they see any fighting and before they sit down to learn the finer points of doctrine. All of this suggests that non-military products and practices matter for how groups recruit and operate.

This book has two objectives: one limited, the other far-reaching. The first is to introduce readers to the jihadi aesthetic universe. We do so by describing, chapter by chapter, seven prominent genres or elements of jihadi culture: poetry, music, iconography, cinematog-raphy, dream interpretation, martyrology, and social practices. Our ambition here is limited insofar as we seek only to explore a selection of genres, not to exhaust the topic. The second and most important objective is to highlight the wealth and significance of jihadi culture and inspire others to do more research on it. We believe there is room and need for an entire research program on the cultural and aesthetic dimensions of jihadism, and later in this introduction I sketch out some possible lines of inquiry.

The big idea in this book is that what scholars have tended to refer to as "ideology" is really two different things: doctrine and aesthetics. Many academics today would say that jihadi poetry and hymns belong to the realm of ideology, for which we already have a lively research program. However, the literature on jihadism has mostly treated ideol-ogy as synonymous with doctrine, that is, a set of ideas transmitted through language and internalized through cognition. Students of jihadi ideology – this author included – have tended to examine texts, dissect-ing their theological or political reasoning in the hope of identifying salient tenets, objectives, and preferences. While things like poetry and music have not gone entirely unstudied, they have certainly received much less attention than doctrinal treatises. Yet poetry and music must do something more or something different than simply convey doctrinal principles, because otherwise activists would not bother creating them, but write terse prose instead. If hymns are doctrine in musical form, what does the sound do? If poetry is theology in flowery language, are the metaphors and cadence all fluff? This book does not purport to know exactly what that "something more or something different" is – though I present some hypotheses below – but it does argue that the only way to find out is to devote more intellectual attention to the cultural-aesthetic dimension of jihadi ideology.

We do not claim to have discovered jihadi culture and aesthetics, because substantial work has already been done on individual elements of it. Some of the contributors to this volume, such as Jonathan Pieslak, Iain Edgar, and Afshon Ostovar, have already written on their respective topics (music, dreams, and iconography) elsewhere.[1] Other important contributions to the literature include Kendall and Holtmann on jihadi poetry, Said and Lemieux and Nill on jihadi music, Holtmann and Weisburd on jihadi iconography, Farwell and El Difraoui on jihadi films, and Sirriyeh on jihadi dreams, to mention just a few.[2] There is also a related literature on other militant Islamist groups; for example, Alagha's work on the music and dance of Hizballah, Pelevin and Weinreich's work on the songs of the Taliban, Alshaer on the poetry of Hamas and Hizballah, and Strick van Lindschoten and Kuehn on the poetry of the Taliban.[3] Looking beyond the Islamist universe, we find many more publications, from Reed's book *The Art of Protest* via Anton Shekhovtsov's work on the music of the extreme right to Cheryl Herr's study of "terrorist chic" in Northern Ireland.[4] Still, relatively few attempts have been made at linking the study of these various cultural expressions and exploring culture and aesthetics as a category of rebellious activity.

A number of academics have identified the broader phenomenon we are describing in this book – or something close to it. Alagha, for example, has written about Islamist uses of – and debates about – "resistance art" and "purposeful art," terms connoting ideologically motivated art forms such as dancing, music, and literature.[5] Halldén has described jihadi poetry as part of the "aesthetic dimension of al-Qaida's culture wars," and Crone has analyzed the role of "aesthetic assemblages" and "aesthetic technologies" such as jihadi videos and hymns in the radicalization of Muslims in Denmark.[6] Writing about salafism in Germany, Dantshke pointed out the development of a "genuine Jihad based youth culture" or "Pop-jihad," with its own music ("Battle-nasheeds"), apparel, and ideological iconography.[7] Several scholars have also talked about the "counterculture" dimension of jihadism in the West and its significant role in drawing young Muslims into extremism. Sageman, for example, notes that "these [jihadi] symbols and rituals amount to a lifestyle, which participants view as 'cool'. Thus they create a 'jihadi cool' counterculture."[8] Hemmingsen concluded her ethnographic study of jihadis in Denmark by noting that they "perceived themselves as sharing something – something which included worldviews, norms, dress codes, language and insights ... this 'shared we' can best be understood as a counterculture."[9] All these scholars seem to have put their finger on roughly the same thing as we are describing in this book, but they did not examine its constituent parts in much detail. The most prominent exception is Herding's recent book *Inventing the Muslim Cool*, which does go into depth, but it looks at Western Muslim youth culture more broadly, not militants specifically.[10]

It is worth noting here that the term "jihad culture" or "jihadi culture" has also been used in the past to describe somewhat different things than what we have in mind in this book. For example, Jessica Stern has written about "Pakistan's jihad culture" in the sense of a culture of armed struggle, and Michael Taarnby and Lars Hallundbæk have described the "culture of jihad" in the Lebanese group Fatah al-Islam, but in the sense of a culture of religious warfare.[11] Similarly, Jeffrey Cozzens employed the term "culture of global jihad" to describe attitudes, values, and beliefs that we in this book would mostly sort under the label doctrine.[12] Gilbert Ramsey's book *Jihadi Culture on the World Wide Web* appears to understand culture in a broader sense of "the entirety of jihadi activity" (my formulation) in the online domain.[13] It is an interesting book that sheds important light on life in the digital jihadi underground, but its definition of culture is substantially broader than ours.

Defining Jihadi Culture

So what exactly are we talking about? Readers will already have noticed a glaring terminological inconsistency. I have already used several different terms to describe our research object, including "the cultural dimension of jihadism," "the soft dimension of military life," "what terrorists do in their spare time," "aesthetic culture," "subculture," "non-military products and practices," and "things like poetry and music." Clearly, whatever we are dealing with is slippery and is not easily captured by existing terminology.

In this book we use the term "jihadi culture" for lack of a better one. It does, however, require some elaboration, because culture is itself a loose and contested concept. The academic literature on culture is vast, and the available definitions equally numerous.[14] Our usage is closest to definition 7a of "culture" in the *Oxford English Dictionary*: "the distinctive ideas, customs, social behaviour, products, or way of life of a particular nation, society, people, or period."[15] However, we have in mind something slightly more specific than that. We are indeed interested in the "ideas, customs, social behaviour, products, or way of life" of jihadis, but only those that do not have an obvious military-strategic purpose. Central to our definition of culture, in other words, is the idea of apparent superfluousness.

We define jihadi culture as *products and practices that do something other than fill the basic military needs of jihadi groups*. This understanding of culture is very close to what the anthropologist Edmund Leach called "technically superfluous frills and decorations." The following passage from his classic study of the Kachins (an ethnic group in northern Burma) is a good illustration of what we seek to capture:

For example, if it is desired to grow rice, it is certainly essential and functionally necessary to clear a piece of ground and sow seed in it. And it will no doubt improve the prospects of a good yield if the plot is fenced and the growing crop weeded from time to time. Kachins do all these things and, in so far as they do this, they are performing simple technical acts of a functional kind. These actions serve to satisfy "basic needs." But there is much more to it than that ... the routines of clearing the ground, planting the seeds, fencing the plot and weeding the growing crop are all patterned according to formal conventions and interspersed with all kinds of technically superfluous frills and decorations. It is these frills and decorations which make the performance a Kachin performance and not just a simple functional act. And so it is with every kind of technical action; there is always the element which is functionally essential, and another element which is simply the local custom, and aesthetic frill.[16]

Now think of a rebel group. It has certain "basic needs," such as the capacity to deploy violence and the ability to muster material resources for its continued survival. These needs can, conceivably, be fulfilled in a minimalist, no-frills fashion: you train, fight, raise funds, purchase weapons, write communiqués, get some sleep, repeat the next day. To put it simply, these are the functionally essential elements of rebellion; everything else is culture. A militant group cannot operate without military expertise or weaponry, but it should be able to do without music or dream interpretation. Soldiers need durable clothes, but they do not need a variety of soft hats. The group may need to communicate its political objectives to enemies and recruits, but it does not need to do so through poetry. Thus, the litmus test for whether something sorts as jihadi culture under our definition is whether it is functionally essential to the military effort.

Militant Islamists do a lot of these unnecessary things, as do probably all other military organizations on the planet. Sometimes they also do things that are not only superfluous, but also outright counterproductive. As we shall see in Chapter 9, jihadi memoirs contain many examples of people insisting on some practice – such as excessive fasting, refusing to lie on the stomach, or shooting in the air to celebrate – even though it made them more vulnerable to enemy attacks. Another indication that something is culture is that it has a starkly different value in another military organization. Functionally essential tasks are largely the same across all militant groups, for there are only so many ways to fire a gun. Culture, on the other hand, varies. Hence poetry can be highly valued in Hamas, while the Israeli military frowns upon poetry as unmanly. (The IDF once refused to let a soldier read poetry on military radio so as not to ruin the organization's image.)[17]

This is all well and good, but what does it mean specifically? Where exactly does the functionally essential stop and the culture begin? This question is very difficult to answer fully, but we can be a bit more specific. Most elements of jihadi culture will be observable products or practices. Products are artifacts such as poems, songs, images, and films. They are static in form and portable from one context to another. Practices are acts, often (but not always) involving the consumption of a product. It is the singing of a song, the performance of a ritual, the wearing of certain clothes, or the talking about dreams. Some elements of jihadi culture combine multiple products and practices. The ceremony of the martyr's wedding, for example (see Chapter 9), combines singing of *anashid*, dancing, shouting *"allahu akbar,"* firing guns in the air (if possible), and the future martyr being well-groomed.

It is important to note that things do not need to be particularly exotic or sophisticated to be cultural. Even though we have so far highlighted poetry and music, we are not seeking to identify a jihadi "high culture." We are equally interested in the ordinary and mundane, such as the cooking, favorite sports, or jokes of militant Islamists. We are even interested in their toilet habits (see Chapter 9). And if silence were an important part of social interaction among jihadis (it is not), we would study that, too, even though it is literally nothing.

Moreover, a product or practice need not be unique to jihadi groups to be considered an element of jihadi culture. Jihadis do a lot of things that also non-militant Muslims do, like pray, play sports, or eat with the right hand. In fact, as we shall see in this book, most elements of jihadi culture are not specific to jihadis; the appreciation for poetry and a penchant for dream interpretation are entirely of the ordinary in the Muslim world. What is specific to jihadis is the particular combination or cluster of practices that they entertain, as well as the ideological tinge to the products they consume. (Poetry as a genre has nothing jihadi about it, but poems praising suicide bombers do.)

The most challenging part of any definitional exercise is treating borderline phenomena, and in the case of jihadi culture, there are several. One is the fascination many jihadis have with war, weapons, and military effects. Military activities really are a very big part of life in a jihadi group, especially those that have training camps or operate in conflict zones. To say that war and weaponry is not part of jihadi culture defies common sense; after all, the willingness to perpetrate violence is one of their defining traits as a social group. Besides, it is not always clear which military practices are functionally essential. Take the soldier who names his gun and sleeps with it. This is a near-universal practice in military organizations, including in jihadi groups.[18] Is it strictly necessary in order to be an effective soldier? Perhaps. That said, the jihadi fascination with things martial sometimes clearly goes beyond the purely functional. In Western cities, for example, radical Islamists often wear military-style camouflage jackets over their Middle Eastern–style robes, even if they are just going to the grocery store. Most jihadis also seem to like exchanging stories about Muslim battle exploits from early Islamic history, even though nobody fights with swords or on horseback anymore. These practices are easier to describe as cultural, but many others defy easy classification.

The same applies in the domain we may call the art of war. There may be more than one way to perform a military task, and a given group may have a preference for one or the other method. Is that variation an expression of culture? For example, when the Islamic State group in Syria executes prisoners by beheading instead of shooting – is that functional or cultural? Bear in mind that some Islamic state supporters defend the practice invoking efficiency, arguing that it is humane because the victim supposedly dies immediately (at least when it's done from the back of the neck in a single stroke).[19] The point to this gruesome example is that there are many military practices where the notion of functionally essential can be debated.

Another important gray area is the intersection between culture and doctrine. We can all agree that poetry or music belongs in the realm of culture, and that, say, al-Qaida's 1998 "Statement of the World Islamic Front for Jihad against Jews and Crusaders" is a doctrinal document.[20] But many examples of texts or propaganda videos mix terse political and theological arguments with more elaborate language, lines of poetry, historical references, or symbolic imagery. It is often difficult, if not impossible, to say exactly where, within a given document, doctrine stops and culture begins. And even if we were able to isolate the key ideas, beliefs, and arguments from the cultural scaffolding, how would we distinguish between those ideas that are "necessary" for the justification of the armed struggle and those that are not? Most of us would probably agree that the belief in dreams as a window into the future is less "necessary" for justifying al-Qaida's armed struggle than the conviction that American troops should not be stationed on Muslim lands. But for many other beliefs, it is a much more difficult call. Take the belief in afterlife rewards for fighters who die in battle. The core idea that something good awaits the fallen may be considered doctrine, because it provides an incentive for individual participation.[21] However, as we shall see in Chapter 8, this core idea is never expressed simply in the sentence "do it because you will be rewarded." It is always accompanied by a plethora of other more specific beliefs about what exactly happens in the afterlife and what specifically happens to the martyr's corpse when he dies. And these beliefs are often conveyed with supporting iconography or citations of poetry and scripture, complicating our classification task even further.

This is fuzzy conceptual terrain, and we do not claim to know exactly where the borders lie.

In this book we have chosen the safe route of treating mainly phenomena that fall in the relatively undisputed center of the jihadi culture category. If there is such a thing as functionally nonessential products or practices, then poetry, music, iconography, and the like are surely among them. In other words, we start in the middle of the category and hope that we as a scholarly community may work our way out to the borders as our understanding of the topic becomes more sophisticated. We expect and indeed hope that other scholars will criticize our conceptualization so that it can get sharper. It may well be that the term jihadi culture needs to be further disaggregated into more precise and operational terms. It may even need to be scrapped altogether for a better alternative. We are happy so long as the rough phenomenon we have sketched out above, whatever we end up calling it, gets more scholarly attention.

Actors and Contexts

Who are the people whose culture we propose to study? The term "jihadi," although now relatively established in the academic literature and news media, means slightly different things to different people. Put simply, jihadi today has both a broad and a narrow definition. In the broad definition, jihadi is a synonym for "violent Islamist" and may in principle apply to Islamist groups of all ideological orientations, so long as they wage violence. That means not only groups like al-Qaida, but also Shiite groups like Lebanese Hizballah and Muslim Brotherhood–affiliated Sunni groups such as Hamas. This is arguably the most parsimonious and logical of the two definitions, but it is the least common.

In the narrow and more frequently used definition, jihadi refers to a subset of particularly violent, conservative, and uncompromising Sunni groups, such as Islamic State and al-Qaida, their affiliates like Boko Haram and al-Qaida in the Islamic Maghreb, or their predecessors such as Egyptian Islamic Jihad and the Algerian Groupe Islamique Armée. These groups are sometimes also referred to as "salafi jihadis" due to their identification with salafism, a literalist approach to Sunni jurisprudence. They also tend to be grouped together for other reasons: their transnational outlook, their rejection of electoral politics, their reluctance to make truces or political compromises, and their near-exclusive focus on armed struggle as opposed to other political activities. The groups in this category also form what we may call an "epistemic community" in the sense that they see each other as parts of the same movement and partake, through online and offline publications, in a global conversation about theological, political, and strategic matters. Groups like Hamas and Hizballah and their supporters are usually not part of this conversation.

In this book, we are concerned with jihadi groups in the narrow sense. We will study the products and practices of al-Qaida, its various affiliates and associates, the foreign fighters who join these groups, and some of the earlier jihadi groups from the 1980s and 1990s. We will not be studying Hamas, Hezbollah, or the Taliban. This is first and foremost a practical decision, because a wider empirical scope would leave us with an unmanageable number of sources, and we would have to sacrifice a lot of depth for breadth. As we shall see, the epistemic community of jihadism is also a cultural one, in the sense that they have many products and practices in common. It takes only a brief look at other types of groups to spot cultural differences: Hezbollah's music, for example, has instruments and sounds very different from al-Qaida's a cappella *anashid,* while the Taliban enjoy traditional Afghan dances, unheard of in the Islamic State group.

Besides, the universe of groups we study in this book is more than diverse enough as it is. We are covering groups of widely different sizes, in different parts of the world, and in different time periods (from the 1980s to the 2010s). Clearly, there will be a broad range of group-specific products and practices, and we should be extremely careful to generalize about "what jihadis do" or "what jihadis enjoy." At the same time, a certain degree of generalization will be necessary, or else this book would come in thirty volumes. What we can do, however, is reflect for a few paragraphs on the ways in which groups in our empirical universe differ.

One obvious source of variation is time. From the 1980s to the 2000s, the technological environment of militant groups changed dramatically. The Internet, the digital camera, and eventually the smartphone made it much easier to produce audiovisual propaganda and exchange information between activists on different continents. The declining relative cost of air travel and the growth of the so-called foreign fighter phenomenon from the 1980s onward also led to more direct social interaction between militants in different regions. Technological change also affected the weaponry available to militants as well as the repressive tools used against them. (Nobody in the 1980s needed to worry about drones or Internet surveillance.)

Despite the increasing level of contact between groups in different regions, most groups have a geographical base and are marked by their environment. Recruits bring cultural references from their upbringing into the organization, and most groups adapt, consciously or not, to their surroundings. Given that culture and customs vary considerably across space, we should expect to see differences in the cultural products and practices of, for example, jihadis in Africa versus Asia, in Egypt versus Libya, and even in eastern versus western Libya.

Groups also differ in type. We shall not linger on group typologies, only highlight the particularly important ideal-type distinction between *large insurgent groups* and *small clandestine groups*. The former include groups such as the Islamic State, al-Shabab, or Boko Haram. These are typically large (thousands of members), hierarchical organizations that control territory and employ a combination of paramilitary and terrorist tactics. These groups tend to be relatively well embedded in the local population, which means that the supply of recruits is relatively high and the constraints on training and preparation relatively low. The *small clandestine groups* include organizations such as the Egyptian Islamic Jihad or the Saudi al-Qaida on the Arabian Peninsula. These are small (low hundreds of members), semi-structured organizations that do not hold territory and specialize in urban terrorist tactics. Their members live in safe houses in cities or towns, often surrounded by a population that does not share their agenda and by highly capable security services that seek to capture or kill them.

To understand the products and practices described in this book, it is also useful to mentally visualize the precise material surroundings in which jihadis spend their time. What we sometimes refer to as the "jihadi underground" can be many things, of course, because jihadis live in different places, and because they are invested in the struggle to different degrees. However, in the sources we examined to write this book, two ideal types of contexts recurred: what we may call the rural base and the urban safe house. The rural base is typically a cluster of brick houses or tents in an isolated location remote enough to allow for undisturbed weapons practice. Life here is rough and austere, often with no electricity, no running water, bad food, and hard physical

training. The urban safe house is an apartment or a house in a popu-
lated area. Inside it tends to be half empty, bachelor pad-style, with the
basic equipment to sleep, cook, study, and prepare operations. Here is
a description of a jihadi safe house in Paris in 2001:

> the two-room apartment was completely run-down. In one room there was
> bedding piled up. The other room was tidier: a foam-rubber mattress on the
> floor, religious books and audio cassettes on the mantelpiece, a stool, a prayer
> mat, a chair, and a military uniform was all that the room contained.[22]

Other videos and testimonies also suggest that the physical environment of the "jihadi underground" is often an aesthetically minimalist
one, reflecting, perhaps, salafi ideals of austerity or these groups'
frequent lack of money.

Our empirical scope has two important limitations. The first is that
we focus primarily on the period from the early 1980s to the early
2010s and therefore do not look in depth at the culture of Islamic State
(IS, aka ISIS or ISIL) or other groups that rose to prominence in the
Syrian civil war. Most of the chapters were written before the Islamic
State's spectacular expansion in mid-2014, and while we did revise the
manuscript to incorporate IS-related material, we chose not to study IS
in depth because it would have meant discarding earlier material to
make space for the new. This would have been unfortunate, because a
good understanding of earlier jihadi culture is a prerequisite for any
serious examination of IS culture.

A second limitation is that we do not study the online lives of jihadis,
but focus on activism in the physical world. Many jihadis are very
active online, and some operate almost exclusively in the digital
domain. Jihadi culture online is a topic that clearly requires in-depth
investigation, as does the relationship between the digital and the offline lives of militant Islamists. Substantial work has already been done
in this field, not least by the above mentioned Gilbert Ramsey, but
more can be done, for this is a rich and fast-evolving domain of social
interaction for jihadis.[23]

Toward a Research Program on Jihadi Culture

One book alone can only scratch the surface of jihadi culture. What we
hope to demonstrate, though, is that jihadi culture constitutes a rich
empirical domain that remains deeply underexplored. This opens up

an entire new research program with numerous intriguing lines of inquiry. We see at least two broad clusters of research questions that we hope will pique the curiosity of future scholars.

First is the task of *description:* What exactly do the jihadis do? The sheer number and complexity of products and practices and the range of groups that perform them mean that there is a substantial descriptive job to be done before any causal analysis can be conducted. We need more granular information about each element of jihadi culture, about what precisely it consists of and how exactly it is consumed or performed in context. This book treats only a small selection of topics, and it does not exhaust any one of them. We also did not conduct ethnographic work inside jihadi groups. This is of course difficult to do, but it should not be impossible for a scholar with the right skills, connections, and a bit of luck. But even without fieldwork, there are enough primary source documents to explore jihadi culture in more depth.

There remains an almost endless list of unanswered descriptive questions, which we can tentatively sort in three categories. First is the exploration of individual groups and individual elements of jihadi culture. What do Boko Haram members do in their spare time? Is there Uighur jihadi poetry? What exactly do jihadis in the West wear, and in which contexts? Do all members of a jihadi group weep, or do leaders do it more?

Better case descriptions should then allow for the examination of variation in time and space. Do different groups listen to different types of *anashid*? Which groups appreciate poetry more? Do Urdu-language cultural products differ from Arabic-language ones? How have the various elements of jihadi culture evolved since the 1980s?

Finally there is the intriguing issue of comparison with other types of groups and communities. How does jihadi culture differ from that of "mainstream" Muslims? How does the culture of al-Qaida differ from that of Hezbollah or Hamas? How is the Sunni-Shia divide reflected in the culture of militants? This is not to mention the comparison with non-Islamist militants, be it neo-Nazis, leftist revolutionaries, Jewish extremists, Basque separatists, or apocalyptic sects. A quick look at the universe of militant groups suggests enormous variation in the cultural domain, but also intriguing similarities. Many, if not all, groups have their own music, for example, and several non-jihadi groups have produced poetry. And it is not just jihadis who weep on a regular basis; some extreme right-wing activists do it too.

The second main cluster of questions revolves around *explanation:* Why do they do it? This is arguably the most important, but also the most challenging task. Within this cluster we have at least two different sets of inquiries. The first is accounting for variation, which, in social science terms, amounts to treating jihadi culture as a dependent variable. Why do different jihadi groups have somewhat different cultures? Why do some groups have more elaborate rituals, weep more, or listen more to *anashid* than others?

The second approach would treat jihadi culture as an independent variable and ask about the effects of jihadi culture, be it on the individual, the group, or the movement as a whole. This is perhaps the most intriguing aspect of the entire phenomenon, at least for social scientists. What does culture do for the jihadis? Why is it that most-wanted terrorists spend time on poetry and dream interpretation when they could be training or raising funds? How do cultural products and practices affect behavior, and by which mechanisms? What is the role of jihadi culture in individual radicalization, and which elements of jihadi culture are more salient in this regard? If jihadi culture does affect behavior, do leaders manipulate or curate their group's culture for strategic benefit?

Two Hypotheses

As already mentioned, this book is mainly about the *what*, not the *why* of jihadi culture. We describe a subset of products and practices and make a few observations about cross-group and chronological variation, but we do not venture far into the domain of explanation.

Still, it may be worth sketching out a couple of hypotheses about the relationship between jihadi culture and violent behavior, if only to illustrate how this topic can be approached by social scientists. The question "what does jihadi culture do?" is obviously extremely complex, and the answer, if there is one, probably depends on which particular product or practice we are talking about. Nevertheless, by drawing on other theoretical literatures, we might engage in some informed speculation about what the function or effect of jihadi culture as a whole might be. Recall here that the key conundrum is why hunted men spend time on apparently unnecessary activities. Let me suggest two hypotheses.

The first, inspired by the literature on signalling and mimicry, is that jihadi culture serves as a *resource for costly signs*.[24] High-risk activists often face a severe trust problem when dealing with new recruits or new interlocutors. The person who is presenting himself may be unreliable or, worse, a government agent seeking to infiltrate the group. Given that trustworthiness and authenticity are unobservable properties, "trusters" have to look for observable signs that are correlated with those properties. A sign can be the way a person looks, behaves, speaks, or something else. Because impostors are actively looking to mimic those same signs to pass themselves off as trustworthy, the sign-reading exercise – otherwise known as "vetting" – is far from than straightforward. Central to the trust game is the notion of sign cost, because some signs are easier to mimic than others. Talk is famously cheap, while congenital features, like skin color, are very hard to mimic. Signaling theory predicts that trusters will look for signs that are too costly to the mimic but affordable to the genuinely trustworthy. What this means in practice is intimately context-dependent, because a sign may be costly in one setting and not in another.

In the case of jihadi groups, displaying knowledge of jihadi culture – for example, a deep command of jihadi *anashid* – may be a costly sign because it takes time to acquire it. Familiarity with jihadi culture can thus be an indicator of time previously spent in the underground. Knowledge of certain products might also only be available in certain places – a particular *nashid* might have been sung only in the trenches of Bosnia – in which case singing that *nashid* is a proxy for the cost previously incurred by going to fight in Bosnia.

By the same logic, jihad culture can also be used to elicit commitment signs from recruits who enter the organization with little prior knowledge. That person's willingness to learn poems, *anashid,* and the finer points of ritual during the vetting period can be used as an indicator of commitment. Of course, displays of cultural knowledge are probably never used as the single indicator of trustworthiness; they likely enter into a broader cluster of signs that includes appearance, locution, personal connections, and much more. From a truster's point of view, however, the greater the range of possible signs to look for, the better. Because the jihadi cultural corpus is so rich and complex, it may well be a useful resource for vetting signs. There is some empirical evidence that this is the case, in both offline and online recruitment contexts.[25] We also know that certain jihadi groups have proved notoriously difficult to infiltrate for intelligence services, and at least one former U.S. intelligence officer has suggested that the complexities of culture have something to do with it.[26]

A second possibility is that cultural products and practices serve as *emotional persuasion tools* that reinforce and complement the cognitive persuasion work done by doctrine. Jihadi culture may help shape the beliefs and preferences of activists, ultimately affecting their decision to join, stay in, or perform certain tasks for the group. A common denominator of several elements of culture – such as music, imagery, storytelling, or weeping – is that they appear to evoke or involve emotion. Primary sources contain numerous examples of activists reporting a particular feeling while listening to *anashid*, watching videos, or reading poetry. We also know that individuals are exposed to cultural products early in their recruitment trajectories, and several explicitly say they were drawn to jihadism more by the videos and the music than by the ideological tracts. Moreover, a number of academic specialists have suggested that emotion may matter more than cognition in the radicalization process of jihadis in the West. Marc Sageman, for example, notes: "I have come to the conclusion that the terrorists in Western Europe and North America were not intellectuals or ideologues, much less religious scholars. It is not about how they think, but how they feel."[27] Claudia Dantshke observes that "The emotional appeal [of *anashid*] reaches mainly adolescents who neither are interested in long sermons online nor [in] visiting the famous 'Islam seminars' of the second generation Salafis."[28]

There are also indications that group leaders use cultural products deliberately for recruitment purposes (see notably Chapter 3). In 2000, a jihadi strategist nicknamed Abu Hudhayfa wrote a letter to Usama bin Ladin suggesting that al-Qaida should videotape a jihadi wedding and use it for propaganda:

the political division could undertake the appropriate preparations by way of featuring speeches, anashid, poems etc … Such an [advertising] product would therefore have profound meanings and psychological rewards that [though their impact] may vary from one person to the other, they would nevertheless flow into a principal [strategic] objective, namely causing [Muslims'] feelings to be moved.[29]

Similarly, the Yemeni-American jihadi preacher Anwar al-Awlaki, in a famous tract titled "44 Ways to Support Jihad," wrote the following about *anashid*:

Muslims need to be inspired to practice Jihad. In the time of Rasulullah (saaws) he had poets who would use their poetry to inspire the Muslims and demoralize the disbelievers. Today nasheed can play that role. A good nasheed can spread so widely it can reach to an audience that you could not reach through a lecture or a book. Nasheeds are especially inspiring to the youth, who are the foundation of Jihad in every age and time. Nasheeds are an important element in creating a "Jihad culture."[30]

And here is a description of a Yemeni jihadi using *anashid* to recruit:

Abeer Al Hassani's ex-husband was famed for his beautiful voice. He used it, she says, singing poetic hymns to martyrdom and jihad to try to draw youth from their neighbourhood of the Yemeni capital into joining Al Qaida. He sang at weddings of fellow members of the terror group, and held discussions with young men at local mosques.[31]

Of course, that videos and music can help persuade by evoking emotion is hardly a new idea; it is what propaganda and marketing is largely about. It is also something that regular militaries do to recruit "our" soldiers.

That said, not all elements of jihadi culture evoke or involve emotion to the same extent. It is easy to see why jihadis might want to have *anashid* with which to seduce recruits, but it is less obvious how this would explain why they are so concerned with dreams or why they dress the way they do. These two hypotheses, even if they both happen to be correct, only take us so far. Much more research will be needed before we understand the why of jihadi culture.

It should now be apparent that jihadi culture is hardly an esoteric subject, but one that has bearing on some fundamental questions about human behavior. How does culture vary across social groups and why? Why do even the busiest men invest time in art? What are the relative roles of cognition and emotion in individual decision making? Why do some people choose to participate in high-risk activism? Research on jihadi culture should therefore interest scholars from a broad range of disciplines, including Islamic studies, anthropology, sociology, psychology, political science, and even economics. In several of these disciplines there already are related research efforts and debates that may inform, and be informed by, the study of jihadi culture.

Research on jihadi culture is also highly policy-relevant, because it can shed new light on why people join extremist groups and why some groups and movements survive longer than others. This, in turn, can generate ideas on how to dissuade recruits and how to weaken the groups. If, for example, it turns out that emotional attraction rivals cognitive persuasion as a mechanism driving the radicalization of young Muslims, then we should, for instance, worry less about jihadi doctrinal documents and more about propaganda, videos, and radical *anashid*. Governments should perhaps also invest less in trying to develop a cognitively persuasive "counternarrative" and more in messaging that targets emotions. Local authorities might want to focus less on improving the economic situation of youth at risk of radicalization and more on offering "substitution activities" that provide emotional rewards similar to those obtained in the jihadi underground. These are but some of the possible policy implications of deeper insights into jihadi culture.

Outline of the Book

 The following eight chapters are each devoted to a discrete element of jihad culture. Chapters are organized roughly according to the complexity of the element in question; hence cinematography comes after music and iconography because it includes elements of both. Martyrology comes late because it involves several different types of cultural genres. There are two chapters on *anashid,* partly because *anashid* are one of the most prominent elements of jihadi culture, and partly because they have both a musical and a lyrical dimension, each of which merits separate treatment. The final chapter on social practices differs from the others in that it explores not one element of jihadi culture in depth, but rather tries to give a broad overview of jihadi daily life and a sense of how the various elements of jihadi culture relate to one another.

  The team of contributors is multidisciplinary and consists of scholars who had done extensive research on their respective cultural genre prior to embarking on this project. In the next chapter, Bernard Haykel and Robyn Creswell explore jihadi poetry, documenting its centrality in jihadi cultural corpus, its major themes and techniques, the role and status of jihadi poets, and its deep significance to its jihadi consumers. In the second chapter, Nelly Lahoud examines *anashid,* tracing the gradual liberalization of jihadi views on their permissibility, their decentralized production process, and evidence of their strategic use for morale-building purposes. In the third chapter, musicologist

Jonathan Pieslak describes emergence of jihadi *anashid* as a musical genre in the 1970s, the musical characteristics of modern *anashid*, and their reception among grassroots jihadis. In the fourth chapter, Afshon Ostovar looks at the jihadi visual culture, presenting major themes and recent developments in jihadi iconography. In the fifth chapter, Anne Stenersen traces the history of jihadi filmmaking since the early 1980s, with a focus on the production process, major themes, and techniques. In the sixth chapter, Iain Edgar and Gwynned de Looijer explore the jihadi fascination with dreams, describing when and how dreams are interpreted and by whom, the role of dreams in individual decision making, and the ways in which dream tradition can be used by leaders to claim authority and justify decisions. In the seventh chapter, David Cook examines the literary, audiovisual, and material products devoted to the celebration of martyrs in jihadi groups, tracing their many substantial changes over the past three decades. In the final chapter, I examine the many different social practices of jihadis, describing their form and relative prominence in the daily life of jihadis as documented in memoirs and other primary sources.

The most striking overall finding in the book is that jihadi culture appears to have become somewhat more "liberal" over time. We document a fascinating chronological evolution from the 1980s, when many radical Islamists were skeptical of hymns and imagery, to the 2010s, when audiovisual material is omnipresent in the movement. Moreover, jihadi culture has taken up more and more elements from the Sufi (Islamic mystical) tradition, which is counterintuitive because jihadis are by their own declaration extremely hostile to Sufism. Jihadis have, over time, developed a stronger appreciation for dream interpretation and weeping – both typically Sufi preoccupations – and martyrs are increasingly treated like liminal figures reminiscent of Sufi saints. They would never admit it, of course, but jihadis have in effect compromised on key salafi principles to accommodate new products and practices. Jihadis are not exactly the compromising kind, so these cultural appropriations must have proved useful in some way. To us, this is another strong indication that jihadi culture matters.

A Caveat

When writing about an understudied topic – perhaps when writing about any topic at all – there is a risk of overselling its significance.

We do not wish to fall into that trap. We realize that in the bigger scheme of things, jihadi culture is but one of the factors that affect the behavior of militant Islamists. If more scholarly attention has thus far been paid to the "hard stuff of rebellion," it is because those factors really do matter for understanding political violence.

Moreover, some primary sources explicitly downplay the significance of jihadi culture. For example, Omar al-Hammami, an American national who became a foreign fighter with al-Shabab in Somalia in the late 2000s, addressed head-on the suggestion that he had been seduced by jihadi culture:

[Question:] some might argue that your journey towards Jihad is more a result of your inclination towards the counter-culture, as opposed to your search for the truth. How do you respond? I'd respond by asking: Who throws away their entire life for counter-culture? Of course when I was first starting to practice the religion, and even when I became acquainted with videos about Khattaab (may Allaah accept him as a martyr), I was highly motivated by a sense of zeal. But you'll note that that zeal never got me across the line. It was only when I had become completely convinced that Jihaad is truly incumbent upon me as an individual that I took it upon myself to make that huge leap. I knew that I was going to become a fugitive for the rest of my life when I made that decision. I was well in to the post-9/11 era. Someone seeking a thrill or a hippy's midsummer's night dream doesn't normally consciously burn his bridges like that.[32]

Another autobiography, this one by an Egyptian foreign fighter named Abu Ja'far al-Masri al-Qandahari in 1980s Afghanistan, suggests jihadi life is not at all as emotion-filled as we have suggested so far:

Jihad – unlike what many people think – does not soften one's heart [but] rather hardens it. Most Mujahidin would complain to me saying how their hearts had become tougher and their tears ran dry. They no longer cried during prayer and even poetry no longer affected them. True, there were still saints among us who would burst into tears during prayer or during any discussion of heaven and hell, but they were very rare cases. Maybe I saw one or two of them throughout my journey.[33]

These testimonies suggest that we should not take for granted that jihadi culture matters to the same extent in all situations or that it affects all people in the same way.

Moreover, we should not have any illusions about being able to *explain* every aspect of jihadi culture. The question of why cultural products and practices take the particular form they do is probably impossible to answer fully, because there is contingency, creativity, and taste behind much cultural production. To some extent, cultures are what they are, and no amount of intellectual effort can explain their form. Take the example of prisons, a popular object of social scientific study. Scholars such as Diego Gambetta have shown that there is much about social life in prison that can be explained – more than lay people probably realize – but there is also much that cannot.[34] We may know that facial tattoos can serve as a costly sign of commitment to prison gangs, but who can say why inmates choose the particular face tattoo designs that they do? As U.S. convict-turned-writer Daniel Genis notes in a grim passage about prisoners' labelling of scars:

There's even names for scars. There's a 'telephone cut,' which goes from your ear to your mouth, which you get for using a claimed telephone. There's a 'buck eighty,' which is a scar [that] requires 180 stitches. There are 'curtains', which are two cuts down the face, which make your eyes look like they have curtains. There's the 'hook,' which puts a hole in the cheek. These things sound horrible, but in reality they kind of show a culture of incarceration has arisen and it shows that human beings really are more than animals – we make culture wherever we go.[35]

In any case, we will not know how significant jihadi culture is – or how much of its specifics we can explain – until we have done the research. It is time to give serious attention to the soft matter of rebellion, and we hope that this book will serve as a modest beginning.

1 | *Poetry in Jihadi Culture*

ROBYN CRESWELL AND BERNARD HAYKEL

The Islamic State (IS) and other jihadi movements such as al-Qaida produce an enormous amount of verse in Arabic, almost all of it online. Most militant websites have discussion forums dedicated to poetry, where postings range from couplets on current events to downloadable collections with flashy graphics and embedded photos. Jihadi magazines regularly feature original verse alongside essays and interviews with movement luminaries. Similarly, many jihadi videos and audio recordings contain poetry recitations. Poetry is central to the self-fashioning and self-presentation of the jihadis; it lies at the core of their identity as well as their ideology, and it represents their most sophisticated cultural product. Most militant leaders and ideologues, including Usama bin Ladin, have written poems of their own and make a point of reciting these, as well as verse by others, in social settings and in propaganda communiqués. The jihadis' poetry is not aesthetically innovative, and it does not try to be. Instead, it highlights the poets' rootedness in *tradition*, presenting itself as an "authentic" expression of Muslim identity in a world that has perverted true Islamic principles.

Analysts have generally ignored these texts, as if poetry were a colorful but ultimately distracting by-product of jihad.[1] Perhaps this is because they are linguistically difficult or because their purpose appears both alien and obscure. But this dismissal is a mistake. It is impossible to understand jihadism – its aims, its appeal to outsiders, and its durability – without looking into its culture. This culture comes in a number of forms, including anthems, documentary videos, and polemical essays, but poetry is arguably at its center. And unlike the slickly produced videos of beheadings and burnings, which are made primarily for foreign consumption, poetry provides a window onto the movement talking to itself, as well as to potential recruits. It is in their verse that militants most clearly articulate the fantasy life of jihad.

When the militants' literary interests are noted, the result is often amused incomprehension. The raid in May 2011 on the Abbottabad compound in Pakistan that killed Usama bin Ladin also uncovered a trove of correspondence. In one letter, written on August 6, 2010, bin Ladin asks a key lieutenant to recommend someone to lead "a big operation inside America." In the following sentence he requests that "If there are any brothers with you who know about poetic meters, please inform me, and if you have any books on classical prosody, please send them to me."[2] Commentating for *Foreign Affairs* on this exchange, an analyst remarked, "Because after a long day of planning to strike fear into the hearts of the infidels, sometimes a guy just wants to take a relaxing bubble bath and read some Emily Dickenson [*sic*]."[3]

It is indeed curious that so many militants, who are some of the most wanted men in the world, should take the time to study prosody and write poems in monorhyme – one rhyme for what is sometimes many dozens of lines of verse. This is far easier to do in Arabic than in English, but it still takes practice. And it is not only jihadi leaders who engage in such activities. On the contrary, poetry is widely practiced in militant circles, and judging by the posts in discussion forums it is also widely appreciated. Certain members of the rank-and-file have been recognized for their literary abilities, earning sobriquets such as "The Poet of al-Qaida" or "The Poet of Jihad." One of these is a young woman whose verse has made her a cultural celebrity among the militants.

"Dreams of Victory": Poetess of the Islamic State

On 12 October 2014, according to Twitter accounts linked to members of IS, a woman going by the name Ahlam al-Nasr was married in the courthouse of Raqqa, Syria, to Abu Usama al-Gharib, a Vienna-born jihadi.[4] IS social media rarely makes marriage announcements, but al-Nasr and al-Gharib are a kind of jihadi power couple. Al-Gharib, whose real name is Muhammad Mahmoud, is a veteran propagandist, originally for al-Qaida and now for IS. He was imprisoned in Austria for four years before an al-Qaida affiliate arranged for his release in 2011 via a prisoner swap.[5] He is the biographer of Turki al-Bin'ali, a prominent IS ideologue from Bahrain, and he is reportedly an associate of the self-proclaimed caliph, Abu Bakr al-Baghdadi.[6] As for Ahlam al-Nasr, an alias meaning "Dreams of Victory," she is better known as "The Poetess of the Islamic State."

Al-Nasr's first book of verse, *The Blaze of Truth [Uwar al-haqq]*, was published online by an IS media outlet in the autumn of 2014.[7]

Al-Nasr was already something of a literary celebrity in jihadi circles, and her poetry collection, equipped with a pair of prefaces by senior ideologues, quickly circulated on social media. Sung recitations of her work, performed a cappella in accordance with IS's prohibition on instrumental music, are easily found on YouTube. In the following lines, from one of those poems made into an IS anthem (*nashid*, plur. *anashid*), al-Nasr infuses her romantic nationalism with sectarian overtones:

> The glory of Islam has returned:
> People, welcome the lions.
> Come, let us build our state
> and bring honor back to our religion.
> The unbelief of Shiites has been defeated;
> the fortress of crime is falling.
> Islam's banners have been raised
> and hope is now rekindled.[8]

The Blaze of Truth consists of 107 poems, including elegies to fighters (mujahidin), laments for prisoners, and victory odes to the armies of IS. There are also short poems, such as one about the flight of rival jihadis from the Syrian town of Deir al-Zor, that were originally tweets. Almost all the poems, including the tweets, are written in monorhyme and classical Arabic meters. This attention to form is typical of militant verse. Like many amateurs, jihadis take delight in virtuosic feats and displays of learning. *The Blaze of Truth* includes footnotes explaining difficult syntax and unusual rhyme schemes, which is a convenient way of drawing attention to their existence.

Little is known for certain about Ahlam al-Nasr. Her mother, Iman Mustafa al-Bagha, is the daughter of a well-known Syrian scholar of Islamic jurisprudence. Al-Bagha was a professor of legal sciences in Saudi Arabia until fall 2014, when she resigned her position and emigrated to IS-held territory. She has since posted a short, biographical text about her daughter, and al-Nasr has published a number of diaristic writings through IS outlets. These sources suggest that al-Nasr is originally from Damascus. Now in her early twenties, she began writing poems in her teens – "she was born with a dictionary in her mouth," according to her mother – often in support of Palestine.[9] When protests broke out in the spring of 2011 against the rule of Syrian president Bashar al-Assad, al-Nasr took the side of the demonstrators. Several poems in *The Blaze of Truth* suggest that she witnessed the regime's crackdown at first hand and may have been radicalized by what she saw:

> Their bullets shattered our brains like an earthquake,
> > even strong bones cracked then broke.
> They drilled our throats and scattered our limbs –
> > it was like an anatomy lesson!
> They hosed the streets while blood still ran
> > like streams crashing down from the clouds.[10]

Al-Nasr fled to a Gulf country, but returned to Syria in 2014, arriving in Raqqa, the de facto capital of IS, in early fall. She quickly became a kind of court poet – she has written poems in praise of Abu Bakr al-Baghdadi, the self-styled caliph – as well as an official apologist for the regime. This is an unusually public role for a woman to play in jihadi movements, though IS has made a point of putting women on the front lines of the propaganda war.[11] (And perhaps not only on the propaganda war: IS has created a female morality police, a shadowy group called the al-Khansa' Brigades, who ensure proper deportment in IS-held towns.) In a written account of her emigration, al-Nasr describes the caliphate as an Islamist paradise, a state whose rulers are uncorrupted and whose subjects treat each other without regard to national or ethnic difference. "In the caliphate," she wrote, "I saw women wearing the veil, everyone treating each other with virtue, and people closing up their shops at prayer times."[12]

Raqqa was also seat of what seemed to be an ascendant Muslim power. When al-Nasr arrived in October, the movement's victories in Mosul and western Iraq were fresh in the militants' memory. In the city streets, "children played with sticks, pretending these were weapons they would use to fight heretics and unbelievers."[13] Al-Nasr celebrated IS's military triumphs as a new dawn for Iraq:

> Ask Mosul, city of Islam, about the lions –
> > how their fierce struggle brought liberation.
> The land of glory has shed its humiliation and defeat
> > and put on the raiment of splendor.
> I hear your weeping, Baghdad, only be patient –
> > your turn with the roaring lions will come.
> The sun is rising over Iraq
> > and she breathes in the blooms of victory:
> Shiite infidels have reaped the rewards of enmity;
> > the cross is broken and disgraced.[14]

Poetry and Performance

Why should it be poetry, of all things, that captures the militant
imagination? The authority of verse has no rivals in Arabic culture.
Al-shiʻr diwan al-ʻarab runs an ancient maxim: "Poetry is the record of
the Arabs" – that is to say, an archive of their historical experience and
the epitome of their literature. Desert nomads composed the earliest
poems in Arabic in the centuries before Muhammad's revelations. The
poems are in monorhyme and one of sixteen canonical meters (here is
the ultimate source for Ahlam al-Nasr's prosody), making them easy to
memorize. The poets were tribal spokesmen, celebrating the virtues of
their kin, cursing enemies, and lamenting the dead, especially those
killed in battle. They also recalled lost loves and boasted of their
drinking prowess. The Qur'an has harsh words for these pagan
troubadours, who were natural rivals to the Prophet. The Surah of
the Poets reads, "Only those who have strayed follow the poets. Do you
not see that they wander lost in every valley, and say what they do not
do?"[15] But the poets could not be written off so easily, and Muhammad
often found it more useful to co-opt them to the new dispensation.
A number of tribal poets converted and became Companions to the
Prophet, praising him in life and elegizing him after his death.

Arabic culture of the classical period – roughly, the eighth to the
thirteenth centuries – was centered on the courts of Damascus,
Baghdad, and Córdoba. Although most poets lived far from the
pasture grounds of the tribal bards, and written texts had replaced
oral compositions, the basic elements of the art lived on. The key
genres – poems of praise and blame and elegies for the dead – were
maintained, and new modes grew out of the old material. The wine
song, which had been a minor episode in the old poetry, became, in
the urbane atmospheres of the Caliphal courts, a full-fledged genre.
Poetic meters were essentially unchanged. These conventions have lost
some of their authority in the present. Contemporary poets writing in
Arabic read and translate all kinds of verse from abroad, and the
older, native models struggle to retain their sway. For many profes-
sionals, free verse and prose poetry are the norm. But to the Western
observer, it is the deep continuity of this poetic culture that astonishes.
For a literate Arab, the language of the classical period, along with the
moods and music of its poetry, is relatively easy to enjoy. The hum-
blest bookseller in Cairo or Damascus will stock editions of medieval

verse, and pre-Islamic poems are assigned to high school students across the Arab world.

Equally astonishing to Western observers is the fact that Arabic poetry is also, or can be, a popular art. Among the most-watched television programs in the Middle East is *Sha'ir al-Milyun [Millionaire Poet,* but also, *Poet of the People],* a program produced and shot in Abu Dhabi and modeled on *American Idol.*[16] Every season, amateurs from across the Arab world recite their own verse in front of a large and enthusiastic studio audience. Winners of the competition receive up to 1.3 million dollars – which, as the show's boosters are fond of pointing out, is slightly more than the amount given to winners of the Nobel Prize in Literature. A typical episode has a worldwide audience of more than ten million viewers.[17]

In formal terms, the verse one hears on *Sha'ir al-Milyun* is highly conventional (in political terms, the show is typical of the Gulf States' efforts to impose conservative cultural norms across the region). The contestants' poems evoke the beauties of the homeland, praise the generosity of local leaders, or lament social ills. According to the rules of the show, they must be metered and rhymed, and the judges' comments often zero in on contestants' technique. Despite this stress on convention – or, more likely, because of it – the show has produced a number of literary celebrities. In 2010, a Saudi contestant named Hissa Hilal recited a poem criticizing hard-line Saudi sheikhs and became an audience favorite (she was also interviewed by Diane Sawyer of ABC News), though she ultimately finished third.[18] During the Arab Spring, an Egyptian named Hisham Algakh appeared on one of the show's spinoffs (*Amir al-Shu'ara', [Prince of Poets]*), reciting several poems in support of the demonstrators at Tahrir. Algakh became a media star, and soon his poems were being recited in the square itself.[19]

Jihadi poetry is a subset of this popular art. It is also sentimental – it is even, at times, kitschy – and it is a communal rather than a solitary pursuit, the sort of thing enthusiasts might do around a campfire. It is as easy to find a video of jihadis sitting in a group reciting poems, or tossing back and forth the refrain of a song, as it is to find a video of them blowing up an enemy tank.[20] Of course, the views expressed in this poetry are more hard-edged than anything on *Sha'ir al-Milyun.* Shiites, Western powers, Jews, and rival factions are relentlessly vilified and threatened with destruction. The culture of jihadi poetry is one in which speakers can articulate all sorts of things – personal animus, political rage, communal boasting – that have been banned from more decorous (and less popular) precincts of literature. In both milieus, poetry is understood as a social art rather than a specialized profession, and practitioners take pleasure in showing off their technique. Indeed, the poems are full of allusions, recherché terms, and baroque devices. Acrostics, in which the first letters of successive lines spell out names or phrases, are especially popular. One of al-Nasr's poems, a declaration of her commitment to IS, is based on the group's acronym: "Daesh" is used by most Arabic speakers in a derogatory sense, so that al-Nasr's embrace of the term is a defiant one (formally, it is not unlike the poets of *négritude* embracing the pejorative *nègre*).[21]

An illustration of this performative verbal culture is a YouTube video of an Egyptian IS recruit who boasts in classical Arabic about the tanks and other heavy armor seized from the Assad regime with little more than automatic rifles.[22] For this militant, the conquests in Syria prove that strong faith is the surest path to victory, and that IS's military campaigns are a harbinger of the Muslims' return to glory. Midway through his speech he breaks into verse, reciting with brio portions of an oft-quoted poem by the Egyptian Mahmud Ghunaym (d. 1972) (appropriations of this kind are common in jihadi circles). Ghunaym's poem is in large part a lament for the decline of Islamic power:

> I remember – and the memory has made me sleepless –
> an inherited glory we have squandered.
> Wherever you turn you find Islam
> like a bird with its wings cut off.
> Those we had power over now overpower us,
> and we are governed by a people we once ruled.[23]

Jihadi poems are best understood not as works of propaganda or recreation, but as performances of authenticity. The poets are taking a turn in the spotlight and telling each other who they are, or at least how they would like to be seen. This work of self-fashioning is a cultural task as much as it is a political one. The militants must tell themselves stories about where they have come from and what their achievements have been, where the borders of their community are and what threats lie outside, what their special virtues are and how they can be handed on from generation to generation. And as with most political communities, the jihadis are eager to convince themselves that their identity is not really new, but very old.

It is the special place of poetry in Arabic culture that explains such performances, which are effectively claims to cultural authority. The militants' evident delight in their own literary expertise – their formal pyrotechnics and flourished erudition – accomplishes a similar function. The poets are making sure we know *they are poets*. Yet behind the swagger, powerful anxieties are at work. All militants have chosen to set themselves apart from the wider society, including their family and religious communities. This is often a difficult choice, with lasting consequences. By casting themselves as poets, as cultural actors with deep roots in the Arab-Islamic tradition, the militants attempt to assuage their worries of not really belonging.

Usama bin Ladin

Bin Ladin was the most celebrated jihadi poet, and he prided himself on his knowledge of the art.[24] The speeches and interviews of the al-Qaida leader are peppered with cited verses, and the name of his first camp in Afghanistan, al-Ma'sada ("The Lion's Den"), was inspired by a line of Ka'b bin Malik's, one of the pagan tribal poets who converted and became a Companion of the Prophet.[25] Jihadis are always careful to cite precedent for their writings, and one prophetic *hadith* they often quote is "In eloquence there is enchantment, and in poetry there is wisdom."[26] Jihadi poetry places a high value on eloquence – in Arabic, *al-bayan* – which is the art of clear speaking and the mastery of rhetorical convention. (Contemporary professional poetry, in Arabic as well as in English, places a higher value on innovation, which is the avoidance of both clear speaking and convention.) A large part of bin Ladin's charisma as a leader was his mastery of classical eloquence, including his ability to compose poetry.

One of bin Ladin's most emblematic compositions is a poem he seems to have written in the late nineties, sometime after his arrival in Afghanistan in 1996 and before the attacks on the World Trade Center. It is a two-part poem, forty-four lines long, the first half of which is in the voice of bin Ladin's young son Hamza. Many jihadi poems use the conceit of a child speaker. It provides them with a figure of innocence and truthfulness, and jihadi poets see themselves as always speaking the truth to power. Hamza begins by asking his father

why their life is full of hardship and why they can never stay in one
place. The rhetoric and mood of this opening section are borrowed
from a pre-Islamic genre called the *rahil*, in which the Bedouin poet
evokes the difficulty of his journey, complains of solitude and danger,
and compares his lot to a series of desert animals:

> Father, I have traveled a long time among deserts and cities.
> It has been a long journey, father, among valleys and mountains,
> So long that I have forgotten my tribe, my cousins, even humankind.[27]

Hamza goes on to recall the odyssey of bin Ladin and his family: their
departure from Saudi Arabia, their stay and subsequent expulsion
from the Sudan, and finally their arrival in Afghanistan, "where men
are the bravest of the brave." Even here, though, the militants find no
peace, for America "sends a storm of missiles like rain." Despite the
poem's lingering over the sufferings of exile, it evokes no nostalgia for
Saudi Arabia. For bin Ladin and other militants, the true homeland
(*watan*) has not yet come into being. Hamza's portion of the poem
ends with a request for fatherly wisdom.

Bin Ladin's response uses the same meter and rhyme letter as the lines
given to his son, lending the poem an air of formality but also intimacy.
Bin Ladin tells Hamza not to expect their life to get any easier: "I'm
sorry, my son, I see nothing ahead but a hard, steep path, / Years of
migrations and travel." He reminds Hamza that they live in a world
where the suffering of innocents, particularly Muslim innocents, is
ignored and "children are slaughtered like cattle." Yet Muslims themselves seem inured to their humiliation – "a people struck by stupor."
This rhetoric of awakening, of arousing the masses to a recognition of
their plight and the true teachings of Islam, is common in jihadi culture,
a trope it shares with reformist strands of Islamism. Bin Ladin's
harshest lines are directed at the impotence of Arab regimes. "Zionists
kill our brothers and the Arabs hold a conference," he jeers. "Why do
they send no troops to protect the little ones from harm?"[28]

Bin Ladin is acknowledging Hamza's complaint, but also reassuring
him that hardship and exile are necessary. This is not only because
injustice is everywhere, but – more significantly – because adversity is
the sign of election. A core belief of all jihadi movements is that they
form the last nucleus of authentic Muslims, a minority referred to in
the tradition as "the strangers" (in Arabic, *al-ghuraba'*). This is also the
name of an IS media outlet, the title of a popular jihadi anthem, and the

nom de guerre of many IS recruits. Abu Usama al-Gharib, the alias of Ahlam al-Nasr's husband, translates as "Usama's Father, the Stranger." The trope has its source in a *hadith* especially important for militants: "Islam began as a stranger and it shall return as it began, as a stranger. Blessed are the strangers."[29]

Islam began as a stranger in the sense that Muhammad's first followers in Mecca were persecuted by the town's unbelievers, which led to a period of hardship and eventually the flight to Medina. For jihadis, their own exile in foreign lands – evoked in Hamza's plaint and confirmed by his father's response – is evidence that they are the strangers of prophecy. In fact, the jihadis consider themselves to be in exile even when living in nominally Muslim states, and their exclusion from mainstream believers only vindicates their own sense of righteousness (a cycle of self-confirmation familiar to many cults). Jihadis are no doubt hoping that those who feel alienated or marginalized in their own societies find this promise of redemption appealing.

The structure of bin Ladin's poem, its division between the voices of father and son, makes the poem into a drama of inheritance. Bin Ladin is passing on to Hamza a political duty as well as an ethical disposition, which is that of a pious vanguard. The handing down of culture across the generations is a constant worry of jihadis. The militants are surrounded by enemies – Arab states, rival Islamists, remote Western powers – and always on the run. The first lines of Hamza's poem are "Where can we escape to, Father, and when will we stay in one place? / Father, did you not sense the circle of danger?" Under these conditions, maintaining the continuity of cultural traditions is extraordinarily difficult.

A further difficulty is that so much of jihadi culture is online, rather than embodied in material things. Virtual culture is volatile and hard to preserve: even the militants' social media accounts are subject to regular hacking, surveillance, and erasure.[30] All this suggests why jihadis, like many diaspora communities, are obsessively concerned with recording their achievements for posterity. The infrastructure of their online archives, such as Abu Muhammad al-Maqdisi's *Minbar al-tawhid wa-l-jihad*, a repository of religious opinions, manifestos, and poetry, is remarkably sophisticated.[31] It represents an immense curatorial effort to establish a canon of jihadi source materials that can be drawn on and appropriated, from the classical poets to the writings and poems of modern Islamists such as Sayyid Qutb, Marwan Hadid, and Usama bin Ladin.

The Jihadis' effort to constitute their own historical archive is also reflected in the forms of their verse. One reason that elegies are the most common genre in the poetry of jihad – the poems are typically composed for fallen fighters, including suicide bombers – is that they memorialize significant events. Bin Ladin himself recited an elegy for the nineteen hijackers of 9/11: "The mounted knights of glory found rest in the embrace of death. / They gripped the towers with hands of rage and ripped through them like a torrent."[32] After his death in Abbottabad, bin Ladin was elegized in turn by many other militants, including the Kuwaiti Islamist Hamid bin 'Abd Allah al-'Ali:

> I have elegized many before you, seeking their intercession,
> and poetry heard my call and came to my aid.
> But now my own poem chokes me,
> like a mother weeping over her precious one.
> I have elegized many great lions,
> but your fate has struck my heart like an earthquake.
> But in my grief I am glad,
> for we have not seen the lion humiliated by chains.
> I thank God sincerely and out loud
> that He has not let the lion spend one night in shackles.[33]

Such elegiac traditions give the militants a common calendar, which has little or nothing in common with the one used by everyone else. For the jihadis, as for the early Christians, acts of martyrdom are the building blocks of communal history.

Rejection of the Nation-State

At the center of bin Ladin's poem, and at the center of jihadi politics in general, is a rejection of the nation-state as a political norm. The map of the modern Middle East, drawn up by Britain and France at the end of World War I, is a constant source of bitterness. One of IS's most striking videos shows jihadis destroying the border crossing between Iraq and Syria, a line established by the infamous Sykes-Picot agreement of 1916.[34] Since the founding of Abu Bakr al-Baghdadi's caliphate, jihadis have taken to the practice of filming the ceremony of foreign fighters tearing up and burning their passports – an act intended to symbolize the rejection of the old order and the birth of a new one.[35] In bin Ladin's poem, Sudan offers the militants no refuge, and the Arab League is powerless before Israel. It is only in failed states such as Afghanistan – or, later, eastern Syria – where the holy warriors find a home. So the poetry of jihad leads to a new political geography, one that ignores or aggressively violates the boundaries set by foreign powers.

This new geography is organized around sites of militancy and Muslim suffering. A poem by Ahlam al-Nasr draws this map with a visionary élan that combines the politics of jihad with the cosmopolitanism of Doctors without Borders:

> My homeland is the land of truth,
>   the sons of Islam are my brothers.
> I do not love the Arab of the South
>   any more than the Arab of the North.
> My brother in India, you are my brother,
>   and so are you, my brothers in the Balkans,
> In Ahwaz and Aqsa,
>   in Arabia and Chechnya.
> If Palestine cries out,
>   or if Afghanistan calls out,
> If Kosovo is wronged,
>   or Assam or Pattani is wronged,
> My heart stretches out to them,
>   longing to help those in need.
> There is no difference among them,
>   this is the teaching of Islam.
> We are all one body,
>   this is our happy creed.
> We differ by language and color,
>   but we share the very same vein.[36]

Ahwaz is the Arabic name for a province of southern Iran where Sunni Arabs have long complained of persecution. Pattani is a Muslim-majority province of Thailand, where a Malay insurgency dating back to the 1960s has become increasingly Islamist. Al-Nasr's empathy for Muslims in far-flung places is a central trait of her literary persona. Among the many elegies in *The Blaze of Truth* is one for a prominent Chechen jihadi and another for a Jordanian preacher (a third is for bin Ladin, a jihadi genre unto itself). These moments of internationalist ecstasy are common in militant verse. The poets delight in crossing borders in their imaginations that are impassable in reality.

The Caliphate of IS, so far recognized by no other country, is itself a provocation to the Westphalian order – a fantasy world of fluctuating borders where anything can happen, including the recapture of past glories. In March 2014, the kingdom of Bahrain declared that all subjects fighting in Syria had two weeks to return home or be stripped of their nationality. A day after the grace period ended, Turki al-Bin'ali, a former Bahraini subject, published "A Denunciation of Nationality," a short poem thumbing its nose at the royals and ridiculing the very idea of the nation-state. "Don't the tyrants know that we are rebels who do not fear the whip?" he writes. "Tell them we put their nationality under our heel, just like their royal decrees." For the jihadis, new frontiers beckon: "Do you really think we would return," al-Bin'ali writes incredulously, "when we are here in Syria, land of epic battles and the outposts of war?"[37] Al-Bin'ali, who is in his early thirties, has emerged as IS's most prominent ideologue, and his orations are easily found on YouTube. In these performances, he shows off his rhetorical abilities in flawless Arabic as well as a prodigious ability for accurately citing Wahhabi texts from memory. He is also the author of the catechism-like booklets on Islamic theology and law for the course that all IS recruits must take before they undergo military training.[38]

Just like the theological and legal principles, the new frontiers of Islam, drawn in defiance of conventional maps, need to be defended. The "outposts" of al-Bin'ali's verse, *ribat*, were garrisons on the frontier between medieval Islamic states and their neighbors – Catholic Spain or Orthodox Byzantium. There are no *ribat* anymore, however. The term is an archaic flourish – like using monorhyme and classical meters – and jihadi culture is premised on such anachronisms. Propaganda videos invariably show the militants on horseback with their swords in the air, flying banners whose calligraphy is modeled on those of the earliest Muslim conquerors. (Such videos have already spawned a cottage industry of YouTube parodies.) And jihadi poetry indulges in similar fantasies. Muhammad al-Zuhayri, a Jordanian engineer whose Internet alias is "The Poet of al-Qaida" – each faction has a court rhymester – captures this martial mood in a poem dedicated to Abu Mus'ab al-Zarqawi (d. 2006), the one-time head of al-Qaida in Iraq. The lines are addressed to an unnamed female:

Wake us to the song of swords,
>   and when the cavalcade sets off, say farewell.
The horses' neighing fills the desert,
>   arousing our souls and spurring them onward.
The knights' pride stirs at the sound,
>   while humiliation lashes our foes.[39]

The culture of jihad is a culture of romance. It promises adventure and pretends that the codes of medieval heroism and chivalry are still relevant. All jihadi poets depict themselves as the protectors of women and children, particularly widows and orphans. Having renounced their nationalities and the community of most co-religionists, the militants must invent an identity of their own. And, indeed, jihadi politics is a type of identity politics – a demand for recognition and a performance of authenticity. The knights of jihad style themselves as the only true Muslims, and while they may be tilting at windmills, the romance seems to be working. IS recruits do not imagine they are emigrating to a dusty borderland between two disintegrating states, but to a caliphate with more than a millennium of history.

Theology and Jihad

Anyone who reads much jihadi poetry soon discovers that it includes a great deal of theology. Religious doctrine is the basic glue of militant culture, and many theologians have written poems. The case of Ahlam al-Nasr, a poet who has become a theologian, suggests how blurry the boundaries are. And, in fact, the jihadis' approach to religious tradition is essentially the same as their approach to literary tradition: just as the poets think of themselves as resurrecting an authentic poetic heritage, so jihadi theologians imagine they are uncovering and bringing back to life the true tenets of their faith. In both instances, this work is conceived of as a raid against intellectual orthodoxy. Although militant groups often have in-house scholars with some formal training, the jihadis are largely self-taught (all canonical texts are now online). And like many autodidacts, militants believe that mainstream thinkers are engaged in a conspiracy to hide the truth – in this case, the truth about Islam, which they accuse clerics of covering up in deference to political despots. The jihadis, on the contrary, are literalists, who promise to sweep away centuries of scholasticism and put individual believers in touch with the actual teachings of their religion. It is remarkable how closely the elements of this scenario resemble those of the Protestant Reformation: mass literacy, the democratization of clerical authority, and methodological literalism. Under these circumstances, anyone might nail their theses to a mosque door.

Among the principles that militants have rescued from the clerics is the principle of jihad itself, which is at the core of militant theology. While armed struggle has long been recognized by the Islamic tradition, it was rarely put at the heart of what it means to be a Muslim: by the twentieth century, many jurists treated it as little more than a relic. For the jihadis, this is the clearest example of clerical treason. They believe that waging jihad is constitutive of Muslim identity. It is an ethical discipline as well as a political obligation, and its neglect is a major cause of what they perceive to be the Islamic world's decline. Broadcasting the truth about jihad is therefore a fixation of militant culture, and some of the most compelling defenses of jihad come in the form of poems.

One of these is Isa bin Sa'd Al Awshan's "Epistle to the Scolders."[40] The poem was published in *Diwan al-'izza [The Anthology of Glory]*, a collaborative volume released in the spring of 2004 by Saudi militants. From mid-2003 to the end of 2006, al-Qaida attempted to bring international jihad home to the Kingdom, attacking local Western targets and oil compounds. The poets included in *The Anthology* were the rank and file of this offensive, which the regime eventually snuffed out (surviving members fled to Yemen, where they teamed up with local militants and relaunched the organization al-Qaida in the Arabian Peninsula). 'Awshan himself was a jihadi propagandist and magazine editor of *Sawt al-Jihad*, the movement's principal online organ. In late 2003, he was number seventeen on the government's list of the twenty-six most-wanted men in Saudi Arabia. 'Awshan was subsequently killed by Saudi internal security forces during a shootout in Riyadh.

The publication of the most-wanted list was the occasion for 'Awshan's "Epistle," which he prefaces with a note claiming that after its release "some of my brothers and friends scolded me, wishing that I had not gone down this road – the road of jihad and struggle against unbelievers – since it is full of difficulties." He explains that he wrote his epistle "to clarify the path I have chosen and the reason for pursuing it." The fifty-two-line poem that follows is an apology for jihad. It begins:

> Let me make clear every obscure truth,
>> and remove the confusion of he who questions.
> Let me say to the world and what is beyond it, "Listen:
>> I speak the truth and do not stutter.
> The age of submission to the unbeliever is over,
>> he who gives us bitter cups to drink."
> In this time of untruthfulness, let me say:
>> I do not desire money, nor a life of ease,
> But rather the forgiveness of God and His grace.
>> For it is God I fear, not a gang of criminals.
> You ask me about the course
>> I have pursued with zeal and swiftness,
> You ask, afraid for my sake, 'Is this
>> the rightly-guided path, the good road?
> Is this the way of the prophet?'

The world of jihad is often thought to be a Manichean one, split between the soldiers of faith and the mass of unbelievers. In fact, jihadis recognize a number of intermediate positions. One is the position of those who consider themselves pious Muslims but are not convinced of the legitimacy of jihad and suspect the militants' impulsiveness puts their communities in danger. This is the attitude of "the scolders" whom 'Awshan addresses in his poem. The scolder, *al-la'im*, is another figure from the old poetry. In pre-Islamic lyrics, the speaker typically styles himself as a lover, a fighter, and a host of reckless generosity. The scolder, by contrast, is a voice of the communal superego, reminding the poet of his tribal duties. "His job," writes Andras Hamori, a scholar of this tradition, "was to try to prevent the protagonist from making the heroic gesture" – in other words, "the willingness to expose the self, to face danger and eventual destruction."[41]

Jihadi poetry is full of such scolders, who counsel caution and implicitly give their blessing to the status quo. They speak the language of quiescent clerics – "the sheiks of deception" (*shuyukh al-tadlil*) as one poet in *The Anthology* calls them[42] – as well as of parental authority. In another poem, a martyr addresses his mother from beyond the grave, telling her not to cry for him (nor to question his judgment). "I've left my blood behind me, mother," he writes, "a trail that leads to paradise."[43] The scolders serve several purposes. They let the poet display his knowledge of literary tradition and create the archaic mood so crucial to these performances. They also function as a choric background against which the poet can strike his lonely, heroic poses. By questioning the advisability of jihad, the scolders allow the speaker to make its virtues clear.

Awshan's poem is a short treatise on eloquence, or the art of making things clear. This is not simply a matter of defending the necessity of jihad against clerics, but of publicly stating one's creed. This act of forthright declaration is at the heart of jihadi ethics. As he writes in the "Epistle":

> My path is the way of Muhammad the Messenger and his Companions.
> I wish to be saved from the dark road.
> My creed is to declare the unity of the enthroned God (*tawhid rabb al-'arsh*)
> and I will not compromise myself for the sake of money.
> Disbelief in a false god (*taghut*) is my creed.
> Without this, true worship is defiled.
> War against disbelievers and apostates –
> this is what it means to hate the wicked enemy;
> And to struggle to expel the Cross and its people
> from the Arabian Peninsula by the sword and bloodshed.[44]

When the rest of the world is against you, and your co-religionists are too timid to speak the truth, coming out as a jihadi – by swearing allegiance to the Emir of al-Qaida, or the Caliph of IS, for example – is a central test of courage. The "Epistle" is full of verbs of exposure and annunciation. After condemning the American invasion of Iraq in 2003, 'Awshan writes:

> I announced there would be no more rest
>   until our arrows smote the enemy.
> I strapped on my machine gun with a mujahid's resolve
> and pursued my course with a passionate heart.
> I want one of two good things: martyrdom,
> or deliverance from despotic power.[45]

For the jihadi, poetry is a mode of manifesto, or bearing witness. There are no prizes for subtlety. The poet's task is to make an open and lucid defense of his faith against all doubters, at home and abroad. He must dare to name the truths that his parents and elders try to hide. Another poem in *The Anthology of Glory* begins with a classical-sounding admonition: "Silence! Words are for heroes / and the words of heroes are deeds."[46] Surrounded by skeptics, the jihadi poet fashions himself as a knight of the word, which is to say, a martyr in the making.

Innovation and Traditionalism

After her arrival in Raqqa in the autumn of 2014, Ahlam al-Nasr was given a celebrity tour by IS public relations. She wrote a long piece in prose about what she saw, addressed to her "sisters" and disseminated through IS media outfits. Walking through the streets of Raqqa, al-Nasr noted that the stalls were full of fresh vegetables and that men encouraged each other to follow the example of the prophet and stop smoking. She was allowed to cook for the militants, which gave her great joy: "Everything had to be clean and wonderful. I kept repeating to myself: 'This food will be eaten by mujahidin, these plates will be used by mujahidin.'" She was also brought to a gun shop, where she learned how to assemble and disassemble Russian- and American-made rifles. "All this happened in Syria, sisters," she writes, "and in front of my eyes!"[47] Here is how she describes the new order in verse:

God's law is light
through which we rise to the stars.
Here we live without humiliation,
a life of security and peace.
Our state has been established
absolutely on the basis of Islam.
Though we battle against enemies,
our state adjudicates by His guidance.[48]

For al-Nasr, the caliphate is an Islamist utopia, not only because it is a place where Muslims behave as Muslims should, but also because it is a place of new beginnings. Raqqa may strike outsiders as the very type of a rigid, even totalitarian, society, but for her and other recruits it is a frontier where everything is in flux and free to be reformulated – not only political boundaries, but personal identities too.

Al-Nasr's own trajectory from poet-in-exile to movement ideologue underscores the possibilities for self-fashioning. In addition to a stream of tweeted poems, she has written several prose polemics published by IS. The most extensive is a thirty-page defense of the movement's decision, in January 2015, to burn Jordanian pilot Mu'az Kasasbeh alive.[49] Al-Nasr's argument, backed by a formidable legal apparatus, is premised on the right of Muslims to retaliate in kind against attackers. Since Kasasbeh's bombs were "burning" the homes of believers, al-Nasr claims that his immolation was legitimate. Along the way, she rebukes a number of jihadi scholars such as Abu Muhammad al-Maqdisi, who scolded IS for its temerity (burning people is generally thought to be something only God can do). Al-Nasr articulates an uncompromising defense of the caliphate, using theological and legal arguments drawn from the canonical texts of the Islamic tradition. Her treatises bear some similarity to articles published in *Dabiq*, IS's English-language magazine, which boast an elaborate critical apparatus of footnotes, precise translations and transliterations of Arabic words, and selected citations. In jihadi circles, many poets embed theological arguments in their verse, and many theologians write poetry. But the emergence of a woman among the highest ranks of IS's propaganda machine is a sharp departure from jihadi precedent. None of al-Qaida's ideologues were women, and no female militant has so audaciously challenged male jurists on their home turf.

Although media accounts of IS's female recruits typically cast them as naïfs signing up for sexual slavery, no other militant group has been as successful in attracting women. In one of the recent issues of *Dabiq*, a female writer encourages women to emigrate to Syria with or without a male companion, a significant departure from traditional Islamic law.[50] This may be a cynical ploy by the movement's leadership – a recipe for runaways – but it is in keeping with the jihadis' suspicion of parental authority as well as its emphasis on individual empowerment, even including the power of female believers to renounce families they do not view as authentically Muslim.[51]

But authenticity is a volatile basis for a political community. And, indeed, the militants' obsession with purity – evident in their use of classical literary forms, their search for the buried truths of religion, their self-consciously archaic imagery – often results in something unprecedented. The al-Khansa' Brigades, the women's morality police that patrol some IS-held cities, is one notable example. Al-Khansa' was a female poet of the pre-Islamic era whose elegies for male relations are keystones of the genre (she too converted to Islam and became a Companion of the Prophet). That jihadis would name a branch of their police force after an ancient poet is not really surprising – on the contrary, it is a typical flourish of militant medievalism. But while the name suggests an institution with deep roots in the past, in fact there has never been anything like the Brigades in Islamic history, nor do they have an equivalent anywhere in the Arab world. It may be that IS's radical traditionalism, in social relations as in poetry, is the formula for something strange and new (whether it will last is another question). The militants see things differently, of course. They view their caliphate as a pure resurrection of the past. In her Raqqa diary, Ahlam al-Nasr describes the IS capital as a place of everyday miracles, a city where believers can go to be born again into the old, authentic faith. In the caliphate, she writes, "There are many things we've never experienced except in our history books."[52]

2 | *A Cappella Songs* (anashid) in *Jihadi Culture*

NELLY LAHOUD

In the late 1980s, an internal al-Qaida document recommended the purchase of "tape recorders and empty tapes on which to record Persian language lessons, Qur'an [recitation] and *nashid*."[1] These and other "essentials" were deemed necessary to "raise the intellectual level of the mujahidin."[2] The same document contained an itemized budget with entries for the purchase of *anashid* and poetry books.[3] Some fifteen years later, in one of the bags left at the airport by the 9/11 hijackers, investigators discovered a handwritten document with advice on how to prepare mentally for the operation. It suggested, among other things, that if "everything comes off well," it would be delightful if one "recited *anashid* to his brothers – as the forefathers used to recite *rajaz* poetry in the midst of the battle – to comfort them and to fill their hearts with the presence of God (*sakina*) and joy."[4] In 2009, in a widely read essay, the American-Yemeni jihadi leader Anwar al-Awlaqi identified *anashid* as "an important element in creating a 'Jihad culture.'" He argued that *anashid* inspire Muslim youth to wage jihad, and that a good *nashid* "could reach an audience that you could not reach in a lecture or a book."[5]

These three snapshots from different points in jihadi history illustrate the importance that al-Qaida and its supporters attach to *anashid*. *Nashid* (plur. *anashid*), as defined by Shiloah, is "a piece of oratory, a chant, a hymn and a form of vocal music" following a poetic metrical rhythm.[6] It is a devotional artistic expression that goes back centuries, but its appeal to contemporary militants shows no sign of waning. On the contrary, as technology allows for more audiovisual jihadi propaganda, jihadi *anashid* are more popular than ever. They are all over the jihadi Internet, and virtually all recruitment videos include *anashid* in their soundtrack.

This chapter examines the role of *anashid* in jihadism from two angles. The first consists of examining what jihadis have said about *anashid*, with a focus on the ideological debates regarding their lawfulness and utility. The second involves studying the *anashid* them-selves; here I analyze the form and content of about seven *anashid* in some depth. These are selected for their representativeness from a larger dataset comprising 636 Arabic-language *anashid* downloaded from a jihadi website in 2011.[7] The dataset predates the declaration of the Islamic State (IS) in June 2014, so my analysis speaks primarily to *anashid* used by al-Qaida and its supporters. However, the latter part of the chapter offers brief observations about IS *anashid* based on a review of about forty Arabic *anashid* produced by IS's media arm, Ajnad.[8]

I argue that jihadi media uses *anashid* as a tool to forge bonds between jihadis and mine their emotions to produce an activist jihadi culture. As such, *anashid* do not strictly belong to the doctrinal realm of jihadism, but rather to a set of practices or technologies that curate the listener's emotions: the melodic rhythms of *anashid* seem intended to give rise to cathartic releases that complement and even substitute for dry ideological dogma. That is perhaps why the ideological litera-ture pays little attention to *anashid*, while training manuals cannot stress their importance enough. In doing so, except for IS media, jihadi media does not always produce its own *anashid* but draws on existing Islamic *anashid*, mostly those that engender militancy. Accordingly, one should not equate "*anashid* about jihad" with "pro-jihadi *ana-shid*" and infer that those who listen to the former sympathize with jihadis. The same, however, may not be said about IS, for the group uses only the *anashid* it produces. This suggests that IS's uses of *anashid* is not limited to producing an activist jihadi culture but also as a tool of state building.[9]

A Brief History of *anashid*

Nashada (n.sh.d) is the verbal root of *nashid* and *unshuda* (singular forms of *nasha'id* and *anashid*, respectively) and of *inshad*, the act of performing a *nashid*.[10] The lexicon *Lisan al-'Arab* by Ibn Manzur (d. 1311) includes two additional meanings: a person performing *inshad*, that is, *munshid* or *nashid* (with a long "a"), could mean either a diviner/fortuneteller (*mu'arrif*) or even a seeker of knowledge (*talib*).[11] Fouad Ephreim al-Bustani observes that *inshad* represented the art of Arabic oral composition during pre-Islamic era (*jahiliyya*) when there was no tradition of literacy in the Hijaz. In its origin, he explains, *inshad* was neither poetry (*shi'r*) nor prose (*nathr*); instead it

was comparable to Homer's *Iliad* and some of the compositions of the
Jewish prophets, such as Solomon's *Song of Songs* (*nashid al-anshad*).[12]
The origin of the genre is disputed, but one modern poet argues that the
practice originated in the enthusiastic cries (*al-sayhat al-hamasiyya*) of
warriors preparing to go to war, cries intended to cause fear and terror
in the ranks of their enemies. *Inshad*, he argues, is therefore about
boosting the morale of fighters on the battlefield.[13]

Irrespective of the precise origin of inshad, the author/composer
(*munshid*) had to be in command of rare skills to engender the
emotional outcome he sought. Al-Bustani explains that the *munshid*
had to bring together emotions (*'atifa*), imagination (*khayal*), and
music (*musiqa*) to command the attention of his audience. To do so
effectively, he had to excel at mastering a range of rhetorical flourishes
(*uslub zakhrafi*) and linguistic tools to facilitate memorization. For
instance, the *munshid* would introduce contrast in meanings (*tadad*),
analogy (*tibaq*), repetition (*takrar*) and especially rhymed prose
(*saja'*).[14] The rhythm, harmony, and melody of this combination is
therefore musical in its output, even if it is not accompanied with
musical instruments; and it is the musical component that makes the
lyrics reach the listener. In the words of al-Bustani, this art of composition "produces an effect in the listeners, causing them to pay attention,
listen and be affected."[15] That is perhaps why a *munshid* at times earned
the status of soothsayer (*kahin*).[16]

According to Henry George Farmer, musical culture was embedded
in early Arab society. "Music," he eloquently remarked, "accompanied
the Arab from the cradle to the grave, from the lullaby to the elegy.
Every moment of his life seems to have had its particular music – joy
and sorrow, work and play, battle-throng and religious exercise."[17] In
Arabic literature, the art of *inshad* evolved and eventually served as the
wellspring of both prose and poetry. Poetry developed with *inshad*-style
sentences assuming the same length and their rhymed prose based on
poetical meters.[18]

Given the rich pre-Islamic *inshad* tradition, it is not surprising that,
with the advent of Islam, its style should leave its mark on Scripture.
Al-Bustani draws attention to sections of the Qur'an that flow in an
inshad-like rhythm, as when a verse is repeated 31 times (Q. 55) as a
pedagogic device, or when a number of comparisons and analogies are
drawn to highlight a single theme (Q. 69; 101). It is perhaps because
the Arabs of the *jahiliyya* made no distinction between poetry and

rhymed prose that some accused the Prophet of being a poet (*sha'ir*) and a soothsayer (*kahin*) (Q. 37: 36; 69: 40–2) when his preaching of the Islamic creed displeased them.[19]

The subsequent development of the Islamic legal tradition saw the musical aspect of *inshad* described as *sama'*, denoting a musical performance.[20] Al-Ghazali (d. 1111 C.E.) defines *sama'* as "sessions that may produce the state (*halat*) in the heart called Ecstasy (*wajd*). Ecstasy in its turn may produce movements of the limbs which are either rhythmically irregular, and called agitated/trembling, or are rhythmically regular, such as hand-clapping and dancing."[21] Classical jurists and theologians differed on whether *sama'* is lawful;[22] as far as al-Ghazali was concerned, "Listening (*sama'*) [to music and song] . . . has a perceptible effect on the mind (*qalb*). Anyone not moved by it is deficient in some quality, lacks an evenly balanced disposition, and is far removed from spiritual insight."[23] Nevertheless, al-Ghazali did not believe that it was possible to give an "unqualified ruling as to whether it is Permissible or Unlawful"; it depended, he held, on the circumstances and the modalities of the singing.[24] Combat is one of the situations in which al-Ghazali considers *sama'* lawful:

The recitation of poems [is Permissible] in the *rajaz* metre by the brave once battle is joined. The purpose of such poems is to keep up the courage of one's self and one's allies, and to stir eagerness for combat among them. The poems recited in this ritual are a celebration of bravery and courage. *When it is done with fine articulation and a beautiful voice it has a powerful impact on the soul/mind.* This practice is Permissible in every conflict that is Permissible, and Recommended in every conflict that is Recommended, but is proscribed in conflicts between Muslims and those of *dhimmi* status, and indeed in every proscribed conflict, because to encourage something proscribed is itself proscribed. [emphasis added][25]

Modern Debates

The medieval debates produced several, seemingly irreconcilable, positions as to the lawfulness of anashid and are echoed in modern debates. Their lawfulness is contested because chanting is associated with music, the permissibility of which is highly debated in Islamic law.

In practice, Muslims today have largely embraced music with and without musical instruments. In Islamic law, however, the permissibility of music remains a contested issue. Progressive legal scholars, such as

Muhammad Abu Zahra,[26] have argued that "we do not see a [legal] reason to forbid chanting [*ghina'*] so long as it does not contain anything that causes sexual instincts to be aroused." Relying on a *hadith*, a report attributed to the Prophet in which he approved the tambourine during marriage celebrations, Abu Zahra concludes that "other musical instruments are also lawful (*mithlu dhalika al-musiqa*)." He nevertheless qualifies this by adding that "it is agreed upon that so long as music does not cause sexual instincts to be aroused and does not distract [the believer] from invoking the Lord's name (*dhikr Allah*) and prayer, then it does not violate [the fundamentals of the religion]."[27]

Islamists, starting with the Muslim Brotherhood, have embraced a pragmatic view on music. Much to the dismay of ultra-conservative religious scholars, they have had no qualms about introducing musical instruments into their *anashid* or even listening to music that is not composed for pious purposes. For example, the Islamist ideologue Sayyid Qutb wrote an article praising the music of the Egyptian composer Sayyid Darwish (d. 1923).[28] Qutb, it should be added, was only interested in promoting what he considered to be tasteful Darwish-like music and would have liked the government to ban tasteless commercial music.[29]

By contrast, Wahhabi scholars forbid musical instruments altogether. When the Saudi kingdom challenged the Ottoman Empire militarily and doctrinally in the nineteenth century,[30] Muhammad Ali, the Governor of Egypt, reportedly took pleasure in "torturing" captured Wahhabis by forcing them to listen to music. H. St. John Philby relates that "Sulaiman bin 'Abdullah, a grandson of Muhammad ibn 'Abdul-Wahhab was subjected to the ignominy of listening to the guitar as preliminary to being conducted to the cemetery and executed by a firing-squad."[31]

Nevertheless, most Wahhabi scholars permit a cappella singing, with a series of qualifications.[32] Ibn Baz (d. 1999), for instance, insists that there is nothing wrong with *anashid* when the content is limited to preaching, reminding believers of doing good deeds, and exhorting them to defend their nations (*awtan*). Nasir al-Din al-Albani (d. 1999) is of the view that *anashid* must not preach extremism (*ghuluw*) and that they must not amount to becoming a religion ('*adam ittikhadhiha dinan*), by which he meant that they must not serve as substitute for the Qur'an.[33] Al-Albani wrote a treatise in which he rebuked progressive Azharite and Islamist scholars such as Abu Zahra,

Yusuf al-Qaradawi, and Muhammad al-Ghazali, who openly admitted that they enjoy certain types of Arabic popular music such as Umm Kulthum and the Egyptian musician Muhammad Abd al-Wahhab.[34] Ibn Uthaymin (d. 2001) is even less flexible. In his mind, not only must *anashid* exclude musical instruments, but their melodies must not imitate those of "insolent songs" (*aghani majina*), by which he meant popular songs, lest the soul gets accustomed to this type of singing and is moved/delighted by it (*tatrab lahu*). He also insists that it is not permitted for *anashid* to be performed by young boys whose voices are seductive and may arouse the listener's sensual desires (*shahwa*).[35]

Jihadis generally anchor their religious teachings in the concept of *tawhid* as articulated by Wahhabi scholars; some jihadi groups, like al-Qaida, also draw on teachings from Muslim Brotherhood ideologues such as Sayyid and Muhammad Qutb. When it comes to *anashid*, jihadis straddle a delicate balance. On the one hand, they clearly seek to satisfy the conservatives by promoting *anashid* without musical instruments. Indeed, many productions by al-Sahab, al-Qa'ida's media production company, begin with a written warning stating, "this is a jihadi product and it is not lawful to play music along with its content." Moreover, jihadi commentators are keen to point out that their *anashid* elevate the morale of jihadis and strengthen their resolve, thereby emulating a practice that the Prophet adopted when he used to bring a *munshid* to spur fighters before going on military expeditions.[36] On the other hand, many of the *anashid* promoted by jihadis make use of what one may consider faux instruments in the form of sound effects that produce upbeat rhythms and melodies. In this respect, they are not entirely faithful to the conservative spirit that rules out the inclusion of *mu'aththirat* (sound effects) as part of the recital.

That is why, even today, *anashid* are not automatically assumed to be lawful by jihadi ideologues, and occasionally the debate flares up again. For example, in 2011 a certain "Azifat al-Rasas asked the Legal Committee of the *Minbar al-Tawhid wal-al-Jihad* website about the permissibility of listening to *anashid* that 'are free of percussion instruments (*iqa'*) and tambourines/drums (*dufuf*).'"[37] A cleric had told the enquirer that it is only lawful to listen to *anashid* that are exclusively devoted to jihad. Al-Rasas was surprised by this response and reminded him of the *hadith* attributed to the Prophet approving the tambourine.[38] Yet Abu Usama al-Shami from the Legal Committee had responded to an earlier query by the same al-Rasas,[39] indicating that that "there is no [legal] objection to listening to a *nashid* that is free of percussion instruments, music, tambourines, and sound effects."[40] He further added, "it is permissible (*mubah*) especially if the *nashid* stimulates enthusiasm [that extols militancy] like the jihadi *anashid*." The Prophet, al-Shami pointed out, was in the habit of listening to the chanting of his caravan leader Anjasha; on another occasion, he extolled "'Aisha to recite a *nashid* during a wedding of one of the *ansar*" (the locals of Medina and early supporters of Islam).[41] Nevertheless, al-Shami warned against intemperance (*israf*), adding that "listening to *anashid* must not take precedence over listening to the Qur'an."[42]

The same concern was reflected in a heated discussion between the prominent al-Qaida operative Fadil Harun and his wife Umm Luqman over the religious education of their children.[43] Harun was relatively pragmatic and open-minded in matters of religious doctrine, and he himself would play *anashid* for recruits during military training.[44] Nevertheless, when he reunited with his wife and three children in Somalia in 2006 after a four-year absence, he was disturbed to find that his four-year-old daughter Samiyya had memorized virtually all the *anashid*, but very little of the Qur'an.[45]

Overall, however, the jihadi ideological literature pays limited attention to *anashid*. One reason may be that the majority of ideologues take their lawfulness for granted. Another reason may be that they wish to avoid all the theological controversies and concerns associated with *anashid*. Perhaps they also wish to be seen as addressing the big geopolitical and doctrinal topics of the day as opposed to what some may consider as questions of art and entertainment. They may not want to be perceived as an *école buissonnière* where young men are free to hang out and *sing* with their friends. Whatever the reason, the "official" treatises of jihadi ideology – those intended for public consumption – seem to skirt the topic of *anashid*.

The Utility of *anashid*

If jihadi leaders skirt the topic of *anashid* in their official documents, they discuss it extensively behind closed doors. Documents intended for internal use contain numerous references to and reflections on *anashid*, although here the issue is not their lawfulness, but they highlight their utility.

For obvious reasons, the outside world does not often get to see these communications; typically it happens when documents are leaked by disloyal members or captured by enemy forces. The U.S. military has captured thousands of internal al-Qaida documents over the years, and some have been declassified and published.

As the opening paragraph of this chapter suggests, internal communications from al-Ma'sada in the 1980s suggest that its leaders saw *anashid* as "essential" for the military effort and worth spending money on. *Anashid* are also discussed in more detail in writings about how to forge an activist jihadi culture. Accordingly, we find the role of *anashid* discussed in letters of advice between jihadi leaders and especially in training manuals. For example, in 2000, a certain Abu Hudhayfa wrote a long and detailed letter to Usama bin Ladin offering advice on how al-Qaida could improve its communication strategy. It included the following passage:

Wedding ceremonies that are performed here [in Afghanistan], may God bless [these unions], may appear on the surface to be an ordinary occurrence, but in reality, they carry significant meanings if they are properly utilized and exploited by the political division [of al-Qaida] to advance its jihadi project. For example, the political division could undertake the appropriate preparations by way of featuring speeches, *anashid* [my emphasis], poems etc. ... during the wedding ceremony. Then the media arm [of al-Qa'ida] would undertake the appropriate technical production of the ceremony, using a suitable/professional motion picture, and [mass] distribute the video. The political investment of such a project serves to show that [although] we are living in the abode of emigration (*dar al-hijra*), we [nevertheless] lead normal lives, including [celebrating each others'] marriages, [partaking in] happy events and enjoying the gift of *hijra* with all its blessings despite the expulsions [we endure] and the war declared [against us] by the [forces] of global unbelief (*al-kufr al-'alami*). Such an [advertising] product would therefore have profound meanings and psychological rewards. [Although the rewards] may vary from one person to the other, they would nevertheless flow into a principal [strategic] objective, namely causing [Muslims'] feelings to be moved, shaking the psyche of those who hesitate to commit to *hijra*, especially as they compare their situation with that of their fellow brethren in the abode of *hijra*, as the latter enjoy happiness, relaxation, and disappearance of worries while they constantly prepare to fight.[46]

Abu Hudhayfa thus believes *anashid* ought to be used to stir Muslims' feelings and emotions and inspire them to take up the life of *hijra* and jihad. In a different part of the letter, he recommends that al-Qaida should follow the example of Hamas and film the testament of men who volunteer to carry out martyrdom operations. The videos can then be broadcast after the operation. Thus, Abu Hudhayfa wants to utilize *anashid* and visual media for propaganda purposes.

Anashid also feature in another genre of internal jihadi communications, namely, training manuals. We often find *anashid* mentioned in sections dealing with audio-visual tools and other means that affect the recruits' emotions (*mu'aththirat*). Thus it is often dealt with separately from issues pertaining to ideological persuasion and indoctrination. One such training manual is entitled *A Course in the Art of Recruiting (Dawra fi Fann al-Tajnid)* by a certain Abu "Amru al-Qa'idi.[47] It devotes a whole section to examples of audio-visual educational tools, highlighting the utility of *Rih al-Janna [Winds of Paradise]*, a series of video recordings by al-Sahab that includes lectures, interviews with jihadis, Qur'an recitation, and *anashid*.[48]

Several other training manuals captured by U.S. forces recommend using *anashid* as a tool to forge a specific cultural mindset. One such manual, found in Abu Hafs al-Misri's house in Kandahar, has a section on "propaganda" in which *anashid* feature as one of seven key techniques for ideological influence:

1. Repetition technique
2. Advising and preaching technique
3. Supplication technique
4. *Rhymes and songs technique* [my emphasis]
5. Slogans technique
6. Comedy/jokes technique
7. Lies technique.[49]

That *anashid* feature in training manuals under propaganda or under *mu'aththirat* is a strong indication that *anashid* have been considered as an important tool and not just as entertainment.

Anashid may have served another, more specific purpose: to prepare suicide bombers. This function cannot be ascertained yet for lack of sources on what happens in the final stages of a suicide attack, but there is at least one prominent example, that of Khalid al-Awhali, one of the two men tasked with bombing the U.S. embassy in Nairobi in 1998, who survived the bombing. According to Fadil Harun, who planned the operation, al-Awhali was to accompany Azzam, the driver of the bombing vehicle, but to jump out shortly before the detonation. Things went according to plan, although al-Awhali was later apprehended. In the subsequent trial, the FBI agent who had interviewed al-Awhali told the court that "on their way Al-'Owhali described to me that he and Azzam were listening to an audio cassette of what he described as chanting poems for motivation in preparing to die on the way to the embassy."[50] Quoting al-Awhali, the FBI agent said:

The interview ended where Mr. al-'Owhali stated that he would like to recite a poem to the investigators and he wanted the official from the Department of Justice to also stay and hear the poem as well. So Al-'Owhali began to say this poem, and it wasn't so much normal speak, it was a chanting, almost a singing-type poem. He was doing it in his – in Arabic, in his language and through the translator I was able to determine that this particular chanting poem questioned whether or not two friends would ever meet again in paradise, and Al-'Owhali explained to me that this chanting poem is what he and Azzam were listening to as they were driving for motivation, they were listening to for motivation as they were driving to attack the U.S. Embassy. And as Al-'Owhali was reflecting on his friendship with Azzam and this chanting poem, he started to cry.[51]

This example suggests that *anashid* may have been used in some (or perhaps most/all) cases to keep up the motivation of would-be suicide bombers.

Islamic or Jihadi *anashid*?

A casual browser of *anashid* on jihadi websites might be forgiven for imagining a Nashville-style industry funded by jihadi tycoons. The sheer number and production quality of *anashid* promoted on jihadi websites is rather impressive. While some *anashid*'s lyrics and tunes are produced for yokels, others are of a higher quality. Indeed, the thinking invested into composing the lyrics of some reflects a profound knowledge of Islamic history, theology, and a discerning sensitivity of the pulse of modern politics on the part of the poet. The caliber of the voices suggests professional singers trained in vocalization. The rhythms accompanying the lyrics can reveal musical talent, and the quality of the productions evokes not training camps or basements, but professional studios.

   The reason for the high production quality is that militants do often not record them. Except for the *anashid* used in the releases by IS, most of the *anashid* promoted by jihadis, even those cited by their leading figures, are not composed or produced by jihadi organizations. While some high-quality productions are the work of jihadi media production companies;[52] most are professionally produced by non-jihadi media outlets. These productions are probably best described as Islamic *anashid* chanting the praises of jihad rather than "jihadi *anashid*."

To put this in perspective, martyrdom and militancy are not alien to the mainstream monotheist traditions, including Islam. For instance, the four-volume *Anashid al-Da'wa al-Islamiyya* (*Anashid* of the Islamic Call) – a written collection of mainstream *anashid* – include entries that extol jihad, laud the bravery of fighters in Afghanistan, foretell of reclaiming Jerusalem, and hail martyrs. One notable *nashid* in this collection, *Unshudat al-Shuhada'*, is written by Amina Qutb, none other than the sister of Sayyid Qutb. The subjects promoted by such *anashid* are likely to appeal to many politically informed Muslims (and some non-Muslims, for that matter); that is why jihadis, among others, have adopted them and put them in the service of promoting their militant causes.[53]

In most cases, *anashid* are to be found on jihadi websites under a section devoted to "audiovisual products" (*qism al-sawtiyyat wa-al-mar'iyyat*). Members on some discussion forums, such as *Shabakat Ansar al-Mujahidin*, may bring a certain *nashid* to the attention of other members by posting a link to it either from YouTube, a file-sharing site, or some other website (not necessarily a jihadi one).[54] In most cases, the *anashid* extolling jihad and martyrdom that are promoted on jihadi websites are produced by non-jihadi media companies and performed by singers who are not affiliated with al-Qaida or other jihadi groups. Indeed, borrowing poetry and *anashid* from non-jihadi authors is common in the jihadi world as long as the content fits the jihadi world-view. In some cases they even borrow poetry from non-Muslims.[55]

It is worthy of note that many of the *anashid* promoted by jihadis are performed by two renowned Saudi artists, Abu Ali and Abu Abd al-Malik, both of whom insist that they have no affiliation with the jihadis. Indeed, in an interview with *Sawt al-Yaman*, Abu Abd al-Malik explicitly dissociated his *anashid* and those of his singing partners from jihadis using his recordings. In the same interview, he remarks that the Saudi Ministry of Information took the decision to disallow media production companies from producing *anashid*. He explains the decision on the basis that "unfortunately, some of our fellow brethren misused these *anashid*: instead of serving as a means to repel oppression and fear, the *anashid* were used and were even [promoted as a] cause to create fear and destabilize security in Muslim countries; and this we disapprove of."[56]

Even *anashid* used in al-Qaida's most official productions need not have been produced by a jihadi media outlet. A case in point is Ayman al-Zawahiri's al-Sahab–produced series of audiovisual statements released in 2011 and 2012 under the title "Missive of Hope and Joy to our People in Egypt." All recordings begin with *Bushrayat*, a *nashid* produced by Taratil, a Saudi media production company,[57] and performed by Abu Ali and Abu Abd al-Malik.[58] Similarly, in his last public statement, bin Ladin recited an excerpt of *Bada'a al-Masir*, a *nashid* performed by the same Abu Abd al-Malik (along with two others).[59] Another compelling example is a popular *nashid*, *Ya Ummati Wajaba al-Kifah* (O My Umma: Fighting Is Now an Obligation), excerpts of which are from a poem by the Egyptian Muslim Brotherhood figure Yusuf al-Qaradawi, who is not a jihadi ideologue. The *nashid* featured in a statement released by Ayman al-Zawahiri in 2009.[60] The excerpt can be roughly rendered:

O billion [Muslims]! When the wounds [of children] appeal for help where/ why do you [hide]?

[Just] give us one million out of the billion, [they would suffice] if they are of sound faith (*sihahan min sihah*)

[With the bravery] of every thousand, we shall conquer and roam every theatre of war.[61]

It should be noted, however, that some *anashid* and recruitment videos are indeed produced by entities that are part of, or closely affiliated with, militant groups. Al-Sahab, for instance, makes use of *Badr al-Riyad*, a video series produced by al-Tajdid,[62] a media arm of a U.K.-based group that at one stage prominently displayed on its website a poem eulogizing bin Ladin.[63] Other *anashid* praising jihadi leaders are clearly produced by jihadi groups, but the number of such *anashid* is not significant in comparison with *anashid* by non-jihadis. For these reasons, one should not equate "*anashid* about jihad" with "pro-jihadi *anashid*" and infer that those who listen to the former sympathize with jihadis.

The same, however, may not be said about the *anashid* produced by IS, which may represent a distinct category. The group has been producing *anashid* since it declared itself the "Islamic State of Iraq" (ISI) in 2006 and announced the establishment of its own media foundation, *Mu'assasat al-Furqan li-al-Intaj al-I'lami*.[64] In the late 2000s and early 2010s, the group produced *anashid* that emphasized its claim to statehood. Since the group declared a caliphate in June 2014, it has polarized the jihadi landscape, and the use of its *anashid* now appears to be limited to its supporters, and the *anashid* feature in the media productions of those groups that have pledged allegiance (*bay'a*) to its leader, Abu Bakr al-Baghdadi.

IS *anashid* may be considered as jihadi *anashid* insofar as they are exclusively produced by a jihadi group. But such a label could be misleading, not least because not all IS *anashid* have a militant theme. It would be more accurate to describe them as "IS *anashid*," for IS is the only jihadi group that relies solely on in-house *anashid* productions. Further, unlike the *anashid* discussed in this chapter, IS *anashid* are not endorsed just for their thematic content but more importantly for the *brand* that they represent.[65] As will be discussed later in this chapter, IS *anashid* appear to be not just about engendering militancy, but also about identity building. In short, when jihadis use IS *anashid*, it is not simply a statement equivalent to "made in/by IS," but rather "we are (or aspire to be) IS."

Common Themes

In its essence, jihadism not only calls on Muslims to join jihad but also seeks to foster a new generation of Muslims who will grow up to love jihad and yearn for martyrdom. The jihadis are not, nor do they wish to be, associated with those Muslims whose political impotence the secular Syrian poet Nizar Qabbani (d. 1998) lamented when he wrote in his famous poem "*Dafatir 'ala Hawamish al-Naksa*," following the Arab defeat in the 1967 Six-Day War:

> Victory is a performance [we enact]
> [How is it possible to achieve it when]
> We [spend our days] sitting around in mosques
> Idlers, lazy
> We compose proverbs or draw up verses of poetry
> And we beg [and hope for] victory against our enemy
> From Him, the Sublime.[66]

The image of idlers is one that the jihadi establishment has revolted against and sought to replace with an activist and self-sacrificial ethos. To this end, jihadi ideologues have advanced elaborate arguments for the necessity of jihad to rid Muslims of "apostate" dictators and expel "infidel" occupiers.[67] However, jihadi strategists may have recognised that appealing to the intellect alone is not sufficient for such an ethos to arise. The lyrics, melodies, and rhythms that combine to form a *nashid*, on the other hand, can touch people's emotions in ways that a dry ideological text cannot.

If the *anashid* that are promoted on jihadi websites cannot be said to be exclusively jihadi, what then is jihadi about them? And what purpose do they serve? Just as ideologues articulated a jihadi ideology by emphasizing militant components of classical Islamic jurisprudence, the jihadi establishment has drawn on the most militant of Islamic *anashid* to form a new, almost exclusively jihad-centred *anashid* corpus. The collection of 636 *anashid* compiled for this study illustrates this point. The collection was posted on the jihadi website *Shabakat al-Mujahidin al-Iliktruniyya*, and it was presented as the largest collection of "jihadi *anashid*" on any forum.[68] It is also the largest collection I have come across in my research. After listening to their lyrics, the *anashid* were coded for their dominant theme. The coding was not always clear-cut as many *anashid* address several topics, and some topics are ambiguous. FIGURE 2.1 shows the distribution by topic.

What follows is a thematic analysis of a selection of *anashid* that are representative of the dominant militant themes.

Tahrid (Incitement) and Tahdid (Threatening the Enemy)

Not surprisingly, the most common theme in *anashid* promoted by jihadis is that of *tahrid* (incitement). *Anashid* of *tahrid* are typically ecumenical in their content, tackling universal motifs such as injustice, oppression, occupation, and the like. For example, "*Lan Udaji*" (I shall not be cowed [into submission]) is a *nashid* whose lyrics are almost guaranteed to move any conscientious listener.[69] It speaks of the pain of those suffering occupation and oppression, and evokes a resilient and defiant spirit that refuses to be cowed into submission. The *nashid* starts by addressing the enemy:

You who are settling
On my soil

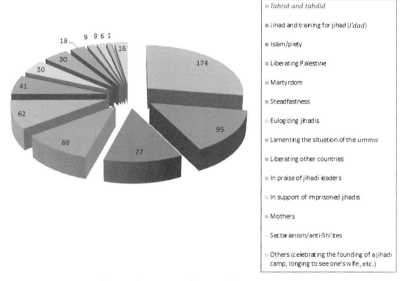

Figure 2.1: Distribution by topic of *anashid* in sample collection

> You who are imbibing
> The blood vessels of [our] necks
> ...
> You who steal away
> The dawn of my country
>
> I shall not be cowed [into submission]

The *nashid* then enumerates what may be considered to be insurmountable obstacles and unbearable grievances, but only to follow them with an audacious stance by the mujahid who refuses to compromise and is unfazed by the hardships awaiting him on the battlefield. Thus, the element of *tahdid* (menace/threat) clearly underlies and indeed sustains its theme of *tahrid*:

> Robbed of my childhood and youth
> I remain radiant despite [life's] darkness
> ...
> Steadfast I [stay on] despite my injuries
> Patient I [prevail] despite my pain
>
> I shall not be cowed [into submission]

Interestingly, *Lan Udaji* does not include any religious references, the words "God" and "jihad" do not figure as part of its lyrics. Hence, it could appeal to anybody concerned by occupation and oppression around the world.

Similarly, the *nashid* "*Bada'a al-Masiru ila al-Hadaf*" (The March to [Victory] Has Begun) draws on idealistic and heroic themes,[70] and although it is not overly religious, it uses terms like "*hadyu al-salaf*" (the guidance of the righteous predecessors). It is noteworthy that Usama bin Ladin chose to recite excerpts of this *nashid* in his last public statement, which addressed the Arab Spring. The central motifs of this *nashid* pertain to freedom and liberty:

> The march to [victory] has begun
> Resolute the free [man] advances
>
> When he sets out on his march, the free
> Is [invincible] – he is tireless, he is unstoppable

Addressing those who consider themselves religious but do not to engage in militancy, *Bada'a al-masiru* appeals to their sense of religious responsibility. More specifically, it alludes to the culpability they must feel for standing idle as their fellow Muslims resolutely join the march to victory:

> He who knows not [God's teachings]
> Is not as blameworthy for not finding the Way as he who knows
>
> He who knows [God's] guidance
> Follows in the footsteps of the salaf

For those who doubt whether the jihadis will be victorious, *Bada'a al-Masiru* has an assuring and calming answer. Victory has the same quality of certitude as:

> The night [that] cannot conceal
> From the eyes the morning when it rises
>
> For the eye does not agree [to see] what
> May have happened, unless it actually happened

The *anashid* of *tahrid* and *tahdid* are not always tasteful. Some call for violence in very explicit terms. The *nashid* "*Udrub Darabataka al-Muntazara*" (Strike Your Awaited Blow) illustrates in word and in melody the call to immediate action:[71]

Strike your awaited blow
And kill as many of the infidels as you go
Our nations a cemetery render
[to bury] the defeated armies of unbelief [as we tear them asunder]
The appointed time of the strike has now come
And the time for victory has also come
Get up, say bismillah and proceed to butcher [the enemy]
Do not slack, do not delay
For falsehood is boisterous, we can no longer put up with its arrogance
. . .
Destroy, repeat, do not negotiate
The glories of Manhattan conquests [iterate]

Jihad

While all *anashid* promoted on jihadi websites are meant to serve as a
form of *tahrid* to take up jihad, one nevertheless may consider that
some *anashid* treat the theme of jihad as a subject in its own right.
These *anashid* focus on the love of and yearning for jihad, the heroism
of "God's knights" on the battlefield, their desire to sacrifice their lives,
and their properties in this world to gain the greater prize of eternal life
in the hereafter. The *nashid* "*Bakat 'Ayni*" (My Eyes Are Shedding
Tears) speaks of powerful feelings that could only be experienced by
performing jihad:[72]

My eyes are shedding tears
[Instead of] rebuking me [why not] take me
To the land of jihad and [say] farewell to me
When I recalled [the obligation] of jihad my eyes flowed with tears
They were inflamed by the humiliation of dependence

The *nashid* "*Fi Kulli Ardin li-al-Ilahi Fawarisun*" (In Every Land God Has
Knights) addresses more explicit heroic themes, drawing on the sacrifices
of modern jihadi warriors as examples to be admired and emulated:[73]

In every land God has knights
[Unshakable] in their fighting the path of sacrifice they pursue
They take pleasure fighting their way through arduous mountain trails
Their blood record [the lyrics] of glory, quenching Muslims' thirst [for dignity]

. . .
Khattab is a symbol of giving and sacrifice
He loved martyrdom

Istishhad (Martyrdom Seeking)

It should come as no surprise that *istishhad* (martyrdom seeking) is one of the key themes represented in this collection. The lyrics of the *anashid* of martyrdom seeking are arguably the most moving and the richest in metaphors. "*Lillahi Darruka*" is a good example:[74] the martyr is one who refuses to put up with *dhull* (humiliation) and has no attachment to this transient world. He is ready to sacrifice his all, knowing that a seat alongside prophets awaits him in the afterlife and damsels are chanting love songs in anticipation of his arrival:

> How awesome you are, you took no liking to our [transient] world
> You refused to follow in a defeated spirit behind false visions
> . . .
> Today the horse of [heavenly] glory met his rider
> [The martyr's] glances were beaming as he fell [in battle] rejoicing
>
> Today the damsel was married to her lover
> He is sated after spending the night in her now familiar quarters
>
> Enchanted the damsel sang love tunes [to her lover]
> Delight in your exuberant and joyful [eternal] life
> . . .
> God promised martyrs a seat
> At the highest rank, alongside the prophets
>
> Lord O Lord my heart is melting away yearning
> To be in paradise, [I pray] you fulfill its wish.

Despite the heroism that these *anashid* invariably evoke in the minds of their listeners, their content is mindful of the pain that death – martyrdom style or otherwise – is likely to cause the family of martyrs, especially their mothers. Jihadi literature in general recognizes the sacrifices of mothers, which may be why some of the *anashid* dealing with martyrdom address head-on the guilty conscience a would-be martyr might suffer from at the thought of picturing his mother mourning his death. One such *nashid*, "*Ummahu Khalli al-Dam'a*" (Mother, Quit Crying) brings up themes of motherly grief, but also of consolation:[75]

> Mother, quit crying and sighing
> Your buried son died a martyr

Mother, do not say that he departed
[Do not say] that your son was lost to the path of sorrow

I am not dead, I am alive in the hereafter
In paradise, I have been reborn
I am here alive, by God I continue to exist
I live happily under God's protection

In God's path I died, what
A joy it was [as] I ascended [to heaven]
And as I saw in my own eyes O mother my seat
Reserved for me in the midst of paradise

God's angels were at my wedding
In a procession they served as witnesses [to my marriage]
I wished I would return to life so that I may be killed
As a martyr many times more in the service of God

Do not shed tears, though we part ways today
This day shall forever be a holiday
If only you knew the honour [through my martyrdom] I attained
You would have used my pure blood as [ink] to compose a *nashid*
[in celebration]

Islamic State *Anashid* and State Building

Although this chapter does not include a systematic study of IS *anashid*, a few observations are worth including. As far as the overall quality is concerned, the production of the *anashid* is professional. The lyrics, the *munshid*'s voices, and the sound effects all suggest that the group is not producing *anashid* on the cheap. Although those accustomed to the militant Islamic *anashid* are likely to miss the moving and upbeat rhythms chanted by Abu Ali and Abu Abd al-Malik. Given the group's use of *anashid* exclusively produced by its own media arm, it suggests that unlike other jihadi groups, IS may conceive of *anashid* not simply as a tool to engender militancy, but also as a way to build group identity. To appreciate better the implications of this possibility, one needs to know whether IS members are forbidden from chanting non-IS *anashid* on a casual basis; and if so, how strict is IS about policing it? And what might be the consequences of those caught chanting them? At this stage, we do not have answers to these questions.

As for the themes of IS *anashid*, the forty Arabic ones I examined are consistent with those of the larger dataset mentioned previously. Among others, they include themes related to piety, yearning for martyrdom, rejecting humiliation, eulogizing martyrs, prisoners, and mother's grief. As one would expect, some celebrate the establishment of the Islamic State and its Imam/leader. Yet despite the group's rigid sectarianism, not least its explicit animosity against Shi'ites, it is surprising that this does not feature as a dominant theme in its *anashid*. Some references to sectarianism exist, but not as a theme in its own right.

Notwithstanding the overall consistency between IS *anashid* and those analyzed earlier in this chapter, the military victories achieved by IS accompanied by gory public display of its practices have imparted a certain realism to those *anashid* that are designed to threaten the enemy (*tahdid*). These *anashid* differ from previous ones by not being simply aspirational; they celebrate threats that have already been carried out. Thus, IS comes across as a group that has not only intent, but also capability.

For example, the *nashid* "*Al-Maliki Ghada Maqhura*" ([Nouri] al-Maliki Has Been Vanquished) is essentially about the many successive victories the group has achieved. The reference in the title to Iraq's former Prime Minister is sure to evoke in the listeners' mind at least two key IS achievements. It recalls both that al-Maliki had to resign and that his resignation was largely caused by the group's capture of Mosul in June 2014, following which the caliphate was proclaimed. The lyrics of the *nashid* enumerate the names of areas that were in the headlines for weeks or months, ones that have either been conquered by IS or where the group put up a serious fight against government forces (e.g., Falluja, Ramadi, Samarra, Tikrit, Beiji, Haditha). The same *nashid* celebrates that IS succeeded in "burning the Sahwat" (the Arab Sunni tribes of Iraq who once collaborated with U.S. forces against the Islamic State of Iraq, as the group was once called); that it defeated the Shi'ites and their Iranian supporters (*al-safawiyya dahar-naha*); and the delight of establishing a territorial state where God's Law reigns supreme. Perhaps the most upbeat *nashid* produced by IS is that which accompanied the video in which the Jordanian pilot was burned. Titled "*Qariban, Qariban, Tarawna al-'Ajiba*" (Soon, Soon, You Shall See Something Wondrous), it spares the listener no detail of the group's gory public practices. The *nashid* speaks of "bearing slaughter and death" to the enemy, and of "beheading," to "break the disgrace [you caused us] . . . so that you may taste humiliation." When this *nashid* was first heard on the execution video published in February 2015, its lyrics went hand in hand with the silent rhythm of the flames that burned the Jordanian pilot, leaving little doubts that the group's threats are indeed actionable.

Conclusion

The powerful impact of rhythm and harmony in shaping people's dispositions was recognized in ancient times. Indeed, in devising an education plan for the "guardians" entrusted with the security and governance of his *Republic*, Plato considered that it would be difficult to find anything better than "physical training for bodies and music and poetry for the soul."[76] He believed that "education in music and poetry is most important . . . because rhythm and harmony permeate the inner part of the soul more than anything else."[77]

The prominent place that *anashid* occupy in the online universe of the jihadis suggests leaders are finding them useful. Indeed, what better means to promote militancy than a tool that is *literally* music to the ear? Although the lawfulness of *anashid* is contested from an Islamic legal perspective, the jihadi establishment has embraced them. As some of the internal jihadi communications discussed in this chapter reveal, *anashid* are recognized by the jihadi establishment as an effective method that contributes to the creation of a jihadi culture.

Their utility is perceived to be multifaceted. *Anashid* can entice new recruits by showing them that there is more to jihadi life than just fighting. *Anashid* can motivate members during the hardship of training and combat. And they can help calm suicide bombers as they enter the final phase of their missions. These are but some of the ways in which *anashid* seem to serve jihadi groups.

But will *anashid* serve to divide jihadis much like ideological differences have? If IS's use of *anashid* that are exclusively produced by its own media arm is an indication that it conceives of them not simply as a tool to engender militancy, but also as integral to its identity, then *anashid* may well deepen the growing schisms among jihadis.

3 | *A Musicological Perspective on Jihadi* anashid

JONATHAN PIESLAK

Music has always held a precarious position within Islam – at times embraced, at others denounced for its sensually arousing potential.[1] The jihadi relationship with music is particularly confusing to outside observers. In the 2000s, for example, al-Qaida produced videos that opened with the words "Attention! Musical Accompaniment Is Not Permitted," but were subsequently filled with melodious recitations of the Qur'an and elaborate a cappella hymns (*anashid*).[2] Similarly, young Islamists in the West might sympathize with groups that prohibit music entirely, yet listen to jihad-themed rap and hip-hop like the song "Dirty Kuffar" or the music of the British Islamist band Blakstone.

This chapter explores the ambiguous jihadi relationship with music by examining the role of *anashid* in the media and culture of al-Qaida. Using tools of analytical and historical musicology – my original field of study – I will look at how jihad-themed *anashid* are constructed, how the genre has developed over time, and how it is received and used by activists. My analysis complements the previous chapter by Nelly Lahoud by treating *anashid* first and foremost as pieces of music. I will show that jihadi *anashid* are often elaborate compositions that are produced with increasing technical sophistication. They appear to function in al-Qaida media as a means of enticing recruits, retaining members, and motivating members to action by eliciting emotion. *Anashid* seem to have a particularly strong ability to create a sense of interpersonal bonds that appear so important to recruitment and membership retention.

The Legal Status of Music

Within the Muslim world, debates have raged for centuries about the permissibility of music (*musiqa*), the use of musical instruments (especially drums), and the distinctions between listening to (*sama'*) and performing music.[3] Although consensus has been elusive, a limited

63

number of legal positions have crystallized. For certain fundamentalist groups, such as al-Qaida, there is no gray area; all forms of *musiqa* are unequivocally forbidden under their interpretation of Islam. In reality, though, this begs the questions What is "music" in Islam? and How can jihadi groups employ and enjoy sound forms that most non-Muslim observers would consider music?

An instructive example to begin answering these questions is the *adhan*, or call to prayer, which is heard every day from minarets throughout the Muslim world. The call to prayer bears a striking similarity to Christian chant as an unaccompanied religious, vocal form. Furthermore, there is a clear melodic structure to the sung vocal articulation, typical markers of what many of us would call "music." In Islam, however, this is decidedly not music (*musiqa*). Instead, the *adhan* and similar forms, including Qur'anic recitation (*qira'a, tilawa*), are considered stylized recitation, vocalized religious chant, or poetry; they are emotive sonic manifestations of the divine truths revealed to the prophet Muhammad, not simple acts of music making. Sacred cantillation is not music as we in the West would define it.

Scripture is unclear or ambiguous on several technical issues pertaining to music – such as a positive definition and the use of musical instruments – and this has produced a contested gray area of musical practices. Muslim theologians seem in agreement that music's danger lies in its agency for sensual (and particularly sexual) arousal. Nonetheless, they have yet to establish a universally accepted definition of what music is and whether or not it should be permitted beyond an unaccompanied vocal recitation of an Islamic text. Rulings on permissibility are highly variable, and the scholarly distinctions between *musiqa* and other sound forms are contested.[4]

One of the principal guidelines directing permissibility is that lawful "non-*musiqa*" has texts addressing some component of Islam, while unlawful "music" does not. The gray areas of Islamic "music" arise when texts start gravitating toward less clearly scriptural themes and musical instruments are added to accompany the voice. Throughout history, the vocal or instrumental music that lay at the fringes of permissibility could gain wider acceptance by adopting some of the musical features of accepted sound forms, particularly Qur'anic recitation, thereby granting it "non-*musiqa*" status. Even so, where is the line that divides permissible (*halal*) recitations from forbidden (*haram*) or unfavored (*makruh*) music? Are instruments allowed?

What about certain types of drums? A sound form granted acceptance within the realm of lawful (non)-music may be virtually indistinguishable from a non-lawful one. What may be "music" to one theologian may be "non-*musiqa*" to another, and their rulings on permissibility may differ so widely that the designation of outlaw-able "music" could be ascribed to something that contains fewer instruments and drums than what another theologian would label as permissible "non-*musiqa*."

Adding to these problems, one of the most common arguments in the debate on the legality of *anashid* is the degree to which *anashid* become their own ends, outweighing the message they are intended to serve.[5] Such dilemmas appear throughout Christian literature as well; both Augustine of Hippo in his *Confessions* (397–398) and John Calvin's introduction to the 1543 edition of the Geneva Psalter express concern that the power of the music itself can easily seduce one away from religious virtue.[6] Augustine and Calvin ultimately approve the carefully monitored use of music in religious service, and in *Tracts on Listening to Music*, Islam scholar James Robson asserts that Calvin's ruling on music "is essentially the same argument as that used by al-Ghazali and other Muslims, who hold that music is lawful."[7]

Finally, it is important to acknowledge the potential influence and historical connection of the *anashid* used by al-Qaida to war songs and the *tabl khanah* (warlike music), which was early military band music that had instruments.[8] These genres are fairly distinctive within the soundscape of Islamic music in that they represent some of the only examples where exceptions were made for instruments (drums and tambourines in particular) seemingly among all interpretations of Islam. The reasons behind this permissibility of instruments are not clear, but it seems sensible to assert that among the justifications included the use of instruments to assist in battlefield maneuvers and commands and an instrument's (particularly the drum's) ability to heighten a combatant's appetite for violence. These reasons, among others, may have proven too useful in the arena of military conquest to be overruled by orthodox religious practice.

A Modern History of Jihadi *Anashid*

Contemporary Muslim usage of the term *anashid* covers almost any musical genre that makes textual mention of Islam. Both fully orchestrated pop songs and solo vocal cantillations bear the title of *anashid*, and the only similarity across the varying languages, geographies, and musical styles in which *anashid* are produced seems to be the semantic reference to Islam. The academic literature in musicology is fairly vague. Most scholars and historians of Islamic music define *anashid* as a vocalized, songlike form, but rarely go into specifics. Musicologist Amnon Shiloah sheds light on the etymology of *anashid*, describing it as a term derived from *inshad*, a raising of the voice usually associated with public recitations of poetry in pre-Islamic times.[9] Shiloah refers to *anashid* as a "religious poetic genre" or a "vocal improvisation."[10] In another study, ethnomusicologist Birgit Berg describes the etymology of *anashid* as being "to lecture or reverberations" and suggests that the genre's principal function was to present "lyrics that promote proper behavior and the fulfillment of religious doctrine."[11] Finally, in an older study from 1929, George Farmer notes that *anashid* ("a recognized vocal form of the olden days") demonstrate rhythmic and unrhythmic structure, presumably meaning that these songs were sung around a somewhat regular pulse, or they were freely vocalized in time.[12] This is not a very informative description because music, being a temporal phenomenon, either exists in recurrent pulse structures or it does not. Examples are unfortunately absent from his otherwise careful study as are any descriptions of pitch.

The most thorough academic treatment of *anashid* appears in Patricia Matusky and Tan Sooi Beng's study *The Music of Malaysia*. They trace the genre's history back to a "first" *anashid*, "*Tala'a al-Badru 'Alayna*" (Oh, the White Moon Rose over Us), which reportedly was sung by a crowd in Medina that gathered to welcome the Prophet Muhammad after his journey from Mecca.[13] From this and a few other early *anashid*, they argue, emerged a distinct performance practice in which *anashid* were used to instill Islamic values as well as express national pride:

Originally nasyid was performed informally at home while seated on the floor in a circle formation after studying the Qur'an. The teachers taught while the students sang nasyid. The process of teaching and learning took place by rote method and in call and response style without using any musical instruments. The voices alone carried the song texts and their messages, as the lessons took place from day to day.[14]

They suggest that the 1950s were a pivotal decade in *anashid* practice in Malaysia. The genre moved out of the home and into the sphere of public entertainment, incorporating musical instruments, which by the 1970s had evolved into *anashid* accompanied by orchestras and synthesizers. Structurally, Matusky and Tan propose that *anashid* were traditionally based on the *maqam* system of pitch that is a part of classical Arabic music (secular art music with roots in pre-Islamic times) with lyrics most often dictating form.[15]

One of the challenges in trying to understand the musical contexts that gave birth to the contemporary *anashid* is that the history of Arabic music is not strongly rooted in notated text. The tradition of musical performance was mostly oral and based on specific systems of pitch improvisation (the *maqam* system) and rhythmic patterns.[16] The need for notation as a necessary means of communicating a musical idea (i.e., musical score) was simply not a feature of Arabic music. As such, tracing the changes, influences, and development of certain musical genres, such as *anashid*, is almost impossible because comparisons are highly limited.

The evolution of *anashid* in the modern era is, unfortunately, not well documented. It is entirely likely that, as Matusky and Tan suggest, *anashid* migrated from the private realm into the public sphere in the 1950s and 1960s throughout the Muslim world. This development was made decidedly more pervasive and had a stronger impact through the changes in audio technology that occurred during this period. To a lesser degree the LP, but especially the audiocassette, created a consumer market for all genres of music, which circulated widely due to the recording technology that made high-fidelity music simpler to produce and duplicate. One might propose that the explosion in music consumption ignited by the LP, and later, the audiocassette catalyzed this move from private to public as well as enabled consumers to listen to music in the privacy of their own home as often as they liked.

It was not until the late 1960s that militant Islamists seem to have embraced the *anashid* genre as an art form of choice. In the wake of the 1967 Arab-Israeli War, the Palestinian group Fatah broadcast songs that professed explicitly violence-endorsing themes intended to foster notions of Palestinian nationalism and the call for armed resistance.[17] According to Middle East specialist Yezid Sayigh, the lyrics of such songs broadcast on the radio during this period included "I am born, live, and die a *fida'i*, until I return, land of ancestors, immortal people," "the Palestinian people is a revolution, take my blood O revolution and give me victories," "Kalashnikoff makes a waterfall of blood ...

O Dayan, drinking blood is the custom of our men," and "I carry my machine-gun that the generations after us may carry a scythe ... I have made my wounds and the blood a river that courses through the plain and valleys."[18]

Later, in the late 1970s and 1980s, a group of Syrian artists began writing *anashid* with lyrics more actively addressing political Muslim causes. These *munshidun*, known as Abu Dujanah, Abu al-Joud, Abu Ratib, and others, were not fighters themselves, but appear to have been inspired by the Arab-Israeli conflict and the unrest in Lebanon and Syria during this period.[19] Their *anashid* differ from modern jihad-themed ones in that these singers used the duff (a frame drum) with other percussion instruments occasionally, and their lyrics are not as explicit as the Palestinian songs mentioned above. Nonetheless, their impact, while not precisely chronicled, seems to have contributed to an overall popularization of *anashid* with themes supporting an activist political Muslim agenda.[20]

By the mid-1980s *anashid* had become a prominent feature of jihadi culture in Afghanistan. John Baily, a noted scholar on the music of Afghanistan, points out that there was a flourishing industry of mujahidin cassettes in Peshawar in the mid-1980s. Baily likewise laments the absence of research and documentation on this music, but notes that these cassettes, "were bought by Mujahideen fighters and taken to Afghanistan for entertainment purposes."[21] Many of the features we now witness in contemporary al-Qaida *anashid* were present in the cassettes Baily describes, long epics about particular groups or fighters and insertions of real (less common) or artificial (more common) gunfire in the recording.[22]

Given the challenges and highly varying religious interpretations surrounding what is permissible in *anashid*, we might understand *anashid* as a catchall genre within the global Islamic community that can be manipulated to fit variable doctrinal interpretations. Because almost any stance on the permissibility of *anashid* and music is possible, even from the legal point of view (i.e., scriptural analysis), any particular *anashid*, ranging from solo vocal melody to pop song, could be allowed depending on the political, social, or other aims of the group. This would clarify the inconsistencies we notice among the music of violence-endorsing, Islamic terrorist groups. Such differences might be explained, in part, by proposing that a group like Hamas is appealing to a more Western-exposed youth culture from which they wish to recruit (hence, their permissiveness of instruments, synthesizers, and even women vocalists). Islam scholar Jonas Otterbeck makes the credible observation that a Western-exposed and consumer-inclined youth culture seems to be growing in Arab nations, and religious authorities have had to address the divide that has grown progressively wider between traditional Islamic values and influences from consumer culture, which are now more than ever accessible to Muslim youths.[23] We might therefore view the spectrum of "music" in global jihad-endorsing culture as being determined by the recruiting goals and cultural backgrounds of distinct groups, held in check more or less by their ideological framework. For instance, Taliban *taranas* (Taliban "songs" as described by Baily) are set in traditional Afghan/Pasto modes and rhythms, not the Arabic *maqam* system, corresponding to the cultural background of those who are members and those they wish to recruit.

Musical Characteristics

I now turn to a musicological examination of the *anashid* presently used and circulated by al-Qaida, addressing aspects of pitch, rhythm, affect, form, text, and production quality.[24] These melodies are stamped with the distinctive features of a cappella vocal music, which means there are no instruments or drums, although vocal harmonizations/arrangements appear. Texts most often address topics related to jihad and martyrdom, and there is occasional overdubbing of sound effects such as gunfire, explosions, animal noises such as lion roars, and shouting. Even within these strict parameters, most pieces are thoughtfully constructed both as musical works and in terms of the production fidelity.

The pitch structure of many of these *anashid* is governed by the traditional system of *maqam*, derived from Arab secular music. Musicologist Habib Touma states that most forms of religious music can be traced back to *maqam*, a musical structure of pitch originating in the secular art music of pre-Islamic times. Thus, Qur'anic recitation is typically based on one of the *maqamat* (*maqam*, plural) of Arabian secular music, often *maqam Bayati*, *Hijaz*, or others. The *maqam* system regulates melodic organization and might be thought of analogously to the system of Western musical modes or scales with a few important distinctions.

Maqamat are typically made up of two distinct tetrachords – collections of four adjacent pitches. Although trichords or pentachords appear, tetrachords are the most common. The subgroups are called the upper and lower *jins* (*ajnas*, plural), and it is more accurate to think of a *maqam* as a product of two or more *ajnas* than a single eight-note scale. We should further note the subtleties of intonation and performance that distinguish *maqamat* from conventional conceptions about musical scales. Many *maqamat*, while employing microtonal intervals (quarter-step intervals), have even further intervallic divisions. For instance, the E quarter flat of *maqam Bayati* is slightly lower than the E quarter flat of *maqam Rast*.[25] Each *maqam* also has different guidelines of performance, dictating melodic development and the emphasis of specific pitches. This means that two *maqamat* may have identical or transposed interval structures, but different pitches are emphasized in performance. Such is the case between the *maqam Nahawand* and *maqam Farahfaza*, which have identical interval content (corresponding to the natural minor scale). Yet the *maqam Farahfaza* places greater emphasis on the third degree and the interior *Ajam* trichord (corresponding to the third, fourth, and fifth degrees).[26]

In terms of rhythm, Touma suggests that a distinct rhythmic organization is not connected to *maqamat*.[27] While it is true that many *maqamat* are freely improvised as are many *anashid*, it does not imply that rhythm is purely the domain of improvisation or compositional personality. Rather, Arabic music is swimming in rhythmic patterns, and it is further elaborated by the Turkish, Persian, and even Greek rhythms that may appear. While a clear metrical and/or rhythmic framework does emerge in some of this music – Matusky and Tan propose that *anashid* "comprise sung poetry using Middle Eastern rhythms" – the degree to which the music is based, in a (pre)compositional sense, on specific Arabic rhythms is not always clear.[28]

Affectively speaking, the pitch structure of *maqamat* represent a "tone space," to paraphrase Touma, in which an instrumentalist or vocalist improvises according to particular parameters.[29] These melodies form what ethnomusicologist Ali Jihad Racy calls an "ecstatic substance" (*tarab* or *saltana*) and have distinct emotional characters associated with them, regulating which *maqamat* may be used for conveying different thematic and emotive content.[30] Throughout the course of a performance, the pitch space may change via modulation to any number of *maqamat*, and the aptitude of a performer is often judged according to their ability to successfully weave among varying *maqamat* in an engaging and seamless manner.

Formally, these *anashid* vary from through-composed epics to a verse-chorus form. Here, too, some forms can be linked to traditional Arabic music. The verse-chorus form might be traced to the genre known as *madih an-nabawi*, a genre of Arabic song dedicated to eulogizing the Prophet Muhammad and structured around a solo singer and a group of men, forming the chorus.[31] The chorus sings in strict rhythmic organization while the soloist is more improvisational, usually singing the same line of text.[32] Also, the call and response style, corresponding to the verse-chorus form, may arise from how Matusky and Tan suggest *anashid* were first practiced, in which students learned Islamic lessons through call and response with their teachers.[33]

For the composers, the poetry or text is often the most significant component of *anashid*. Abu Ratib, one of the most recognized *anashid* singers in the Muslim world, summarized this point in an e-mail correspondence with this author: "One important aspect about nashed [*anashid*] is it prioritizes the lyrics. The words and meanings of the songs are the most important part, even more important than the 'maqams'."[34] Thus we need to keep in mind that *anashid*, at least in theory, are intended to transmit the messages of the texts above all else.

In sum, then, historically and musically speaking, *anashid* can be defined as a metered or free rhythm vocal genre traditionally structured on the *maqam* system of pitch. Evolving from pre-Islamic, public recitation with a loud or raised voice, these melodies most likely incorporated degrees of improvisation in performance. Perhaps most important to observe is that this genre originates with the text or poetry, which fully determines the musical structure.

This look at *anashid* in musicological terms provides the necessary background to assert that the *anashid* used by al-Qaida in videos released by al-Sahab, as well as many other jihadi groups, are typically based on *maqamat*. A survey of al-Sahab's almost hour-long documentary *The Red Mosque* provides a suitable example.[35] The video is peppered with excerpts from *anashid* built on *maqamat*, seemingly suited to the meaning and emotive content of the texts. In one example, the following *anashid* is sung (quotation from the English subtitles):

Chorus: "Rise! Oh defenders of my religion, let's rebel against this regime of vice"

Verse: "It is the need of the time that we take a sword in hand, and crush the worshippers of falsehood, Let's accustom ourselves to continuous struggle, And begin to love the world of dust and blood."[36]

The pitch structure reveals the *maqam Farahfaza*, a *maqam* within the larger family of *Nahawand* (*Nahawand* is both a specific *maqam* and a term for a larger family of *maqam*).[37] The *Nahawand* family of *maqam* is described by one Islamist forum member as, "motivating and dynamic, suit[ed to] the Jihadic Nasheeds."[38] While technically not a *nashid*, Qur'an verse 5:51 is recited earlier in the video, cast in *maqam Hijaz* – a typical *maqam* for Qur'anic recitation. Other *anashid* in the video are consistent in terms of their *maqam* structure. The texts are inspirational calls to defend the faith or rousing musical eulogies to martyrs based on *maqamat Farahfaza/Nahawand*, while the Qur'anic recitations (*qira'a*) are set to *maqam Hijaz*. The *anashid* and *qira'a* in the above-mentioned al-Sahab video, "The West and The Dark Tunnel," are similarly composed.[39]

Is there a connection between a *nashid's* stylistic features and its topic or content? Probably not. A closer analysis does not reveal a connection between *maqam* (or other musical features) and the theme of the song. I studied a sample of fifty *anashid* from a compilation circulating on jihadi websites and found no clear correlations between content on the one hand and *maqam*, form, duration, harmony, production quality, background effects, or other features on the other.[40] Certainly, *maqamat* are selected based on their emotion/meaning in a general way, but the kind of categorical nuance Lahoud provides does not reveal a pattern or connection between *maqam* and theme. For instance, *maqamat Nahawand* or *Farahfaza* adequately suit any number of themes as identified by Lahoud, such as Jihad, Iraq, Martyrdom, or Mujahideen, and indeed these *maqamat* are used to express these themes within the sample examined. This should come as no surprise; most of the emotion or meaning within the *maqam* system is flexible enough so as to embrace many themes.

Finally, most jihad-themed *anashid* are recorded in studios and avail themselves of a variety of sound enhancement and manipulation techniques to improve the quality of the recording. Producers take full advantage of the opportunities offered by contemporary recording technology and techniques. Recordings typically involve subtle and not-so-subtle uses of reverb, delay, stereo panning, and occasionally the overdubbing of sound effects, all of which attempts to add to the overall impact of the message without violating the instrument-free mandate.

A close examination of a jihad-themed *nashid*, "Amerna Abkek," posted on tawhed.net, nicely demonstrates many of these devices at work.[41] Listening to this *nashid* with headphones reveals that the primary vocal line is panned in the center. To the right side of the stereo field is the same vocal line articulated slightly after the main vocal melody but drenched in reverb and delay and at a lower volume. To the left of the stereo field is the same line, again drenched in reverb and delay and slightly softer, but heard just after the melody on the right side. The result is a carefully crafted sonic texture in which the main vocal line moves about the stereo field, in time from right to left, effected by reverb, delay, and volume so as to literally resound the message in the listener's ears. While the use of such recording effects is quite common on vocal parts in many recorded music genres (albeit not with such a heavy hand), we might assume that such techniques are intended to emulate the sonic environment of a mosque in which recitation can reverberate off the walls. Sonically speaking, this may endow the recording with the solemnity of religious service. Such techniques are quite common among contemporary jihad-themed *anashid* and represent a full realization and use of recording techniques to enhance the effect of the music.

The Reception of Jihadi *Anashid*

If al-Qaida are so conservative, we might ask: why do they bother with *anashid* at all? From a theological viewpoint, they could simply stay out of the debates surrounding *anashid* altogether – an idea that is certainly possible and much safer.[42] Presumably, they are promoting and utilizing jihad-themed *anashid* for a reason, and I would argue that these *anashid* are dynamic cultural catalysts in recruitment, membership retention, morale, and motivation for action.[43] Although it would indeed be challenging to prove such an assertion scientifically, we can make a strong case for it by demonstrating the potency of music to forge interpersonal bonds and emotionally impact listeners, and then to examine what the jihadis themselves report about their responses to *anashid*.

Starting with a survey of online discussions, it is interesting to note that quite often the extra-textual features of jihad-themed *anashid*, such as the vocal timbre and arrangement, melody, and rhythmic structure, create the initial connection or enjoyment among listeners, not the lyrics. Most threads about one's preferred jihad-themed *anashid* almost invariably point to the quality of the singing, the beauty of the melody, even the "thumpin'" rhythm, as the reasons for any *anashid* to break into one's favorites list. The poetry or text, while not ignored or absent from these discussions, seems to run second to the timbral and musical components of the *anashid*. In fact, many non-Arabic speaking listeners probably do not understand the lyrics and thus make an initial connection to the music on extra-textual level, even if they later request a translation. Specifically, rhythm is a highly valued component of many *anashid* within jihad-supporting culture. Those demonstrating vocal lines with repeated beat patterns and driving rhythms are the most popular among listeners of this music.

Islamic discussion forums often include threads where users discuss their favorite jihad-themed *anashid*, and the most popular appear to be those that have an up-tempo and/or clearly articulated beat. For example, the Ummah.com forum included a thread entitled "the best of Jihadi Nasheeds," which ran from July 4, 2005, until it was closed on June 21, 2007, and included 1,166 posts. One of the opening posts was by a certain "Rashid," who wrote: "Anyway, I'm back, and want to build my nasheed collection. ☺ Anyone have some nice, fast paced, Jihad nasheeds?"[44] When this thread hit 1,000 posts, a new one was set up, and this latter thread included more than 3,000 posts when I last accessed it in March 2007. Surveys of other threads, such as "my favorite Jihad nasheeds" on http://wup-forum.com, reinforce the impression that pace matters, because the majority of links and videos contain up-tempo, invigorating *anashid*.[45] The sounds, timbres, and cultural resonances of the genre generate much of the initial and sustaining appeal, particularly to non-Arabic-speaking audiences, the message and ideology are seemingly along for the ride.

Without doubt, the Internet has become a very important platform for the dissemination of jihadi propaganda products. But it has also raised challenges for radical Islamists because it exposes Muslim youth to ideas and products of Western, secular culture. Muslim societies are inundated with Western music, television, and movies, and this effect was palpable during the so-called Arab Spring in 2011, when many protesters expressed their dissent with Western-inspired cultural genres. In Libya, for example, Western music (Pink Floyd and hip-hop) became the soundtracks of the resistance against Ghaddafi. Jihad-themed *anashid* thus cannot be understood in a vacuum; they are in permanent competition with secular cultural impulses over the attention of young people. No doubt, the producers of jihad-themed *anashid* or those *anashid* selected for propaganda must abide by the ideological guidelines of the group – al-Qaida is not going to start using *anashid* with instruments no matter how appealing – but there may be certain timbre, sonic, or pitch/rhythm elements that render any given nashid more relatable.

This may also help explain why jihadi hip-hop and rap have been so important to Western-exposed Muslim audiences. The music reaches the youth from which future jihadis may emerge with a message presented in a musical language they are predisposed to enjoy, even when it appears as a musical genre of the culture they oppose. Additionally, as mentioned above, many listeners of traditional jihad-themed *anashid* (those without instruments) are not altogether attracted to this music because of its message, but through the quality of the singing, melodic beauty, and driving rhythmic structure. Thus, when attempting to draw people to radical ideology, do not lead with the ideology if you can find a more attractive garment in which to dress the message. And music provides very fashionable clothes.

But why *anashid* over other aesthetic forms? Part of the answer probably lies in music's ability to foster interpersonal bonds. In *Music in Everyday Life*, musicologist Tia DeNora proposes that one of music's principal functions is to serve as "a device for clarifying social order, for structuring subjectivity (desire and the temporal parameters of emotion and the emotive dimension of interaction) and for establishing a basis for collaborative action."[46] Music unites people through the shared experience of enjoyment, and this unifying quality can be a powerful means of recruitment and strengthening the sense of community among members. While the processes of recruitment and membership retention in groups such as al-Qaida is enormously complex, many recent studies of extremist groups suggest that membership is less the result of ideological appeal than of interpersonal bonds. Studies by various authors point to social relationships as the initial and sustaining aspects of the stages of member recruitment, with ideological acceptance coming as a final step.[47] In an examination of recruitment into cults and sects Stark and Bainbridge conclude, "Rather than being drawn to the group because of the appeal of its ideology, people were drawn to the ideology because of their ties to the group – final conversion was coming to accept the opinions of one's friends."[48]

When understood in this fashion, the sounds of jihad-themed *anashid* are a fruitful means of attracting listeners, but they also carry an added potency to forge interpersonal bonds, something that is demonstrated in many online communities supportive of jihad-themed *anashid*. Online discussion forums provide a staggering abundance of links, downloads, resources, and, most importantly, personal support for jihadi causes, and *anashid* are often at the center of long discussion forum threads. Recent research by Madeleine Gruen, Thomas Hegghammer, and Gabriel Weimann supports the idea that the Internet is a fertile ground for terrorist recruitment and support, and jihad-themed *anashid* are often the focal points around which forum members communicate and offer ideological reinforcement.[49]

Interestingly, this is not particularly new. The process of interpersonal bonding created among combatants and their supporters through the shared enjoyment of music has a long and rich history, transcending culture, geography, and religion. This is nicely illustrated by the musical environment that existed among U.S. soldiers during the Iraq War (2003–10), where music often established social circles, operated as a pretext for action, served as "entertainment," and was a way of honoring those killed.[50] Music (or in al-Qaida's case, *anashid*) has a profound ability to catalyze the process of interpersonal bonding that appears so important to recruitment, membership morale, and sustaining motivation during war operations.[51]

Anashid are an excellent way of forging interpersonal bonds – the glue that holds groups like al-Qaida together perhaps more so than ideology. In *Breaking the Silence*, a Western-produced documentary about music in Afghanistan, a former mujahidin fighter in Afghanistan is quoted as saying,

Although it was a holy war, we still listened to music. We were not narrow-minded. Music was our entertainment. Here is an example of what we used to listen to [turns on tape of an a cappella mujahidin song]. There was the sound of weapons firing. These tapes calmed us down when we were fighting. When we sat with our friends, this was our entertainment.[52]

This statement, while brief, is quite instructive. Not only does the mujahidin fighter suggest that "music" is permissible "entertainment" even in the context of "a holy war," but he suggests that "music" was the focal point during periods of socialization. Moreover, his declaration that "These tapes calmed us down when we were fighting" clearly underscores the idea that the music had a meaningful emotional impact on listeners – an idea that is frequently articulated by present-day discussion forum members who similarly discuss jihad-themed *anashid*'s emotional impact.

Yet, a contradiction arises. One of the main reasons jurists warn against music is its ability to excite the senses and arouse the emotions, particularly leading to sexual misconduct. However, a *nashid*'s ability to arouse emotion may be precisely what makes it such a valuable tool in propaganda, recruitment, membership retention, morale, and motivation to action.[53] It is useful to note that most contemporary studies of hate crimes, terrorism, or genocide identify emotion as an important catalyst in instigating violent behavior or hostility toward a person or group.[54]

While I have argued for the importance of non-textual elements in al-Qaida *anashid*, the message of this music should not be discounted. Most al-Qaida *anashid* glorify aspects of jihad, extol martyrs, call for the defense of Islam, and the best combine these thematic elements. The following text is a verse-chorus form (call and response) veneration of martyrdom sung to *maqam Farahfaza* from "The West and The Dark Tunnel." The video includes scenes from an apparent suicide bombing in which the drivers of a truck detonate an explosive device at a military outpost (quotation from the English subtitles).

> (verse): Who dares to stand in front of them? They are those who sacrifice for their Prophet, They are Khalid and Dharaar.
> (chorus): Our path, our path, this is our path! The jihad and more jihad.
> (verse): They advance seeking death, and when they see it, they will smile. They are aware of the danger, yes. But they have no fear.
> (chorus): Our path, our path, this is our path! The jihad and more jihad.
> (verse): They leap like lions into the lines of the enemy. The aid of Allah is with you today, O Mujahideen![55]

These themes resonate with the *anashid* texts presented earlier in this chapter from "The Red Mosque," as well as the *anashid* excerpts below which are interspersed throughout the documentary, often playing in the background and brought to the forefront in order to underscore key moments in the narration and video (quotation from the English subtitles).

We endured oppression for so long, and became today able to pay back and avenge, Oh martyrs, it is because of your benevolence that we are able to hold our heads high ... The promise that we made to the Truth continued to be dutifully fulfilled, bullets kept being fired and the obligation continued to be fulfilled, the eyes of the sky will be witness on the Day of Judgment to the criminal oppression committed upon the innocent ... Desecration of the Qur'an and at the hands of vain louts! O God! O Avenger! To You we complain! ... Fire and pillage and plunder prevailed on that side, while the Truth was proclaimed and remembrance of Allah persisted here ... The prayers of the People of Truth, on that night of the gallows, the passion of the heart, the melancholic spirit kept burning up into supplication ... gratitude is seen in the scorching sun of sacrifice and preference, the stages on the way to the destination kept being crossed.[56]

The themes we see in al-Sahab videos are by no means exclusive to al-Qaida. Indeed, the veneration of martyrdom and the call to defend Islam through violence resound persistently through most of the jihad-themed *anashid* I have examined. Considering now the jihad-themed *anashid* used in al-Qaida media, a connection might be drawn: studies demonstrate that emotion plays a significant role in cultivating and perpetuating violence, and music is often a powerful mediator of emotion. This helps explain music's Janus-faced history. It can represent the pinnacle of human artistic expression, or it can be commandeered to etch a particular message in one's mind by playing on emotional responses that circumvent a critical reflection of the message itself. The ability of music to invest the listener with emotion, at the possible expense of a rational contemplation of its message, is one of the principal reasons why the art form has been afforded a prominent position in the propaganda efforts of almost every nationalist, religious, or ideologically driven group in history.

Thus, the seeds of violence are planted, taking root in the fertile soil that music provides. The textual messages of the threat to Islam and the Muslim community, and death in glory for the defense of God, reinforced by the emotions of fear, resentment, and anger over injustice, become an even more toxic elixir when they appear in the form of music. Why? Because music can present those messages in emotionally charged ways, preying upon culturally conditioned perceptions of music that render the audience more vulnerable to the message.[57] As Augustine noted in his *Confessions*, "when they are sung these sacred words stir my mind to greater fervour and kindle in me a more ardent flame of piety than they would if they were not sung." And it is worthwhile mentioning that listening to music is not a simply passive act. Recent studies of the processes at work when people listen to music have shown that we possess neurological and biological responses to music, such as alterations of blood pressure, adrenaline, and brain chemistry. Further elaboration on this topic is beyond my area of expertise, but there is extensive research suggesting that the arousal of emotion through music has a neurobiological basis.[58]

The Case of Arid Uka

A valuable example of the potency of jihad-themed *anashid* can be seen in the case of Arid Uka, the twenty-one-year-old who shot and killed two U.S. soldiers at the Frankfurt airport in March 2011. According to the German police investigation, Uka frequently participated in Islamist "friends" networks on Facebook, enjoyed first person shooter video games ("Call of Duty" was a favorite), and actively praised jihad-themed *anashid* through YouTube commentary and online discussions, and posted links to such music on his Facebook wall.[59] One report of the incident noted,

The ex-rapper Deso Dogg from Berlin, who converted to Islam and now calls himself "Abu Malik," was particularly influential to Arid U. "I love you for Allah!" said the German-Kosovan [Arid U.] in response to one of the former musician's videos [an *anashid*]. Abu Malik, who preaches the "True Religion" of the Salafi missionary movement, recently released a controversial song [*anashid*] in which he extols jihad and martyrdom.[60]

In the *nashid*, Abu Malik praises Usama bin Ladin and sings, "your name flows in our blood." He also praised Arid Uka's actions, saying "the brother (Uka) hasn't killed civilians, he has killed soldiers who had been on their way to kill Muslims."[61]

An article in *Der Spiegel* suggested that Uka's radicalization occurred very quickly and was almost entirely Internet-based:

a large number of people, many of them well-known Islamists, became Facebook friends of Arid U. just in the two weeks immediately preceding Wednesday's attack. Investigators suspect that the wave of new contacts could have something to do with the airport assault. One theory holds that Arid U. radicalized extremely quickly and became part of a scene that urged him to act ... In real life, such connections were not nearly as apparent.[62]

While Uka told German police in interrogation that he acted against U.S. military personnel out of revenge for the wars in Iraq and Afghanistan, it was ultimately a scene from the 2007 movie *Redacted* that brought him to violence, a film about a U.S. military unit charged and convicted in the rape of a girl and killing of an Iraqi family in Mahmoudiya on March 12, 2006.[63] The day before the assault, Uka watched a YouTube video entitled "Americans raping our sisters! Wake up Ummah!" which showed the rape scene from the film. Although the scene was a reenactment, Arid Uka believed it showed the actual rape.[64] He had found the link to the video on an Islamist website, with which he had recently become familiar through his circle of Islamist Facebook friends. He later told German police that the images disturbed him so profoundly that he was compelled to action the next day.[65]

Interestingly, he harbored doubts about going through with his plan. He recounted in a Frankfurt courtroom, "On the one hand, I wanted to do something to help the women and on the other I hoped I would not see any soldiers."[66] But as he sat on the bus to the airport on the day of the attacks, he had his iPod with him and his reluctance would not hold up to the power of what resonated in his ears: "It (the jihad-themed *anashid*) made me really angry," Uka explained to the judge.[67] These jihad-themed *anashid* may have been the final push that motivated him to follow through with the attacks. Later in the courtroom Uka would condemn this music, the videos, and all the jihadi media that he voraciously consumed up to the attacks as "lying propaganda."[68]

The case of Arid Uka is unusual in the sense that he took action alone, without training, membership in a terrorist group, or advanced planning, but it does demonstrate the broader challenge of online radicalization. In real life, Uka demonstrated few signs of radicalization; online, however, he was a rhetorically vicious radical, supported and inspired by the community of jihad sympathizers with whom he communicated. Music was clearly a major factor in his radicalization, and the interpersonal bonds he initiated and maintained online often revolved around sharing *anashid* and videos posted on Facebook, YouTube, and other websites.[69]

Conclusion

The uncertain legal status of music in Islam has led to a variety of interpretative sonic practices within the Muslim world. Al-Qaida's use of jihad-themed *anashid*, set in the most conservative arrangements as unaccompanied vocal melodies, negotiates the gray areas between outlawed "music" and permissible "non-*musiqa*" so as to present the group as ideological purists. While the musical characteristics of *anashid* vary enormously, those appearing in al-Qaida media and culture typically display features associated with traditional Arabic music, such as the *maqam* system of pitch organization. Regrettably, the history of *anashid* and the development of jihad-related texts within the genre are not well documented; further inquiry, while challenging, would help fill many of these historical gaps.

Considering the controversial debates that surround music, al-Qaida (and most jihadi groups in general) seem aware that completely eliminating *anashid* from their media and culture – and thereby sidestepping the problem altogether – is not a productive strategy to promote their goals. The reception of jihad-themed *anashid* suggests part of the answer as to why: music carries a distinct potency to recruit, forge social bonds, reinforce a message, animate it with emotion, and potentially motivate the listener to action. Music's functioning in these ways sheds light on the value and purpose behind jihad-themed *anashid* within al-Qaida culture.

This chapter makes a case for the careful examination of music's role in terrorist and extremist cultures, a role that is not purely theoretical or academic but can be seen in cases like Arid Uka or Khalid al-Awhali (see Nelly Lahoud's chapter in this volume). Understanding music beyond the framework of mere benevolence can illuminate the ways in which those involved in terrorism and extremism (as well as ourselves) are subject to its power.

4 The Visual Culture of Jihad

AFSHON OSTOVAR

Islamist organizations use a variety of means to articulate their worldviews, and text is only one of them. Visual elements, such as photographs, artwork, and emblems, are a crucial part of Islamist messaging but have not received nearly the same attention as texts. As the advertising industry realized long ago, images can be extremely effective at grabbing attention and communicating ideas through simple forms of symbolism.[1] Jihadi propagandists seem to have realized it too. They use imagery extensively to transmit ideas and perspectives on everything from the nature of jihad to global affairs.[2] By employing visuals, jihadist organizations are able to distill their views into a rudimentary symbolic language that appeals and is readily accessible to sympathetic audiences across linguistic barriers. Such visuals are an important aspect of broader jihadist culture and an important site for the articulation of jihadist identity.

This chapter explores the main patterns and characteristics of jihadi visual culture. It focuses on still images as opposed to moving ones, although many of the same visual motifs carry through in jihadi cinematography, as Anne Stenersen will show in the next chapter. For space considerations I limit this inquiry to the contemporary period, well aware that there is much to be said about the historical evolution of jihadi iconography – and Islamist visuality more broadly – in the second half of the twentieth century. Also, although this chapter concentrates on images associated with contemporary jihadist organizations, especially those associated with al-Qaida, visuals from other Islamist organizations are at times mentioned for comparative purposes.

I will argue that jihadist visual culture is based on a network of visual images, symbols, and themes widely used by the jihadist community and familiar to its supporters. Groups, media organizations, and artists deliberately draw from this "visual network" to create compositions that represent and resonate with the jihadist community. The main themes in jihadi visual culture closely correspond with the political and religious tenets of the movement itself. Images depicting austere religiosity, war, antagonism toward enemies, as well as honor, fraternity, chivalry, and justice, are all conveyed through the lens of jihadist belief and often shaped by the political context of the moment. The jihadist visual lexicon – like that of other political movements – stresses simplicity; however, it is also adaptive and evolving. Jihadist groups tend to favor symbols familiar across the movement – regardless of ethno-linguistic background – but variations between groups also exist. The tendency toward straightforward, widely understood visual symbolism has made jihadi visual culture a powerful and effective form of communication across the movement's diverse membership.

Most of the images discussed in this chapter originated on the Internet. They were collected from a variety of websites between 2005 and 2013 and are part of the author's personal collection. A few images come from the Militant Imagery Project, an online database first published in 2006 and maintained by the Combating Terrorism Center at West Point.[3] Because of the clandestine nature of the groups that produce these images and the fickle state of the jihadi Internet, it is often very difficult to know where and from whom these images first originated. If pagination is clear, it is usually mentioned; otherwise no citations or specific URLs are provided for the images.

In the first half of the chapter I discuss the notion of visual networks through the example of organizational emblems and flags. These sections look at how official insignia of militant organizations and jihadist groups are used to communicate organizational identities and to build association with broader movements. The next part of the chapter looks at particular visual themes in jihadist artwork: the mujahid, hero, martyr, and heavenly paradise. These are central themes in jihadist propaganda and are examples of how visual imagery is used to communicate a variety of messages. The final section is a brief discussion on the growing role of graphic design in Internet forums and its impact on jihadist visual culture.

Visual Networks and Organizational Identities

Visual symbolism is an important aspect of how organizations under-stand and express themselves. The particular symbols an organization chooses to include in its materials, and how those symbols are ordered and displayed, can be revealing about the group's worldview and objectives. Although visual communications are more effective when viewed from inside the same linguistic and cultural communities from which they originate, political imagery also has the advantage of transcending some linguistic and cultural barriers. Basic symbolism and visual techniques, such as markers of armed resistance, ideological affiliation, or even color choice, can communicate or at least suggest meaning across place and time. More complex symbolism, which might draw from cultural tradition or insider political dynamics, can be difficult if not impossible for those outside of the target audience to understand. Nonetheless, because political imagery is meant to communicate ideas without language, it can be an effective and powerful tool for political organizations. Political posters, for example, were a rich and vibrant place of ideological contestation in Lebanon's civil war and in the Iranian revolution. In both contexts, imagery was used to craft identity, promote ideology, and disparage rivals. Imagery in these contexts was successful because it advanced ideas quickly and succinctly for the viewer. Visuals unburden the viewer from the time and effort required to read and digest textual arguments.[4]

It is for such reasons that Islamist organizations regularly employ visuals in their branding and propaganda campaigns. Some organizations employ visuals consistently, enabling them to cultivate an easily recognizable visual profile. Groups such as Lebanon's Hezbollah, for instance, have a robust media effort and a recognizable brand centered on a fixed organizational emblem. Other organizations, however, are less deliberate with their visual aesthetic, which makes their visual identity more a sum of its parts rather than a coherent statement.

In establishing visual identities, Islamist organizations generally draw from a rather limited set, or network, of symbols. Aside from the names these groups adopt, which, especially when written in the Arabic (or Persian, or Urdu, etc.) script, can also serve as a powerful visual statement, the symbolic elements that they use to decorate their emblems, flags, and propaganda are often not unique but rather typical for Islamist groups and militant organizations in general. For instance, many Islamist groups will employ rifles in their materials as a way to communicate their dedication to armed resistance. Such imagery is used by groups across cultures and, by itself, is no more evocative of Islam or Islamist politics than it is of a host of other political and ideological orientations.[5]

Figure 4.1. Flag of the Tamil Tigers and the emblem of al-Shabab

Taken together, the political groups that employ these symbols can be said to be a part of a shared visual network. For the purpose of illustration, I contrast two types of visual networks – casual and deliberate – that are, above all, a way to explain intentionality behind the adoption of certain symbols and imagery. In a casual visual network, visual imagery can be shared by both affiliated and unaffiliated groups. Casual networks are unsuccessful at articulating a unified movement because they are not intended to do so. Imagery used within a deliberate network, however, is intended to highlight affiliation between groups or to express solidarity within a movement.

For example, the images in Figure 4.1 are the official emblems of two very different organizations: the Liberation Tigers of Tamil Eelam (Tamil Tigers) of Sri Lanka and the Harakat al-Shabab al-Mujahidin (al-Shabab) of Somalia. Although both of these groups used crossed rifles in their emblems to express notions of armed militancy, they did so in support of different ideologies – Marxist-Leninism (Tamil Tigers) and jihadism (al-Shabab) – and at different times and places – beginning in the 1970s (Tamil Tigers) and 2000s (al-Shabab). Because mutual use of this symbolism is not intended to express or imply an affiliation between these groups, it would be an example of a *casual* visual network.

By contrast, shared imagery can reflect political allegiance and cooperation between groups. The similarity in the emblems (Figure 4.2) of Iran's Revolutionary Guards, Lebanese Hezbollah, and Iraq's Kata'ib Hezbollah is not coincidental, but rather an intentional testament to the actual close affiliation and cooperation of these organizations.[6]

Figure 4.2. Emblems from left to right: Revolutionary Guards, Lebanese Hezbollah, and Kata'ib Hezbollah

Figure 4.3. From left to right: flag of Jamaat-ud-Dawa, Jaysh-e Muhammad, Sipah-e Sahaba

The flags of the Pakistani militant organizations Jamaat-ud-Dawa (the political front for Lashkar-e Taiba), Jaysh-e Muhammad, and Sipah-e Sahaba are also an example of a deliberate network – albeit one that is perhaps more based on a shared political cause than on intergroup collaboration or patronage.[7] Although each flag (Figure 4.3) is distinct, they are linked both visually and politically by the black and white bars on each flag. These bars represent the bars of the Kashmiri flag (in its official and unofficial iterations) and are used to symbolize the fight to liberate Kashmir from Indian occupation.

Groups can self-consciously strive to be a part of a visual network even if they have no actual affiliation with the major organizations that give the network its resonance. This can enable smaller groups the ability to associate themselves *visually* with more important organizations and larger movements, even if they lack any literal ties to them. Radical leftist groups in the 1960s and 1970s are a good example of this phenomenon, where organizations around the world adopted imagery such as five-pointed stars, raised fists, automatic rifles, and the color red to suggest association with the more renowned liberation movements of the era.[8] However, deliberate networks in their most overt form represent the conscious shared adoption of visual symbols between organizations for the purpose of constructing, expressing, or inventing a larger, more unified movement. These shared symbols can reflect actual political allegiances (as they do in the case of the Revolutionary Guards and Hezbollah) or simply signify affinity and shared goals.

Like the groups above, jihadis draw from a limited pool of symbols and imagery to construct their visual identities. The images discussed below show some of the more common elements of what I suggest is a jihadi visual network. On their own, these images can represent a single organization, idea, or issue, but collectively they form the body of a specific and evolving visual culture.

Black Flags

Official insignia are a view into an organization's self-conception. They are used by organizations to distill politics and ideology into a visual expression of identity. These types of images can be used in a variety of ways. Organizations that control territory or are able to operate openly in the public sphere might use flags and signs that carry an official emblem to advertise their presence. The emblem of Hezbollah, for instance, is widely displayed publicly on flags throughout the group's areas of control and on an innumerable assortment of para-phernalia – from official publications to kitsch (e.g., cigarette lighters and tea cups). Hamas's official emblem is likewise prominent through-out Gaza, and groups such as al-Qaida in the Arabian Peninsula (AQAP), the Taliban in Afghanistan, and Somalia's al-Shabab have publicly displayed their flags and other propaganda to highlight their control over territory. The Islamic State (formerly known as the Islamic State in Iraq and ash-Sham, or ISIS) is a prominent example of this phenomenon. The organization routinely places its official flag atop buildings, hillsides, vehicles, and other landmarks as a way of marking territory under its control or announcing the presence of its forces. Official insignia are also used as branding elements in media distributed on the Internet.[9] In these forms, emblems enable organizations to advertise their existence and politics, mark their (online) territory and products, and make official the videos, messages, and materials distributed in the group's name.

The flags used by al-Qaida and associated jihadist groups are examples of this. Unlike many other militant organizations, al-Qaida does not have an organizational emblem per se. Instead, variations of the Islamic banner are used to represent it and many other (aligned or independent) jihadist organizations in a variety of forms and contexts. Jihadist flags, which are generally black, are meant to represent the battle standards (e.g., *al-raya*) carried by Muslim forces in some of the earliest armed conflicts in Islamic history. Historical descriptions of the banners used by the earliest Muslim forces differ. They were said to have no consistent color or pattern. They could be white, green, yellow, or black and sometimes included the Muslim proclamation of faith.[10] Without a clear notion of the Prophet's true flag of choice, jihadist groups have been left to interpret history for themselves. The flags they adopt are manifestations of those interpretations and say as much about the group's modern sensibilities as their appreciation for historical purity.

Although they reflect contemporary sensibilities, these flags are meant to evoke the battles fought by Islam's earliest generations – which succeeded in transforming the Islamic community into a powerful, expansive empire and transnational religious community – and, by extension, symbolize Islam in its purest and most earnest stage. Flying the Islamic standard enables jihadist groups to connect themselves with Islam's revered first generations and the religion's early history.[11] It projects the image of religious authenticity, unobscured by modern political ideologies or ideas. Also, because Islamic flags are associated with religious battle and conquest, they have come to represent righteous and legitimate jihad.

The central element of the Islamic flag is the Muslim proclamation of faith, or *shahada*, in Arabic: "*la ilaha ilallah muhammad rasulullah*"

Figure 4.4. The Islamic State's flag

(There is no God but God, Muhammad is the messenger of God). On its own, such a flag does not denote jihadism. The official flag of Saudi Arabia, for example, contains the shahada as well as a sword that signifies the rule of the House of Saud. It is nonetheless the most potent visual symbol adopted by jihadist groups. Some versions of the flag carry only part of the shahada, whereas others include it in its entirety. The flag of the Islamic State (Figure 4.4) includes the phrase in two parts. The first ("There is no God but God") is at top, and the second half ("Muhammad is the messenger of God") appears in a white circle. The leadership of what was then known as the Islamic State of Iraq promoted this image as the nascent organization's official symbol and to distinguish it from al-Qaida in Iraq, the organization from which it emerged. The group hung its flags throughout Iraqi neighborhoods during periods it either controlled or operated in those areas, and later it did the same as it expanded into Syria. The Islamic State explained its design in a statement posted on jihadi discussion forums. The organization claimed that the flag was an accurate recreation of the Islamic standard from the Prophet Muhammad's era. It said the white circle and its text were the official seal of the Prophet as contained in

Ottoman records, and the ordering of the words (from top to bottom: god, messenger, Muhammad) followed Islamic oral traditions describing Muhammad's seal.[12] Writing on the Islamic State's usage of the symbol, McCants argues that the "Islamic State's leaders had to choose among conflicting scriptures and histories from their religion's past to craft a vision of what they aspired to in the present and future." He continued:

Their choices display the cultural biases and modern sensibilities they try so hard to displace. They selected a stark black for the flag rather than green, yellow, or white; the color suits their Manichean worldview, which permits no gray areas between the binaries of right and wrong, believer and unbeliever. The white scrawl across the top, "No god but God," is deliberately ragged, meant to suggest an era before the precision of Photoshop even though the flag was designed on a computer.

The blackness of the Islamic State's flag (as well as other flags used by jihadist groups) is worth noting. Black is regularly used as a color of protest, both within the Islamic world and more globally. However, in the Islamic tradition black flags most often evoke the black standards flown during the eighth-century Abbasid Revolution, which overthrew the corrupt rule of the Umayyad clan and replaced it with a new caliphate based in Iraq. The Abbasids ushered in the Golden Age of Islam, but their revolt also played upon certain prophetic expectations of the coming of the Mahdi – the Muslim savior who is expected to appear before the apocalypse and restore justice to the Islamic community. McCants argues that the Islamic State chose to make its flag black precisely to suggest its apocalyptic expectations.[13] The black flags of other jihadist groups can be seen as suggesting similar connotations, albeit less explicitly than the Islamic State.

Since its appearance in Iraq, the Islamic State's flag has become one of the most widespread jihadist symbols and has been used by groups such as al-Shabab, AQAP, and Nusra Front (al-Qaida's Syrian branch). Its common association with these groups had made the flag regularly referred to as al-Qaida's flag. These groups, however, more often referred to it as the "banner of monotheism (*tawhid*)" – a term jihadis sometimes use to describe black flags in general. Yet, after the Islamic State's political break with Nusra in Syria, and its vigorous expansion in both Syria and Iraq, the symbol became inseparable from its own project and therefore distanced from previous associations with al-Qaida. The flag has been adopted by affiliates of the Islamic State, who use it to mark their formal ties and allegiance to the caliphate of Abu Bakr al-Baghdadi, as well as to signify their break with other previous alliances (such as with al-Qaida).

Although this flag became a clear demarcation of jihadist affiliation, it also gained currency outside of the jihadist context. Like the Palestinian *keffiyeh*, the flag of Islamic State has had some crossover appeal as a symbol popular of protest. Its distinctive design might be seen as capturing a certain Islamic cultural authenticity, and its stark black and white coloring corresponds well to conceptions of protest and revolt, both within Islamic history and more globally. The flag appeared as a symbol of Islamist resistance and protest across parts of the Middle East during the Arab Spring. It was flown at political demonstrations in Kuwait, during anti-Mubarak protests in Cairo, raised atop buildings in Benghazi, and held by protestors in Tunis. It was a central symbol of the 2012 U.S. Embassy takeover in Cairo, where protestors replaced the embassy's American flag with it on the eleventh anniversary of 9/11. As such, the flag has served not only as an official marker of the Islamic State and al-Qaida affiliates, but also as a symbol of revolutionary Islamist protest in the Middle East and North Africa. It is impossible to say whether or not the flag will continue to have resonance outside of jihadist circles. Its appeal to non-jihadists was likely stronger before the Islamic State's 2014 expansion into Iraq and its widely publicized legacy of brutality. The success or failure of the Islamic State's project in Iraq, Syria, and elsewhere will probably determine the resonance the flag will have on the future of the jihadist movement.

Many similar flags are used by jihadist groups. The examples in Figure 4.5 (clockwise from the top) are but a few and represent the following entities: al-Tawhid wa'l-Jihad (a precursor to the Islamic State), Caucasus Jihad (an umbrella group of various allied Islamist organizations in the Russian Caucasus region), Sepah-e Sahabah-e Iran (a small jihadist group based in Iranian Baluchistan), and *Yarmuk* Magazine (an Afghanistan-centric jihadist magazine). These flags are meant to signify two fundamental aspects of each entity: their Islamic identity and their involvement in the jihadist movement. Although each flag is a little different, the contexts in which they appear and the groups they represent are generally sufficient for them to effectively communicate the intended core message. Some jihadist flags, like the one used by Caucasus Jihad, add a depiction of a sword (or other

Figure 4.5. Flags of al-Qaida and associated jihadist groups

symbols of armed violence) along with the *shahada* to emphasize the group's militancy. Others make the jihadist association more overt, such as the *Yarmuk* emblem, which literally spells out its association with the jihadist movement in Afghanistan by including a geographical representation of Afghanistan with the word *al-jihad* printed on it.

The visual imagery of the Islamic flags is meant to be easily recognizable and understood by supporting, sympathetic, and even outside audiences. Although these flags technically require a familiarity with Arabic (or Persian, in the case of the flag of Sepah-e Sahabah-e Iran) and Islam to be read accurately, they can also be effective markers for jihadist militancy to the uninitiated. This is achieved both by the context in which these flags appear and by the communicative power of the visual network of which they are a part. That is, because many jihadist organizations (and even non-jihadist Islamist organizations) have adopted flags like these as a central visual statement in their materials and activism, Islamic flags have collectively become markers for both these individual groups and for the militant Islamist movement more broadly. It is no coincidence that al-Qaida affiliates such as al-Qaida in the Islamic Maghreb (AQIM), Nusra Front, and AQAP use versions of the black flag in nearly all of their imagery (from video statements, to photographs of leaders, etc.) and that groups associated with al-Qaida, such as al-Shabab in Somalia, Caucasus Jihad, and others, do the same.

The Islamic flag has a rich and varied history that stretches back to the early days of the religion, but because of the flag's appropriation by jihadist organizations, and especially because of the consistent, repeated, and perhaps increasing use of the flag as the de facto emblem for a number of militant Islamist groups, the black flag has become the foremost marker of the jihadist movement in the contemporary period. Its adoption by Islamist organizations is a simple but powerful way for them to mark association with the jihadist movement. Thus, these flags not only help define a visual network, they comprise an inexorable and important component of jihadi visual culture.

Central Themes in Jihadi Imagery

Jihadi visual culture incorporates a variety of subject matter. Jihadi propagandists have used visuals to comment on current affairs, enter into intercommunity debates, and advance all sorts of religious or political ideas.[14] Visuals used in this spectrum can be diverse, but in general the jihadi visual language is fairly limited. Some themes have endured as central components of jihadi visual culture over time. Islamic flags are one example. Below I discuss a few others: the muja-hid and hero, the martyr, and the promise of heavenly paradise. These are not the only motifs in jihadi visual culture, but they are prominent themes and examples of how certain visuals are used to communicate notions of virtue, heroism, and divine reward – the building blocks of jihadi identity and activism.

Mujahid and Hero

The *mujahid* or Muslim soldier is a prominent fixture in jihadi visuals. This generic figure can be articulated differently, depending on the artist or organization behind the image, but in general it is used to represent the rank-and-file jihadist, a specific group, or the jihadist movement more broadly. Beyond this usage, the figure of the mujahid can also symbolize certain attributes such as bravery, strength, and religious devotion. This is done by presenting the figure in a form or context suggestive of these attributes for the viewer.

Figure 4.6. Minbar al-Tawhid wa'l-Jihad (c. 2011), Kuwait jihad (c. 2005)

In one form, abstractions of the mujahid can take on a premodern guise, depicting the fighter along with other symbols such as horses and swords to evoke connotations of Islam's past. Figure 4.6 shows two examples of this type. The first (on the left) is the emblem for a jihadist Internet forum called the "Minbar al-Tawhid wa'l-Jihad" (Pulpit of Monotheism and Jihad). In addition to the name of the forum at the bottom of the image, there are a few other evocative symbols. In the middle of the piece you see the earth with Eurasia and Africa visible. Superimposed on the earth is a solid black figure atop a rearing horse holding aloft a sword and a flag. Above the figure is a partial verse from the Qur'an (4:84), which reads "Urge the believers to fight. It may well be that God will keep back the might of the infidels."[15] The figure here can be seen to symbolize the jihadist movement in general, with the globe, and perhaps more specifically the eastern hemisphere, as the scope or aspiration of its enterprise. The horse, battle standard, and sword evoke connotations of religious battle and Islam's early history, making the mujahid (the image's central figure) the primary catalyst for the hopes contained in the image and implied by the Qur'anic verse.

The next image is less straightforward. It shows a figure on a horse, holding what looks to be a flag, superimposed on an isolated outline of Kuwait. The text in Arabic reads: "Rain down upon Kuwait, O my hope." Although this image might be confusing to an outsider, within the context of the jihadist forums where it was distributed, its meaning is clearer. It expresses the desire for the jihadist movement to galvanize and become (at the very least) more active in Kuwait. In this context the black figure is immediately recognized as a mujahid, with the

Figure 4.7. Nusra Front, "Day of the Infiltration" (2012)

trappings of the horse and standard evoking the same connotations as suggested above.

Conjuring the past is not just done through abstraction. Jihadist organizations employ similar motifs in videos and photographs to associate themselves with the legacy of Islam's founding generations. Photographs of Usama bin Ladin, for instance, often showed him clad in white, traditional garb and riding a horse to that effect. The Nusra Front, the Al-Qaida affiliate in Syria, uses similar symbolism in its propaganda. The image in Figure 4.7 is the cover art for a digital video distributed on Internet forums. The video, entitled "Day of the Infiltration," is a statement by Nusra Front detailing a 2012 attack on Syria's Interior Ministry. At top, the group brands the image with a black flag that includes the group's name below the traditional *shahada*. On the right is the title and description of the video. Emerging from the center of the image and moving to the left is a row of black-clad jihadist fighters, carrying automatic rifles, seemingly jogging in lock-step behind a commander, who leads the unit riding a horse and holding a black flag with his right hand. The horse and the flag, again, are tropes used to evoke Islamic history. However, unlike the images above, Nusra's fighters or mujahids are modern in their attire and weaponry. The symbolism then is used to link the present to the past and in a sense establish an authenticity for Nusra (and their campaign) similar to that enjoyed by Islam's early warriors.

The black-clad fighters in the above image are familiar across jihadist propaganda. Countless images posted to Internet forums include similar depictions of the mujahid. The masked, faceless warrior is an intimidating sight, one that projects an aura of strength as much as it does violence or anonymity. The black suggests that the modern mujahid, more than his forbearers, operates in secrecy, working from the shadows to engage his enemy. It furthermore draws attention to the tactics of terrorism and insurgency favored by jihadists.[16]

The masked, black-clad mujahid is a common archetype. Jihadist groups seem to favor this type of depiction because the figure can conjure up many of the attributes (e.g., anonymity, violence, strength, power, mystery) they associate with themselves and their enterprise. Some of these themes can be seen in the images in Figure 4.8. The first example, on the left, is a rather crudely composed image (from around 2009) of a masked mujahid holding what looks to be a rocket-propelled grenade. Smoke and fire, seemingly from an explosion, appear behind the fighter, indicating the violent operations conducted by the group, Jundallah (Army of God), responsible for the image. The group's full name, the "Popular Resistance of Jundallah" is written in Persian above the figure, with the phrase "Come to Jihad" in Arabic placed at the top. The purpose of the poster is made evident through

Figure 4.8. Jundallah poster (c. 2010) and Global Islamic Media Front advertisement (c. 2005)

the interplay between text and visual imagery. It is akin to the famous "Uncle Sam" posters produced by the U.S. government to recruit volunteers to join the fight in World Wars I and II, except in this case it is a call for volunteers by a small militant group fighting the Iranian government in a desolate region of Iran's southeast.[17] Unlike most of the groups associated with al-Qaida that often have access to a cadre of designers and media specialists, Jundallah seems to have produced most of its images in house, generally posting these and other materials to its websites rather than to more popular Internet fora.

The next image is an advertisement for a well-known al-Qaida–affiliated propaganda organization, the Global Islamic Media Front, which circulated on the Internet beginning around 2005. Here the mujahid wears a black uniform, cut more in the fashion of traditional Muslim garb than modern attire, with a vest and arm patches that give the outfit a military quality. The mujahid is again masked and anonymous. Unlike the other examples discussed so far, this image presents the mujahid as victor. He stands on a map of Iraq next to a black Islamic flag planted in the heart of the country as if he has conquered the land himself in the name of Islam. This sort of view reflects the aspirations of the jihadists that aimed at creating an Islamic state in Iraq.

Such exaggerated depictions can make the mujahid appear larger-than-life, like a superhero for the Muslim community. This is a popular motif and one made more explicit in other images, such as in Figure 4.9. The image on the left was posted in 2012 to the Ansar al-Mujahidin forum by one of its regular contributors. At the center of the image is an imposing, mysterious figure. He is masked in a traditional *keffiyeh* scarf, wears what seems to be a military uniform with an armored breast plate, and carries a large military-style automatic rifle and a holstered side arm. On his left arm is the Islamic State flag. He is partly hidden and obscured by the darkness that surrounds him, again playing on the theme of operating from the shadows. Written at the top in calligraphic Arabic is "Islamic State of Iraq" and at bottom is a menacing message targeted at Shi'ites: "We lie in wait for you, O rejectionists."

The image imagines the jihadist as a shadowy, but impressive, military fighter. He looks like he could be a part of an elite special forces unit and would not be out of place as a character in any popular first-person-shooter video game.[18] He is an idealized figure, one meant to portray strength and resolve, as well as to strike fear in the heart of

Figure 4.9. Mujahid as superhero (left), Marvel's The Punisher (right)

his stated enemy (i.e., the Shi'a). It is unsurprising then that the designer of this image drew direct inspiration from a genre well known for its cultivation and celebration of armed heroes: comic books. Indeed, in this case the jihadist image is adapted from a drawing of The Punisher, a popular character from the Marvel Universe famous for his murderous vigilante campaign against organized crime. By blending the images the designer utilizes the familiar symbolism of the comic to achieve something both menacing and distinct, a reimagined jihadist hero – one perhaps meant to be relatable and attractive to young males immersed in popular culture on the Internet.

Lionizing Martyrs

Martyrs are generally depicted in ways that magnify them and their role in jihad campaigns. This is done by using well-known tropes of Islamic and/or local culture to honor a fallen comrade. For this reason, Islamist organizations can differ in the ways in which they celebrate their martyrs. However, some tropes are common to most jihadist groups. One example is the lion, which is used to highlight the bravery

Figure 4.10. "Khattab, Lion of Chechnya …" (c. 2005)

and valor of both important living jihadists and martyrs. The lion has rich meaning in Islamic history and culture. A famous Islamic tradition (*hadith*), for instance, refers to Ali ibn Abi Talib, the Prophet's cousin and later successor, as the "Lion of God" (*asad allah*) for his courage and success in the battle of Badr. Jihadists use the metaphor of the lion to similar effect in honoring the heroes of their community.

The example in Figure 4.10 is one such occurrence of this. The image is dedicated to the famous jihadi commander Samir Salih Abdallah al-Suwaylim, better known by his nom de guerre Ibn Khattab, or simply Khattab. Khattab was a Saudi citizen who went to Afghanistan to fight the Soviets in the 1980s and never looked back. His career as a fighter and commander also took him to Tajikistan, Bosnia, and Chechnya, where he became a renowned warlord, military strategist, and close advisor to former Chechen rebel leader Shamil Basayev. Khattab was killed by Russian intelligence in 2002 and soon after became one of the more eminent heroes in the jihadist community.[19]

As we can see, Khattab was a striking figure, almost like a jihadist Che Guevera. The image highlights Khattab's legacy as a successful military commander. To an outsider it seems plain that the individual in the image is a revered soldier or military leader. For the insider, it is explicit. The lion in the background combined with the Muslim *shahada* at top and the crossed RPGs at bottom imply that the figure was a courageous fighter and faithful mujahid. The text spells this out: "Khattab: Lion of Chechnya, Lion of the Battlefield." The map in the background seems to be used for context, although it centers on Europe instead of the Caucasus and is from World War I instead of the present era. It is not clear why this particular map was used. It could be the designer's way of making reference to the break-up of the Ottoman Empire following the war. It could have also been less deliberate. At the bottom of the image is the designer's email address, included to elicit comments or requests for additional work.

Khattab is one of the more widely celebrated heroes in the jihadi cannon. However, honorifics like the lion are also used to memorialize lesser known martyrs and increase their stature in the community. One individual who briefly garnered a lot of attention from the online jihadi community was Muhammad Ahmad Qanita. Qanita, also known by his nom de guerre Abu Umar al-Maqdisi, was a Gaza-based commander in the Al-Qassam Brigade of Hamas. Reports suggest that he left Hamas to join the jihadist Ja'amat al-Tawhid wa'l-Jihad organization shortly before leaving Gaza for Syria. In Syria, he became a trainer and fighter associated with jihadists operating in Idlib alongside units of the Free Syrian Army. He was killed in late December 2012 in an operation aimed at seizing the Idlib airport from Syrian government forces.[20]

Qanita's death was widely discussed on jihadi forums and other sites associated with the Syrian conflict. He was regularly described as a martyr-hero (*al-shahid al-batal*) and as the "Falcon" (another

Figure 4.11. "Lion of Tawhid: Abu Umar al-Maqdisi" (2012)[21]

powerful motif in Islamic and Arab culture) of al-Shati Refugee Camp (the part of Gaza he was from). The image in Figure 4.11 is one of many depicting Qanita as a martyr-hero. In it, Qanita, referred to by his nom de guerre, is called a "Lion of Tawhid," which is a term often used by this group to describe their martyred comrades. The fiery stylizing of the lion's mane adds to Qanita's aura, amplifying his significance as a faithful mujahid, commander, and martyr.

A Call to Paradise

The path of jihad is commonly described as one of sacrifice. To participate fully in jihad, a mujahid must forsake family, material possessions, and the possibility of a normal future. The achievement of martyrdom – to die or be killed in the path of jihad – is considered an honor and a heroic deed by jihadists, who believe that it is afforded by God to only those most deserving of the spiritual bounty.[22] Just as martyrs are celebrated, the act of martyrdom is encouraged in jihadi imagery.

A common method to promote martyrdom uses references to or depictions of heavenly paradise (*janna*). Visual allusions to heaven or the afterlife can be subtle, such as by placing foliage or water next to a known martyr. Such natural associations are drawn from Islamic culture and rooted in the Qur'an, which describes heaven as a lush, verdant, Garden of Eden–like paradise.[23] Figure 4.12 is an example of this. In this image, taken from the first issue of *Inspire* – al-Qaida in the Arabian Peninsula's English-language magazine – a photo of a waterfall accompanies a short message on martyrdom. The message

Figure 4.12. "O Martyr, You Have Illuminated!" (2010)[24]

Figure 4.13. "Calls" to Paradise Jama' (c. 2005) and AQAP (c. 2011)

persuades the reader to reflect on the meaning of life, stating: "The fact is that every soul is going to come to an end, completing the test of this world. Those who prepare with their utmost will be greeted with success. Those who lag in their preparation will have to face the consequences." Success here is an allusion to the rewards of the after-life and heavenly paradise, something brought into focus for the reader with the accompanying photo of the waterfall surrounded by lush green plants. The text further emphasizes the relationship between martyrdom and the gift of paradise: "The martyr who fights and dies in the path of Allah, undoubtedly has the greatest chance of meeting his lord as a victor. So what will your excuse be for restraining yourself from Paradise?"

Visual "calls" or invitations to paradise are meant to be evocative and powerful. Figure 4.13 provides two very different examples of how this can be attempted. The top image was designed by a propa-ganda organization linked with al-Qaida in Iraq. It shows a bright blue sky, white clouds, verdant trees, and foliage. In the center is a pair of hands holding a leaf and a scroll that reads: "A call to paradise." The context for this image, which was posted to jihadist forums during the

Figure 4.14. Iranian Baluch martyrs (c. 2010) and Usama bin Ladin in Paradise (2010)

height of the Iraq war (c. 2005), makes its meaning evident: it is meant to encourage fighters to jihad (or in this case Iraq) with the indirect promise of heavenly paradise as a reward for the sacrifice of martyrdom. Paradise is evoked both by its explicit mention in the text and, more impressionistically, by the natural imagery.

Next is an Internet banner by al-Qaida in the Arabian Peninsula. It carries the group's name at the bottom right and their flag on the left. The text at top reads: "Arise to paradise which is as vast as the heavens and the earth." This line comes from a famous Islamic tradition wherein the Prophet inspires one of his followers to fight and die in the battle of Badr.[25] The image is darker than most paradise-centered pieces, with elements such as the gas mask and assault rifle more suggestive of the violence behind the message than of a paradisiacal garden. The natural elements of paradise are also present; but instead of blues and verdant greens, the natural setting here looks to be viewed during the haze of sunset, perhaps alluding to the physical death (e.g., the setting sun) required for the immortal soul to live on in heaven.

Allusions to paradise are a popular way to honor martyrs and heroes. As mentioned and seen above, this can be done through simple, yet suggestive symbolism. Trees, green grass, flowers, water, rain drops, and the like are all used to connote heavenly paradise. I have included two examples that illustrate how this symbolism works in martyr iconography. The image on the left, which was posted to a website associated with the Jundallah organization, is devoted to two ethnic Baluch activists killed in Iran. Here we see a bright blue ocean in the background. In the foreground is a verdant hill out of which emanates a staircase lined with colorful flowers that proceeds into the sky and culminates in a burst of light. At the end of the staircase hover, as if in spirit form, the heads of the two martyrs being honoured, the idea being that they have entered heaven via the path (i.e., staircase) of martyrdom.

The next image is an homage to Usama bin Ladin. It contains familiar visual themes all meant to evoke notions of a martyr rewarded with heavenly paradise. We see blades of green grass, a bright blue sky, and fluffy white clouds. The sun shines brightly and reflects off pictures of bin Ladin contained in circular bubbles, seemingly floating in the breeze. (I would suggest that the bubbles are used as a stand-in for water, and not meant to simply connote the soap bubbles beloved by children.) The text at the top of the image reads "We will miss you, our shaykh."

An Evolving Culture

Jihadist art has gradually evolved, particularly in the online context. What had once been the domain of amateurs, whose work often reflected their lack of training, is now increasingly being done by quasi-professional designers working in support of various jihadist groups and online entities. The change in quality over the years has been dramatic. Although not all jihadist groups have benefited from the service of trained and experienced designers, the look of jihadist propaganda in general has improved across the spectrum. The Islamic State and the groups aligned with al-Qaida, which are the most prominent on the Internet and have the most robust media efforts, generally have the more sophisticated design. But even groups that have run comparably rudimentary media operations in the past, such as Iranian-based Baluchi groups, have begun to produce higher quality material.[26]

Progress in design has been fueled by increased appreciation for visual propaganda on internet forums and on social media, especially Twitter. Forums such as Ansar al-Mujahidin have devoted parts of their site to media operations and graphic design.[27] Headed by in-house designers, the site has an "audio-visual department" with sub-forums on images, design tools, and archived material. Each subforum has countless moderator- and member-driven discussion threads, which focus on everything from images of martyrs to how to make money as a professional designer.

Perhaps the most interesting feature of this forum is its emphasis on creating sophisticated images. The site's main designer, a moderator called "Gharib," has dedicated a large portion of his subforum to providing forum members with instruction on basic design. In addition to providing links to downloadable pirated versions of design software, Gharib has provided lessons on a variety of topics, such as how to integrate images, how to balance colors, and on learning various techniques in Photoshop.[28] The efforts of Gharib and other designers on the site, who also host instruction threads, have made the forum a place of interaction and engagement with visual material. Forum members are encouraged to ask for assistance and to post their own work for feedback from the moderators and regular participants. Members regularly critique and praise each other's work and hold the known designers on the site in high esteem.

A prime example of this interaction takes place during the site's periodic art competitions. In these threads, the moderator introduces a particular image or theme and encourages submissions that incorporate the element into a unique design. The moderator narrows down the submissions to a group of finalists and then asks forum members to comment and vote on their favorite. Most of the comments by members are filled with praise, but occasionally there are more constructive remarks as well. For instance, in the third iteration of this contest the moderator presented members with a photograph of a young boy holding a large bunch of helium-filled balloons. The picture seems to be taken at sunset, with haze and dust obscuring almost all color from the scene except for the balloons, which visually pop in oranges, purples, and blues against the bland backdrop. It is a beautiful photograph with no violent or jihadist connotations.

Members were asked to use this photograph and create a design appropriate for the forum. Out of an untold number of submissions, the moderator selected eleven finalists, two of which are shown here. The submissions all clearly bore the hallmarks of jihadi art. Many included images of violence, such as automatic rifles, soldiers, or mujahids. Others included poems, Islamic texts, or messages related to jihad. All of the submissions were commended by the voters, with most posts asking God to bless the designers for their work. One voter commented on the professional quality of one piece (at bottom in Figure 4.15), while others were more conflicted, expressing how worthy each design was before casting a vote for a particular favorite. In the end, a design by forum member "Salafi 92" got the most votes (at top in Figure 4.15) and received first place honors from the moderators.

Figure 4.15. Ansar al-Mujahidin Internet forum art competition submissions

Conclusion

From the outside, jihadi visual imagery may appear shallow and simplistic. However, this betrays the meaning and significance these images hold in the jihadi community. In a sense, this imagery reflects the religious fundamentalism of the jihadists themselves. It is stripped down and uses plain symbols and themes to articulate its messages.

I have argued that this collection of symbols, motifs, themes, and moods forms a network, or visual lexicon, of images that jihadist rely on and draw from for visual productions. It is this network that defines and articulates jihad to its own community. It is how they understand their movement and how they express it to themselves visually. Although some of the elements in jihadi images are shared across Islamic, Islamist, and other radical visual cultures, their meaning and use are specific to the jihadi community. The value of this network is its success in meaning making, which is what makes it the foundation of jihadi visual culture.

The boundaries of jihadist visual culture are not fixed. Even though jihadi visuality is at times unrefined, growing interest and sophistication in graphic design within the community is expanding the parameters of jihadi visual culture. This is moving jihadi designers away from the clipart-like reliance on familiar symbols toward something more inclusive and expressive. The jihadist community still stresses the value of violent symbols such as guns, and culturally significant motifs such as lions, yet there appears to be a growing embrace of less generic, perhaps more abstract, aesthetics as well. This might be a symptom of the interrelated universe of the Internet, where good design is vibrant and appreciated; but it is also suggestive of a possible looseness in jihadi culture, which allows an otherwise rigid movement the ability to change and adapt to the world around it.

5 | A History of Jihadi Cinematography

ANNE STENERSEN

Jihadi films incorporate many of the visual motifs described by Ostovar in the previous chapter, but they represent a much more complex format – notably allowing for storytelling and the inclusion of sound – and therefore merit separate treatment. This chapter traces the history of jihadi filmmaking.

The existence of jihadi videos is somewhat paradoxical, given that conservative Islamists have often been sceptical of the production of moving images.[1] Nevertheless, militant Islamists have been producing videos since the early 1980s. The number of videos increased exponentially in the 2000s, in line with technological developments that made production and dissemination of homemade videos a mass phenomenon. Today, jihadi videos are mainly found on the Internet, either as downloadable files or on video-sharing websites such as YouTube or Dailymotion. They can be divided into genres such as operational videos, ideological speeches, martyr wills, or hostage executions. Another genre is the lengthy feature film, which combines several genres into one to present a grand narrative of whom the jihadis fight and why. Jihadi videos serve a variety of purposes, not least to attract new recruits by appealing to their emotions.[2]

Jihadi videos can be seen as part of the broader phenomenon of war propaganda. Jihadi feature films use similar narratives as the newsreels and documentaries made by the warring parties during the Second World War. For example, Nazi Germany's *Triumph of the Will* from 1935 presented a grand narrative of suffering German people, a battle between good versus evil, and the Nazi party that will come to their rescue. Although it depicts a different political context, the victim narrative is essentially the same as in al-Qaida's major productions.[3]

Jihadi videos are among the least well-studied bodies of war propaganda relative to the size of the corpus.[4] We lack, in particular, a historical analysis of how jihadi videos have evolved over time; it is this gap I hope to fill with this chapter. The chapter has two objectives.

The first is to trace the history of jihadi video production and give a sense of its scale and content. The second aim is to discuss how jihadi videos can be seen as an expression of jihadi culture more generally. The study will not analyze the reception or radicalizing effect of jihadi videos, as this would require a different methodology and hard-to-get sources.[5] The main sources used here are the jihadi videos themselves, in addition to court documents, autobiographies, and other sources that say something about the historical context in which the videos were made.[6]

The chapter has four parts. The first part discusses early jihadi video production in the 1980s and 1990s during the wars in Afghanistan, Bosnia, and Chechnya. The second part is concerned with the history of al-Sahab, al-Qaida's official media company, and how in the early 2000s they pioneered the development of the lengthy feature film. The third part discusses the effect of the Iraq War from 2003 on jihadi video production. The fourth part is concerned with developments from 2006 onwards, with examples drawn from the video production of al-Shabab in Somalia and the Islamic State (IS) in Iraq and Syria.

Origins of the Jihadi Video (1981–2000)

The history of jihadi film production goes back to the early days of the Afghan-Soviet war. Afghan mujahidin reportedly brought cameras to the battlefield as early as 1981. The purpose was not primarily to make artistic products, but to document results on the battlefield. This in turn would generate more supplies and funding for the group.[7] Foreign and local journalists also came to Afghanistan in this period to make pro-mujahedin documentaries.[8]

Arab foreign fighters also filmed in 1980s Afghanistan. In some cases their motives were personal. Afghan commanders certainly viewed some of the Arabs as war tourists who filmed themselves simply so they could impress people back home. One Afghan commander complained in 1987 that he "had some Arabs who were with us for jihad credit. They had a video camera and all they wanted to do was to take videos. They were of no value to us."[9] Another commander described the Arabs bluntly as "prima donnas who were more interested in taking videos than fighting."[10]

Other Arabs shot videos for a purpose. Around 1987, Usama bin Ladin invited the Saudi Journalist Izzam Diraz to make an Arabic-language documentary about the Arab fighters in Afghanistan for fundraising purposes. The documentary, entitled *The Arab Supporters in Afghanistan*, was published in 1988.[11] The forty-nine-minute video shows clips of the Afghan leader Abd al-Rabb Rasul Sayyaf and bin Ladin and footage from bin Ladin's al-Ma'sada base in Paktika.

Some iconic video clips were also recorded around this time, notably a series of speeches of Abdullah Azzam in Peshawar around 1988–1989. The clips were produced by a group calling itself the Black Banners Studios (*markaz al-rayat al-sawd lil-intaj*). They produced several videos featuring speeches by Abdullah Azzam, including a well-known lecture called *The Solution*, taped around 1988. Later, the studio produced another jihadi classic, the *Lovers of Martyrdom*, an hour-long video featuring old clips of Abdullah Azzam along with clips of the first foreign fighters killed in Bosnia in 1992.[12]

The First Jihadi Filmmakers

In the 1980s and early 1990s, films were often recorded by TV teams and journalists brought in for the sole purpose of filming.[13] However, by 1992 the jihadis had started using their own fighters as cameramen. This development happened as hand-held camcorders became more accessible to private consumers. One of the first jihadi cameramen appears to have been Abu Musa al-Almani, a German national of Turkish origin.[14] An excerpt from a biography describes how he worked in the field:

Abu Musa had some experience in making video films and editing, and so in Bosnia they made him the cameraman. Therefore, along with his Kalashnikov he would carry his camera. He was witnessed in front of the attacks with his camera, fighting and even reaching the bunkers of the Serbs before the rest of the brothers. He would be standing on top of the bunkers of the Serbs and the Serbs would still be shooting. He said to a brother, that when he reached the bunker, "*I thought whether I should throw a grenade inside or put the camera inside,*" and he chose to put the camera inside so that he could get the best possible pictures, mix the best possible film and send it back to the other Muslims that do not know anything about Jihad. Then, they could see the Jihad on their television sets and find out and learn about this obligation that the Muslim World had forgotten about.[15]

Another cameraman who seems to have played a prominent role in the mid-1990s is the French-Beninese Masood al-Benin. He joined the Chechen mujahidin toward the end of the first Chechen war in 1996.

There was a lull in the fighting at the time, so he spent the next few years using his IT skills to assist local mujahidin. Among other things, he set up computers for use by the local Sharia courts. In addition he was a correspondent for the Qoqaz.net website. With the start of the Second Chechen War in 1999, he was able to participate in battles again. Like the German-Turkish Abu Musa, he appears to have played multiple roles as cameraman, fighter, and video editor.[16] It was only in the 2000s that jihadi groups started creating separate "media cells" that would film battles and edit videos, but not participate in the fighting themselves. This development was a result of the new standards on jihadi video production set by groups fighting in Iraq from 2003, discussed further below.

Distribution and Audiences

In the early days of jihadi film making, propaganda videos were spread mainly through mosques, charity organizations, bookshops, and Islamist street vendors. In the United States, the two Muslim charities al-Kifah Refugee Center and Care International distributed audio and videotapes from the mid-1990s onwards.[17] In Britain, jihadi propaganda videos could be bought in Islamic bookstores such as Maktabah al-Ansar located in Sparkhill, Birmingham. According to court documents, the bookshop "became the exclusive distributor of the Azzam Publications books, videos and tapes glorifying violent jihad."[18] Another venue that sold jihadi propaganda was the Four Feathers Club near Baker Street in London. The venue served as a base for the radical preacher Abu Qatada al-Filistini.[19]

One of the first Web pages to distribute videos from Bosnia and Chechnya was the U.K.-based Azzam Publications (www.azzam.com), founded by Babar Ahmed in 1997.[20] Azzam.com may have been the first virtual jihadi media organization; the group stated on their page that they existed only on the Internet and had no street address. However, they had a P.O. box address in London. To order videos, audios and books, people had to send them cash in an envelope.

Among the volunteers who helped run the Azzam website was a certain Suraqah al-Andalusi. According to his biography,

Suraqah was part of the team that translated and typeset the script for the video *The Martyrs of Bosnia*. He was also part of the team that conducted interviews, translated and researched the material for the Jihad Lands section of Azzam.com, namely the lands of Afghanistan, Uzbekistan, East Turkestan (China) and Central Asia. He translated an entire book on the Jihad in Central Asia by himself, written by a Mujahid in Afghanistan, even though Arabic was not his mother-tongue.[21]

In fact, *The Martyrs of Bosnia* was advertised as "the first of its kind in the English language."[22] It suggests that Azzam.com were pioneers when it came to translating jihadi propaganda videos from Arabic to English for Western audiences. Azzam.com was also a pioneer in distributing jihadi videos on the Internet. According to an archived version of the Azzam webpage from 2000, some of the jihadi video clips could be viewed directly online, just by clicking on a link.

However, Internet distribution was rather uncommon at the time, given the low bandwidth available. Instead, potential recruits watched videos during public events and social gatherings. According to a former militant Islamist, the videos from Bosnia and Chechnya in the 1990s had a profound effect on their audience.[23] What cinematographic techniques were used to exaggerate this effect?

Video Content

Simple, cinematographic techniques were used from the very start of jihadi filmmaking. On Azzam.com we find one of the earliest jihadi video recordings from Bosnia: a five-minute clip of a Saudi fighter named Abu Zubayr al-Madani, claimed to be recorded in Bosnia in 1992.[24] The video is an example of the "martyr video" genre. It has some of the features that have become standard in later jihadi video production. Most notably, it includes footage of the martyr before and after his death. Parts of it are in slow motion, a technique commonly used in movies to create suspense or highlight a particular element. Furthermore, the footage of the dead martyr shows his face styled in the way that was common on martyr photographs and posters at the time. Another, typical feature of this film is the sound track made up of a medley of Qur'an recitation, speeches, gunshots, and, of course, *anashid* (see Pieslak and Lahoud's chapters in this book). At the end of the video, the screen goes black while the soundtrack plays a recording of a *nashid* allegedly sung by the dead fighter.[25]

The film about Abu Zubayr did not present a grand narrative, but this has become more common in later jihadi productions. Among the first jihadi films to present such a narrative was *The Battles of Badr in*

Bosnia (*ma'arik badr al-bosna*), produced in 1995 by the Mujahidin Brigade (i.e., the foreign jihadi fighters) in Bosnia.[26] The video contains standard elements of war propaganda in that it presents a diagnosis, followed by a prognosis. First, a narrator tells the story of the Bosnian conflict, accompanied by images of Islamic preachers, Western rulers, and foreign fighters in Bosnia. Next, the video describes the mujahidin's preparations: commanders planning an operation, fighters walking to the battlefield and setting up a forward base. We observe their daily activities at the base, such as cooking, eating, and grooming. The third part of the video shows the actual battle and ends with fighters gathering and praying in the sunset.

The best-known jihadi films from Chechnya were made during the Second Chechen War in 1999–2000. In March 2000, the "video library" of the Qoqaz.net website contained titles such as *Jihad in Dagestan* (August 1999), *Massacres in Chechnya* (October 1999), and *Chechnya: Destruction of a Nation* (December 1999).[27] The first video featured operational footage of jihadi fighters, while the two latter titles claimed to depict "civilians massacred by Russian forces." Jihadi films from Bosnia and Chechnya tended to depict either operations or atrocities against civilians, while in later jihadi productions these two themes were combined into one and the same narrative.

The Chechnya film that got the most attention among Islamists in the West was probably *Russian Hell in the Year 2000*, produced by a group called "The Islamic Army of the Caucasus."[28] The composition of the story in *Russian Hell* is similar to that of *The Battles of Badr in Bosnia*. The film starts with a narrator's voice explaining the background for the Chechen war. Then the film shows clips of Chechen commanders preparing for the operation. We see the fighters walking to the battlefield and setting up camp as the darkness falls. In the early morning hours, the operations begin. Between the attacks we see the mujahidin being welcomed into a local village by locals. The film ends with footage of the battlefield and a tribute to the fallen. Here, too, a sunset concludes the film.

Russian Hell employed all the cinematographic techniques seen in earlier productions: a soundtrack with *anashid*, speeches, and battle sounds, and pictures of soon-to-be martyrs are played in slow motion. Interestingly, the film not only shows the smiling face of the dead martyr, but his entire – often heavily mutilated – body.

Russian Hell also contains some innovations. For one, the film shows a live execution of a Russian soldier. This seems to have been the first videotaped execution in jihadi cinema, but it was certainly not the last. A second innovation of *Russian Hell* is the clever use of contrasting images. The cold, snowy landscape of Chechnya is contrasted with images of burning enemy vehicles. The use of burning vehicles as visual symbol is a direct allusion to the title of the film, *mahraqat al-rus*: The Arabic word *mahraqa* may be translated as Hell, pyre, or Holocaust.

Another contrasting image is the look of Khattab's rough, seasoned fighters, compared with the Russian Army's young, clean-shaven, and uniformed soldiers. Khattab's fighters are sporting long hair and beards and no particular style of uniform, except that they include some style of camouflage jackets and pants. Some of the fighters are wearing Western-style wool caps, others are wearing Afghan *pakhols* – giving the impression that the person is a seasoned jihadi fighter with experience from the Afghan-Soviet war. The contrasting imagery reinforces the "us" versus "them" narrative of the film.

Al-Sahab's Early Productions (2000–2004)

Al-Sahab was founded in 1999 to serve as the official video production company of al-Qaida. The name al-Sahab, which means "The Clouds" in Arabic, was allegedly chosen by Usama bin Ladin himself.[29] Al-Sahab's main task was to produce official propaganda videos for al-Qaida, in addition to videotaping speeches by bin Ladin and other important al-Qaida leaders.[30] In February 2001, Khalid Sheikh Muhammed was appointed to be al-Sahab's leader.[31] He likely continued in this position until he was arrested in Rawalpindi, Pakistan, in 2003. Since then, al-Sahab has been run by unknown al-Qaida members, probably from somewhere in Pakistan, and has continued to function as al-Qaida's official mouthpiece.

The inner workings of al-Sahab were long unknown to the outside world, but new details have trickled out after the interrogation records of Ali Hamza al-Bahlul, who was captured and sent to Guantanamo in 2002, were made public. During interrogations, he gave a detailed account of the production of al-Qaida's first and perhaps most famous full-length feature, *The Destruction of the American Destroyer USS*

Cole, also known under the title *State of the Umma* (hereafter referred to as *The USS Cole* video).[32]

The Making of The USS Cole *Video*

According to al-Bahlul, the order to make the *USS Cole* video came directly from bin Ladin himself. The final result was an almost two-hour long propaganda film, the main purpose of which was to present al-Qaida's aims and ideology and encourage Muslims to join al-Qaida's training camps in Afghanistan.[33] The *USS Cole* attack itself was only briefly mentioned in the video. In fact, the video does not say explicitly that al-Qaida perpetrated the attack, presumably because doing so would have caused problems for the Taliban regime.[34] However, the main point was that the *USS Cole* attack had ensured al-Qaida publicity. Al-Bahlul himself stated to interrogators that the purpose of the *USS Cole* video was "to awaken the Islamic Umma to revolt against America ... he hoped new recruits would come to Afghanistan and join the jihad."[35]

Bin Ladin was directly involved in the production of the *USS Cole* video. Al-Bahlul said that bin Ladin revised the video several times, and he instructed him to include a certain audio clip at the start of the video. The audio clip was a Qur'an recitation by Mamdouh Mahmud Salim, who had been indicted in the 1998 East Africa embassy bombings and was in prison in the United States.[36]

Al-Bahlul said that al-Sahab's offices were fully equipped with VCRs, computers, satellite TV, and a library of video and audiocassettes. But the video editing software was far from professional: It consisted of a Windows PC and Adobe Premiere Pro video editing software. Al-Bahlul's handwritten notes, recovered by U.S. troops during the 2001 invasion, indicated that he often ran into technical difficulties with the software. In the end, it took about six months to finish the *USS Cole* video, and it was released sometime in the spring of 2001.[37]

Before its release, the video went through a thorough review and approval process. According to al-Bahlul, this was standard procedure at the time. Videos of bin Ladin were reviewed by al-Qaida's Security Committee, while training camp footage was to be approved by al-Qaida's Military Committee. The final product was approved by bin Ladin himself before being disseminated.[38]

Al-Bahlul stated that several of his videos were "sent through Bin Ladin to the Al-Jazira [*sic*] channel."[39] Videos were also distributed directly to foreign journalists who came to Afghanistan. In June 2001, the MBC correspondent Bakr Aytani was given a copy of the *USS Cole* video when he was in Afghanistan to interview bin Ladin and Ayman al-Zawahiri. Clips of the tape were subsequently shown on MBC.[40] The *USS Cole* video was also available in the West, through Islamic bookstores such as Maktabah al Ansar in the United Kingdom. Finally, al-Sahab videos were used internally by al-Qaida to indoctrinate foreign recruits who came to Afghanistan. After the U.S. invasion in 2001, a flier was found in one of al-Qaida's guesthouses advertising a screening of the new *USS Cole* video. "Please let us know your comments and suggestions," the flier stated.[41]

Al-Sahab's Contributions to the Jihadi Film Genre

Between 2001 and 2004 al-Sahab issued at least two other full-length films, *The Nineteen Martyrs* (2002) and *American Hell in Afghanistan and Iraq* (2003). In addition, they issued some videos on behalf of al-Qaida in Saudi Arabia, notably *The Wills of the Heroic Martyrs of the Two Holy Cities* (2003), *Martyrs of the Confrontations* (2003), and *The Battle of Badr in Riyadh* (2004).

In their form, al-Sahab's videos resemble the older videos from Bosnia and Chechnya. *Anashid* are used extensively, especially when showing preparation and battle scenes, and when commemorating dead fighters. However, there are several innovative aspects to al-Sahab's initial productions. First, they combine diagnostic and prognostic messaging in a more explicit way than before. At the beginning of the *USS Cole* video, a text appears on the screen stating that "after revealing the illness, [the video] goes on to describe the cure." The first twenty-five minutes of the video are dedicated to showing atrocities against Muslims in different parts of the world. The second half of the video starts, unequivocally, with displaying the heading "The Solution." In comparison, *Russian Hell 2000* spent only a few minutes explaining the background for the Chechen war, while most of the video was dedicated to operational footage.

The second important contribution is that al-Sahab's videos started including clips from many different conflicts across the world, while earlier films focused on one or just a few. This geographical diversification in the diagnostic framing reflected al-Qaida's globalized worldview. The selection of clips also reflected current events. For example, the *USS Cole* video was produced during the al-Aqsa intifada in 2000. It was the first jihadi video to make use of a famous video clip from the intifada: the footage of the Palestinian boy Mohammed al-Durrah allegedly being killed by Israeli soldiers.[42] The al-Durrah image became an icon of the second intifada and appeared on t-shirts, posters, and wall murals. Several Arab countries issued postage stamps carrying the image, and one of Baghdad's main streets was renamed The Martyr Mohammed Aldura Street.[43] The picture became a symbol of Israel's oppression of the Palestinians.

For al-Qaida, the timing of the event was perfect. The al-Durrah incident happened only ten days before the *USS Cole* bombing, and shortly after that, al-Bahlul started working on the *USS Cole* propaganda video for bin Ladin. Al-Sahab exploited the al-Durrah incident for all it was worth. The filmmakers highlighted the al-Durrah clip by showing it repeatedly, each time with the sound of a gunshot and the name "Muhammad" in Arabic letters popping up on the screen. In the background, emotional voices of preachers denounce the killing.

The al-Durrah image has been used in numerous subsequent jihadi videos. For example, it appeared in the infamous video clip showing the beheading of the journalist Daniel Pearl in Pakistan (2002), in the al-Sahab documentary *The Manhattan Raid* (2006), and in *The Bouchaoui Attack* (2007), produced by the media wing of Groupe Salafiste pour la Prédication et le Combat (GSPC) in Algeria.[44]

The third of al-Sahab's contributions is the introduction of suicide bomber testaments. We recall from the Bosnian and Chechen wars that the "heroes" were seasoned guerrilla fighters, portrayed at camp and on the battlefield, within the framework of another day of fighting. When they died, they were commemorated through slow-motion film and images of their face after death, combined with martyrdom *anashid*. Sometimes, films would include some kind of "martyrdom testament," a speech or statement by the fighter recorded before his death, but this was rather uncommon.

Al-Sahab, who probably took inspiration from Palestinian groups such as Hamas, made it obligatory to record such martyrdom testaments. All of the 9/11 hijackers recorded a statement before their death, and these were included in subsequent al-Sahab productions. They were not always comfortable with this; one of the 9/11 hijackers,

Ziad Jarrah, reportedly required several takes before managing to deliver a speech that showed sufficient "passion and enthusiasm."[45]

For al-Sahab, it was important to sell the new jihadi hero to their audience, in order to continue recruiting operatives for martyrdom attacks against Western targets. Through visual effects, al-Sahab attempted to portray these new jihadi heroes as equal to the classical mujahidin of Bosnia and Chechnya, in order to sell bin Ladin's fighting doctrine to the coming generation of fighters. Arguably, al-Sahab has not been entirely successful in this. A majority of jihadi recruits who have gone to training camps abroad after 2001 have wanted to fight in a "classical jihad" – that is, to take part in guerrilla fighting against a non-Muslim occupant of Muslim lands. On the other hand, many jihadi guerrillas have started to employ suicide bombers and to make sure that his testament – and if possible, his last moments – are preserved on tape.

Al-Sahab's film from 2004, *The Battle of Badr in Riyadh*, included all the elements of a classical suicide bomber video. The video depicted the bombers who carried out the devastating attack on the al-Muhaya housing complex in Riyadh, Saudi Arabia, on November 8, 2003. *The Battle of Badr in Riyadh* was probably the first jihadi video to use a cell phone camera for filming an operation. Cell phone cameras were a novelty at the time; the first models started to appear on the world market only in 2002.

The cell phone video depicts two of the attackers in their truck as they drive to the target. We hear their voices, gunshots, and shouts of "*Allahu Akhbar*" before the screen goes blank. In later productions, it became common for attack teams to employ a cameraman to film the actual suicide truck explosion from a safe distance. We would see this technique used extensively during the Iraqi insurgency.

The Iraq War Effect (2004–2006)

The Iraq war was the first conflict in which a substantial part of the jihadi propaganda campaign was waged on the Internet. Between 2004 and 2006, most Iraqi groups established a presence on the Web, and they released statements and videos on jihadi web pages and discussion forums on a regular basis. Abu Mus'ab al-Zarqawi's group *Monotheism and Jihad*, later known as al-Qaida in Iraq (AQI), pioneered online distribution of audio-visual propaganda.[46] A majority of the videos were short, operational films that showed a single attack by a rocket, sniper, or (most commonly) an improvised explosive device (IED).[47]

The attack videos from Iraq differed fundamentally from the full-length feature films of al-Sahab. Attack videos seldom contain a narrative justifying the group's actions. On the other hand, they appear to have served as proof that the group in question had carried out the attack. Thus the videos served the same instrumental purpose as the first videos emanating from Afghanistan in the 1980s. Both Afghanistan in the 1980s and Iraq after 2003 were complex battlefields with several guerrilla groups competing for influence and resources. Moreover, the Iraq War coincided with a series of technological developments that made it easier to upload and share video files online. These factors contributed to the exponential growth in the number of jihadi videos in the 2000s.

Video Producers and Distributors

Al-Qaida in Iraq's Internet-based propaganda campaign was initiated in early April 2004.[48] The mastermind behind the campaign appears to have been Muhannad al-Sa'idi (aka Abu-Maysara al-Iraqi), a Shiite who had converted to Sunni Islam and joined al-Zarqawi's group in or before 2003. In addition, "there were also a few figures from the Arab Maghreb who had the capability and the enormous energy to use the Internet, computers, tactics, and montage, particularly from Algeria. This is how the media issue started, until Al-Furqan [AQI's official media company] was established."[49]

AQI's media operation relied not only on operatives inside Iraq but also on sympathizers elsewhere who would upload the videos to jihadi discussion forums. In 2004, AQI started using the Web forum Muntada al-Ansar as their primary channel for publication of videos. Al-Ansar had existed since May 2002 but reached prominence in 2004 when al-Zarqawi's group started using it on a regular basis. It was administered by an individual named Mohibb al-Shaykhain al-Tunsi, in addition to a U.K.-based Moroccan named Yunus Tsouli, who called himself "Irhabi 007" (Terrorist 007).[50] The al-Ansar forum stayed open until October 2005, when other similar forums, such as Al-Hisba and Al-Firdaws, replaced it. The important thing was that

AQI continued to have access to online venues on which to upload statements and videos.

In November 2006, an online media company named al-Furqan became the official video producer of al-Qaida in Iraq. In 2007, the United States carried out a series of raids against al-Furqan offices and operatives, which gave an indication of the size of al-Qaida's media operation in Iraq at the time. As one U.S. spokesperson noted at the time, "Since the surge began, we've uncovered eight separate al Qaeda media offices and cells, have captured or killed 24 al Qaeda propaganda cell members and have discovered 23 terabytes of information."[51] By now, it is safe to assume that jihadi groups had started to set up separate "media cells," as opposed to in previous conflict theaters where fighters had doubled as cameramen and producers.

Content and Contributions to the Jihadi Film Genre

One of the first videos produced by al-Qaida in Iraq was the beheading of Nicholas Berg, published in May 2004.[52] It was followed by a series of similar videos published between May and December. It is unknown why AQI ceased issuing these videos at the end of 2004. One theory is that al-Zarqawi stopped because he was criticized by the al-Qaida leadership in Pakistan. Another explanation could simply be that the beheading videos had outplayed their role. The main purpose of the videos had been to get media attention, and by the end of 2004 AQI had clearly established itself as a prominent player on the Iraqi insurgent scene.[53]

From 2004 onwards, AQI issued a number of other videos from Iraq. The most striking new feature of these videos was their extensive use of short clips. Videos were either very short (under ten minutes) showing one single operation, or long (forty minutes to an hour and a half), but comprising a number of shorter clips. AQI's first operational video, *The Winds of Victory*, was released in July 2004 and was six minutes fourteen seconds in length. It was built upon the pattern of earlier documentaries, showing a group preparing for battle. They are seen reading the Qur'an, training, and listening to a motivational speech by their leader. The video ends with a scene of the fighters praying together at dawn. The battle itself is not shown, presumably because the group was not able to capture any footage.[54] *The Winds of Victory* is built upon a familiar narrative, but each phase is compressed so that the film is just a little longer than six minutes in total. This preference for short films likely reflects the shift to online video distribution. In 2004, jihadi producers were no longer dependent on having to fill a whole VHS cassette or CD-ROM, because the videos were digitalized and uploaded directly to the Internet. Given that bandwidth was limited, shorter clips would be more easily accessible.

The groups in Iraq also produced longer films for distribution on CD-ROM, but even in these films the narrative tempo was much higher than in previous jihadi productions. While Khattab's *Russian Hell* covered three different operations in a two-hour video, AQI's *Lions of the War* from 2005 presented twelve different attacks within the first twenty minutes.[55] Another technique introduced by AQI was to film attacks from multiple camera angles. An early example of this is from December 24, 2004, during a suicide attack on an American base in Mosul.[56]

Another characteristic of AQI's films, which followed the trend started by al-Sahab, was their casting of the suicide operative as the principal character of the video. A good example is the film *The Expedition of Shaykh Umar Hadid* from 2006.[57] Incidentally, this video was one of the first AQI videos to be translated into English. The translator, U.S.-born Tarek Mehanna, said he selected the video because he thought it would have a powerful impact on its audience.[58] The eighty-minute video features suicide operatives from a larger AQI offensive in and around Baghdad in 2005. The most innovative aspect of AQI's martyr videos, compared to al-Sahab's first videos, is the use of computer graphics. AQI notably started manipulating pictures of its fallen martyrs with Photoshop and other techniques to make the corpses look cleaner and "happier."

The increased use of graphics and photoshopping is obvious in *The Expedition of Shaykh Umar Hadid*. A considerable part of the video shows pictures of the martyrs floating over the screen while *anashid* are playing in the background. Later there is a scene where footage of the martyr speaking is superimposed over footage from the suicide operation – as if he is talking to us from the hereafter.[59] At the end of the video, portraits of martyrs are superimposed over a cloudy sky, again depicting them as if they were in heaven. The clip ends with footage of bin Ladin speaking of sacrifice in God's path, superimposed over a pictorial illustration of Paradise.

Another feature of the *Expedition* video is that occasionally, the martyrs are shown speaking directly to the camera – making eye contact with the audience watching the tape and addressing them directly. The recruitment agenda is obvious. One of the individuals states that "Whoever who sees this CD should come and join the lands of jihad!"[60] Another, responding to a question about whether he has a message to those who shirk the duty of jihad, fixes his eyes on the camera as he says, "You have no excuse."[61]

It is difficult to know how these videos affect their intended viewers. Occasionally, however, we can observe their reception through declassified surveillance videos. For example, during a terrorism trial in the United States in 2006, the prosecution presented an audio recording of a group of radicals watching and discussing a martyrdom video from Iraq:

See, look. This is the guy who committed, May God be praised, the martyrdom [operation] driving the car... This is a brother who made martyrdom car bombing on the bridge of Khalidya. Look brother, after – after the whole blow... explosion; when they returned him. My brother, look at his face. I swear to Allah he is smiling ... And the whole explosion. Glory be to Allah. Look, I mean Praise be to God, he's still in one piece.[62]

While the infamous decapitation videos from 2004 served to attract global attention to al-Qaida in Iraq, more sophisticated productions such as *The Expedition of Umar Hadid* were probably more important for recruitment.

Toward a "Jihadi Hollywood"?

The last part of this chapter discusses some of the developments that have taken place within jihadi video production in recent years. The topic is too broad to be studied in detail, and so this section is therefore limited to discussing how new, visual styles inspired by mainstream Western media have inspired jihadi filmmaking in such diverse places as Somalia and Syria.

Al-Shabab and the "MTV Jihad"

Al-Shabab, which officially joined al-Qaida in 2012, can be described as an "ideological hybrid" – a local Islamist guerrilla that has embraced al-Qaida's global ideology. This dual agenda shines through in their video productions. The group has produced videos in the local language, Somali, in addition to videos in English and Arabic. The design and quality of al-Shabab's videos vary greatly, suggesting that several different production teams have produced videos in al-Shabab's name.

When al-Shabab started making propaganda videos for English and Arab speakers, they sought to emulate classical jihadi films from the 1990s and early 2000s. A typical example is *Hell of the Apostates in Somalia* from November 2006. The title is inspired by *Russian Hell* and later productions with variations of the same title ("Hell of the X in area Y"). The film opens with graphic pictures of dead civilians, followed by speeches by ideologues justifying the war. Next are training and preparation footage, followed by combat scenes. Both preparation and battles are accompanied by familiar Arabic *anashid*. Interviews with guerrilla leaders and fighters feature at regular intervals throughout the film. Curiously, the video features an interview with a fully veiled woman, which was quite unusual for jihadi recruitment videos at the time.[63]

An al-Shabab video that is even more reminiscent of *Russian Hell* is *The Blessed Dinsur Battle*, released in May 2008. It includes scenes with commanders planning the battle on a map, a commander giving the fighters a pep talk in the field, and fighters singing a *nashid* together before going into battle. After the battle the camera dwells on the bodies of dead enemies and vehicles blazing with fire. The fighters are greeted and applauded as they ride into a nearby village with the symbolic black banner mounted on the vehicle.[64]

Hell of the Apostates in Somalia and *The Blessed Dinsur Battle* are only two of many videos released by al-Shabab from 2006 onwards. They illustrate how al-Shabab's video production was inspired by and – whether consciously or not – copied the visual motifs and narrative from earlier videos recorded thousands of miles away. It suggests that a distinctive cinematographic style had established itself within the world of global jihadism. By emulating this style, al-Shabab sought to associate itself with and become part of the transnational jihadi movement.

In addition to emulating existing patterns of jihadi film making, al-Shabab were one of the pioneers in introducing stylistic elements from Western culture into jihadi videos. This development, dubbed the "MTV jihadism" was possibly reflecting the influence of a small group of American citizens who joined al-Shabab in the late 2000s. The most

prolific among them was the Syrian-American Omar Hammami, also
known as Abu Mansoor al-Amriki.[65]

The videos made by Hammami and others are characterized by
short clips, fast tempo, and vivid colors – much like in a commercial
music video. For example, the English-language video *The Beginning
of the End: A Response to Barack Obama* released in July 2009 opens
with a 3D animation of al-Shabab's name and logo followed by a
series of fast-moving clips. By contrast, an al-Sahab video featuring
al-Qaida's leaders would typically open with al-Sahab's vignette and
one or more Islamic or jihadi symbols – a Qur'an, Kalashnikovs, a
cross that explodes, or a burning American flag. The introduction to
The Beginning of the End is virtually stripped of such effects, save for
the words "In the Name of God, the Merciful, the Compassionate," at
the very beginning.[66]

Another attempt to merge jihadi culture with American youth
culture is apparent in Abu Mansoor's self-composed "jihadi rap" – a
combination of an English-language *nasheed* and rap-style verses –
which is included in the soundtrack of *Ambush at Bardal* (2009).[67]

However, the innovations introduced by Hammami and others were
limited to a few videos, and it never became the trademark of al-
Shabab's video production. Besides the rap song, *Ambush at Bardal*
contains many of the more traditional audio clips and visual images of
jihadi filmmaking – such as the sound of a neighing horse and Qur'an
recitation, the image of a martyr's face, his grave in the dark, and a
superimposed picture of Usama bin Ladin talking about martyrdom.

While al-Shabab's films in 2009 experimented with introducing
some elements of Western pop culture into the films, the Islamic State
in Iraq and Syria (ISIS), later known as the Islamic State (IS), took it a
long step further. Films issued by IS have a distinct visual style –
presumably aimed at capturing a new generation of consumers accustomed to high-resolution video games, TV, and Hollywood movies.

The Islamic State's Video Production

In the West, IS is perhaps best known for their videos of hostage executions and other abhorrent acts. However, IS propaganda is a much wider
phenomenon. Since its foundation in 2013, IS has waged a propaganda
campaign that is highly sophisticated relative to that of other jihadi
groups, in both quality of content and methods of distribution.[68]

The sophistication of IS propaganda content is especially evident in their video production. Propaganda videos by IS have been described as "slick," "sophisticated," "professional," and even "Hollywood-style."[69] The size of IS's video output is too massive to be treated in any comprehensive way here: according to one study, IS released no fewer than twenty-four videos during one particular week of data collection.[70] However, a quick look at some of IS's productions from 2014, such as the full-length feature film *Flames of War: Fighting Has Just Begun* and a series of short clips known as the *Mujatweets* series, suggest that the group has indeed created a new visual style that differs from that of older videos.

The main difference between IS propaganda and that of other groups is probably the increased professionalism at all stages of production – from shooting, to editing, to uploading and distribution. As outlined by Dauber and Robinson, "ISIS is systematically working to use visual standards that will give their videos an underlying professional look to someone whose eye is accustomed to a European or North American industry standard."[71] They do this by using a variety of techniques such as color saturation, professional lighting, and a shallow depth of field. IS videos appear to be more carefully scripted and edited than other movies, using camera angles, sound effects, graphics, and other techniques to imitate the cinematographic techniques of Western blockbusters and news broadcasts. This has also been done before, but IS is arguably the first group to do it in a systematic and repeated fashion; thus we may talk about the "IS visual style" as a distinct phenomenon.

An example of this "Hollywood-like" editing can be found in *Flames of War*, published by the IS-affiliated media company *Al Hayat* in September 2014. It is a fifty-five-minute full-length feature film, presenting a diagnosis-prognosis narrative similar to that of earlier jihadi films. The sound track is also relatively familiar – mixing anashid, ideological speeches, and battlefield sounds. However, the film mimics shooting and editing techniques of professional moviemakers to a degree that has not been observed before. For example, at one point a fighter is seen firing an anti-tank grenade at Syrian regime troops. The firing of the grenade is shown in slow motion – an effect used since the early days of jihadi filmmaking – but in addition the fighter is filmed from a first-person perspective and from below, as if he sees the firing through the eyes of a fighter laying on the ground. As the grenade fires, sound effects are used to simulate ringing ears, heavy breathing, and a beating heart – again, creating a sensation that the viewer is right there on the ground, next to the shooter.[72] While these techniques are standard in commercial filmmaking – and technically possible to replicate for talented amateurs with off-the shelf equipment and software – they do require a certain level of artistic ambition not previously seen in jihadi groups.

For all their "slickness" and sophistication, though, IS's video production does not represent a watershed event in the history of jihadi filmmaking. On the contrary, it follows a predictable pattern in which jihadis make use of new technologies (in this case, modern camcorders and editing software) that are already available off-the-shelf. While IS, for now, has succeeded in creating a distinct visual style, it is to be expected that other jihadi groups will follow suit – especially those who seek to appeal to Western audiences.

Conclusion

This brief, historical overview has shown that jihadis are adept at taking advantage of new technologies to produce and disseminate audiovisual propaganda. Since the 1990s, jihadi videos have increased in importance relative to traditional propaganda products such as books, pamphlets, and magazines. This development is not unique to militant Islamism but follows general trends in consumer preferences and technological innovation across the globe.

We have seen that the most common visual symbols and cinematographic techniques have been present in jihadi videos from the very beginning. There have been some changes, such as when al-Sahab in 2001 changed the main protagonist from the guerrilla fighter to the suicide bomber. Similarly, the "grand narrative" changed their focus from specific territorial conflicts to encompassing the whole Muslim world. These developments were not unique to the video genre. Rather, they were necessary adaptations of jihadi propaganda content to suit al-Qaida's new narrative of a global struggle between Muslims and the West.

The introduction of suicide operatives required new techniques for video production in order to uphold the myth of martyrdom. Previously, the most viable "proof" of the martyrdom myth was the divine signs appearing in connection with the martyr's body. But when the martyr's body was not available – which was commonly the case after a suicide bombing – other icons of martyrdom had to be created. This is when computer-generated animation started to appear in videos on a large scale. Initially, animated techniques were used to depict the martyr in paradise. Later, they were used for various other purposes such as replaying operations.

On the one hand, editing techniques have evolved to resemble those of modern-day television and movies – with fast clips, crisp and clear images, and rapid scene changes. On the other hand, it is noticeable how the form and symbols of the older jihadi videos have been retained. For all their minor variations, jihadi videos are quite conformist and predictable. There is not much room for creativity, which is probably why we find no individual jihadi filmmakers known for their distinctive style. This may prove to be a weakness in the long run.

6 The Islamic Dream Tradition and Jihadi Militancy

IAIN R. EDGAR AND GWYNNED DE LOOIJER

The Prophet, now quite ill, is carried into the mosque on the shoulders of two companions. He tries to lead the prayer, but is too weak. He delegates his duties to Abu Bakr. And as he leaves, proclaims: "[When I am gone] there shall remain naught of the glad tidings of prophecy, except for true dreams. These the Muslim will see or they will be seen for him."

Prophetic Hadith[1]

I kept hearing these stories, no big military operation can happen unless he gets his instructions in his dreams; he was a big believer in dreams.

Rahimullah Yusufzai about Mullah Omar[2]

Muhammed [Atta] told me that Marwan [al-Shahhi] had a beautiful dream that he was [physically] flying high in the sky surrounded by green birds not from our world, and that he was crashing into things, and that he felt so happy.

Ramzi bin al-Shibh to Yosri Fouda[3]

Mr. Robert ... one of our brothers had a dream. He dreamt that you came to us one day on a horse, that you had a beard and that you were a spiritual person. You wore a robe like us. This means you are a true Muslim.

Usama bin Ladin to (a terrified) Robert Fisk[4]

In this chapter we will show that there is a long tradition of dream interpretation in Islam that has been wholeheartedly adopted by contemporary militant Islamists. As the quotes above suggest, jihadis attach great significance to dreams, and some even say they let dreams inform their real-life decisions. Indeed, one may argue that contemporary jihadism cannot be fully understood without considering the role dreams play. Yet the subject of jihadism and dreams remains largely understudied.[5] Many scholars of Islam have written about the history, tradition, and theology of jihad, and some have studied dream interpretation, but we know little about the relationship between jihadism and dreams.[6]

As this chapter shows, the presumed revelatory potential of the dream in Islam is key to understanding the significance that modern jihadis attach to dreams. We will show, with a range of examples, that dreams affect jihadi behavior in at least two important ways. First, at the individual level, dreams appear to help activists make sense of the world by providing a rationale for past decisions and events. We cannot verify the frequent claim that dreams alone inspire new decisions – such as joining a group or launching an operation – but we can safely say that militants find comfort in retroactively claiming that they did. Second, and more importantly, Islamic dream theory seems to help some militant leaders establish authority over followers by allowing them to claim special revelatory powers. The perceived ability to obtain and/or to interpret true dreams seems to bestow a special kind of charisma in a culture that acknowledges the "taste" and reality of "hidden worlds." The chapter consists of two main sections. In the first, we trace the history of Islamic dream interpretation, from the Prophetic example to Ibn Sirin and other medieval sources, showing how the dream interpretation tradition came into being and how its reception changed over time. The second part explores the role of the dream in contemporary jihadism, as revealed through a wide range of textual sources.

Dreaming in Islam

The jihadis' relationship with dreams cannot be grasped without knowledge of the historical foundations and cultural specificity of dream interpretation in Islam. The Islamic dream tradition holds that the interpretation of dreams, especially true dreams (*al-ru'ya*), can help to reveal the real world surrounding us. In other words, dreams can be messages from God and may be interpreted to make sense of present-day and future realities. To many Muslims, including jihadis, dreams are a vital part of the constant engagement with the mysteries of life and the search for its meanings. It is said that the Prophet Muhammad had a habit of starting the day by asking his companions about their dreams; this tradition seems to have become commonplace among many Muslims today.[7] In this tradition, dreams are to be seen as a potential guidance for the pious Islamic wayfarer, as dreams are considered to originate beyond human consciousness, beyond the normal concourse of the daily imagination and human desire. The critical evaluation of the manifest meaning of the dream is thus an integral part of the spiritual practice for Muslims almost regardless of their theological orientation.

However, in the Islamic tradition, not all dreams are seen as divinely inspired. A distinction is always drawn between three categories of dreams. First are "bad dreams" (sing. *hulm*, pl. *ahlam*), which are typically based upon human desire and which are designed to lead the dreamer astray. These dreams are thought to be demonic or satanic. Second, there are "divinely sourced" dreams (sing. *ru'ya*, pl. *ru'an*). The Arabic for the latter is "derived from the verb *ra'a*, 'to see', meaning a vision seen in either a dream or waking life."[8] A third category of dreams can be identified as "normal" everyday dreams (*manam*), which are often the result of one's own thinking. Dreams thus enjoy different statuses, as either "true" (in the case of *ru'ya*) or "false/meaningless" (in the case of *hulm* and *manam*). The content of the dream can be also categorised as either *symbolic*, that is, in need of interpretation, or *literal* and therefore clear.[9] The understanding of these two types of dreams developed in their own distinct ways and historically played different roles in the legitimization process of the dream as a revelatory guidance tool and in the changes over time with regard to the prerequisite background of the dream interpreter. Moreover, the meaning and function of the "true dream" in Islamic tradition differ in important ways from the Western (psychoanalytic) view, according to which dreams reveal the unconscious and the inner world of the dreamer.[10] Lamoreaux elegantly summarizes this difference between the Western and Muslim opinions regarding dreams: "Dream interpretation offered Muslims a royal road that led not inward but outward, providing insight not into the dreamer's psyche but into the hidden affairs of the world. In short, the aim of dream interpretation was not diagnosis, but divination."[11]

Dreaming in the Qur'an

Even though many sources point out that the Prophet Muhammad was a great dreamer and he practiced dream interpretation among his companions on a regular basis, the Qur'anic textual evidence of this is sparse. According to Lamoreaux, almost a hundred years passed after the Prophet's death before the first traces of a dream tradition can be observed.[12] However, textual analysis of the Qur'an provides us with strong indications that dreams, visions, and divination were an integral part of the Prophet's account of God's revelation to him. Whether the Prophet explicitly advocated dream interpretation is unclear, but we are certainly able to trace Qur'anic foundations for a dream interpretation tradition.

As a holy text the Qur'an presents itself as firmly rooted within the Abrahamic tradition. The One God chose Abraham (Ibrahim) because he was righteous and the first believer in the Oneness of God. By grounding Abraham within a prophetic tradition, revelation through distinct forms of divine communication implicitly became an indication of a person's religious authority. Hence, Muhammad's authority as a Messenger (Prophet) of God is established through the recognition of his ability to receive God's message, just like the great prophets in the Abrahamic tradition before him. In short, the Qur'an portrays the Prophet Muhammad as if he were created in the image of his predecessors.

The Qur'an notably portrays Muhammad's prophetic predecessors as having had the ability to receive and demonstrate their unique connection to God through various forms of divination: dreams, visions, and miracles. First, Abraham is said to receive divine dreams: the command to sacrifice his son Ishmael was given to him in a dream (*fi al-manam*, Sura 37:102), while Sura 37:105 describes God recognizing Abraham's fulfillment of that dream (*al-ru'ya*). Interestingly, even though in the Hebrew Bible the binding of Isaac is connected to Abraham's submission to God's will, His command to Abraham to sacrifice his son presumes a form of direct verbal communication instead of communication through dreams (cf. Genesis 22:16). Also, the Angel that prevents the sacrifice in God's name does not mention this sense of dream fulfillment as found in the Qur'an. This distinction between the two traditions might point to a Qur'anic preference for the dream as God's way of communicating.

Second, even though the Qur'an does not speak of dream interpretation as an important and integral part of Islam, the importance of dream interpretation might be implicitly observed by the prominent place of Joseph within the Holy Book. Sura 12/6 narrates that God himself will provide Joseph with the skill to interpret his dreams correctly. By contrast, in the Joseph narrative in the Hebrew Bible, dream interpretation belongs to God, as Joseph's words to Pharaoh indicate before he interprets his dreams: "I cannot do it [interpret dreams], but God will give Pharaoh the answers he desires" (Genesis 41:16, 40:8). This notion of dreams as messages from God, and of dream interpretation as a prophetic skill, strengthens Muhammad's stature as a prophet: This "what happened then also happens now" scenario is a well-known literary strategy in Antiquity and establishes a lineal transmission of sacred traditions.

Having shown that the Prophet Muhammad's authority as a diviner is firmly rooted within the Abrahamic tradition, we now turn to those instances in the Qur'an in which the Prophet's own dreams are narrated. Those instances are few and mostly rather vague. First, Sura 8/38–44 (esp. 43) describes the dream that the Prophet had before the Battle of Badr, in which God shows the enemy forces smaller than they actually are, thus giving him and his army confidence:

> Remember in thy dream Allah showed them to thee
> As few: if He had shown them to thee as many,
> Ye would surely have been discouraged,
> and ye would surely have disputed in (your) decision:
> but Allah saved (you): for he knoweth well the (secrets) of (all) hearts.[13]

Another example is Sura 48/27–29, which is said to anticipate the Treaty of Hudaybiyya, which permitted the Prophet and his followers to return to Mecca in order to perform *Umra* (the small pilgrimage):

> Truly did Allah fulfil the Vision/Dream of His Messenger:
> Ye shall enter the Sacred Mosque, if Allah wills
> With minds secure, heads shaved
> Hair cut short. And without fear
> For He knew what ye knew not
> And He granted a speedy victory.

The famous *Isra* and *Mir'aj*, or Night Journey, might be another example of the Prophet's true dreams. However, in the scholarly debate the Isra and Mir'aj are often explained literally, even though some scholars interpret the Prophet's journey as a vision or a dream (Sura 17/1):

> Glory to (Allah) who did take His Servant
> For a journey by night
> From the Sacred Mosque to the Farthest Mosque

Whose precincts We did bless, – in order that We
Might show him some of Our signs:
For He is the One who heareth and seeth (all things).

Apart from the dream narrative found in the Joseph Sura and the tales
about Abraham, these are the only references to dreams and their
interpretation in the Qur'an. What is clear from these sporadic references is the notion of divine intervention: It is God who guides
Muhammad, for "He knew what ye knew not" and "for Allah hath
power over all things." The Prophet's reaction to this divine interaction
is different in each case: In the case of the Treaty of Hudaybiyya, the
Prophet decides to leave all weapons behind and march to Mecca as
pilgrims. However, in the case of the Battle of Badr, he leads his men
into action, an action that is often assumed to be the first jihad or holy
war. If this assumption is correct, Sura 8/38–44 is the only Qur'anic
instance that combines the notion of dreams as divine messages with
that of jihad.

However, the Qur'an does not inform us whether God instructed the
Prophet's actual reaction or conduct with regard to his dreams. Moreover, it is God's all-knowing greatness and transcendental knowledge
that determines the dream vision; as such, no information is provided
as to the Prophet's level of autonomy or predetermination in "choos-
ing" warfare (at Badr) or truce (at Hudaybiyya). Hence, in the Qur'an,
divine intervention through dreams is scarce, and the dream's form,
content, purpose, and meaning are concealed from the human realm:
only God knows all and can foresee human reactions to His divine
messages. Surah 8/43 gives clear evidence of God's intention to encourage by making the enemy forces look small, knowing Muhammad's
certain discouragement without His dream intervention. As such, military action is not divinely sanctioned nor actively sought after on the
basis of dreams. Moreover, no evidence of divine guidance as to the
human *interpretation* of these dreams can be observed.

The First Receptions: Dreaming in the *Hadith*

From our brief investigation above, we learned that the Prophet
Muhammad's reputation as a great dreamer must have been developed
outside of the primary source of the Qur'an, most likely in the *hadith*,
the sayings of the Prophet. Dream interpretation seems a notable topic
in the canonical collections of prophetic traditions as in fact most

collections have an entire chapter on dream interpretation. According
to Lamoreux, the *hadith* establishes a basis for the growing importance
of dream interpretation in Islam, since they hold "that dreams are a
part of prophecy, that they are the successors of Qur'anic revelation,
and that a good Muslim can expect to receive from God messages in
dreams."[14] In the background of Lamoreux's observation stand the
early traditions' reports of the Prophet saying that "prophecy had
come to an end and no prophet will be after me," but that "the glad
tidings remain."[15] Here the earliest traditions demonstrate an interest
in constructing the beginnings of a dream tradition, as they connect the
end of prophecy with the particular interpretation of the "glad tidings"
as referring to "true dreams." In fact, Sura 10/64, in which these "glad
tidings" are mentioned, states only that believers "will have glad
tidings in the life of this world and in the next." However, many
traditions allow the possibility that these "glad tidings" refer to true
dreams, while some of them explicitly narrate the Prophet explaining
that they are "the Muslim's dream (*ru'ya*); it is part of prophecy."[16] In
Bukhari this notion of the dream as prophecy is further developed by
the implicit suggestion that part of the Qur'an already came through
dreams: the tradition expands on Sura 48:27 ("Truly did Allah fulfil
the Vision/Dream of His Messenger") by connecting it to the recorded
sayings of three separate traditions, which state that "a good dream is
1/46th of prophetism."[17] Hence, the early and most authoritative
hadith construct a tradition, which legitimizes (certain) dreams as the
bearers of prophetic wisdom.[18]

Kinberg argues for two more strategies used in the *hadith* to construct and legitimize a dream tradition. First, the *hadith* emphasize the
Prophet's personal interest in dreams. An example is the report of the
Prophet's wife Aisha commemorating that Muhammad's divine inspiration – leading up to the reciting of the Qur'an – started with good
(righteous) dreams.[19] Another example is the Prophet's alleged practice
of asking his companions about their dreams in the morning, a habit
reported in several *hadith* traditions. The identification of the Prophet
Muhammad as an interpreter of dreams par excellence is further
established by various traditions that mention not only many of The
Prophet's dreams, but also his interpretation of symbols that appear in
these dreams. Second, Kinberg finds that the traditions provide a basis
for the subsequent view that a dream vision of the Prophet himself
equals his actual presence.[20] Hence, by ascribing dream narratives and

interpretative examples of dreams directly to the Prophet, his presence in his believers' dreams in a way preserves his prophetic guidance, even though he has died.[21] As Kinberg has argued, it seems that, through this strategic move, (true) dreams become a "third tradition" of sacred knowledge and divine revelation, no less important than the *hadiths*.

With the early development of a dream tradition as a source of divine revelation arise a number of questions regarding the origin and interpretation of dreams: Who is the dreamer, and is he trustworthy? Which dreams are good, and which are bad? Who may interpret and who cannot? In the *hadith*, we observe early negotiations about these important issues. For instance, Bukhari contains three distinct and distinguishable dream categories: unimportant dreams, which reflect one's thoughts and experiences during wakefulness; false dreams, originated by Satan to frighten the dreamer; and true dreams, the aforementioned "glad tidings" from God.[22] Other traditions are less clear-cut and take other things into account, such as the piety of the dreamer and the credibility of the dream.[23] Together with the beginnings of differentiation in *types* of dreams and their content (literal, symbolic, and legislative), these considerations demonstrate the preoccupation with and discussion about the desired level of authority and legitimacy of the dream as a possible source of divine revelation.

Ibn Sirin, Ibn al-Musayyab, and the Emergence of Dream Manuals

Medieval Muslims interpreted dreams by using dream manuals that their contemporaries composed.[24] The number and size of these manuals bear witness to the importance of this form of divination to Muslims in this period.[25] Moreover, we have seen that the *hadith* transmit certain dream interpretation traditions. Interestingly, as we have seen above, dreams and their interpretation do not have a prominent place within the primary source of Islam, the Qur'an. This raises the question of where the ideas in the manuals came from. Lamoreaux has argued that the Islamic dream interpretation tradition may have its origins in an oral culture that developed partly independently of the scriptural tradition. He suggests that these oral dream traditions may have informed the *hadith* collectors. Chronologically, both traditions must have developed alongside one another.[26] Lamoreaux finds

written evidence of anecdotal dream narratives from the eighth century
C.E., which by the mid-tenth century C.E. were being compiled into
dream manuals.[27]

In addition to the above discussed development in the *hadith*, we
can observe the gradual growth of a dream tradition in several sources:
In the 10th century C.E., for example, al-Khallal produced a large
dictionary in which he listed all the known dream interpreters, from
the early prophets via the Prophet Muhammad to his companions and
successors, followed by a large number of contemporary interpreters.
Interestingly, the latter category consisted of individuals from different
kinds of traditions, socioeconomic backgrounds, and geographical
areas.[28] Clearly one of the objectives must have been to establish
legitimacy for a firm dream interpretation tradition. Despite the
number of dream interpreters, not many textual sources have survived;
only two out of well over a hundred of the medieval dream manuals
survived in extant form: those of Ibn Qutaybah (828–889 C.E.) and
Khalaf b. Ahmad (d. 1008 C.E.).[29]

However, a thorough investigation of the formation of dream
manuals is hindered by the fact that most of them are anonymous
or use pseudonymity, especially under the name of Ibn Sirin. The
historical Ibn Sirin lived from 654 to 728 C.E., but even though many
dream manuals are attributed to him, he most likely never wrote a
single dream book. Nevertheless, the tradition made him the uncon-
tested founder of the Muslim dream interpretation tradition. Indeed,
Lamoureaux argues against actual authorship, but he has also found
indications that Ibn Sirin was indeed interested in dream interpretation
and most probably "put in circulation a great deal of dream lore."[30]
He cites three traditions that tie Ibn Sirin's capacity to interpret dreams
to the skills of the prophet Joseph, for instance, this one:

[Ibn Sirin] said: In a dream I saw Joseph the prophet over our prophet. To
him I said: Teach me the interpretation of dreams. He replied: Open your
mouth. This I did. He then spat into it. When morning dawned – behold
I was an interpreter of dreams.[31]

The tradition describes Ibn Sirin as a dream interpreter who ties his
interpretations to citations of the Qur'an. Also, he is said to read the
dream symbols in line with what the tradition says about the Prophet
Muhammad's interpretation of symbols. Even today, dream interpretation dictionaries attributed to Ibn Sirin are published throughout the

Islamic world and are commonly used by Muslims seeking help in understanding their dreams.

Another notable figure in this tradition is Ibn al-Musayyab (712 C.E.), who is said to be "a famous Medinese *muhaddith* [*hadith* expert]" with great ability to interpret dreams.[32] Lamoreux finds that Ibn al-Musayyab's interpretation of dreams rests solely on his personal authority and reputation – that is, on the fact that he is thought to stand in a direct lineage of prophetic tradition going back onto Abu Bakr and ultimately to the Prophet Muhammad. For our purposes, it is most interesting how Ibn al-Musayyab interpreted dreams without the hitherto necessary Qur'anic citation and without establishing a connection with what the *hadith* ascribe to Muhammad. As we shall see later, this form of authoritative interpretation, which seems solely based on charisma and status, resembles the manner according to which later jihadi leaders such as Usama bin Ladin and Mullah Omar function as dream interpreters.

A final and crucial element to the dream interpretation tradition is added by Ibn Qutayba (828–889 C.E.), who introduces a methodology of dream interpretation as a safeguard against improper interpretation of dreams. He ties his views to the lineage of prophetic transmissions, while emphasizing the extreme complexity of dream interpretation. His dream manual describes nine legitimate methods for interpreting dreams, a framework that has remained in use by Islamic dream interpreters to this day:

1. Etymology of the dreamer's name and the object in the dream
2. Interpretation via meaning; an interpretation of the meaning of the dreamt object
3. Connections to the Qur'an
4. Connections to the *hadiths*/Muhammad
5. Connections to earlier prophets
6. Interpretation through opposition or inversion
7. Interpretation through increase and decrease
8. Time of day
9. State of the dreamer (for instance the dreamer's religion or occupation).[33]

This systematic approach to dream interpretation and the formalization of loose traditional materials into dream manuals reflect the growing importance, in the medieval period, of dream interpretation in Islam. Over time, a tradition developed in which dreams no longer were only connected to the earlier prophets, the Prophet Muhammad and the prophetic traditions but also to elaborate methodologies that mustered Qur'anic citations and symbols to support the interpretation. Moreover, Ibn Qutayba's dream manual implicitly established an ethical component to dream interpretation, as he prescribes that a dream interpreter is required to act and behave properly, even regarding how he sleeps, eats, and worships. He also gives advice about the correct ethical behavior of the dreamer who seeks interpretation of his dreams. Hence, dream interpretation becomes a source of guidance and ethics, a way to seek insight into God's will.

In some sense, dream manuals also served to democratize divination. Of course, the main exponents of the dream interpretation tradition were leaders and notable members of society, the same educated people who "compiled collections of prophetic traditions, commentaries on the Koran, accounts of Muhammad's life, legal treatises, and the like."[34] However, the authority to interpret dreams was no longer connected to prophecy, nor to the identity of the interpreter. The dream manuals provided anyone who can read with the knowledge required to interpret dreams. Moreover, the only requirement for the interpreters of dreams is their piety, alongside the observance of certain precautions, such as eating the proper food. Thus the dream interpretation tradition is opened up.

Over time, a dream tradition would develop in which dreams might be seen as a form of prophecy and revelation, a tool of God to communicate His will to the individual believer. True dreams came to be seen as the only communication channel to the divine available to man after the revelation of the Qur'an. In the developments of the dream tradition as described here, we see the first contours of the basis for linking dream interpretation to military activities. No longer need a charismatic leader or interpreter of dreams be connected to prophecy. Instead, Ibn Qutayba's manual introduces every verse of the Qur'an as a possible explanation of dream symbolism.

Islamic Dream Interpretation Today

In Islam today, dreams have several functions or meanings based upon the above mentioned true dream tradition. The dream can be a source of metaphysical knowledge, divination, and spiritual revelation. It is considered to provide a practical and alternate way of knowing, which can give information about invisible worlds and about people's future spiritual state. Indeed, dreams in Islam can be seen as providing guidance for ethical and religious practice both to the individual and to the community. In Sufism in general, a dream is a founding narrative: in many biographies of the great Shaykhs one can find dreams as revelatory signs of their future greatness.[35] *Istikhara*, Islamic dream incubation, is a widespread practice found across Islamic societies as a way of divining the future, especially with regard to marriage choice.[36] Gilsenan writes similarly of the power and role of dreams in contemporary Egyptian society:

In dreams begin responsibilities. Judgements were made. Commands issued. Justifications provided. Hope renewed. Conduct was commented on by Holy figures, by the Prophet himself, by the founding Sheikhs who had died some years before but who appeared with his son and successor. Dreams were public goods, circulated in conversational exchanges, valorising the person, authoring and authorising experience, at once unique and collective visual, verbal epiphanies. Dreams thus constituted a field of force and framed interchange between the living, and between the living and the only apparently dead.[37]

In this section we have explored the socio-historical foundations within which the Islamic dream tradition developed from a limited amount of source material in the Qur'an, to a more elaborate set of textual witnesses in the *hadiths*, and finally gaining its strength in the medieval dream interpretations, the tradition took shape. The second part of this chapter explores the role of the dream in contemporary jihadism, as revealed through a wide range of textual sources.

Jihadis and Their Dreams

In late 2001, in one of his first pronouncements after the 9/11 attacks, Usama bin Ladin spoke about a follower's night dream as a favorable omen:

Abu'l-Hassan al-Masri told me a year ago: "I saw in a dream, we were playing a soccer game against the Americans. When our team showed up in the field, they were all pilots!" He (Al-Masri) didn't know anything about the operation until he heard it on the radio. He said the game went on and we defeated them. That was a good omen for us.[38]

In previous studies, Edgar described some of the narrative patterns found in jihadi dream accounts.[39] Militants often appear to be inspired by what they consider to be true dreams from God. They believe that such dreams can constitute a direct access point to divine revelation and that they offer strategic and tactical guidance in war, as we will see below.

Real or Imagined?

Cynics might argue that jihadi leaders and their followers manipulate dream narratives for propaganda purposes, in the knowledge that faithful Muslims believe in the possibility of such divinely inspired night dreams. While this may sometimes be the case, we would contend that the sheer range and number of such dream narratives found in the traditional sources suggest that there is more to the story than manipulation only. Moreover, even if it were the case that all our reported jihadi dream narratives have been fabricated, the fact that Muslims often believe them, and can be mobilized to jihad partly on their account, seems of significance.

Dreams of sacred figures and direct commandments from God's spiritual representatives conveyed through dreams also seem to generate a special kind of intimacy or proximity to and feelings of belonging to the early golden age of Islam. According to Yosri Fouda, who spoke at length with two senior al-Qaida figures in 2002,

Dreams and visions and their interpretations are also an integral part of these spiritual beliefs. They mean that the Mujahideen are close to the Prophet, for whatever the Prophet dreams will come true. ... He (Binalshibh) would speak of the Prophet and his close companions as if he had actually met them.[40]

This report seems to reflect a fusion of inner and outer worlds. In her ethnographic study of dreams among contemporary Egyptians, Amira Mittermaier quotes a Shaykh Qusi, who describes how this imaginative identification with the sacred figures of Islam takes place:

If you imagine a friend, you can bring him into presence, even if he's not here. You have to use your imagination. You have to imagine the Prophet and the Prophet's companions. You imagine what they were like and what it was to live at that time. Then through your imagination you make them real. They're around you.[41]

For Shaykh Qusi, visions and visionary dreams are real imagined experiences: "The Prophet and his companions are already around us, yet it is through the imagination that we can perceive them … it is more akin to a tuning-in."[42]

In Islamic dream interpretation we find that, unlike in Western Freudian theory, the literal content of a dream is as important as its latent or implicit meaning.[43] For example, when the Taliban leader, Mullah Omar, declared that he had been visited by a sacred figure to save Afghanistan and implement Sharia Law, the dream interpretation was the congruent manifest meaning of the dream, that is, to "save Afghanistan" in an Islamic manner. According to the Islamic dream tradition, if a believer receives such a powerful direct command, he will usually interpret the dream as an absolute imperative. Hence, unlike the past-focused Freudian dreamwork theories, Islamic dreaming is future-oriented.

Interpreting "Message" and "Command" Dreams: The Dreams of Mullah Omar

In 2005, Edgar interviewed Rahimullah Yusufzai, the Peshawar-based editor of the *The News International* newspaper and correspondent of the BBC's Pushto and Urdu services in Pakistan. He was one of very few reporters to have met Omar frequently and was at the time Omar's main conduit to the Western media.[44]

Yusufzai described how Omar was thought by his followers to get strategic warfare guidance in his dreams:

I kept hearing these stories, no big military operation can happen unless he gets his instructions in his dreams; he was a big believer in dreams; he told me he had been entrusted with a mission, a holy mission and the mission is to unite Afghan, to save it from divisions and to restore order and enforce Sharia law … I was told by so many Taliban leaders, commanders, fighters: look, you know, Mullah Omar is a holy man and he gets instructions in his dream and he follows them up.[45]

Yusufzai also said that on one occasion the Mullah Omar had telephoned him to ask about a dream that his (Omar's) brother had dreamed:

[He] asked me if I had been to the White House and I said yes; "can you tell me about it?" and I said yes, and I told him about the White House in Washington and Omar said in Pashto, "white house, white palace … look,

my younger brother had a dream and he was telling me that a white palace
somewhere is on fire ... I have a belief in dreams and this is what my dreams
are saying and if you have been there, then this description by my brother of
a white palace/house means it will catch fire" and this was before 9/11. I am
convinced that Mullah Omar was not aware of Osama bin Ladin's plans to
attack on 9/11.[46]

These reports contain what are now familiar threads: divinatory communication from sacred figures; followers' belief in true dreams as
indicating the dreamer's holiness; and the relationship between dreams
and events, as in Omar's brother's "White House" dream. The Mullah
Omar anecdote illustrates an important aspect of dream interpretation,
namely, the social practice of sharing dreams. The content of one's
dreams are sensitive, intimate matters and should not be shared with
just anyone. Moreover, dream sharing usually takes place in the morning
after daybreak. As stated earlier, the Prophet Mohammad is said to have
started the day by asking who had had an interesting dream. Yusufzai
noted that morning dream interpretation is commonplace among Pash-
tuns: "very often in the morning, somebody is narrating his or her
dream; it is part of our lives; you don't know how to interpret it."[47]

Literal Dream Interpretation: The Case of Zacarias Moussaoui

Usama bin Ladin also interpreted his and others' dreams. A detailed
account of bin Ladin's dreamwork can be found in the testimony of
Zacarias Moussaoui, a French citizen of Moroccan origin also known
as the "20th hijacker" due to his alleged involvement in the 9/11
plot.[48] In 2006 Moussaoui was tried in the United States and sentenced
to life imprisonment without parole. In the trial, Moussaoui described
his dreams and their influence on him once they had been interpreted
by bin Ladin:

Basically, I had, I had a dream, and I had more later, but I had a dream, and
I went to see Shaykh Usama bin Laden, and I told him about my dream. He
told me, "Good". Maybe, I don't know, a few days later, I have another
dream. So I went again, I saw him, and I told him about this. This was after
I had declined, I was asked before. Then I had this dream. Then maybe a
week, a short time, Shaykh Abu Hafs (Mohammed Atef) came to the guest
house and asked me again if I wanted to be part of the suicide operation, me
and Richard Reid, and this time I said yes.[49]

Here we have an insight into the role that dreams – and their interpretation by an influential leader – can play in the radicalization and recruitment process. Later in the trial Moussaoui talked about having dreams of maps with the White House highlighted as a target.[50] This account illustrates the crucial influence wielded by bin Ladin the dream interpreter on Moussaoui's thinking:

And I say this to Shaykh Osama Bin Laden, and we – talked to him. . . . I talk to him about this, it was the first time, it was something middle of 2000, it was March or something like that, okay? And when I came back from Malaysia, we talk about it again because there was – I had another dream with more metaphorical, and I used to go see him each time I had dream, okay, to – because people have more knowledge, understand more because you explain the dream by the Qur'an. You don't explain it because you just think like that, okay? You have to incorporate your explanation with statements you find in the Qur'an or statements you find from the prophet Mohammad. And this book will deal specifically with interpretation of dreams. So I refer to Shaykh Osama Bin Laden and some other Shaykh there to explain to me the reality, but the dream about the White House, it was very clear to me.[51]

Thus we see that a sequence of dreams were integral to Moussaoui's move from contemplation to commitment and violent action. Further, the report shows his awareness of the central role of the Qur'an in dream interpretation and of the requirement that the interpreter be trustworthy. Moreover, it becomes equally clear that dream interpretation should not just be egotistical and related to wish fulfilment, but based upon the teachings of the Qur'an and the statements of the Prophet Mohammad, as mediated by one's shaykh. Again, we see that sometimes dream content can be very clear and explicit, even directive and experienced as a command. This is not always the case; some dreams require metaphorical interpretation, as we shall see below.

Metaphorical Dream Interpretation: The Case of Richard Reid.

Richard Reid, aka the "shoe bomber," is the British radical Islamist convicted of the attempt to blow up a transatlantic flight midair in December 2001 with explosives concealed in his shoe (the attempt failed because Reid needed several matches to light the fuse, allowing fellow passengers to intervene). Reid also appears to have been influenced by dream interpretations. In one of his last emails before the operation, Reid described how he had divined special meaning about his role as a militant jihadi from dreams.[52] We have been unable to obtain a copy of these emails, but they were mentioned in the trial of Moussaoui. Donahue summarizes these emails as follows:

In his dream, [Reid] wrote he was waiting for a ride. A pickup truck full of people came along. Reid couldn't get in because it was too crowded. He was upset. A smaller truck came along. "I now believe the pickup truck was 9/11. I was upset at not being sent."[53]

There is little evidence of how exactly Reid interpreted this dream. However, this brief narrative suggests that he believed his dream to be a true dream that contained guidance. Reid interprets and translates the symbolism of the pickup truck into that of the airplane; both are forms of group conveyance. The fact that he is upset in the dream relates to his real-world loss of the 9/11 attack opportunity.

Dreaming about Paradise

In the Islamic dream tradition, the only way that one is thought to possibly obtain a pre-experience of heaven and hell is by the true dream. Kinberg's detailed study shows how dreams in Islam have historically been considered as a "communicative technology" between the living and the dead.[54] She defines two types of dreams: (1) dreams emphasizing rewards bestowed upon the pious in the after world and (2) dreams in which the dead answer the questions of the living about the process of dying, or about the most rewarding deed.[55] The dreams included in these categories share one common ethical purpose: to show believers the right way of conduct.

In the first type, dreams illustrate specific rewards such as "magnificent palaces, beautiful women, closeness to God, a state of ease and luxury, protection from pain and torture." Kinberg quotes many examples, one of which is that of a dream by the Prophet Mohammad:

Likewise the Prophet informed his companions about ar-Rumaysaa and Bilaal being in paradise based upon one of the Prophet's dreams. Jaabir ibn Abdillah related that the Prophet said: I saw myself (in a dream) entering paradise, and saw Aboo Talhah's wife, ar-Rumaysaa. Then I heard footsteps and asked, "Who is it?" Somebody said, "It is Bilaal." Then I saw a palace with a lady sitting in its courtyard and I asked, "to whom does this palace belong?" Somebody replied, "It belongs to Umar." I wanted to enter it and look around, but I remembered your (Umar's) sense of honor (and did not). Umar said, "Let my parents be sacrificed for you, O Allah's messenger. How dare I think of my sense of honour being offended by you?"[56]

Hence, insight into Paradise and knowledge of other worlds are thought to be available via the portal of dreams. This example of the Prophet Mohammad's dream is echoed in many biographies of fallen jihadis. Hafez's study of martyrdom mythology amongst jihadis contains several dream report examples of fallen martyrs appearing in the dreams of the living, as well as the following paradise dream,

Abu Hamza al-Kuwaiti (Said al Hajari) also had a dream: I saw myself swimming in a river with other people. The river led to a cave or a tunnel on which it was written: 'To the Highest Paradise.' The closer I came to the tunnel the fewer the swimmers. When I approached, something was dragging me to the bottom of the river. It was a beautiful young maiden of paradise. We hugged each other underwater.[57]

In this example, the dream imagery is understood as referring to a paradisiacal "other" world. Al-Kuwaiti appears to be drawn to this envisioned world and its consummate promise. The Islamic *houri* narrative (the tradition of the seventy-two black-eyed virgins of paradise that await the martyr) is one that seems to preoccupy many Islamists and has given rise to the controversial claim by some Western observers that sexual frustration is a driver of jihadism. This is hard to prove, but we do know that jihadi recruiters and propagandists regularly highlight the prospect of a union with the virgins of paradise. A good example can be found in the famous "9/11 hijacker letter" that instructed the hijackers on what to do in the final days and hours before the operation: "You should know that the Gardens [of paradise] have been decorated for you in the most beautiful way, and that the houris are calling to you: 'friend of God, come', after dressing in their most beautiful clothing."[58] Such beliefs are very widespread among militant Islamists. For example, a *Sunday Times* journalist abducted by jihadi insurgents in Syria in 2012 later said his guard had lectured him about the rewards of martyrdom: "And we kept receiving sermons from the Koran, When you die you will be taken to paradise by a green bird. You will see Allah and his thrones, in a house made of gold and silver. Your family will meet you up there. You will have 72 wives."[59]

David Cook traces the dream-martyrdom connection back to the VII century C.E., when Muslims were also reporting dreams about martyrs, as recorded by Ibn Abi al-Dunya (d. 994–995).[60] Cook concludes his survey of early Islamic martyrdom as follows:

All of these dreams – only a small selection of those available – are common throughout the Muslim martyrdom tradition. The general themes of the martyrdom literature serve to confirm the status of the martyrs after their death, to demonstrate their satisfaction with their fate and to influence others to follow them.[61]

The connection between dreaming and martyrdom for contemporary jihadis is illustrated by Cook's chapter in this volume, as well as by Sirriyeh's documentation of dreaming and martyrdom accounts from the conflicts in Bosnia, Iraq, and Palestine.[62] We may add another set of examples from the jihadi website www.azzam.com (described by Anne Stenersen in this volume). The website included many martyrdom biographies from Bosnia and elsewhere with similar stories of dream-mediated communication between living fighters and dead martyrs (*shuhada*').[63] In the following report we find an example of how literally the promise of the *houris* in Paradise can be understood: shortly after the death of a fighter named Abu Muadh in Bosnia in 1995, one of his companions dreams that he is "interviewing" him about his martyrdom experience. This narrative is an example of Kinberg's second type of dream in which the dead answer the questions of the living. The in-dream conversation proceeded as follows:

'Abu-Muadh, why are you here? Are you Shaheed or not?'
He replied, 'Yes, I am Shaheed.'
I asked him, 'What is martyrdom like?'
He replied, 'On the day of the operation a window opens in the sky from Paradise and all the Mujahideen that are going to be killed that day pass through this window straight into Paradise.'
I then asked him, 'What does the actual martyrdom feel like?'
He replied 'You do not feel a thing. As soon as you are killed, you see two beautiful blonde-haired girls who accompany you up to Paradise.'
I asked him 'What is the Paradise like?'
Abu-Muadh replied, 'It is not one Paradise but it is many Paradises!'
I said, 'What about enjoyment and pleasures?'
He replied, 'Every day and in every place.' Abu-Muadh then said, 'Now let me go'.

Dreams about Paradise also reportedly occur to the parents of prospective jihadis, as the following example from Pakistan demonstrates. Mariam Abou Zahab has described how new Pakistani militants fighting for Kashmir have to wait for parental permission which often follows a parent, usually the mother, having a dream of seeing her child in Paradise.[64] Reports of many Muslims experiencing motivational dreams at the same time and for the same jihad also appear. Reports from the 2007 siege of the Red Mosque in Islamabad regard dreams as being influential, even decisive, in bringing young female student recruits from the country to join the movement in the Mosque.[65] BBC correspondent Barbara Plett wrote about the siege and its supporters:

It was easy to dismiss the burka-clad students of the Red Mosque as a bunch of fanatics, especially when they started talking about their dreams. The Prophet Mohammad appeared to them, they told me in interviews a few months ago, handing them swords, telling them to conduct jihad against General Pervez Musharraf. "When we are getting such signs," they asked, "how can we not act?"[66]

Likewise there are reports of the resistance leader in the Red Mosque, Sheikh Abdul Aziz Ghazi, as saying that the Prophet Mohammad "brought me good news and told me 300 times in my dreams to move to implement the Shari'ah of Allah."[67] Edgar quotes several other such examples from across the Islamic world including Britain, Canada, and Germany.[68] There is, in other words, substantial evidence that the remembered dream, when handled and interpreted in certain ways, can facilitate recruitment.

Dream from Detention: The Guantanamo Bay Example

For many religious Muslims, dreams seem to become more important in times of crisis. Islamists in prison appear to be particularly interested in dreams, possibly because prison and its outward restrictions facilitate self-reflection.[69] We can see this clearly in testimonies from detainees at Guantanamo Bay. For example, in May 2005 the following dream narrative from a Pakistani detainee appeared in a Pakistani newspaper:

A Guantanamo ex-prisoner named Qari Badruzzaman Badr said in an interview that at Guantanamo many Arabs had dreams in which the Holy

Prophet (PBUH) personally gave them news of their freedom and called them the People of Badr. The Prophet said that Christ will soon arrive. One Arab saw Jesus who took his hand and told him that Christians were now misled. Later the other prisoners could smell the sweet smell of Jesus from his hand. His hand was rubbed on all the prisoners.[70]

Again the dream message is explicit. It is immediately communicated, not only by word of mouth but also by touch, presumably to transfer the *baraka* (blessing) from the dream. In another retrospective account, a British former inmate, Jaram al-Harath, said that his release from Guantanamo had been foretold to him in a dream two years earlier.[71] Likewise, Ibrahim Sen, a Turkish detainee, has written about how inmates experienced dreams of the Prophet Muhammad and of angels that watched over them.[72]

There is some evidence that Islamic State (IS) members similarly relate to night dreams. Edgar has explored some examples from the online IS English language magazine, *Dabiq*, and from IS websites.[73] Dreams seem to inspire, aid and justify IS Jihadi actions and motivations. For example, Elton Simpson, one of the two perpetrators of the gun attack on the Muhammad cartoon exhibition in Garland, Texas, in May 2015 appears to have been sharing a recent dream that he had had about a woman wearing a hijab on an IS dream interpretation website days before his attack.[74] While that website has been closed down, another similar one discussing dreams is, at the time of writing, online.[75]

Conclusion

Everyone we are watching in our area is into dreaming as crucial to their jihadi membership, progress and their final decision, via Istakhara/Islamic dream incubation, as to whether to go on militant jihad.

Anonymous Western intelligence official[76]

This chapter has looked at the possible connections between the dream as prophetic revelation of God's will and jihadi action. We started our inquiry with a textual analysis of the historic foundations in the holy scriptures of Islam, and found that the Qur'an and the *hadith*, especially the latter, ascribe importance to dreams and dream interpretation. Later the proliferation of dream manuals changed the authoritative chain of transmission and "democratized" dream interpretation. No longer did a Muslim need to be in close lineage to the Prophet and his followers in order to legitimately interpret dreams, nor did the interpretation of dreams solely depend upon the precedent set by the Prophet in the *hadith*. This is what would later allow lay, charismatic figures such as Usama bin Ladin to consider themselves qualified to interpret his followers' dreams.

While Sufis have traditionally paid the most attention to dreams, the more literalist Salafis are surprisingly interested in dreams, as indicated by the many dream interpretation guides circulating on Salafi websites today.[77] Shaykhs Al-Salman and Al-Abdurrahman, authors of a Salafi dream interpretation book, write:

Salafis view the tradition of vision and dream interpretation as being rooted in Islam and having been inherited from the Salaf. Indeed, it has been inherited from the Prophets (peace be upon them), so any insinuation that Salafis are in some way opposed to vision interpretation in its totality would be incorrect.[78]

In Sufism dreams are understood as showing spiritual progression toward union with God.[79] Militant jihadis similarly seek union (in Paradise) with the one God, and some of their dreams are considered key steps on the way. In fact, however, a preoccupation with dreams appears to be a constant across all sects and subgroups within Islam.[80]

Inspirational dreams are a recurrent theme in many jihadis' narratives of their militant careers. Dreams are a significant and accepted part of jihadi group membership behavior and identity. Through dreams some jihadis experience close empathy and even imaginative interaction with early Islamic heroes. Interestingly, jihadis seem to relate to their night dreams in exactly the same way as the great majority of other non-militant Muslims who relate creatively to their dreams. Dreams can be from God, Satan, or more often from the self (*nafs*). The literal manifest meaning of dreams is particularly important, but not at the expense of the need to interpret dreams metaphorically. Islamic sacred figures and their auditory commands as represented in dreams are particularly significant. The appearance of the Prophet Muhammad in a night dream always indicates a true dream. Dreams can be a legitimated means of divine revelation, a way of delving into the future and into what will be righteous conduct in that future. Dreams can offer foretastes of paradisiacal and hellish worlds. The tradition of the dead appearing in dreams and speaking the truth is honored. The sacred Qur'an and its narratives have gradually become a symbolic and literary treasure house source for dream interpretation, and the *hadith* with their chapters on dreaming and interpretation also form a crucial source of information and legitimation. Militant jihadis interpret their dreams and their significance fully within the beliefs and practices of the Islamic tradition as believed to be revealed to the Prophet Muhammad and the great prophets before him in true dreams.

Where jihadis differ from other Muslims is in their use of dreams to justify – to themselves or to others – violent action. Dreams in some cases seem to serve as a catalyst for joining a militant group. For some jihadi recruits, dreams appear to be a more powerful persuasive agent than any ideological pamphlet or recruiter pitch.

At the same time, our analysis showed that the *interpretation* of dreams seems to be at least as important as the dream itself. In the causal chain, if we may call it that, from dream-based inspiration to action there is often an intervening factor in the form of an interpreter, who tells the recruit what the dream signifies. When that interpreter is himself an activist, the dream is presumably more likely to be interpreted as a call to action. Dream narration and interpretation are thus closely related to leadership dynamics in jihadi groups, as we saw in the examples of Usama bin Ladin and Mullah Omar. Leaders derive spiritual, political and social status from telling their followers about "seen-in-dreams" sacred figures of the Islamic spiritual cosmology. Dreams are thus important, but so are their earthly custodians.

7 | *Contemporary Martyrdom: Ideology and Material Culture*

DAVID B. COOK

This chapter covers the Muslim doctrine of martyrdom, both in its classical Sunni and Shi'ite versions, as it relates to contemporary Salafi jihadism. Although martyrdom has been a component of Islam, in Sunnism it has never previously been a major one. With the rise of Salafi jihadism, there has been a revival of a salvational style of jihad that emphasizes martyrdom, bringing out themes of bodily sanctity, visions of the martyr, processes of commemoration, and hagiography associated with the movement. Within Shi'ism, martyrdom has been a major component of the belief system, but such martyrdom was traditionally focused upon the family of the Prophet Muhammad and early supporters of the imams rather than upon common believers. However, with the rise of the Islamic Republic of Iran, and especially since the early 2000s, the focus upon martyrdom has been broadened considerably. These changes in both Sunnism and Shi'ism will be the focus of this chapter.

Martyrdom can viewed as the process by which a human becomes material – material in the sense that because of the death of the martyr, because of the meaning accorded to that death by the audience (both present and future), there is a material legacy to what would otherwise be an ideological message. That corporeality is both the body of the martyr, the message that he or she left (ideally) or in cases where there is no immediate message then the message that is assumed, and most importantly the mythology that will come to surround the martyr.

Muslim martyrdom in its classical phase is very closely linked with that of Judaism and Christianity in that by means of a set process of suffering and death one can *testify* (hence the parallel etymology: both the Greek *martys* and the Arabic *shahid* mean "witness") on behalf of the veracity of something, usually an idea or an ideology, but sometimes a person. In Islam, with the exception of the very earliest history of the community in Mecca, where it was a persecuted minority, the dominant discourse of martyrdom has linked it to fighting "in God's path" or jihad; warfare with the sanction of God. This can be easily seen in Qur'an 9:111:

Allah has bought from the believers their lives and their wealth in return for Paradise; they fight in the way of Allah, kill and are killed. That is a true promise from Him in the Torah, the Gospel and the Qur'an and who fulfills His promise better than Allah? Rejoice then at the bargain you have made with Him; for that is the great triumph."[1]

While this verse provides the Muslim with the contractual basis of jihad, and its assurance of paradise for the martyr, this promise is not significantly different in the Qur'an from the promise of paradise accorded to all believers. Neither does the standard Qur'anic citation lauding martyrdom in 3:169–70 give us a concrete sense of the difference between martyrs and other believers:

And do not think those who have been killed in the way of Allah as dead; they are rather living with their Lord, well-provided for. Rejoicing in what their Lord has given them of His bounty, and they rejoice for those who stayed behind and did not join them; knowing that they have nothing to fear and that they shall not grieve.[2]

However, this latter verse is usually connected with the Battle of Uhud (625 c.e.) in which large numbers of Muslims were killed and was the first of the early Muslim battles in which there was need to explain that martyrdom was special and that its rewards placed the martyr on a different level from the other believers. According to the *hadith* literature,

When your brothers were struck at [the Battle of] Uhud, Allah placed their spirits in the insides of green birds, who go to the rivers of paradise, eat from its produce, and then alight upon candles of gold in the shadow of the Throne. When they [the martyrs] realize the goodness of their drink and food, and the beauty of their rest, they say: "Would that our brothers knew what Allah has done with us, so that they too would devote themselves to *jihad*, and not abstain from battle." Allah most high says: "I will tell them of you."[3]

This selection begins to convey the differentiation of the martyr – for example, the story of the "green birds" is found first here – however, while lauding the pleasures of heaven it does not go far enough to make people want to die specifically as martyrs. The most significant

movement in that direction is to be found in al-Tirmidhi's *al-Jami`
al-sahih*, which states:

In the sight of God the martyr has six [unique] qualities: He [God] forgives
him at the first opportunity, and shows him his place in paradise, he is saved
from the torment of the grave, he is safe from the great fright [of the
Resurrection], a crown of honor is placed upon his head – one ruby of which
is better than the world and all that is in it – he is married to 72 of the houris,
and he gains the right to intercede for 70 of his relatives.[4]

Here we have the elements of the martyrdom mythology needed. The
martyr is actually different in that his forgiveness is complete, he has
direct access to the vision of paradise, from which we can derive the
superhuman visionary qualities so closely associated with classical and
contemporary martyrs, and he receives a special crown. However, the
elements in this tradition that are the most important for the corporeality of martyrdom are the fact that he is saved from the torment of the
grave, that he will be married to seventy-two *houris*, and that he has the
right of intercession. Each of these elements has profound ramifications
for this world and very conveniently lends itself to a martyrology.[5]

First of all, the martyr is free from the "torment of the grave" and his
body, unlike the bodies of other Muslims, does not need to be washed
but is placed within the grave *as is*. Unlike other Muslims, the martyr
will not be tormented by the two angels Munkar and Nakir, whose
hostile questioning in the immediate wake of death is of great concern
to Muslims (hence the process of extreme unction, or *talqin*).[6] When
this fact is coupled together with the idea that the martyr will continue
to be garbed in blood at the Day of Resurrection[7], smelling of musk,
we can see the roots of the belief in the incorruptibility of the martyr's
body and its concurrent sweet smell that was to be developed so
markedly during the medieval period and then marketed by Abdallah
Azzam (discussed below). It is even possible to extrapolate from the
exemption from the torment of the grave the idea that the ground in
which the martyr is buried is itself holy and free from evil.

Second, the marriage to the *houris* mentioned in the tradition,
despite the frequent denials of apologists, is one of the most significant
and tangible aspects of the martyr. As Ibn al-Nahhas al-Dumyati
already pointed out in the 1400s in his massive book on jihad, the
marriage to the *houris* divorces the martyr from human women, who
he states are disgusting in any case,[8] and makes the martyr into a

liminal figure. Promoting the idea that paradise has a major sexual component, graphic details of which are contained in all of the classical and contemporary literature on paradise, provides a secondary life for the martyr – one that is free from any human constraints either of disgust, duration, or to some extent quantity. Although it is not necessarily true that sexual rewards for the martyr are *the* primary driver in a desire or willingness for martyrdom, one cannot deny their omnipresence in the martyrologies (although not in the videos as will be discussed). Because of the importance of marriage in Muslim society, the martyr is given the illusion of wedding festivities either before or after his death in order to visualize the fact of his being married. These wedding festivals have the additional benefit of denying any aspect of mourning to the commemoration of the martyr, something that is strongly supported by the jihad literature.

Third, and perhaps most importantly, is the question of intercession. Although it is evident that in the popular perception the sexual rewards of the martyr are the ones that gain the most attention, it is my personal belief that the rewards of intercession, specifically for seventy of the martyr's relatives, are the most influential. Intercession is a very controversial idea in Islam, with no obvious consensus as to its veracity having been reached. Pretty naturally, Salafi jihadis are predisposed to be opposed to the idea, as it renders personal piety unnecessary, and points the way to the type of Sufi "holy men" intermediaries the movement rejects. However, because of this tradition and others, it is compelled to accept the idea of limited intercession, which once again highlights the holiness of the martyr and the possibility that one could venerate his memory and *possibly even him* – so as to receive the intercession – after his martyrdom. For it is clear that the number seventy means "a reasonably large number," rather than a specific number. Given that assumption, there is no complete clarity as to how many people the martyr can lend his intercession. As Azzam himself documents when he discusses the issue of the incorruptibility of the martyr's body, by the 1400s the doctrine of the intrinsic holiness of the body had become well-rooted in Islam.

Abdallah Azzam and the Development of Radical Sunni Martyrology

When we discuss the material aspects of martyrdom in contemporary Sunni jihadi thought, the figure of Abdallah Azzam (assassinated in

1989) is the central figure. His biographical details need not be presented here, but the most important fact about him for our discussion is that his clerical education was a mainstream Sunni one and that he had at his fingertips, in contradistinction to other radical Muslim figures, an excellent command of the *fiqh* literature (not to speak of the Qur'an and the *hadith*).[9]

Azzam's development of the concept of martyrdom is a central one within his overall affirmation of a salvational brand of jihad[10] and is summarized by the following statement:

The life of the Muslim Ummah is solely dependent upon the ink of its scholars and the blood of its martyrs. What is more beautiful than the writing of the Ummah's history with both the ink of a scholar and his blood, such that the map of Islamic history becomes colored with two lines: one of them black ... and the other one red ... History does not write its lines except with blood. Glory does not build its lofty edifices except with skulls. Honor and respect cannot be established except on a foundation of cripples and corpses. Empires, distinguished peoples, states, and societies cannot be established except with examples. Indeed, those who think that they can change reality or change societies without blood sacrifices and invalids, without pure, innocent souls, they do not understand the essence of this *din* [religion] and they do not know the method of the best of Messengers [Muhammad].[11]

What Azzam is trying to say here is that there is a close linkage between the suffering and death that is accomplished by the martyrs, and the subsequent success of the *umma*. If there is no willing self-sacrifice on behalf of Islam, then the religion as a religion and as a civilization cannot develop. It is a rather social Darwinian construct to closely connect violence with success in such an inextricable form, as if it is so impossible to visualize success attained through any other more irenic means. It is also not easy to see how this particular statement can be rationalized within the context of mainstream Islam – one would think that sacrificing "pure, innocent souls" would cause the author some pause.

But apparently it does not, and Azzam proved that as one can see from the numerous articles on martyrs in his edition of the journal *al-Jihad* during the period 1985–1989, usually entitled *ma' al-shuhada'* (With the Martyrs).[12] Examination of the columns reveals the growth of the martyrdom mythology. Development of the mythology of martyrdom was continued after his death, as is evidenced by the July–August 1991 column where a certain Muhammad Ali al-Somali is listed, at whose death, "those present witnessed (*shahida*) a sweet smell that emanated from him, and his witness/martyrdom influenced many of the people, but they were certain (*ayqanu*) that God choses those of praiseworthy qualities and true hearts."[13] Others from Bosnia exhibited similarly the "good smell."[14] With a number of martyrs there is an emphasis on their avoidance of marriage: one Adib Sa'di Dhu al-Qarnayn al-Turki was said to have been ordered to "Get married! But he said: If God wills I will be martyred and I will be married to the *houris* in paradise, so leave me alone!"[15] Similarly, Khalid be al-Walid (Umar Hayyat) is said to have "chosen 70 of the *houris*, forgiveness and intercession which is promised" over marriage.[16] Note how this is also said to have been true of Abu Adam Jibril al-Amriki, an African American convert who was killed in Kashmir: "when he left this *dunya* [world] he was still a virgin, something that is very rare for an American youth."[17]

It is clear that the martyrologies promote a rejection of human women as an ideal for the fighter. For example, in the "In the Hearts of Green Birds," a compilation of martyrdom accounts from the Bosnian conflict, we read about Abu Maryam al-Afghani (killed at Ilyash in 1992) that

his wife Umm Maryam was originally German, and she was happy when she learned that she was a *mujahid* woman, and she was patient at the news. Abu Maryam's brother used to want to marry her. She said: Whoever marries me has to fulfill one condition, that he will stay with me for 15 days, and then he will go for jihad. Abu Maryam's brother refused. Her sister, who used to be a non-Muslim, accepted Islam when she saw the patience she had, she is married and her husband is in the jihad.[18]

The life of the wife of a fighter is to merely be a receptacle for future fighters, while she waits for her husband to become a martyr. Her spiritual reward will come as a result of the *sabr* or patience that she exemplifies by giving up worldly familial pleasures. If she actually lived with her husband for a protracted length of time, then presumably she would anchor him to this world in a way that would deny him the crown of martyrdom. This type of marriage can be found with other martyrs as well – note the testimony of Sajida Rishawi, who was part of the Amman suicide attacks in November 9, 2005. She, while married to one of the attackers, had never consummated the marriage.[19]

But for the most part the descriptions from the Bosnian war are those of seeing the *houris* rather than marriage to human women – in the account concerning Abu Zayd al-Qatari (killed in Operation Black Lion, May 1995):

This brother was so young, but so innocent, and this brother, he even saw the *hur al-'in* not in his sleep but at his position on the mountain. Every night as he used to look to the sky, he used to see a woman come to him, a beautiful woman. But he never told anybody about this except one brother and this brother told us afterwards ... there are many instances in the time of the Salaf [pious ancestors], and even during the time of Muhammad himself where the *hur al-'in* would come and manifest themselves to the Muslims to make them steadfast in His path.[20]

One Abu Muadh al-Kuwaiti describes the process of dying in a dream:

On the day of the operation, a window opened in the sky from Paradise, and all of the Muslims that would be killed, *mujahidin* that would be killed that day, they pass through this window straight into Jannah. I said: What is the mark and what does it feel like? He said: You don't feel a thing. As soon as you are killed you see two beautiful blonde girls, they come and sit beside you, and they go to Jannah with you.[21]

All of these martyrologies continually affirm the sweet-smelling nature of the body, the smell of musk that emanates from the corpse, and its absence of decomposition.[22] *Al-Jihad* further allows for the appearance of miracles (*karamat*) associated with the martyr, such as that of Ihsan Hammu Siddiq 'Arif in Kurdistan, "two days after his burial his pure corpse was conveyed to the region of 'Ababyali, a village close to Halabcha, to be reburied there, in accordance with the request of his family, and the blood was witnessed flowing from his body in spite of the fact that his corpse had been underneath the ground for two days."[23]

Probably the most influential martyrological document that Azzam ever penned was the short *Ayat al-Rahman fi jihad al-Afghan* (Signs of the Merciful One in the Afghani Jihad), which gives us a complete doctrine bringing all of the miracle stories connected with martyrs together, and places them, like in so many of Azzam's other works, within a historical Muslim perspective.[24] In Azzam's introduction to the booklet he is at some pains to demonstrate the importance of miracles and signs, that they are not because of a given person's desires, but because of the will of God, and he overwhelms the reader with examples of them from the time of Muhammad and the Companions. This point, which takes up almost half the document, releases most of the doctrinal issues that a Salafi might have with Azzam's work, as it does sail perilously close to the world of Sufism (at one point he even cites al-Junayd and Abu Yazid al-Bistami!).

The examples that Azzam gives follow the paradigms laid down above: he narrates in a *hadith* style on the authority of Umar Hanif (an Afghan fighter) that he "has never seen a single *shahid* whose body has changed or gave off a bad odor." Dogs do not touch the bodies of the *shuhada* although they devour the bodies of the Communists. Hanif continues saying that he has opened twelve graves of *shuhada* three or four years after their deaths – he does not state why he would do such a thing – and did not find any change in their odor. And, last, he states that the wounds of the *shuhada* continue to exude blood even after a year has gone by.[25] Many other similar examples are given, and they are all testimonials; Azzam does not claim to have seen or experienced any of this for himself.

It would seem that the desire to promote the mythology and hagiography of the martyr's body stems from first of all the need to attest to the reality of one's being a *shahid*, which is problematic because of a number of *ahadith* that affirm this knowledge belongs solely to God.[26] However, the performance of such miracles would have the effect of not only confirming the reality of the martyrdom of a given individual – which in itself is tautological, since both Azzam and his narrators have already decided that these figures are martyrs and unlike in the classical material there are virtually no cases of disconfirmation – which would have implications for the holiness of the conflict itself. Through the miraculous preservation of the body the sacrality of the jihad is assured. The body also represents a victory, a consecration, as it were, of the earth, which receives the blood of the martyr on a regular basis after his death, and is infused with the musky odor that he exudes. Plot by plot the martyr conquers and holds the ground in which he is buried and is the permanent reminder of the sacrifices involved in order to maintain Islam on the earth. His corporeal remains are bastions of heaven on earth and serve as conduits for heavenly communications to humanity.[27]

Azzam also gives examples of these heavenly communications. One man slain, Ibn Jannat Jal, is said to have been addressed by his father who stated: "Oh my son, if you truly are a *shahid*, show me a sign thereof?" All of a sudden the *shahid* raised his hand, made *salam* to his father, and continued to clasp his father's hand for fourteen minutes, and then placed it back on his wound.[28] Other martyrs are said to either supply their weapons (still in their dead hands) to the living mujahidin, to occasionally fight with them against the Russian enemy, and to exude light.[29]

The spirits of the martyrs that continue to fight are represented by birds that accompany the mujahidin. Most likely this trope is taken from the tradition that speaks of the souls of the martyrs being in the hearts of green birds in paradise. It is also possible that the idea is connected to the spirit of pre-Islamic vengeance that is often said to be lodged in birds, most specifically owls.[30] Horses and horsemen are also an important symbol of virility and warfare, such as in the common tradition "Horses, in their manes, is the good until the Day of Resurrection."[31] Although horses rarely make appearances in later post-Iraq videos, in the pre–September 11th video material they are an important symbolic expression of the jihad that links the Arabs to the glories of the pre-Islamic and early Islamic period.[32]

Light toward heaven is also an important manifestation of God's favor. About one of the mujahidin named Abd al-Ghafur in Helmand who was martyred it was said "Every night a light would extend from him [his corpse] until the sky, and would remain for about 3 minutes then descend. All the mujahidin saw this light," and, further, a light would illuminate the house of a martyr.[33] From other Afghani martyrologies we read about the story of Abu Asim al-Iraqi, who came to Pakistan and then went to Afghanistan to fight. "The operations in the province of Baghlan intensified [and] Abu Asim enlisted his name with the commander in charge of operations, [who] looked at Abu Asim once and then with a smile wrote the words [*sic!*] *shahid* next to his name." When the commander was asked about this, he said "I do not know the unseen, but look at his forehead. I swear by my Lord! I can see the *nur* [light] of *shahada* [martyrdom] shine on it."[34] This light appears to be strikingly similar to the light of Muhammad, which mystically shone on the foreheads of his forefathers back to the time of Adam and heralded his future prophethood.[35] Light as a confirming substance for various religious issues in Islam is fairly common, and given the elevated status of the martyr that Azzam sought to promote, it is hardly surprising to find it in his martyrology.

The theme of light is also found in martyrdom descriptions after Azzam, as in the story told of a British brother and sister who were converts to Islam and who were captured by U.S. forces in the immediate wake of the 2001 invasion of Afghanistan. As they were being transported in a truck to Kabul the woman carried out a martyrdom operation, from which her brother was able to save himself, and saw

a bright, concentrated beam of light shining from the truck into the sky whilst the truck was otherwise in flames ... [he] confirmed that the two Crusaders [Americans] did not survive ... as for the martyred sister, he saw her noble, pure body largely intact despite the explosion, and he was satisfied that perhaps that beam of light he saw earlier must have taken care of her body.[36]

In general, the lines of the martyrology laid down by Azzam and his successors associated with the Afghani, Bosnian, and early al-Qaida periods is as follows: the martyr is a liminal figure, not subject to worldly whims and passions. His direction, foreordained, is toward paradise, and he is not focused upon the material pleasures of this world, such as women, families, and goods. His character is elevated beyond those of his comrades, and he has a sense of detachment from their pettiness and occasional irreligiosity. When his death arrives, it is a surprise to no one, and some will have seen him in dreams either beforehand or afterwards as a confirmation of his martyr status (as Edgar and de Looijer describe in detail in this book). And, finally, his body remains unchanged from its final traumatic moments, as a connection between this world and the next, a connection that is continually affirmed by the ability of the martyr to influence events on behalf of the mujahidin or to provide them with moral support in their times of need.

Mainstream Martyrology, Sunni and Shi'ite

It is important to note that Azzam did not write in a vacuum: as he was developing the martyrology associated with radical Islam during the 1980s, martyrdom was coming into focus once again after having been neglected by mainstream Islam for almost a century. So we should examine the parallel developments between radical Islam and mainstream Islam (both in its Sunni and Shi'ite variants) and see what the relative influences have been. While martyrdom is crucially important to mainstream Shi'ism because of the sacrifice of al-Husayn (d. 680) and the other imams according to Shi'ite beliefs, it is nowhere near as important in Sunnism. Traditionally martyrdom and martyrdom narratives provided an important social bond within Shi'ism which was shared by the entire community during the course of the *Ashura* and other commemorations, and was closely connected to both literary as well as material developments within the religion and the society.

In contrast, while there was public commemoration of martyrs in traditional Sunnism, such commemoration was never a bond that held the community together or even a secondary focus of the religion, but more of a monument to its glory. This is in sharp contrast to Shi'ism, where martyrdom is closely connected to grief (strictly prohibited in mainstream Sunnism) and a sense of failure, of justice denied or postponed until the Day of Resurrection. But most of all, in both Sunnism and Shi'ism martyrdom had an antiquarian aspect to it: contemporary martyrs have never received anything like the level of attention that classical martyrs did. Few felt that the ranks of martyrs needed to be continually replenished, and in Sunnism there were few means by which martyrs could be generally recognized. With the exception of those martyrs connected with the time of Muhammad and his immediate successors, Sunni martyrdom is more of a local event than as it is in Shi'ism a pan-community event.

There is no doubt that the Islamic Revolution in Iran and most especially the Iran-Iraq War (1980–1988) and the concurrent rise of Shi'ite liberation organizations such as Hezballoh have changed the antiquarian nature of martyrdom for Shi'ites. In this aspect one can call these movements truly revolutionary, and they may have been influenced to some degree by the writings of Sunni radicals. But it is still important to note the differences between the mythology developed by Azzam and that current among Shi'ites, however revolutionary. First of all, the Iranian martyrologies from the period of the Iran-Iraq war are lacking in miraculous elements and are very battlefield-centered. Their ideological need is to connect the immediate war with the eternal battle of good versus evil, al-Husayn versus Yazid.[37] The Hezbollah martyrdoms are all from the perspective of families or final letters from the martyrs and do not contain any direct description of the actual deaths.[38] Most probably the reason for this difference is that overt martyrdom events in Shi'ism are very focused toward the imams, and there is little room for aggrandizement of other figures.

The one section of the Arab world that has produced its own martyrology that can compete with that of radical Islam is the Palestinian conflict. Vast numbers of martyrologies commemorating the deaths of Palestinians have been produced; the standard *Intifadat al-Aqsa* martyrdom series runs to ten volumes and contains 904 entries. Apparently the editors simply gave up in 2004. However, the problems with such a martyrology from an Islamic point of view are obvious: not all of the slain are Muslims, many are secular Palestinians, and some listed, such as Rachel Corrie,[39] are not Palestinians or Muslims at all. None of these martyrologies have any of the characteristics myths of radical Islam: I have been unable to find even one case where the body of the martyr is said to smell sweetly, or where there is evidence of lack of decomposition. Sometimes there are dreams and visions, but very rarely. This absence of Islamic mythology is true also of specific martyrologies available of prominent Hamas leaders, such as the martyrologies of Ahmad Yassin, 'Abd al-'Aziz al-Rantisi, Yahya 'Ayyash, and Salih Shehata.[40] Not one of these lists off any particular miracles associated with the martyr, in spite of the fact that their Muslim character is affirmed in every way (the 1996 assassination of Hamas bombmaker Yahya 'Ayyash, e.g., is compared to the murder of John the Baptist).[41]

What is maintained and affirmed in the Palestinian popular lore about martyrs is that they are going through a wedding ceremony. Time and again, there are celebrations that are associated with martyrdom that emphasize its close connection with the joy of the wedding. It is an interesting parallel: there is the dowry (the bomb or the explosion – compare with that of Abu Mu'awiya al-Shimali in "Fatima's Fiancee" from the Iraq conflict below), there is a fundamental transformation, an "entrance" similar to the *laylat al-dukhul* (night of entrance) in a traditional wedding, and a bride (or a number of brides), all within a heavenly context. But there is none of the hostility toward earthly women that characterize the Azzam-derived radical Muslim martyrologies. On the contrary, those few videos that actually picture the martyrs meeting the *houris* seem to be affirming that the women are actually female martyrs.[42]

General martyrologies such as the five-volume *Mawsu'at shuhada' al-haraka al-Islamiyya [Encyclopaedia of the Martyrs of the Islamic Movement]*, which focuses upon the Muslim Brotherhood from the 1930s until the 1960s and then the Palestinian Second Intifada

(2000–2007), lends a number of its entries a radical Islamic character. For example, in the entry on Abdallah Azzam, it states that "the
martyr was buried the day of his martyrdom, and the participants,
who were thousands, noted the smell of musk which emanated from
his pure blood until the end of his burial," an element that is not
included in other obituaries of Azzam.[43] Comparing the notices of
the *Mawsu'a* with *Intifadat al-Aqsa*, one sees the usually expected
elements: Shadi Salman al-Nabahayn (killed May 19, 2003) refuses
to get married, saying that "he will marry one of the houris,"[44]
while Imran Umar al-Ghul (killed June 27, 2003) predicts his own
death and also refuses marriage,[45] and Ra'im al-Riyyashi (killed
January 14, 2004), who carried out a martyrdom operation, is said
to have been "carried to her wedding to the houris" (*wa-qad zaffat
ila al-hur al-'in*), which raises some interesting questions.[46] All of
these individuals were associated with Hamas or Islamic Jihad.
However, at the same time as these more mainstream groups were
still using conventional tropes, new developments were breaking on
the radical Sunni scene in Iraq.

Abu Mus'ab al-Zarqawi in Iraq and the Age of Online Videos

There can be no reasonable doubt that although Azzam and others laid
down the basic lines of radical Sunni martyrology, one of its greatest
popularizers has been Abu Mus'ab al-Zarqawi (d. 2006), the Jordanian radical whose transformation of the Iraq conflict into an apocalyptic Internet-based spectacle has become paradigmatic.[47] Zarqawi's
contribution to the jihadi culture was to take the myth-making narratives promulgated by Usama bin Ladin and other Salafi jihadi leaders
that had been dependent upon the whims of television producers and
place them within the uncontrolled environment of the Internet. Bin
Ladin and others could rail about how *al-Jazeera* during the critical
years of 1998–2002 filtered out their complete messages sent to the
television station (and others), but they ultimately had no control over
how the myth-making of martyrdom would be played out to the
broadest television audience. Zarqawi and his associates took the Iraq
materials and following in the footsteps of CNN and others sought to
create an immediacy to the warfare, a sense whereby their audience
could participate in the front row seats of the jihad, as Anne Stenersen
describes in this book. Although YouTube and other sites eventually

began to ban these types of videos, their ban has always been half-hearted and their distribution widespread.

The material culture of the Internet jihad is the martyrdom video. Although one can reasonably point to other elements such as video statements (by figures such as bin Ladin and al-Zawahiri), Internet chat forums, poetry, and pictures, the fact remains that martyrdom videos in their essence capture and disseminate the message that Salafi jihadis need to propagate. Al-Zarqawi laid down his basic ideology in his most important statement concerning the meaning of martyrdom (citing Ibn Qayyim al-Jawziyya [d. 1350]):

Martyrdom in the eyes of God is among the highest levels of his friends (*awliya'*), and the martyrs are his intimates and those closest of his servants to Him – after the level of being a *siddiq* there is nothing but martyrdom. He likes to take martyrs from His servants, to spill their blood in the love of Him and His favor, as they prefer His favor and His love to themselves (or their souls). There is no way to gain this level but through estimation of the circumstances that lead to it, namely overpowering the enemy.[48]

It is clear from the use of the term *awliya* that al-Zarqawi, like Azzam before him, was more than willing to utilize terms that had been associated with Sufism. In any case, al-Zarqawi was not in any doubt as to the importance of martyrdom in following the path of the Salaf: he states that the *sahaba* (the Prophet's Companions) suffered over 80 percent martyrdom, a figure that he is at some pains to back up.[49] Further, he states that it is the very nature of the imposition of the Sharia that there will always be opposition and fighting involved, and that waging this type of war is the most important thing that a Muslim can do.[50] The purpose of the war in Iraq, according to al-Zarqawi is: "We believe that the jihad in Iraq is a tribulation (*fitna*), a trial, and a purification process from God to differentiate the righteous from the liar, the evil from the good."[51]

From a comparatively early period in his time in Iraq, al-Zarqawi emphasized martyrdom and its importance. In his *Ilhaq bi-l-qafila* message of January 4, 2004, which is obviously a reference to Azzam's well-known booklet of the same name, he cites a number of verses and *hadiths* extolling the importance of jihad and martyrdom.[52] He held out as an example the figure of Abu Ubayda Abd al-Hadi Dighlas. However, al-Zarqawi in his delivered martyrologies of both Dighlas and his other close companion Abu Anas al-Shami does not extol the circumstances of their deaths, or even give any details of them. He instead speaks of their spiritual circumstances and personal courage in the form of a eulogy,[53] and then lays down the methodology by which he intends to create the chaos from which the Salafi jihadis can benefit: "as for the Shi'ites (*rawafid*) terror (*nikaya*) among them will be with the permission of God through martyrdom operations and car-bombs."[54]

The martyrology laid down by al-Zarqawi and his successors was one that emphasized a very set trajectory to martyrdom. Whereas previously Palestinian martyrdom videos had usually consisted of a statement by the perpetrator, the Iraqi martyrdom videos modified that to almost an informal chat with the martyr.[55] The latter would make their statement, sometimes the video-photographer would participate or interject comments or expostulations, and the whole scene would be one that exuded intimacy. The viewer would be right in the face of the prospective martyr. At every point, the martyr and the video would emphasize the Islamic quality of the martyrdom: the martyr would usually be in white garments, sporting a beard, and sometimes be decorated with Islamic slogans on a headband. The overall picture would be that of a heroic figure, who would be exiting to battle, single-handedly, as a champion, and this attitude would often be highlighted by contrasting it with the collective and generally cautious methodology of the American forces.

It is important in the Iraqi narratives to demonstrate that the martyr is comparatively happy and at peace with what he or she is doing. This fact undoubtedly comes from concerns that the martyr is *actually* committing suicide, a charge that radical Muslims are at pains to deflect.[56] If the martyr is actually a failure or does not have a reason to live, then their sacrifice does not highlight the belief system for which they are dying and does not incriminate the pampered political and religious Muslim elites that for radical Islam are the true target. The fighter must exemplify the heroic and religious qualities that will make his martyrdom an effective one in the eyes of his primary audience, Muslims, and in the eyes of his secondary audience, non-Muslims, who must see the martyr as being impossible to combat.

Usually the videos are divided very starkly into two sections: first, the initial statement by the martyr or the interview with him, followed by the process by which he becomes increasingly liminal as he goes toward the vehicle (in the case of car-bombings), and as his comrades bid him farewell; then the second part, which is filmed by a support crew that enables the audience to participate in the drama. Ideally, the lead-up time will be small, but enough so that suspense can build, because the actual explosion of the car is necessarily very brief and has to be replayed several times for effect. It is striking how rare videos are of a non-VBIED (vehicle-borne improvised explosive device), such as walking suicide attackers (which we know exist). Perhaps they are not as dramatic. Occasionally, the explosion will be followed by some type of exhortation by the leader of the group, or by some positive results as to what the operation accomplished serving as a finale (see Stenersen's chapter in this volume).

In many cases the video is accompanied by *anashid*, hummed ditties that have their roots in the type of tribal poetry, the *hija'*, that accompanied pre-Islamic combat (see Jonathan Pieslak and Nelly Lahoud in this volume). These are of both an Arab and an Islamic character; in other words, it is perfectly possible to have both *anashid* that do not obviously mention Islamic themes, but are entirely of a Bedouin nature, as well as *anashid* that are almost devotional in nature. But for the most part they address martial themes and serve to both build suspense as well as to focus the sense of purpose behind the martyrdom (which sometimes is not apparent). Sometimes there will be other, comparatively discordant elements, such as printed comments that "all civilians were warned to stay away from this area, so that the *mujahidin* do not spill innocent blood," although it is questionable whether these precautions were taken in reality.

Once again like the early Afghani and al-Qaida martyrologies and videos, but unlike the Palestinian ones, al-Zarqawi does not overemphasize the marriage of the martyr. One could perhaps hazard a guess that the commonality between the early al-Qaida materials and al-Zarqawi is that the warfare in Iraq was overwhelmingly taking place in a situation where the population was at best indifferent and sometimes hostile to the methods and sometimes to the goals of the jihadis. Therefore, unlike in the Palestinian situation they could not count on the support of the populace, nor could they create, as in Afghanistan and in Bosnia, memorials for the *mujahidin*. Perhaps these constraints were the ones that pushed al-Zarqawi and others to rely so heavily upon the Internet, and in doing so create one of the first mass Internet martyrologies in history.

Low-Technology Conflicts: Afghanistan, Pakistan, Africa

Although Iraq represents the best effort that jihadis have made thus far in their martyrology, it is fairly easy to see that few conflicts have had the resources or the technology (or perhaps the artistic inventiveness) to fully emulate it.[57] This fact can be ascertained first of all by examination of the conflicts in Afghanistan and Pakistan, both of which have been heavily influenced from a tactical and a media point of view by Iraq. In Afghanistan suicide attacks made a massive upswing in 2005–2006, a trajectory that has continued since that time.[58] However, neither the mass casualties that characterized the Iraqi conflict nor its media aspects have accompanied this trajectory. Most of the videos that are available on the Internet are of the long-statement variety, and virtually none show the actual operation in real time the way that Iraqi videos mostly did.

At least the Afghan conflict can be said to command some national and popular support as long as foreigners are the ones killed by suicide attacks (most protests so far have occurred as a result of mass-casualty Iraqi-style attacks on civilians or mosques or accidents). The same cannot be said to be true in Pakistan, where the suicide attack campaign began in earnest in the wake of the operation against the Lal Masjid in Islamabad in 2007. Although suicide attacks had been utilized by radicals prior to 2007 in Pakistan, for the most part the targets were smaller sectarian populations such as Shi'ites. But the martyrdom operations after 2007 had the Iraqi stamp all over them: attacking mass civilian gatherings, tribal and religious leadership, mosques and holy shrines, especially of a Sufi character, targeted assassinations (such as that of Benazir Bhutto), and especially attacks upon the military-intelligence infrastructure. Unlike in Afghanistan, few of the suicide attacks were directly against military forces in combat situations, but tended to be directed against the soft targets of bases, recruiting centers, convoys, and organizational headquarters.

It is clear that these types of suicide operations are only targeting Muslims, or apostate Muslims (according to the Salafi belief system), and do not command the support of the Pakistani population. Therefore, there is no attempt to identify the martyr or to develop the Afghani- or Iraqi-style martyrology, and the Pakistanis do not appear to be Internet-savvy. The exception to this rule is those martyrdom operations carried out in Indian Kashmir.[59] However, surprisingly few

of these are available, most likely because the heyday of suicide operations in Kashmir was in the 1990s, prior to the age of Internet videos,
and although this struggle continues to the present it has lost a good
deal of the radical Muslim character it had during the past.

Probably the most obviously developing field is in Africa, where
both al-Qaida in the Maghreb and the al-Shabab in Somalia produce
Internet videos that ape the Iraqi model. Best known is perhaps the
video *Lovers of Hoor*, which shows a suicide operation in Algeria.[60]
From a technical point of view it is reasonably well done, although the
statements associated with the martyr are just too long to be effective.
Much of the photography of the type of life that the mujahidin leads is
obviously designed to demonstrate the close-knit character of the
community. However, the most disappointing aspect of the video is
the fact that at the moment of martyrdom, the explosion is obscured by
a hilltop, so one does not see the actual deed but a cloud of smoke . It is
clear that the videomakers had not considered the need to see the target
being obliterated. Following the August 26, 2011, suicide attack
against the UN headquarters in Abuja, Nigeria, the local radical
Muslim group Boko Haram produced a video as well, although it
has not been popularly distributed.[61]

Somalian martyrdom operation videos are becoming comparatively
common. They also feature the statement, a vision of the vehicle
speeding to its destination (or one assumes as much), and then an
explosion in the distance.[62] While the Algerian and al-Qaida in the
Maghreb videos are often translated into French, the Somalian ones
appear to be entirely for local consumption as they do not move
beyond Somalian linguistic borders. It is apparent that the affiliations
of these various African groups are indicated by their presentation of
martyrdom.

Conclusion

One of the most interesting aspects about contemporary Salafi
jihadism has been its openness to adopting ideas from its ideological
opponents, Shi'ism and Sufism. This is quite evident from its embrace
of the doctrine of *al-wala wa-l-bara* (love and hatred on the basis of
Islam) – a doctrine that has no documented existence in Sunnism prior
to the time of Ibn Taymiyya (d. 1328), and did not achieve any
prominence until the middle of the twentieth century, but has obvious

affinities to the Shi'ite doctrine of *walaya* and *bara'a*[63] in the classical period. So, too, has been the gradual embrace during the past twenty years of the *mut'a* or temporary marriage, which although it is called by different other names, such as *misyar*, is essentially an expedient for close relations between the genders that do not involve permanency. It is clear that both of these doctrines were originally adopted by Shi'ites because of the fact that they were a tiny and persecuted minority that had to assume that opposition was all around it, and that many of its supporters were in fact hidden. Temporary marriage as well was the result of the revolutionary impermanence inherent in early Shi'ism. It is interesting to note that as these factors have become true for radical Islam, more and more it has adopted the doctrines of Shi'ism in order to facilitate success.

The principle of borrowing from one's enemies is evident with regard to contemporary radical Muslim martyrology. It is apparent even to a casual observer that the most obvious affinities for the martyrology developed by Azzam are not to the Salafi world but to the world of Sufism. It is clear that the martyr according to the radicals is designed to become the "holy man" whose example is supposed to motivate others. Salafis of course cannot be held responsible if populations such as that of Kandahar actually treat their martyrs as holy men,[64] as do those in Kashmir.[65] In spite of all the parallelism in the doctrines concerning the Sufi holy men and the radical Muslim martyrs, neither Azzam nor any other Salafi writer known to me actually endorses or promotes the use of relics. The bodies of the martyrs are considered to be pure, they are venerated and seen as conduits to heaven, and the doctrine of intercession is clearly accepted, but beyond this level into pure saint worship the Salafis have not and presumably will not go.

From a material point of view, the martyr has a duality: his or her body has a location and a permanence (whether actual or mythological), and, second, a permanence in the realm of hagiographical myth. The figure of the martyr is a permanently liminal figure, hovering between earth and heaven, continually called from one to the other according to the need. Martyrdom videos are, as previously noted, a reflection of the marginality of a given radical group with regard to the territory in which it operates (Iraq produced large numbers of videos because the groups there were marginal, the Palestinians far fewer because their groups are mainstream). Symbolically, using Azzam's two categories of scholar and martyr, the one represents the preservative, conservative side of the faith, while the other represents the active and aggressive side. Of course, Azzam blurred the lines between these two categories, as is well known. In both the cases of the scholar and the martyr, there is a corporeal as well as a disembodied side to their functionality. The scholar preserves the tangible tradition but also embodies the ideal of the tradition, while the martyr bears witness both through his body and through the ideals for which he stands, and continues to embody the ideal after his death.

8 | Non-military Practices in Jihadi Groups

THOMAS HEGGHAMMER

What do jihadis do when they are not fighting? In this final chapter I will use memoirs and other primary sources to create an inventory of the main non-military practices found inside jihadi groups in the 1980s, 1990s, and 2000s. The main purpose is to get a better sense of what life inside these groups looks like in between the battles and the training sessions. By drawing out the range of non-military practices and assessing their relative prominence, I hope to also illustrate how the individual elements of jihadi culture treated earlier in this book fit together.

The inquiry aims to strike a balance between the broad and the deep, that is, to say something general about "what jihadis do" while staying reasonably close to the primary sources. This is a difficult exercise, because, as I wrote in the Introduction, there have been many jihadi groups, each with its own specificities. Moreover, it is in the nature of the balance-striking exercise to sacrifice both some breadth and some depth. As a result, this chapter has several important limitations. First of all, due to space limitations, my aim is primarily descriptive: I ask *what* people did in these groups, not so much *why* they did it. Some might find this cataloguing of behaviors a bit simplistic, but I consider it an important stepping stone for further research. After all, we cannot know why they do certain things before we know what it is they do. Second, the overview is not exhaustive: I present only the most prominent practices within a selection of groups. Third, I do not describe each practice in much detail: I leave much unsaid regarding the history, connotations, cross-group variation, and individual subjective experience of each practice.

My methodology is document analysis, not direct observation, and this raises some obvious problems. Given that both participant and non-participant observation of al-Qaida and similar groups is almost impossible, I had to work with what the activists and other close observers chose to tell us in their memoirs and videos. I was thus observing them through a thick epistemological filter with many possible biases, such as the tendency for authors to ignore what they take for granted, underreport sinful activities, and overreport virtuous ones. In my approach – which might be described as a form of "ethnography by proxy" – I try to take these biases into account, but I am well aware that the picture I draw is at best a phantom drawing compared to that obtainable through direct observation.

I define "non-military practices" as repeated activities with no obvious operational benefit. "Practices" are understood here in a loose sense, capturing a broad range of social phenomena, including gestures, manners, habits, conventions, rituals, and ceremonies. I am aware of the heated definitional debates on several of these terms, not least the term "ritual," which is why I prefer the vaguer term "practices."[1] To be a little more precise, my definition of "practice" contains two key elements. First, I understand it as an *observable activity*. It may include just speech, but it excludes beliefs and ideas. It includes the act of consuming cultural products, but not the products themselves (i.e., the singing, not the song). The second element is *repetition*: practices are not ad hoc, but occur repeatedly, though not necessarily at regular intervals. *Non-military* practices are those that have no obvious and immediate effect on fighting capability. This excludes, of course, fighting itself, but also training, recruiting, fundraising, and propaganda production.

The rest of this chapter consists of five parts. I begin by describing my sources and methods. Part two examines devotional practices such as prayer and invocations, part three looks at recreational activities like hymn-singing and storytelling, while part four describes identity markers such as dress and gestures. The final part reflects briefly on what we are *not* seeing.

Sources and Methods

Scarcity of sources is a key challenge in this type of inquiry. Clandestine groups are poorly documented in general, and non-military practices are particularly unlikely to make it into the sources. Media tend to report on the most salacious aspects of rebellion, and academic datasets mostly record the groups' military activities.[2] Non-military activities are also underreported in primary sources, because they are not among the things that activists are most interested in communicating. Most jihadi texts are primarily about military, political, theological, or organizational matters, and, as we saw in Stenersen's chapter, the majority of jihadi videos depict military operations.[3]

Still, it is possible to find information about non-military practices if we just look closely enough. There notably exist a small, but growing number of insider accounts by active or former militants. Many of these accounts – which come in the form of memoirs, interviews, court testimonies, and the like – include descriptions of daily life in a jihadi group. Another important source is propaganda videos, some of which contain footage from inside training camps or safe houses. Quite often, clues about social practices appear "between the lines" of the source at hand. A text that is primarily about something else – say, a series of military operations – may contain scattered references to socio-cultural matters. And in the case of videos, revealing clues about social practices may appear in the background or at the end of a scene about something else. For example, as we saw in Cook's chapter, films depicting suicide operations can show the behavior of the attacker in his last hours or his comrades' celebratory reactions to the explosion. Even though such segments are often short and disparate, they can be aggregated, which is what I do in this chapter.

The fact that relevant data are thinly spread out over a large number of sources introduces a source selection problem, for the universe of jihadi primary documents is vast and expanding. Examining all sources is unfeasible, while picking anecdotes at random would make the research opaque and non-replicable. My approach therefore consisted of establishing a corpus of core documents and then extracting relevant data from this corpus.

My procedure began with stating some basic selection criteria. Documents had to (1) describe events in the 1980s, 1990s, or 2000s, (2) pertain to a transnational jihadi group, (3) contain relatively lengthy descriptions, (4) stem from a first-hand source, and (5) offer the perspective of a low- or mid-level activist. To locate such documents, I browsed my personal collection of jihadi literature, searched bibliographic databases, and asked other academics for suggestions. Having established a shortlist of some forty to fifty documents, I then selected documents based on a second set of criteria for the set as a whole. First, the corpus had to include a variety of different *types* of documents – from diaries to interrogation transcripts – in order to limit reporting bias. Second, the corpus had to cover most of the main locations and periods in which jihadi groups have operated over the years, so as to be broadly representative of the jihadi movement. All else equal, I chose the documents with the lengthiest descriptions of underground life. I ended up with a corpus of twenty documents, distributed as follows: ten autobiographies, three sets of court documents, three jihadi videos, three documentaries, and one hostage account (see Table 8.1 for details).

Reliability is always a key concern with primary sources on militant groups. I consider the whole corpus authentic, but we can never exclude the possibility of forgery. Moreover, even if an item is genuine, the content may be distorted, biased, or at least inaccurate, because it was relayed by people with agendas and usually recorded long after the events described. Videos are harder to manipulate, but they are all edited for effect – none are fly-on-the-wall recordings. In addition, each document comes with its own set of biases, most of which should be obvious from the document descriptions in Table 1. I shall not elaborate on these biases, for I assume that the reader understands that disgruntled defectors differ from active militants, that al-Qaida propaganda videos differ from TV documentaries, and that interrogation transcripts are produced under special circumstances. All these problems notwithstanding, the sources should be taken seriously. Descriptions of non-military practices are presumably less likely than other types if information to be tainted or manipulated, because they are less incriminating. An author might underplay his past involvement in terrorist attacks, but he has fewer reasons to lie about what he did in his spare time.

Another concern is that individual sources may not be representative. The documents cover a wide range of different time periods and locations, so practices found in one context need not have occurred in another. For example, London in 2010 differs in every way imaginable from the Afghan countryside in 1985, so we should not expect activists in these two places to be doing the same things. Moreover, the sources portray different *types of activism*, each of which may involve slightly different social practices. Most of the memoirs, for example, are written by foreign fighters training for traditional guerrilla warfare, while the court documents involve people convicted for mass-casualty terrorist attacks. Two of the videos depict rural training camps, while the third takes us into an urban safe house. Moreover, while most of the documents describe people who used (or tried to use) violence, two of

Table 8.1: *Key primary source documents*

1. **Abu Ja'far al-Qandahari,** *Memoirs of an Arab Afghan* **(2002).** 326-page memoir (in Arabic) of an Egyptian who fought in Afghanistan in the 1980s and subsequently demobilized though without changing his Islamist convictions. Published as a book.

2. **Khaled al-Berry,** *The World Is More Beautiful than Paradise* **(2009).** 189-page memoir of an Egyptian former member of al-Jama'a al-Islamiyya in Egypt in the late 1980s and early 1990s. Published as a book (and translated into English) after he broke with his Islamist past.

3. **Nasir al-Bahri and Georges Malbrunot,** *In Bin Ladin's Shadow* **(2010).** 293-page book (in French) presenting a transcribed interview by a French journalist with a Saudi-Yemeni al-Qaida member who served as Usama bin Ladin's bodyguard in Afghanistan in the late 1990s.

4. **Aukai Collins,** *My Jihad* **(2002).** 280-page memoir of an American convert describing his stints as a foreign fighter in Chechnya and Kosovo in the late 1990s. Published as a book after he became disillusioned with jihadism.

5. **Omar Nasiri,** *Inside the Jihad* **(2006).** 357-page memoir of an anonymous Belgian-Moroccan who claims to have infiltrated a North African militant network in Europe and an al-Qaida camp in Afghanistan in the late 1990s on behalf of French intelligence. Published as a book after the author broke with his handlers.

6. **Omar Guendouz,** *Islam's Lost Soldiers* **(2002).** 141-page book (in French) presenting detailed life stories of two young men, a French-Algerian and a French convert, who trained with al-Qaida in Afghanistan in the late 1990s. Authored by a French journalist who interviewed the activists at length.

7. **Fadil Harun,** *The War against Islam* **(2009).** 1,158-page memoir (in Arabic) of a Comoro national describing his twenty-year career as an al-Qaida member in Afghanistan and East Africa in the 1990s and the 2000s. Published as a pdf document on jihadi websites.

8. **Abu al-Shaqra al-Hindukushi,** *From Kabul to Baghdad* **(2007).** 159-page memoir (in Arabic) of an anonymous individual who fought in Afghanistan before traveling to Iraq to join al-Qaida there. Published as a pdf document on jihadi websites.

9. **Erich Breininger,** *My Road to Paradise* **(2010).** 108-page autobiography-cum-recruitment pamphlet (in German) by a German convert who trained in al-Qaida camps in Waziristan in the late 2000s. Published as a pdf document on jihadi websites days after he was killed by Pakistani troops.

10. **Omar Hammami, *Story of an American Jihaadi, Part 1* (2012)**. 127-page memoir of an American convert who traveled to Somalia in 2006 and fought there till his death in 2013. Published as a pdf document on jihadi websites.

11. **East Africa Bombings trial (USA 2001)**. Transcript from the trial of the men accused of bombing the U.S. embassies in Nairobi and Dar-es-Salaam in 1998. Includes lengthy testimonies by individuals who trained in al-Qaida camps in Afghanistan in the 1990s.

12. **Tawhid plot trial (Germany 2003)**. Court documents (in German) from the trial of a group accused of plotting attacks against Jewish targets in Germany in 2001. Features lengthy testimony by Shadi Abdallah, a Jordanian who trained in Afghanistan around 2000.

13. **New York subway plot follow-up trial (USA 2012)**. Transcript from the trial of the men accused of plotting an attack on the New York subway in 2009. Features lengthy testimonies by several individuals who trained in al-Qaida camps in Waziristan in the late 2000s.

14. ***Martyrs of Bosnia* (2000)**. 130-minute video (in Arabic) praising the contribution of the Arab mujahidin in the war in Bosnia (1992–1995). Includes interviews with fighters and footage from training camps. Originally recorded on VHS, later digitized and published on jihadi websites.

15. ***The Badr of Riyadh* (2004)**. 91-minute video (in Arabic) documenting in detail the preparations for a suicide bombing in Riyadh in November 2003 by a cell from al-Qaida on the Arabian Peninsula. Published on jihadi websites.

16. ***Diaries of a Mujahid* (2011)**. 82-minute video (in Arabic) depicting the daily life of foreign fighters in Afghanistan and Pakistan. Features interviews with fighters and footage from training camps. Published in seven successive parts on jihadi websites.

17. **Saudi Ministry of Interior, *Inside the Cell* (2005)**. 22-minute segment (in Arabic) of program aired on Saudi TV in 2005 featuring interviews with detained members of al-Qaida on the Arabian Peninsula.

18. **Mohamed Sifaoui, *Islamist Infiltration in France* (2003)**. 60-minute documentary (in French) by a French-Algerian journalist about his alleged infiltration of a radical Islamist network in Paris and London.

19. **Robb Leech, *My Brother the Islamist* (2012)**. 57-minute documentary by a British filmmaker about his stepbrother's life as a radical Islamist in London.

20. **Robert Fowler, *A Season in Hell* (2011)**. 320-page book by a Canadian diplomat who was held hostage by al-Qaida in the Islamic Maghreb from December 2008 to April 2009 in northern Mali.

the TV documentaries portray Islamists who are not strictly speaking militants, but who "merely" express sympathy for jihadi causes abroad. We thus have to be careful not to generalize on the basis of individual reports. Still, as we shall see – and have seen in previous chapters – many practices and activities do in fact recur in many different contexts, suggesting that they are elements of a shared culture.

There is also the methodological challenge of determining how to process the data once we have them. This is tricky because the object of study – non-military social practices – is so vaguely defined. I want to find out what jihadis do when they are not fighting, but that something could be almost anything. How, then, can I identify relevant practices, and how do I know which are significant? My approach was fairly straightforward. To identify practices, I reviewed each document, noting all references to non-military activities and behaviors that appeared with some regularity. This involved some subjective judgment, and I may have been particularly sensitive to the phenomena that my co-contributors were already working on (*anashid*, poetry, films etc.). I may also have missed certain practices, especially those not explicitly mentioned in the sources. To assess the significance of the practices, I paid attention to the frequency with which they appeared and the significance that militants appeared to ascribe to them. Note that practices did not have to be specifically "jihadi" to be included; as we shall see, jihadis do many of the same things as other Muslims, other rebels, and other young men in general.

Finally there is the problem of organizing and presenting the data. The sheer number of practices that emerged from the sources meant there was no getting around some analytical categorizing. This was challenging for several reasons. For one, the range of phenomena is very wide indeed. Moreover, many practices are multifaceted and partly overlapping, which means they can be categorized in several equally sensible ways. Third, most typologies impute something about the function or purpose of the practices being categorized, which may lead to premature conclusions about the function and interrelationship of the various practices.

I settled for a framework that distinguishes between three main types of practices: *devotional*, *recreational*, and *identity-marking*. Devotional practices are things like prayer and invocations; they have God as their main referent and appear to be performed out of duty.

Recreational practices include things like singing and storytelling; they are usually performed together with fellow activists for apparent aesthetic or social pleasure. Identity-markers are things like dress and manners; they are the external signs that set activists apart from non-activists. This typology is tentative and should be understood more as a presentational device than as a theoretical claim. It is not the only possible conceptualization, and it comes with several problems. Some practices fit more than one category (for example, hymn-singing can be both devotional and recreational), while other practices (such as weeping) do not really fit any of them. Still, for the purpose of initial exploration, the typology works reasonably well.

Devotional Practices

I start with devotional practices because they appear most frequently in the sources. Militant Islamists are often accused of religious insincerity; for example, of exploiting religion for political aims, or of leading morally sinful lives behind a façade of piety.[4] My sources suggest that, on the contrary, they take religion – or at least the ritual aspects of religion – extremely seriously. In the following, I describe six of the main types of devotional practices that transpire in the sources: prayer, invocations, ablution, Qur'an recitation, fasting, and exorcism. There is nothing specifically jihadi about any of these practices, of course; they are staples of ordinary Muslim religious life.

Prayer

Prayer (*salah*) was the most pervasive non-military practice in the sources I reviewed. Militants appeared to observe the five Islamic daily prayers very rigorously, in the morning (*fajr*), at noon (*dhuhr*), in the afternoon (*'asr*), at sunset (*maghrib*), and at nightfall (*'isha*). They prayed just like other Sunni Muslims, that is, by performing, preferably in a group, a series of combinations of utterances and movements that include prostration on the ground in the direction of Mecca, a process that usually takes between ten and thirty minutes depending on the prayer.

The five daily prayers seemed to structure life in the camps and safe houses. "From sunrise, the rhythm of the day is defined by prayer," noted an Arab volunteer in Bosnia in 1995.[5] In training camps, the morning prayer served as the bugle call that got the soldiers up in the morning. Here is a scene from the Jihadwal camp in Afghanistan in 1993:

When the *azan* sounded over the loudspeakers, the seemingly deserted camp came to life. Mujahideen streamed out of the tents and mud shacks all over the camp to create a sort of rush-hour traffic headed toward the mosque ... the camp would be quiet for an hour or so afterward. Many of the mujahideen sat in groups of three or four to recite verses from the Qur'an.[6]

The names of the daily prayers also denoted times of the day. Jihadi authors often located events on the prayer cycle rather than on the twelve-hour clock, saying, for example, "we did it after *fajr* prayer" rather than "we did it around 6 A.M." By the same logic, training camp schedules would be organized by prayer times, as in this timetable from a camp in Pakistan around 2009:

[After] *fajr* prayer: *dhikr*, sports, stretching, 1 minute for breakfast, weapons knowledge, memorization. [After] *dhuhr* prayer: Tactics and close-quarter combat. [After] *'asr* prayer: again 1 minute for eating, weapons knowledge quiz, *dhikr*. [After] *maghrib*: Qur'an class. [After] *'isha*: one hour sentry duty.[7]

The militants in my sources seemed to perform all five prayers under virtually all circumstances, be it in training camps, on the road, or on the battlefront. Orthodox prayer rules allow Muslims to shorten the prayer during travel or in the midst of combat, but jihadis often insisted on the full prayer. At the Jihadwal training camp in Afghanistan in the 1990s, recruits were "taught how to observe religious duties under battlefield conditions, how to clean yourself when no water was available, what constituted a suitable place to pray, and how to make the five mandatory daily prayers even when under direct fire from an enemy."[8] Some militants ignored the risks of prayer in combat. According to an Arab fighter in late 1980s Afghanistan, the Russians "sent aircraft at noon because they knew the mujahidin would be performing the group prayer regardless of the circumstances."[9]

He said that at one point, he and his comrades were performing the noon prayer in a grenadine field near the post, when the aircrafts emerged with a deafening sound much like thunder. Thanks to Allah, none of us left the prayer although the bombs fell close to us and we were showered with fragments.[10]

More pragmatic militants would make use of the provision that allows
believers to combine the noon and afternoon prayers, or the sunset and
nightfall prayers, in a single session.[11]

Some jihadis prayed more than the required five times a day, usually
by adding the optional night prayer (*witr*) between nightfall and morning. Some militants night-prayed on a regular basis and acquired a
reputation for special piety. The late Usama bin Ladin was one:

Sheikh Osama usually wakes up an hour before dawn, for night prayer . . .
two guards . . . accompany him to the camp mosque. We pray with him, and
he keeps his Kalashnikov. He stays in the mosque till sunrise, reading
Qur'anic verses, repeating hadith verses or simple incantations. Then he goes
home for breakfast.[12]

Not everyone was equally enthusiastic about this practice, however.
Omar Nasiri was annoyed to get a night-praying roommate in his
Brussels safe house in 1995:

I woke up a couple of hours later. I heard noises in the room. When I opened
my eyes, I saw Tarek reading his Kur'an with a flashlight and praying
quietly . . . he woke me up again before dawn when he performed the dawn
salat. It was the same for every night after that . . . sometimes Yasin and
Amin would sleep in my bedroom as well, and all three of them would wake
up during the night to read and pray.[13]

While some night-prayed regularly, others did it in times of crisis. For
example, after narrowly escaping death in the Kenyan wilderness,
al-Qaida member Fadil Harun thanked God, noting that "we never
omitted Witr when we were in the forest, nor did we fail to perform the
two prayers at dawn despite our fatigue."[14] Similarly, in Egyptian prisons
in the 1980s, al-Jama'a al-Islamiyya members organized "days of
bonding," which were days "when certain selected brothers met together
to pray through the night and recite the Qur'an until the dawn prayer."[15]

Another occasion to perform supplemental prayers was the month of
Ramadan, when many religious Muslims stay up for the optional
Ramadan night prayers, known as *tarawih*. Ramadan prayers are much
longer than regular prayers, and they are often combined with extensive
Qur'an recitation. In the words of an Arab fighter in Bosnia in 1993:

when the month of Ramadan came, it added to that place's spirituality . . .
the young men passed the time in religious studies and reading the Qur'an.
They helped each other stay up late at night and pray and encouraged each
other to remain committed.[16]

Invocations

Jihadis also engaged in two other acts of worship known as "remembrance of God" (*dhikr*) and "supplication" (*du'a*). The two are closely related and are often both translated in English as "invocations." They are forms of prayer, but unlike the five daily prayers (*salah*), remembrance and supplication are optional. They both consist of reciting, aloud or silently, certain set expressions praising God. The main difference, put very simply, is that a supplication usually requests something (such as forgiveness or protection) from God, while remembrance expresses general gratitude or praise. However, their uses overlap: remembrance can be motivated by a desire for divine assistance, and some supplications express general praise.

Remembrance usually involves the repetition, for several minutes or more, of God's name or of relatively short phrases such as "*allahu akbar*" (God is great) or "*la illaha illa allah*" (there is no god but God). In the sources examined here, remembrance was performed typically, but not exclusively, in situations of stress. For example, Fadil Harun, fearful of being searched at a checkpoint in Kenya, "began to remember God's name so that he would save us."[17] Another memoir offered advice for walking through thick thorny bushes: "always keep your arms in front of your face ... keep your mind busy with Dhikr (especially long phrases that you've intentionally ordered in such a way to keep your brain focused)."[18] We also know from videos of suicide attacks that suicide bombers often say remembrance in the hours and minutes before the attack.[19] The famous 9/11 letter instructed the hijackers to "remember God" in the execution stage.[20]

Supplication, by contrast, usually consists of pronouncing the desired phrase only once, but the range of phrases that can be uttered is much larger. There is a whole literature on supplications in Islam, with different supplications recommended for all kinds of situations: not just for safety in battle or travel, but also for entering a house, going to the bathroom, and much more.[21] In the sources, we see jihadis performing supplications for all kinds of needs. Arab fighters in Bosnia prayed "Allah, make us shoot accurately."[22] When a group of Arab mujahidin got lost in Kenya and thought of giving up, they performed supplications to make the negative thoughts go away.[23] An Algerian militant in France explained that "there are invocations for letters, for visa applications ... it's easy, you throw the letter on the ground and

you say 'allahu akbar,' you do like this."[24] When Karim Bourti took
the Eurostar from Paris to London and was not stopped at immigra-
tion, he attributed this to a supplication that made God blind the
border guards.[25] Some also believe supplications can bless objects.
The 9/11 Letter, for example, describes a procedure consisting of
reading verses of the Qur'an into one's hands, and then rubbing the
hands on the object or body part for which the blessing is sought.[26]

Most common, however, is the supplication for guidance (*du'a' al-
istikhara*), which is used in many types of situations. Some do it before
or during a perilous journey. For example, when Fadil Harun was
about to flee Somalia he prepared himself for hardships and "requested
everybody to recite the supplication for guidance ... We slept peace-
fully until 9 am and then performed *istikhara* prayers for our travel to
Kenya."[27] The group ended up being lost, and during the whole
journey Harun and his comrades prayed *istikhara* many times every
day. Others do *istikhara* when faced with a difficult choice. As we saw
in Edgar and De Looijer's chapter on dreaming, *istikhara* is often used
to "incubate" dreams that in turn can inform important decisions.
However, the guidance need not be mediated through a dream. Khalid
al-Berry explains how, during a prison transfer in Egypt, a fellow
inmate prayed *istikhara* to decide whether or not the group should
shout slogans to the people outside, knowing full well that they would
be beaten by the guards if they did.[28]

Ablution

Another frequent practice is ablution, a purification act of which there
are two main variants. Most common is the partial ablution (*wudu'*),
which involves washing the feet, lower arms, and face with water.
(When water is not available, dust or clean soil can be used instead,
and the procedure is called *tayammum*.) Partial ablution is a prerequisite for prayer and recommended for handling the Qur'an. In theory,
one ablution can last the whole day, but certain acts or exposures
(including urination and defecation) render the ablution void, so
observant Muslims, including jihadis, end up performing *wudu'*
(or *tayammum*) many times a day.[29]

The other variant is the full ablution (*ghusl*), in which the entire
body is cleaned with water. In Islam, a full ablution is required after
sexual activity or emission of semen, and it is recommended in a few

other circumstances, such as before important prayers. Jihadis appear to observe these rules, either by performing the full ablution or by avoiding the situations that generate a need for it. A jihadi in Afghanistan expressed relief at being unmarried so he did not have to perform *ghusl* on a regular basis.[30] Teenage jihadis faced a related problem, described by a member of the Egyptian al-Jama'a al-Islamiyya:

> [A consequence of sexual maturity] was having to perform a complete ritual ablution before setting off to say the dawn prayer if one woke up having experienced a nocturnal emission; this was particularly hard in the cold of winter ... [This] was a problem to which I could find no solution other than masturbating the night before, then washing, then going to sleep, in which case I would not have any wet dreams.[31]

As with prayers, some jihadis in my sources performed ablutions more often than necessary. They were hypersensitive to perceived impurity and believed that the state of ritual purity (*tahara*) could be rendered void by the slightest impure exposure, utterance, or thought. For example, a radical Islamist in France performed full ablution immediately after being released from prison, as if incarceration had soiled him.[32] Robert Fowler noted that his Al-Qaida in the Islamic Maghreb (AQIM) captors went to great lengths to avoid touching him, as if contact with an infidel rendered them impure.[33] Another radical Islamist in France refused to pronounce the name of a political enemy because the very act of mentioning the name would, in his view, void his ablutions.[34] Concern with purity is a universal feature of religion, of course, and in Islam it is taken to great lengths by salafis in particular. Richard Gauvain described how some (non-jihadi) Islamists in Cairo performed ablutions more often than required in Islamic law, believing, for example, that ablutions were necessary after lying, becoming sexually aroused, or encountering a Jew.[35]

Qur'an Recitation

Another ubiquitous feature of jihadi life as described in the sources was Qur'an recitation, which was often performed in connection with prayer, but could also be done at other times. In any group of jihadis there would be at least one copy of the Holy Book, and it seemed to be consulted every single day. For example, Fadil Harun notes that in the morning after breakfast, "we started reading the Qur'an, like we did on a daily basis, and prayed for God's guidance on several matters."[36] Similarly, a Western convert training in Kashmir recalled that "after morning prayers everyone sat around reading the Qur'an for about an hour, followed by an hour of exercises and a run up one of the ravines."[37]

There appeared to be at least two variants of Qur'an recitation, formal and informal. The first is a group activity in which one person reads aloud or chants in the particular elocution (*tajwid*) reserved for Qur'anic verse while others listen. Some groups have a designated reader, while others take turns. Several of the groups did Qur'an recitation sessions every day, regardless of the circumstances. In times of hardship, some would intensify the practice, as they did with prayer. During Ramadan, as noted earlier, many would spend the night in communal prayer and Qur'an recitation. One source recalled how, in Bosnia during Ramadan in 1993, the Arab fighters "stayed up late in prayer and read the Qur'an constantly during the days of fasting."[38]

The sources contain a small number of references to Qur'an recitation during combat. One group of Arabs in 1980s Afghanistan recited the Qur'an on loudspeakers as a form of psychological warfare against the enemy.[39] In another battle, in Somalia around 2006, Fadil Harun recited the Qur'an to boost the morale of his own men.[40]

Proper Qur'an recitation requires training, and some militants invested time in it. Training camps sometimes offered courses on Qur'an recitation, as did the Khalden camp in Afghanistan in the mid-1990s: "after dinner, we divided up into small groups to practice the tajwid, the recitation of the Kur'an."[41] Good readers – that is, people with strong *tajwid* skills and a pleasant voice – were appreciated by their peers. For example, Khalid al-Berry said of a comrade's Qur'an recitation: "The chanting of the Qur'an in that voice full of submission and with that face inscribed with fear and awe that I myself could feel conjured up before my very eyes the embodiment of faith."[42]

Some jihadis also spent time listening to recorded Qur'an recitation. Such listening was often done individually, but it could also be a group activity. Recordings could be the object of careful listening, or they could be played in the background. For example, in Mohamed al-Sifaoui's undercover documentary on the French-Algerian radical Karim Bourti, we hear Qur'an recordings being played often inside the car.

In addition to the ceremonial Qur'an recitation at full voice, there is the equally common practice of reading the Qur'an to oneself at low voice. Many militants seemed to do this every day, and some were described as doing it at every available opportunity. Omar Hammami, the American foreign fighter in Somalia, wrote,

A brother gave me his Mus-xaf [Qur'an] so I didn't have to wait for other people to finish anymore. I took that opportunity to memorize a few more chapters of the Qur'aan in between my chores, and it really helped to keep me sane and focused.[43]

Weeping

Judging by the sources studied here, jihadis weep a lot, especially in devotional settings. Weeping is a common Islamic practice associated with, but not limited to, Sufism. The medieval Sufi theologian al-Ghazali (d. 1111) included weeping as one of the ten rules for the recitation of the Qur'an:

The sixth rule is the rule of weeping. It is laudable to weep while reading the Qur'an and if this does not happen spontaneously, one should force oneself to weep. This is possible by way of remembering the threats and warnings in the Qur'an against the sins and failures of man. Should one feel no inclination to weep, then one has full reason to cry over one's lack of grief and tears.[44]

For radical Islamists, devotional weeping is appreciated as evidence of the believer's "fear of God." They see no contradiction between man-liness and devotional weeping. Omar Hammami, for example, noted about his brutal trainer that "despite his tough appearance, he used to cry in the prayers when he heard the verses of the Quraan recited."[45]

The jihadis in my sources wept in a variety of situations, but most commonly during Qur'an recitation and prayer. Here is first-person account by a training camp recruit in late 1990s Afghanistan:

The al-Jum'a prayer was always the most intense of the week ... sometimes, a brother would be so overcome by faith that tears would well up in his eyes. I was overcome too. Standing amidst these mujahidin, I could feel the spirit of God fill me completely. I was swept up as the others by the feelings of love and fellowship and brotherhood. I was part of a community, a community of complete devotion to God.[46]

Interestingly, in a given group of jihadis, only some individuals would weep, and those who did not expressed envy at those who did. Egyptian al-Jama'a al-Islamiyya member Khalid al-Berry lamented,

An acquaintance of mine had changed to a startling degree recently ...
Suddenly this young man started fasting every day and when he came to
the prayer, he only had to hear the Qur'an to start weeping loudly, on one
note, like a long cry of pain. I felt that the sound was sincere and contained a
suppressed complaint and I felt that it contained something I lacked.
I wanted that sound. I wanted it to come out of me, for if it did so, it would
relieve me of many things.[47]

Another common theme in the sources is that of militants weeping
upon being denied martyrdom or an opportunity to fight. For example,
when Nasir al-Bahri had to return to base to recover from an injury, he
"started weeping. I felt that in the middle of the war there was no use
for me."[48] Similarly, an Arab fighter in Bosnia recalled,

One of the brothers told me that he stayed up at night, weeping bitterly and
praying to God to grant him martyrdom in the coming operation ... On the
night prior to the operation he led us in prayer at night and I swear that he
made us cry by the way he supplicated God for victory and implored him
constantly to grant him martyrdom.[49]

The third main type of weeping situation reported in the sources was
when militants were moved by images or information about Muslim
suffering. Nasir al Bahri said he cried over a video from Bosnia in
1993, and a certain Abu al-Zubayr al-Kabili was known for collapsing
in tears "whenever he heard of a calamity affecting the Muslim nation
or a tragic story that had occurred in Bosnia."[50] However, we also
read of weeping for other, less devotional reasons, for example, in
response to relief, separation, reunion, death, or arrest.[51]

Fasting

Another common devotional practice was fasting (*sawm*), that is, the
abstention from food and water between sunrise and sunset. Fasting
during Ramadan is one of the pillars of Islam and seems to be
rigorously observed by all jihadis. In addition, many jihadis also fast
voluntarily on the optional Islamic fasting days. Of these, fasting on
Mondays and Thursday of every week appears to be most common.[52]
Some did it even more: bin Ladin, for example, used to fast "on
Monday and Wednesday [*sic*], as well as on the ten days preceding
Eid and six days after Ramadan."[53] Erich Breininger, a German foreign fighter in Afghanistan, noted that many of his fellow recruits did

"David's fast," that is, fasting every other day. It was the same people, he wrote, who would get up two hours before dawn to pray.[54]

As with prayer, some jihadis insisted on fasting even when it compromised their security. For example, an Arab fighter in Bosnia in 1993 recounted,

We continued our march until dawn. We prayed morning prayers and the commander gave his order to everyone to have breakfast even though it was Ramadan. The men were tired and it was not known how long the battle would take. However, Abu Dujana al-Sharqi insisted on maintaining his fast.[55]

There is some evidence that suicide bombers fast on the day of the attack, regardless of the day of the year.[56] This practice may stem from a belief that fasting increases the probability that God will recognize them as martyrs.

Exorcism

While most devotional practices were about praising God, jihadis also did things to chase the devil and evil spirits. Two such practices appear in the sources, although neither appears very widespread.

The first was a gesture consisting of spitting three times to the left. This was typically done when a person has sinful thoughts or dreams believed to be the work of Satan. He would then spit three times to the left to make the devil's influence go away. For example, when Khalid al-Berry for a moment doubted the existence of the afterlife, he "spit three times to [his] left, this being the prophetically approved behaviour should Satan send ideas into the mind of the believer designed to seduce him."[57]

The second was exorcism (*ruqya*) in the traditional sense, whereby a person chases spirits from another person's body. Some jihadis seemed to believe that certain individuals have a gift for exorcism. Fadil Harun noted that "Brother Abu Wafa was famous for reading the Qur'an and for exorcising by touch anyone possessed by the devil."[58] Khalid al-Berry relates a story about a comrade possessed by a genie and relieved through exorcism:

Our friend Mohammed ... had started seeing a female genie, who came to him at night and slept with him and treated him just like a husband ... she came to him each night in a different shape ... Muhammad told the brothers about her and they decided to bring a brother from Minya to cast her out. I was too scared to attend this expertise in spiritualism, but our mutual friend told me afterward, in terror, that Muhammad had spoken to the exorcist in a woman's voice, and that he had clapped his hands and sung in her silly tones, 'I love Muhammad and he loves me.' The genie had told them that she was sixty-four years old.[59]

Recreational Practices

While the jihadis in my sources spent a lot of energy meeting ritual obligations, they also did things for aesthetic or social pleasure. I call these practices "recreational," not because they are necessarily about relaxation or entertainment, but because they are elective and not primarily about praising God. I will discuss six such practices: *anashid* singing, poetry reading, video watching, storytelling, dream interpretation, and sports.

Anashid Singing

The jihadi appreciation for a cappella religious songs (*anashid*) has been treated extensively in the earlier chapters by Nelly Lahoud and Jonathan Pieslak, so here I shall discuss only the ways in which they were "consumed" by militants in the field.

In my sources, *anashid* were often used as cadence calls during training or on marches. An Arab recruit attending an Afghan training camp in the late 1980s recalled that "every morning we would start running enthusiastically while Abu Harith chanted Palestinian *anashid*."[60] They are also sung for relaxation. For example, Fadil Harun mentions that "one Friday evening, during the break, brother Abu Mansur al-Shishani began to chant *anashid*."[61] Chanting can also be part of an ideological instruction programme. Omar Hammami recalls how his camp received a visit by a highly respected Yemeni jihadi named Abu Mansur al-Yamani:

He had a beautiful character and my days with him are from my most cherished moments in Jihaad ... he was giving motivational talks in the evening before gathering the brothers for Nashiids ... It was not strange to find him or the other brothers shedding tears for love of Islaam. Afterwards he would have me translate the Arabic words of the oldies Nashiids that he loved so much. He wasn't a big fan of the new wave Nashiids with more of a focus on how it sounds then the actual literal content. He memorized almost all of the Qawaafil ash-Shuhadaa' Nashiids and his voice was actually preferable to the original on many occasions. Till this day there are numerous Nashiids that instantly remind me of him and take me back to those bitter-sweet moments.[62]

In a typical *anashid*-singing session, one member would do most of the singing, while the others listen or occasionally join in on the chorus. Some militants specialized in hymn-singing and built reputations as singers. For example, Omar Hammami recalls,

When I reached the other side the Arab brother, Abu Xafs … was singing Nashiids for the brothers crowded around him. This guy was absolutely amazing when it came to Nashiids. He would even pretend to re-wind the "tape player" by making the squealing rewind sound. He had been in a Tunisian jail for terror charges.[63]

As we saw in Lahoud and Pieslak's chapters, *anashid* are also recorded, so the listening has become a practice in itself. The following extract from Fadil Harun's memoir shows how *anashid* were consumed in context and indicates that they could indeed be considered as entertainment:

I had a Qur'an tape and another with inspirational Islamic hymns. We would switch between them according to the atmosphere in the car. When it was calm and quiet we put on the Qur'an, otherwise the hymns. What amazed me was that my little girl Sumayya had memorized all the hymns, even though she was only four years old. I was angry with her mother because I only listen to those hymns at specific times, during training, to get the young men worked up. In normal circumstances I listen to the Qur'an more than to hymns and she knows that. I did and still do encourage memorizing the Qur'an before the hymns.[64]

Jihadis also listen to *anashid* in operational settings. During a terrorism trial in Denmark in 2009, the prosecution produced a secret surveillance video showing the accused, Hammad Khurshid, building a bomb while listening to hymns to his computer and singing along. He "repeated the song a few times, while moving upper body back and forth, with his hands folded in front of him. Then he got up and started shouting in the air: Allahu Akbar, Allahu akbar."[65]

Poetry Reading

Anashid are closely related to poetry, which, as we saw in Haykel and Creswell's chapter, is a prominent element of jihadi culture. Jihadi publications and websites are full of it, and several active militants, including Usama bin Ladin, wrote poems. The sources examined for this chapter are no exception: for example, Fadil Harun includes a poem in his memoir, and one of the Arab interviewees in the film *Martyrs of Bosnia* recites a poem to honor a fallen comrade.[66]

However, I found relatively few descriptions of poetry-reading sessions. One exception is the following anecdote from late 1980s Afghanistan:

> It was extremely hot during that time of the year and we used to go swimming in one of the nearby ponds at noon, hunted a few birds then returned to perform the afternoon prayer. In the evening and after we had tea, we would sit in the calm night and its soft breeze while Abdul Razeq recited religious poems, urging us to recite Arab ones then asking us about their meaning.[67]

The limited evidence of collective poetry recitation may be coincidental, but more likely it indicates that poetry is consumed in other ways, perhaps through individual reading or, as we saw in Pieslak's and Lahoud's chapters, through *anashid* singing.

Video Watching

A more widespread pastime was video watching. We saw in Anne Stenersen's chapter that jihadis have been producing propaganda videos since the early 1980s, and that the number of productions has skyrocketed in the digital age. Here I shall briefly examine the ways in which active militants consume such videos.

One observation is that jihadis in my sources frequently viewed videos together. In fact, video screenings go back a long time. Khalid al-Berry notes that "in the summer of 1987, I started going to movies shown by the Jama'a at the Jam'iya Shar'iya mosque. There were pictures of children disfigured during the war against the Muslims in Afghanistan that would have wrung tears from a stone."[68] Similarly, "one evening in 1993," Nasir al-Bahri recalls, "a Palestinian friend who did jihad in Afghanistan invited me to view a film on the battle of Sarajevo."[69]

Another finding is that jihadis seemed to watch propaganda videos at all stages in their careers, not just in the enlistment phase. Here is a recruitment account from late 1990s Brussels:

I went to a Moroccan brother who had done jihad. After completing our religious duties – prayers and invocations – I told him about myself. I stated my desire to fight alongside my Muslim brothers. After a very long discussion with other brothers, he gave each of us a book of sermons and showed us videos on crimes committed in Algeria or Chechnya.[70]

Videos were also played in training camps. Omar Nasiri describes the Darunta camp in Afghanistan around 1996:

we would watch films in the mosque. There was a huge array of propaganda videos we could watch any time. I had always loved watching movies, and I realized that I had missed watching television when I was in Khalden. I spent a lot of time in the mosque during those early weeks, going through the huge collection of films about the mujahidin during the Soviet-Afghan war.[71]

They also continued to watch propaganda videos long past the training stage. Here is Robert Fowler's description of "video night with al-Qaida" in the Malian desert in 2009:

Just as we had begun to doze off, we heard a great commotion around the front of the track, a metre from our heads. The hood was opened and three large, heavy tires were thrown into a pile. By the time we had sat up to figure what was going on, somebody had placed a laptop computer on the stack of tires and was plugging it into the cigarette lighter socket in the engine compartment ... with some ceremony, a DVD was produced and inserted into the laptop drive and we were chivvied around to have pride of place in front of the screen ... each time an episode of mayhem and destruction occurred on the screen, the crowd pressing around Louis and me shouted "Allahu Akbar!"[72]

Storytelling

Another common practice was storytelling, a practice in which a group of militants gathered to exchange stories or listen to a keynote speaker. Given that jihadis shun popular entertainment and often stay in remote areas, the prevalence of this practice it is not surprising.

A common topic was personal life stories. Here is a campfire scene from Afghanistan around 2000:

On the first night after the attack, we were seated around the fire in one of our positions. It was a cold night. One of the brothers suggested that each of us should tell the story of how he became guided to the right path and joined jihad. Some agreed to do so while others were too embarrassed. The young men began to tell their stories one after the other. The third person to do so was Umar al-Adani ... His story greatly moved the brothers that night, to the point that they wept.[73]

However, the most popular topic appears to have been contemporary battle stories. As Omar Nasiri recounts from late 1990s Afghanistan:

at night, we would sit together in the barracks and talk. We had only gas lamps for light ... we would shroud ourselves in blankets to stave off the bitter cold night air, and the mujahidin would tell us stories from the front lines. I was transfixed by these stories, by the detailed descriptions of famous battles I had only read about.[74]

Note that while the previous quotes depict spontaneous storytelling between trainees, there is also evidence of organized storytelling to socialize recruits. For example, an Arab volunteer in a jihadi safe house in Pakistan in 1995 recalled,

I spent my time reading books and leaflets ... I watched numerous jihadist movies that had been filmed in Afghanistan during the fighting. I sat in the gatherings of the brothers who had fought in Afghanistan for a long time. I listened to their war stories and heard about the martyrs who were killed in battle.[75]

Some fighters excelled in storytelling. One AQIM narrator charmed even his Canadian hostage:

Omar was one of the most natural and entrancing storytellers I have ever encountered. I felt as if I had been transported back in time and was listening to a troubadour from the Middle Ages. The younger mujahideen couldn't get enough of his tales, which all had a religious theme: either his animation of Qur'anic stories, his account of his missionary activities and religious conquests, or his vivid re-creations of numerous *hadith*.[76]

Dream Interpretation

As Edgar and de Looijer explained in Chapter 6, jihadis take dreams very seriously as potential messages from God. Here again, we are not dealing with an exclusively jihadi phenomenon, because dreams remain important in the Muslim world more generally. In the sources examined here, jihadis thought and talked about dreams a lot, and some seemed to discuss dreams on a daily basis.[77] Dreams are considered an intimate, sensitive topic, so they were usually only discussed in pairs or small groups. A few individuals are described as being obsessed with dreams. One memoir from late 1980s Afghanistan portrays a fighter who

wanted to follow [his fallen comrade] by any means, and he started to have martyrdom visions almost every day. He once dreamt he was trapped in a destroyed house ... he opened one door and reached a magnificent garden ... I explained to him that his martyrdom was imminent, and his joy was indescribable.[78]

Most dream accounts in my sources appeared to have an element of post-facto rationalization. For example, Omar Hammami's memoir recounts a number of dreams and concludes that "in hindsight, all of these dreams seemed to have been the foretelling of my future role with the Shabab."[79] Similarly, several jihadis said they had martyrdom premonitions for fallen comrades, as in this account:

Allah sent me a vision through which I knew that Abdul Razeq was going to be martyred ... He was wearing white clothes, a white turban, his face was lit up, and his body full of health ... When I learned what had happened to him, I realized the meaning of the vision.[80]

Several individuals claimed to have taken consequential decisions based on dreams. Some said they joined after a dream; the Bahraini Muhammad Fatih, for example, was allegedly "convinced of the need to go to the land of Bosnia by a dream."[81] Others decided to continue fighting because of dreams. Omar Hammami said he thought of defecting, "but it was really a few dreams that tipped the scales and caused me to stay."[82] Yet others said dreams informed tactical decisions: Fadil Harun writes that when he was lost in the Kenyan wilderness, he relied on a friend's dream to find a way out.[83] An Arab fighter in 1980s Afghanistan refused to fire mortars and insisted on joining a sniper unit because he had a dream in which, to his horror, he had fired mortars on a mosque.[84]

Some jihadis seemed to specialize in dream interpretation and were consulted more frequently than others. Robert Fowler mentions that one of his captors "was much intrigued by dreams and constantly inquired about ours in order to exercise his training in interpretation."[85] An Arab in Afghanistan noted that one of his comrades "had a vision which he related to me the next morning after I acquired a reputation in the interpretation of dreams."[86]

Sports

Jihadis also appreciate sports. Swimming, horseback riding, and archery (interpreted today as shooting) are explicitly encouraged in the *hadith* (Prophetic tradition), so these activities are particularly visible in the sources. For example, in the al-Qaida video *Diary of Mujahid* there are several swimming scenes, at least one horseback-riding scene, and, of course, innumerable shooting scenes.[87] Similarly, an Arab Afghan fighter recalls that "we would pray in the morning, then listen to religious lessons before having breakfast. Then, we headed towards the woods where we could swim in small lakes all day long."[88]

Although a few radicals (including the main character in *My Brother the Islamist*) believe that recreation should be *limited* to these three activities, most seemed to have nothing against other sports.[89] Soccer and martial arts have been particularly popular in jihadi circles. Khalid al-Berry explains that he and his al-Jama'a al-Islamiyya friends in 1980s Egypt played a lot of soccer, and they used it for both recreation and recruitment.[90] Other militants are described in the sources as being proficient in Kung Fu and kickboxing.[91]

Festivities

Despite their reputation for stern fundamentalism, jihadis sometimes celebrated. One occasion was Id al-Fitr, the holiday marking the end of Ramadan. For example, the film *Diaries of a Mujahid* included several long scenes from a lively Id party among Arab fighters in Afghanistan around 2010. We see mujahidin mingling, smiling, and eating good food. Later they sit in a circle singing hymns while a man first performs a brief dance, then they all shout "*allahu akbar!*" while another man fires a Kalashnikov in the air.[92]

Some also celebrated weddings. When the children of two senior al-Qaida members married in late 1990s Afghanistan, they held "a splendid wedding during which sheikh Usama [bin Ladin] gave a speech. There were chants and popular dances performed by the brothers from Yemen, which made everyone happy."[93]

Identity-markers

A third set of practices consists of little things that people wear, say or do. These things I call identity-markers because they affect appearance and distinguish activists from non-activists. There is probably more inter-jihadi variation in this domain than in the two previous ones, as each group and regional context has its own characteristics.

Dress and Grooming

There appears to be no universal jihadi uniform or "look"; militants seem to wear roughly whatever is worn in the area they operate. There are some exceptions; in the 1980s and 1990s, it was not uncommon for Arab veterans of the Afghan jihad to wear their old Afghan clothes outside Afghanistan. As late as the early 2000s, some radicals in the West wore a conspicuous combination of traditional dress and combat gear. In Bosnia in the 1990s, some Arab fighters wore the green headbands commonly associated with Hamas in Palestine.[94] In Middle Eastern countries, jihadis often wear what other conservative Islamists wear, namely, an ankle-length gown or loose shirt/trouser combination, modeled on the Prophet Muhammad's dress. They often follow related Salafi customs, such as carrying a *miswak* (a tooth-cleaning twig from the Arak tree), wearing strong non-alcoholic perfume, wearing the wristwatch on the right wrist, and avoiding gold jewelry.[95]

Beards seem almost mandatory. Those who cannot sport a full beard grow what they can. The seventeen-year old British convert in *My Brother the Islamist* used beard serum to improve growth.[96] Interestingly, shaving to avoid detection is surprisingly rare. Khalid al-Berry, for example, relates how al-Jama'a al-Islamiyya members in Egypt would grow beards, knowing full well that it made them more vulnerable to police repression.[97] In return, they got a stronger sense of group identity:

The feeling of being a group became even more entrenched when it evolved into a common look that made the members of the group recognizable to one another wherever they might go. They would let their beards grow, ungroomed and uncut, to the breadth of a fist … From the pocket of one's jallabiya (which we called a 'shirt') peeked the tip of a miswak, or chewing stick, with which we cleansed our mouths … and those same mouths were never used to whistle.[98]

To the Western eye, jihadis may seem rugged, but they take cleanliness very seriously and are not averse to grooming, even in the battlefield. Robert Fowler recalls that "in the middle of the desert,

Omar Two used cologne and applied Kohl to highlight his large, wide-set and menacing eyes."[99] Those about to undertake a suicide bombing or a high-risk operation often make a particular effort to look good. An Arab fighter in Bosnia noted of a friend that "a few days before the operation, [he] was seen to take great care of himself. And he wore his best clothes as if he knew he had an appointment with the beautiful women of paradise."[100]

Noms de guerre

One of the most conspicuous and consistent jihadi practices is the adoption of a nom de guerre (*kunya*) at the beginning of a military career. Names usually follow the formula "Abu + <name> + <origin>", as in "Abu Hasan al-Iraqi." When Omar Nasiri presented himself with his real name in a Pakistani safe house, a murmur went through the room:

Brother, we never use our real names. When you come here, you must leave everything behind – your home, your family, your identity. You must take a new name.' ... I decided to take the name Abu Bakr.[101]

Slogans

In social interactions, jihadis make frequent use of set religious expressions such as "*la illaha illa allah*" (there is no god but God), "*subhanallah*" (God is glorious), and various forms of "*tahmid*" (praising God). These are all common Islamic expressions – in fact, they are technically a form of remembrance (*dhikr*).

   One such expression – the so-called *takbir*, or the saying of "*Allahu akbar*" (God is great) – is pronounced in a particularly performative way. It is a group act that begins with one person shouting "*takbir!*" whereupon all other members present respond by shouting "*allahu akbar!*" The sequence is usually repeated four times. Jihadis in my sources did *takbir* in all kinds of situations: when doing the inspection call, exercising, firing a gun, seeing the enemy, completing a task, receiving a good piece of news, greeting fellow militants, embarking on a journey, celebrating victory, or for no apparent reason at all.[102] In Bosnia, some fighters carried loudspeakers to amplify their *takbir* shouts against the enemy.[103]

Manners

Jihadi groups have norms for everyday manners and etiquette. The types of prescriptions and the extent of regulation seem to vary between groups: some appear relatively pragmatic, while others expect members to follow precise behavioral blueprints in all walks of life. The Egyptian group al-Jama'a al-Islamiyya was a case of the latter. According to a former member,

> they discuss what is forbidden and what is permitted, they discuss prayer, the rules governing fasting, the rules governing how to look at a woman and listen to music, the limits to be places on the exposure of the body, the acts that render ritual ablutions void, and those that require the ritual purification of the whole body, the proprieties to be observed when bathing and when eating … everything would turn into a mechanical activity … when I got home, I'd say the prayer for entering the house, and it was the same when I entered the bathroom, where I would use my left hand only to clean myself and not say a word, even if someone called to me. Nor would I forget the prayer when I came out. I ate sitting on the ground using three fingers and not two … or five … Even when walking down the street, I would try to walk as [the Prophet Muhammad] … was described as having walked.[104]

Several of these practices are found in other jihadi groups. For example, reserving the left hand for unclean things is very common; in the film *My Brother the Islamist*, the radical convert Salahuddin will use his left hand only to shake non-Muslims' hands – even that of his own step-brother. Jihadis also seem to be generally rather prudish. The swimming in *Diary of a Mujahid*, for example, is always done with clothes on, and Robert Fowler said he "never saw even a naked torso" in five months of living with AQIM.[105]

Rare Practices

Before I conclude, let me briefly consider what the jihadis in my sources did *not* do, or did *less* of than expected. First, there really does seem to have been little "sex, drugs and rock 'n' roll" in the jihadi underground. I have already noted their conservatism in sexual matters, and alcohol and drugs were obvious taboos.[106] They did not smoke cigarettes; only Afghan mujahidin in the 1980s and 1990s seem to have indulged.[107] They neither performed nor listened to music with instruments, in line with the norms described in Pieslak's chapter in this book. They did not produce or watch stage art, unlike the Muslim Brotherhood in Egypt, which produced "Islamic drama" for a long time.[108] Jihadis did not watch network TV, except, perhaps, for newscasts. Dancing was also rare; there was no sign of the Sufi *sama'* ritual with its whirling dervishes, but there are brief references to the Afghan *atan* dance and the "walking under the Qur'an" ritual of Afghan mujahidin.[109]

Second, and perhaps more surprising, militants did little to cultivate a distinct jihadi "look." Other than beards, conventional signs of group membership are rare. Unlike many other paramilitary organizations, the jihadi groups studied here did not have uniforms with badges or insignia. Unlike gang members, they did not expect each other to get tattoos or other body modifications.[110] There was no evidence of secret handshakes or other codified gestures.

Third, and perhaps most important, jihadis seemed to have few ceremonies of their own. One might have expected a violent religious group such as al-Qaida to develop elaborate and idiosyncratic ceremonies, but it seems not to have done so. Most ceremonial practices reported in the sources were conventional rituals of mainstream Sunni Islam.

One partial exception was the pledging of allegiance (*bay'a*). This is a traditional Islamic ceremony of individual submission to political authority. It was adopted as an initiation ritual by al-Qaida in Afghanistan in the 1990s. Although ceremonial in form, the pledge appears to have been elective and without formal implications. It was not a prerequisite for access to training, salary, operations, or even the upper echelons of the group.[111] Here is a sample account by Nasir al-Bahri:

Bin Laden handed me a text, and I swore allegiance. Even though, until then, I had been a de facto full member of al-Qaida, I attached importance to this ritual, which takes place without much ceremony. I raise my hand before Bin Ladin, declaring, 'I swear before God to assist you and to support you, without considering my personal interest or my own ideas, in good times and bad times, forgetting my personal well-being, and I promise not to challenge your leadership.' Although this does not change anything in my daily life, it does affect my state of mind.[112]

Interestingly there is little evidence of pledge ceremonies from other jihadi groups or indeed from al-Qaida itself after 2001. The sources studied here contain only one other reference, from Omar Hammami in Somalia around 2006:

Immediately I recognized Xasan Turky … I knew … that he must be the Amiir … By that point the only thought in my mind was whether or not I should give him Baycah at that moment or wait a bit later when there were only few brothers around! … Nevertheless, Baycah or not, when this group got up … we thought it was wise to stick with them.[113]

The only jihadi-specific ceremony I observed in the sources was the "martyr's wedding," a practice in which suicide bombers are celebrated on the day before the attack. The celebration imitates a wedding party and symbolizes the martyr's coming union with the virgins of paradise. It has no clear precedent in the Islamic tradition, but may be an adaptation of the "funeral-as-wedding" celebrations held for fallen fighters in Palestine.[114] The jihadi ceremony is documented in at least two videos, one from Saudi Arabia in 2003, the other from Afghanistan around 2010.[115] Both show a group of ten to fifteen militants singing a cheerful *nashid* (the same in both scenes) and smiling to the bombers. It is not clear how widespread the ceremony is. On the one hand, the two films are recorded seven years apart in two different places, suggesting the practice has migrated and endured. On the other hand, I have seen little evidence of this practice in other sources, which suggests it was relatively rare.

Conclusion

This chapter has offered an inventory of the main non-military practices in jihadi groups as observed through a selection of primary sources. Beyond the unsurprising finding that jihadis do much more than just fight and train, the chapter provided several important insights. One is that the jihadis in these sources did take religion very seriously. Devotional practices and recreational practices with religious content seemed to take up the overwhelmingly largest part of their spare time. These same practices suggest that few if any jihadis doubt the existence of God, Satan, evil spirits, the afterlife, and the prophetic potential of dreams. This is significant, because it undercuts the frequent claim by non-militant Muslims – and their non-Muslim supporters – that extremists lack genuine faith. Militants are often accused by moderates of being either ignorants who have just discovered Islam, opportunists who exploit religion for personal or political ends, or hypocrites who really lead sinful lives behind a facade of piety. It may be true that many militants have a non-observant past, but my investigation suggests that once they are in a militant group, they take ritual observance very seriously. Nobody can know the depth of their faith, but we should not assume that their belief is less intense just because they know little about theology.

Second, and relatedly, the jihadis studied here were surprisingly orthodox in their ritual practices. They seem to have invented few ceremonies of their own; instead they did mostly what other Sunni Muslims do, only with greater than average frequency and intensity. Given their deviance from norms about violence, one might have expected them to deviate in their ritual practices too, but in general they did not. This is important because it suggests jihadi groups have not had to sacrifice all that much cultural authenticity on their way to extreme political action. This in turn may help understand why people join. In the eyes of prospective recruits from a conservative religious background, jihadi groups can appear as culturally relatively authentic. This is in contrast to other subcultures, such as the Ku Klux Klan or the skinhead movement, which, culturally speaking, represent complete innovations and sharp breaks from the mainstream.

Third, the militants were more emotional and artistically sensitive than their reputation as rugged terrorists suggests. Aside from weeping in all kinds of situations, they appreciated *anashid* and looked up to warrior-poets. The atmosphere in the jihadi underground appears to differ markedly from Western tabloid presentations of jihadi groups as nests of cold-blooded sadists. This is not to say that jihadis are all sensitive poet types who have been mistaken for religious Rambos all along, but to say that in jihadi groups you can be both at the same time. This is in contrast to the warrior culture of modern Western militaries, in which displays of emotion and interest in the arts are usually seen as feminine traits at odds with those of a true warrior. At a more general level, then, these observations tell us something about notions of masculinity in different cultures.

Fourth and finally, as Cook also noted in his chapter, jihadis appear to have been influenced to a surprising degree by Sufism, and the Sufi influence seems to have grown over time. Weeping and hymn singing, for example, were rare in the 1980s, but are common today. Jihadis seem to have compromised, consciously or not, on their Salafi principles, presumably because the imports carried benefits that out-weighed the cost of the doctrinal concession. This is, along with the sheer amount of time jihadis spend on non-military activities, perhaps the strongest indication that culture benefits their military struggle in some important way.

The precise ways jihadi culture helps the fight remain unclear and will require more research. The big causal questions about how jihadi culture affects individuals and groups and what shapes the culture of different groups are beyond the scope of this chapter and indeed of the book as a whole. As noted in the introduction, the purpose of this book was to survey the jihadi cultural universe and provide a starting point for more research into the cultures of rebel groups. We hope we have succeeded in describing the broad features of the phenomenon and in inspiring others to explore this rich topic further. The Introduction sketched out three possible lines of future inquiry: more description of militant cultures (what they consist of), research into culture as a dependent variable (what shapes culture), and research into culture as an independent variable (what culture does). It also proposed some hypotheses about how cultural practices might affect behavior: for example, that they trigger emotions that strengthen recruits' commit-ment to the cause or that they serve as a resource for costly signalling. In addition, the various chapters in the book have offered a range of observations and ideas pertaining to specific elements of jihadi culture. We trust that future thinkers will build on these insights and find new and creative ways to address the puzzles of jihadi culture.

Most of all, we hope that the book will spark reflection on larger questions about how humans engage with each other and the world. The study of militant cultures may have some practical value for counterterrorism and the like, but it is first of all an investigation into some of the most mysterious dimensions of human existence. Why do we like music so much? What are dreams for? Why do we laugh and why do we weep? Why is religion so important to us? To rewrite Bill Shankly's famous quote about football: the study of culture is not about life and death; it is much more important than that.[116]

Bibliography

Ahmed, Khalid. "TV Review." *Daily Times*, May 23, 2005.

Alagha, Joseph. "G. Banna's and A. Fadlallah's Views on Dancing." *Sociology of Islam* 2, no. 1–2 (November 21, 2014): 60–86.

"Jihad through 'Music': The Taliban and Hizbullah." *Performing Islam* 1, no. 2 (2013): 263–289.

al-Albani, Muhammad Nasir al-Din. *Tahrim alat al-tarab [(Legal Rulings) Forbidding Musical Instruments]*. 2nd ed. al-Jubayl al-Sina'iyya, Saudi Arabia: Maktabat al-Dalil, 1997.

al-Amriiki, Abu Mansuur. "The Story of an American Jihaadi – Part One," 2012. https://azelin.files.wordpress.com/2012/05/omar-hammami-abc5ab-mane1b9a3c5abr-al-amrc4abkc4ab-22the-story-of-an-american-jihc481dc 4ab-part-122.pdf [Accessed October 31, 2015].

al-Awlaki, Anwar. "44 Ways to Support Jihad." *Authentic Tauheed*, January 2009. www.authentictauheed.com/2009/12/44-ways-of-supporting-jihad-imam-anwar.html [Accessed March 20, 2015].

Al 'Awshan, 'Isa. "*Risala ila al-la'imin*" [Epistle to the Scolders]. *Diwan al-'izza: majmu'at qasa'id hamasiyya fi'l-jihad*, n.d.

al-Bahri, Nasser, and Georges Malbrunot. *Dans l'ombre de Ben Laden: Révélations de son garde du corps repenti*. Paris: Michel Lafon, 2010.

al-Berry, Khaled. *Life Is More Beautiful than Paradise: A Jihadist's Own Story*. Cairo: American University in Cairo Press, 2009.

al-Bukhari. *Sahih*. Vol. 3. Beirut: Dar al-Fikr, 1991.

al-Bustani, Fouad Ephreim. *Al-shi'r al-jahili [Pre-Islamic Poetry]*. Beirut: al-Matba'a al-Kathulikiyya, 1967.

al Faruqi, Lois Ibsen. "Music, Musicians and Muslim Law." *Asian Music* 17, no. 1 (1985): 3–36.

Al-Ghazali. *Al-Sama' wa'l-wajd [Listening (to Music and Songs)]*. Translated by Anthony H. John, forthcoming.

Al-Harbee, Shaykh Abdullah Ateeq. "Glad Tidings to the Strangers (Ghur-aba)." *Islamic Treasure*. www.islamictreasure.com/788-glad-tidings-to-the-strangers-ghuraba/ [Accessed December 3, 2015].

al-Hindukushi, Abu al-Shaqra. "*Min Kabul ila Baghdad*" [From Kabul to Baghdad], 2007. http://archive.org/details/fromcaboltobagdad [Accessed November 2, 2012].

al Huneidi, Samar. "Prince of Poets Competitor Causes Stir." *The National*, January 26, 2011.

Ali, Ahmed. *Al-Qur'an: A Contemporary Translation*. Princeton: Princeton University Press, 1993.

al-Khalidi, Usama. "*Risalat shahid ila ummihi al-ghaliya*" [A Martyr's Letter to His Beloved Mother]. *Diwan al-'izza: majmu'at qasa'id hamasiyya fi'l-jihad*, n.d.

Allen, Emily. "Kosovan Shot Dead Two U.S. Airmen Because He Thought Facebook Clip of Movie Showing Muslim Woman Raped by American Soldiers Was Real." *Mail Online*, September 1, 2011. www.dailymail.co.uk/news/article-2032133/Frankfurt-Airport-shooting-Arid-Uki-shot-dead-2-US-airmen-seeing-Brian-De-Palma-clip.html.

al-Mihrawi, Wi'ab. *Al-wa'd al-sadiq [The True Promise]*. Beirut: Dar al-Qari, 2007.

al-Muhajira, Umm Sumayyah. "The Twin Halves of the Muhajirun." *Dabiq*, no. 8 (March 2015): 32–37.

al-Muttaqi, al-Hindi. *Kanz al-'ummal [Treasury of Rulers]*. Vol. iv. Beirut: Mu'assasat al-Risala, 1987.

al-Nasr, Ahlam. *Akhiran rabbuna kataba al-samaha [At Last Our Lord Has Decreed (the Caliphate) Permissible]*. al-Ghuraba' li-l-I'lam, 2014.
 Uwar al-haqq [The Blaze of Truth]. Fursan al-Balagh li-l-I'lam, 2014.
 Bal ata'na Allah idh ahraqnahu ya 'abid al-rafahiyya [We Have Obeyed God by Burning Him, Oh Slaves of Luxury]. al-Ghuraba' li-l-I'lam, 2015.

al-Qa'idi, Abu Amru. "A Course in the Art of Recruiting," revised 2010. http://archive.org/stream/ACourseInTheArtOfRecruiting-RevisedJuly2010/A_Course_in_the_Art_of_Recruiting_-_Revised_July2010_djvu.txt [Accessed June 17, 2016].

al-Qandahari, Abu Ja'far al-Misri. *Dhikrayat 'arabi afghani [Memoirs of an Afghan Arab]*. Cairo: Dar al-Shuruq, 2002.

al-Rahman, Mustafa 'Abd. *Anashid laha tarikh [Anashid with a History]*. Cairo: Dar al-Sha'b, 1974.

al-Raqab, Salah. *Al-shaykh al-shahid Ahmad Yasin: shahid al-fajr [The Martyr Shaykh Ahmad Yasin, the Dawn Martyr]*. Beirut: Dar Ru'ya, 2005.

Al-rumh al-thaqib li-jawaz qatl al-murtadd min al-aqarib [The Piercing Spear Allowing the Killing of the Apostate Relative], n.d. http://justpaste.it/mf99 [Accessed December 1, 2015].

Al Salman, Shaykh Abu 'Ubaydah Mashhur bin Hasan, and Shaykh Abu Talhah 'Umar bin Ibraheem Al 'AbdurRahman, *Introductory Salafi*

Themes in the Interpretation of Visions and Dreams, e-book (Salafi Manhaj, 2009), http://download.salafimanhaj.com/pdf/SalafiManhaj_ Dreams.pdf [Accessed February 16, 2017].

Alshaer, Atef. "The Poetry of Hamas." *Middle East Journal of Culture and Communication* 2, no. 2 (2009): 214–230.

"The Poetry of Hezbollah." In *The Hizbullah Phenomenon: Politics and Communication*, edited by Lina Khatib, Dina Matar, and Atef Alshaer, 119–152. New York: Oxford University Press, 2014.

al-Shafi'i, Muhammad. "*Jadal bayna al-usuliyyin hawla istikhdam ashritat 'al-hur al-'ayn' li-tajnid muqatilin li-l-qa'ida'*"[Debates between Fundamentalists Concerning the Use of [anashid] Tapes about Damsels to Recruit Fighters for Al-Qaida]. *Al-Sharq Al-Awsat*, September 27, 2003.

Al-Tamimi, Aymenn Jawad. "'The Cheers Surge' – Nasheed Plagiarised by The Islamic State [IS], n.d. www.aymennjawad.org/2014/11/the-cheers-surge-nasheed-plagiarised-by [Accessed February 2, 2016].

al-Tirmidhi. *Al-Jami' Al-Sahih*. Vol. 3. Beirut: Dar al-Fikr, n.d.

al-Wa'i, Tawfiq Yusuf. *Mawsu'at shuhada' al-haraka al-islamiyya [Encyclopaedia of the Martyrs of the Islamic Movement]*. Vol. 1. Cairo: Dar al-Tawzi' wa-l-Nashr al-Islamiyya, 2006.

Mawsu'at shuhada' al-haraka al-islamiyya [Encyclopaedia of the Martyrs of the Islamic Movement]. Vol. 5. Cairo: Dar al-Tawzi' wa-l-Nashr al-Islamiyya, 2006.

al-Zuhayri, Muhammad. "*Wa amatara al-ghaym al-dima*" *[The Clouds Have Rained Blood]*, n.d. https://archive.org/details/zhiri-0–001 [Accessed November 30, 2015].

'An African American Shaheed." *MyUmmah*, March 13, 2008. http:// myummah.co.za/site/2008/03/13/an-african-american-shaheed/ [Accessed December 31, 2016].

"Austrian Jihadist Poses in Front of Corpses." *The Local*, November 5, 2014. www.thelocal.at/20141105/austrian-jihadist-poses-in-front-of-corpses [Accessed February 16, 2017].

Awan, Akil N. "Virtual Jihadist Media Function, Legitimacy and Radicalizing Efficacy." *European Journal of Cultural Studies* 10, no. 3 (August 1, 2007): 389–408.

Azami, Dawood. "Kandahar's Cemetery of 'Miracles'." *BBC*, January 17, 2008. http://news.bbc.co.uk/2/hi/south_asia/7193579.stm [Accessed February 16, 2017].

Azzam, Shaykh Abdullah. *Ayat al-rahman fi jihad al-afghan [Signs of the Merciful in the Jihad of Afghanistan]*. Peshawar, Pakistan: Markaz al-Shahid Abdallah Azzam, 1990.

The Signs of Ar-Rahman in the Jihad of Afghanistan. Edited by A. B. al-Mehri. E-book. Birmingham, U.K.: Maktabah. https://islamfuture .files.wordpress.com/2009/11/signs-of-ar-rahman-in-jihad-of-afghanistan .pdf [Accessed February 22, 2016].

Azzam, Sheikh Abdullah. "Martyrs: The Building Blocks of Nations." *Religioscope*, n.d. www.religioscope.com/info/doc/jihad/azzam_martyrs .htm [Accessed May 11, 2011].

Bacharach, Michael, and Diego Gambetta. "Trust in Signs." In *Trust and Society*, edited by Karen S. Cook, 148–184. New York: Russell Sage Foundation, 2001.

Baily, John S. *Can You Stop the Birds Singing? The Censorship of Music in Afghanistan*. Copenhagen: Freemuse, 2003.

"Music and Censorship in Afghanistan, 1973–2003." In *Music and the Play of Power in the Middle East, North Africa and Central Asia*, edited by Laudan Nooshin, 143–163. Aldershot, U.K.: Ashgate Publishing, 2009.

Baines, Paul R., Nicholas J. O'Shaughnessy, Kevin Moloney, Barry Richards, Sara Butler, and Mark Gill. "Muslim Voices: The British Muslim Response to Islamic Video-Polemic – An Exploratory Study." Research Paper. Cranfield School of Management Research Paper Series. Bedford, U.K.: Cranfield School of Management, 2006.

"The Dark Side of Political Marketing: Islamist Propaganda, Reversal Theory and British Muslims." *European Journal of Marketing* 44, no. 3/4 (April 6, 2010): 478–495.

Balzani, Marzia. "Dreaming, Islam and the Ahmadiyya Muslims in the UK." *History and Anthropology* 21, no. 3 (September 1, 2010): 293–306.

Bartsch, Matthias, Matthias Gebauer, and Yassin Musharbash. "Facebook Jihad: The Radical Islamist Roots of the Frankfurt Attack." *Spiegel Online*, March 3, 2011.

Barzuq, Mukhlis Yahya. *Fada'il [Merits]*. London: Filistin al-Muslima, 2001.

Becker, Judith. *Deep Listeners: Music, Emotion, and Trancing*. Bloomington: Indiana University Press, 2004.

Becker, Olivia. "ISIS Has a Really Slick and Sophisticated Media Department." *VICE*, July 12, 2014.

Berg, Birgit. "Authentic Islamic Sound? Orkes Gambus Music, the Arab Idiom, and Sonic Symbols in Indonesian Islamic Musical Arts." In *Divine Inspirations: Music and Islam in Indonesia*, edited by David Harnish and Anne Rasmussen, 207–240. Oxford: Oxford University Press, 2011.

Blazak, Randy. "White Boys to Terrorist Men Target Recruitment of Nazi Skinheads." *American Behavioral Scientist* 44, no. 6 (February 1, 2001): 982–1000.

Blee, Kathleen M. *Inside Organized Racism: Women in the Hate Movement.* Berkeley: University of California Press, 2003.

Bodansky, Yossef. *Chechen Jihad: Al Qaeda's Training Ground and the Next Wave of Terror.* New York: Harper, 2007.

Bohn, Thomas W. *An Historical and Descriptive Analysis of the 'Why We Fight' Series: With a New Introduction.* New York: Arno Press, 1977.

Bolt, Neville. *The Violent Image: Insurgent Propaganda and the New Revolutionaries.* New York: Oxford University Press, 2012.

Bonney, Richard. *Jihad: From Qu'ran to Bin Laden.* Hampshire, U.K.: Palgrave Macmillan, 2004.

Boudali, Lianne Kennedy, Afshon Ostavar, and Jarret Brachman. *Islamic Imagery Project: Visual Motifs in Jihadi Internet Propaganda.* West Point, NY: Combating Terrorism Center, 2006.

Boyd, Douglas A. "Saudi Arabian Television." *Journal of Broadcasting* 15, no. 1 (December 1, 1970): 73–78.

Broughton, Simon. *Breaking the Silence: Music in Afghanistan.* Documentary, 2002. www.amazon.com/Breaking-Silence-Afghanistan-Simon-Broughton/dp/B002HMDEI4 [Accessed December 31, 2016].

Bunzel, Cole. "Bin'ali Leaks: Revelations of the Silent Mufti." *Jihadica.com.* www.jihadica.com/binali-leaks/ [Accessed June 15, 2015].

Burkhardt Qureshi, Regula. "Sounding the Word: Music in the Life of Islam." In *Enchanting Powers: Music in the World's Religions*, edited by Lawrence Eugene Sullivan, 263–298. Cambridge, MA: Harvard University Press, 1997.

Calvert, John C. "The Striving Shaykh: Abdullah Azzam and the Revival of Jihad." *Journal of Religion and Society*, Supplement series no. 2 (2007): 83–102.

Cantlie, John. "Are You Ready to Die?" *Sunday Times*, August 5, 2012.

Chelkowski, Peter, and Hamid Dabashi. *Staging a Revolution: The Art of Persuasion in the Islamic Republic of Iran.* New York: New York University Press, 1999.

Chesler, Phyllis. "Why Are Jihadis So Obsessed with Porn?" *New York Post*, February 17, 2015.

Cohen, Gili. "IDF Brigade Refuses to Let Soldier Read Poetry on the Radio So as Not to Ruin 'Fighter's Image'." *Haaretz.com*, June 18, 2013.

Collins, Aukai. *My Jihad: The True Story of an American Mujahid's Amazing Journey from Usama Bin Laden's Training Camps to Counterterrorism with the FBI and CIA.* Guilford, CT: Lyons Press, 2002.

Conway, Maura. "Terrorism and the Making of the 'New Middle East': New Media Strategies of Hezbollah and Al Qaeda." In *New Media and the New Middle East*, edited by Philip Seib, 235–258. Palgrave Macmillan

Series in International Political Communication. New York: Palgrave Macmillan US, 2007.

Conway, Maura, and Lisa McInerney. "Jihadi Video and Auto-Radicalisation: Evidence from an Exploratory YouTube Study." In *Intelligence and Security Informatics*, edited by Daniel Ortiz-Arroyo, Henrik Legind Larsen, Daniel Dajun Zeng, David Hicks, and Gerhard Wagner, 108–118. Lecture Notes in Computer Science 5376. Berlin: Springer, 2008.

Cook, David. "Suicide Attacks or 'Martyrdom Operations' in Contemporary Jihad Literature." *Nova Religio* 6, no. 1 (2002): 7–44.

   Martyrdom in Islam. Cambridge: Cambridge University Press, 2007.

Cozzens, Jeffrey. "The Culture of Global Jihad: Character, Future Challenges and Recommendations." Future Action Series. London: International Centre for the Study of Radicalization, October 2008.

Crone, Manni. "Religion and Violence: Governing Muslim Militancy through Aesthetic Assemblages." *Millennium – Journal of International Studies* 43, no. 1 (2014): 291–307.

Dajani-Shakeel, Hadia. "Jihād in Twelfth-Century Arabic Poetry: A Moral and Religious Force to Counter the Crusades." *The Muslim World* 66, no. 2 (April 1, 1976): 96–113.

Dam Press. "Details of the Death of Muhammad Qanita …" *Dam Press*. www.dampress.net/index.php?page=show_det&category_id=7&id=24552 [Accessed December 29, 2012].

Dantschke, Claudia. "'Pop-Jihad': History and Structure of Salafism and Jihadism in Germany." Working Paper. Berlin: Institute for the Study of Radical Movements, n.d. www.istramo.com/index.php/publications/working-paper-series [Accessed June 29, 2014].

Dauber, Cori E., and Mark Robinson. "GUEST POST: ISIS and the Hollywood Visual Style." *Jihadology.net*. http://jihadology.net/2015/07/06/guest-post-isis-and-the-hollywood-visual-style/ [Accessed July 6, 2015].

Dawlat al-'Iraq al-Islamiyya [Islamic State of Iraq]. "Al-i'lan 'an insha' Mu'assasat al-furqan li-l-intaj al-i'lami" [A Statement Announcing the Founding of the Furqan Foundation]. Ana Muslim, October 31, 2006. www.muslm.org/vb/showthread.php?184654 [Accessed March 7, 2016].

DeNora, Tia. *Music in Everyday Life*. Cambridge: Cambridge University Press, 2000.

'Diwan al-'izza: majmu'at qasa'id hamasiyya fi'l-jihad" [The Anthology of Glory: A Compilation of Zealous Poems about Armed Struggle]. *Sawt Al-Jihad [Voice of Jihad]*, n.d. www.slideshare.net/AladeebShaker/ss-28041859 [Accessed July 20, 2015].

Donahue, Katherine C. *Slave of Allah: Zacarias Moussaoui vs. the USA.* London: Pluto Press, 2007.

Duw'ar, Ghassan. *Salah shihata: amir al-shuhada' [Salih Shihata: The Commander of Martyrs].* Beirut: Dar Ruy'a, 2005.

Edgar, Iain. "The 'True Dream' in Contemporary Islamic/Jihadist Dream-work: A Case Study of the Dreams of Taliban Leader Mullah Omar." *Contemporary South Asia* 15, no. 3 (2006): 263–272.

    "The Inspirational Night Dream in the Motivation and Justification of Jihad." *Nova Religio* 11, no. 2 (2007): 59–76.

    "A Comparison of Islamic and Western Psychological Dream Theories." In *Dreaming in Christianity and Islam Culture, Conflict, and Creativity*, edited by Kelly Bulkeley, Kate Adams, and Patricia M Davis, 188–199. New Brunswick, NJ: Rutgers University Press, 2009.

    The Dream in Islam: From Qur'anic Tradition to Jihadist Inspiration. New York: Berghahn Books, 2011.

    "The Dreams of Islamic State." *Perspectives on Terrorism* 9, no. 4 (July 31, 2015): 72–84.

Edgar, Iain, and David Henig. "Istikhara: The Guidance and Practice of Islamic Dream Incubation through Ethnographic Comparison." *History and Anthropology* 21, no. 3 (2010): 251–262.

Edgar, Iain R. *The Dream in Islam: From Qur'anic Tradition to Jihadist Inspiration.* New York: Berghahn Books, 2011.

Edwards, David B. "Images from Another War in Afghanistan." *Nieman Reports* 55, Winter 2001.

El Almani, Abdul Ghaffar. "Mein Weg nach Jannah." 2010. www.scribd.com/doc/31071994/Schaheed-Abdul-Ghaffar-al-Almani-Mein-Weg-Nach-Jannah [Accessed November 20, 2012].

El Difraoui, Abdelasiem. *Al-Qaida par l'image: la prophétie du martyre.* Paris: Presses Universitaires de France, 2013.

El Difraoui, Asiem. "Al Qaida par l'image ou la prophétie du martyre. Une analyse politique de la propagande audiovisuelle du jihad global." Ph.D. dissertation, Sciences Po, 2010.

Elefheriou-Smith, Loulla-Mae. "Escaped Isis Wives Describe Life in the Punishing All-Female Al-Khansa Brigade Who Punish Women with 40 Lashes for Wearing Wrong Clothes." *The Independent*, September 23, 2015.

Ellis, Robert. *The Games People Play: Theology, Religion, and Sport.* Cambridge: Lutterworth Press, 2014.

Elster, Jon. "Motivations and Beliefs in Suicide Missions." In *Making Sense of Suicide Missions*, edited by Diego Gambetta, 233–258. Oxford: Oxford University Press, 2005.

Epstein, Dena J. *Sinful Tunes and Spirituals: Black Folk Music to the Civil War*. Urbana: University of Illinois Press, 2003.

Fakhry, Majid. *The Qur'an: A Modern English Translation*. London: Garnet, 1997.

Falkoff, Marc. *Poems from Guantanamo: The Detainees Speak*. Iowa City: University of Iowa Press, 2007.

Fallows, James. "Who Shot Mohammed Al-Dura?" *The Atlantic*, June 2003.

Farmer, Henry G. "Ghina." In *Encyclopedia of Islam*, 2nd ed. Brill Online, n.d.

  "Music." In *The Legacy of Islam*, edited by Sir Thomas Arnold and Alfred Guillaume. Oxford: Clarendon Press, 1931.

Farmer, Henry George. *A History of Arabian Music to the XIIIth Century*. London: Luzac, 1929.

Farwell, James P. "Jihadi Video in the 'War of Ideas.'" *Survival* 52 (2010): 127–150.

  "Jihadi Video in the 'War of Ideas.'" *Survival* 52, no. 6 (December 1, 2010): 127–150.

Fielding, Raymond. *The American Newsreel, 1911–1967*. Norman: University of Oklahoma Press, 1972.

Finsnes, Cecilie. "What Is Audio-Visual Jihadi Propaganda? An Overview of the Content of FFI's Jihadi Video Database." Norwegian Defence Research Establishment (FFI), March 20, 2010. www.ffi.no/no/Rappor ter/10-00960.pdf [Accessed 16 February 2017].

Fisk, Robert. *The Great War for Civilization: The Conquest of the Middle East*. London: Fourth Estate, 2005.

Flade, Florian. "The Double Life of Arid U., The Frankfurt Airport Gunman." *Worldcrunch*, March 4, 2011. www.worldcrunch .com/double-life-arid-u-frankfurt-airport-gunman/world-affairs/the-double-life-of-arid-u.-the-frankfurt-airport-gunman/c1s2613/ [Accessed March 14, 2011].

Fouda, Yosri, and Nick Fielding. *Masterminds of Terror: The Truth behind the Most Devastating Terrorist Attack the World Has Ever Seen*. London: Mainstream Publishing, 2003.

Fowler, Robert. *A Season in Hell: My 130 Days in the Sahara with Al Qaeda*. Toronto: HarperCollins, 2011.

Fujii, Lee Ann. "The Puzzle of Extra-Lethal Violence." *Perspectives on Politics* 11, no. 2 (2013): 410–426.

Galanter, Marc, and James J. F. Forest. "Cults, Charismatic Groups, and Social Systems: Understanding the Transformation of Terrorist Recruits." In *The Making of a Terrorist*, edited by James J. F. Forest, 2: 51–70. Westport, CT: Praeger, 2005.

Gambetta, Diego. "Deceptive Mimicry in Humans." In *Perspectives on Imitation: From Neuroscience to Social Science*, edited by Susan Hurley and Nick Chater, 221–241. Cambridge, MA: MIT Press, 2005.

Making Sense of Suicide Missions. Oxford: Oxford University Press, 2005.

Codes of the Underworld: How Criminals Communicate. Princeton: Princeton University Press, 2009.

Ganor, Boaz, Katharina Von Knop, and Carlos Duarte. *Hypermedia Seduction for Terrorist Recruiting*. Vol. 25, NATO Science for Peace and Security Series: Human and Societal Dynamics. Washington, DC: IOS Press, 2007.

Gattinara, Pietro Castelli, and Caterina Froio. "Discourse and Practice of Violence in the Italian Extreme Right: Frames, Symbols, and Identity-Building in CasaPound Italia." *International Journal of Conflict and Violence (IJCV)* 8, no. 1 (April 16, 2014): 154–170.

Gauvain, Richard. "Ritual Weapons: Islamist Purity Practices in Cairo." *ISIM Review* 19 (2007): 40–41.

Gerecht, Reuel Marc. "The Counterterrorist Myth." *The Atlantic*, August 2001.

Gilsenan, Michael. "Signs of Truth: Enchantment, Modernity and the Dreams of Peasant Women." *Journal of the Royal Anthropological Society* 6, no. 4 (2000): 597–615.

Glyn Williams, Brian. "Allah's Foot Soldiers: An Assessment of the Role of Foreign Fighters and Al-Qa'ida in the Chechen Insurgency." In *Ethno-Nationalism, Islam and the State in the Caucasus: Post-Soviet Disorder*, edited by Moshe Gammer, 156–178. London: Routledge, 2007.

Goldsworthy, Rupert. "Revolt into Style: Images of West German 'Terrorism' from 68–77." *Aftershock Magazine*, winter 2006. http://aftershock magazine.com/goldsworthy68.html [Accessed February 17, 2017].

Gruen, Madeleine. "Innovative Recruitment and Indoctrination Tactics by Extremists: Video Games, Hip Hop, and the World Wide Web." In *The Making of a Terrorist*, edited by James J. F. Forest, 1: 28–46. Westport, CT: Praeger, 2005.

Guendouz, Omar. *Les soldats perdus de l'Islam: les réseaux francais de Ben Laden*. Paris: Editions Ramsay, 2002.

Hafez, Mohammed M. "Martyrdom Mythology in Iraq: How Jihadists Frame Suicide Terrorism in Videos and Biographies." *Terrorism and Political Violence* 19, no. 1 (January 1, 2007): 95–115.

Halldén, Philip. "Jihad, retorik och poesi i digitaliseringens tidsålder: estetiska dimensioner i Al-Qa'idas kulturkamp." *Samlaren – Tidskrift För Litteraturvetenskaplig Forskning* 131 (2011): 330–352.

Hamori, Andras. *On the Art of Medieval Arabic Literature*. Princeton: Princeton University Press, 1974.

Haqqani, Husain. "The Ideologies of South Asian Jihadi Groups." Carnegie Endowment for International Peace, 2005. http://carnegieendowment .org/2005/04/13/ideologies-of-south-asian-jihadi-groups [Accessed February 17, 2017].

Harun, Fadil. *Al-harb 'ala al-Islam [The War against Islam]*. Vol. 2, 2009. www.ctc.usma.edu/v2/wp-content/uploads/2013/10/The-Story-of-Fazul-Harun-Part-2-O.pdf.

Hasim Kamali, Muhammad. "Muhammad Abu Zahra." In *Encyclopedia of Islam*, edited by Gudrun Krämer, Denis Matringe, John Nawas, and Everett Rowson, 3rd ed. Brill Online, n.d.

Hegghammer, Thomas. *Dokumantasjon om Al-Qaida: intervjuer, kommunikéer og andre primærkilder, 1990–2002 [Documentation on Al-Qaida: Interviews, Communiqués and Other Primary Sources, 1990–2002]*. Kjeller: Norwegian Defence Research Establishment (FFI), 2002.

Jihad in Saudi Arabia: Violence and Pan-Islamism since 1979. Cambridge: Cambridge University Press, 2010.

"The Recruiter's Dilemma: Signalling and Rebel Recruitment Tactics." *Journal of Peace Research* 50, no. 1 (2013): 3–16.

"Can You Trust Anyone on Jihadi Internet Forums?" In *Fight, Flight, Mimic: Identity Signalling in Armed Conflicts*, edited by Diego Gambetta. Oxford: Oxford University Press, forthcoming.

Hemmingsen, Ann-Sophie. "The Attractions of Jihadism: An Identity Approach to Three Danish Terrorism Cases and the Gallery of Characters around Them." Ph.D. dissertation, University of Copenhagen, 2010.

Herding, Maruta. *Inventing the Muslim Cool: Islamic Youth Culture in Western Europe*. Bielefeld: Transcript-Verlag, 2014.

Herr, Cheryl. "Terrorist Chic: Style and Domination in Contemporary Ireland." In *On Fashion*, edited by Shari Benstock and Suzanne Ferriss, 235–266. New Brunswick, NJ: Rutgers University Press, 1994.

Hillenbrand, Carol. "Jihad Poetry in the Age of the Crusades." In *Crusades Medieval Worlds in Conflict*, edited by Thomas F. Madden, James L. Naus, and Vincent Ryan, 9–24. Farnham: Ashgate, 2010.

Hinds, Martin. "The Banners and Battle Cries at Siffin." In *Studies in Early Islamic History* 4, 97–142. Princeton: Darwin Press, 1996.

Hizbullah: al-muqawama wa-l-tahrir [Hizbullah: Resistance and Liberation]. Vol. 2 and 3. Beirut: al-Safir, 2006.

Holtmann, Philipp. "Casting Supernatural Spells and Fostering Communitas: Abu Yahya Al-Libi's Qasida Poetry." In *Jihadism: Online Discourses and Representations*, edited by Rüdiger Lohlker, 103–120. Vienna: Vienna University Press, 2013.

"The Symbols of Online Jihad." In *Jihadism: Online Discourses and Representations*, edited by Rüdiger Lohlker, 9–64. Vienna: Vienna University Press, 2013.

Horowitz, Donald L. *The Deadly Ethnic Riot*. Berkeley: University of California Press, 2003.

Husain, Ed. *The Islamist: Why I Joined Radical Islam in Britain, What I Saw Inside and Why I Left*. London: Penguin, 2007.

'Interview of Ibrahim Sen, a Turkish National Detained in Guantanamo." *Vakit*, November 10, 2006.

Intifadat al-aqsa [The Al-Aqsa Infifada]. Vol. 6. Amman: Dar al-Jalil li-l-Nashr, 2003.

Jalali, Ali Ahmad, and Lester W. Grau. *Afghan Guerrilla Warfare: In the Words of the Mujahideen Fighters*. St. Paul, MN: MBI Publishing, 2001.

Janata, Petr. "The Neural Architecture of Music-Evoked Autobiographical Memories." *Cerebral Cortex* (January 1, 2009): 2579–2594.

Jarar, Husni. *Ma'an ila al-janna: Shahid al-fajr wa-saqr filistin [Together to Paradise: The Dawn Martyr and the Falcon of Palestine]*. Amman, 2004.

Jarar, Husni Afham, and Ahmad al-Jada, eds. *Anashid al-da'wa al-islamiyya [Anashid of the Islamic Dawa]*. Vol. 4. Amman: Dar al-Diya', 1990.

Johnston, Winifred Josephine. *Memo on the Movies; War Propaganda, 1914–1939*. Norman, OK: Cooperative Books, 1939.

Kathir, Ibn. *Tafsir Ibn Kathir*. Vol. 1. Beirut: Alam al-Kutub, n.d.

Kendall, Elisabeth. "Yemen's Al-Qa'ida and Poetry as a Weapon of Jihad." In *Twenty-First Century Jihad: Law, Society and Military Action*, edited by Elisabeth Kendall and Ewan Stein, 247–269. London: I. B. Tauris, 2015.

Khalili, Laleh. *Heroes and Martyrs of Palestine: The Politics of National Commemoration*. Cambridge: Cambridge University Press, 2007.

Kimmage, Daniel. "The Al-Qaeda Media Nexus: The Virtual Network behind the Global Message." Washington, DC: Radio Free Europe/Radio Liberty, 2008. http://docs.rferl.org/en-US/AQ_Media_Nexus.pdf [Accessed February 17, 2017].

Kimmage, Daniel, and Kathleen Ridolfo. "Iraqi Insurgent Media: The War of Images and Idea." *Central European Journal of International and Security Studies* 1, no. 2 (2007): 7–89.

Kinberg, Leah. "Interaction between This World and the Afterworld in Early Islamic Tradition." *Oriens* 29/30 (1986): 285–308.

"Literal Dreams and Prophetic 'Hadîts' in Classical Islam – A Comparison of Two Ways of Legitimation." *Der Islam* 70, no. 2 (1993): 279–300.

Kippenberg, Hans G. "Translation of the Spiritual Manual." In *9/11 Handbook*, edited by Hans G. Kippenberg and Tilman Seidensticker, 1–9. London and Oakville: Equinox Publishing, 2006.

Koet, Bart J. "Discussing Dreams in a Prison in Amsterdam." In *Dreaming in Christianity and Islam Culture, Conflict, and Creativity*, edited by Kelly Bulkeley, Kate Adams, and Patricia M. Davis, 226–235. New Brunswick, NJ: Rutgers University Press, 2009.

Kohlberg, Etan. "Bara'a in Shi'i Doctrine." *Jerusalem Studies in Arabic and Islam* 7 (1986): 139–175.

Kohlmann, Evan F. "Expert Report II: U.S. v. Amawi et al." Expert Report. New York: NEFA Foundation, January 2008.

"Inside As-Sahaab: The Story of Ali Al-Bahlul and the Evolution of Al-Qaida's Propaganda." New York: NEFA Foundation, December 2008.

Kreinath, Jens. "Virtual Encounters with Hızır and Other Muslim Saints: Dreaming and Healing at Local Pilgrimage Sites in Hatay, Turkey." *Anthropology of the Contemporary Middle East and Central Eurasia* 2, no. 1 (September 22, 2014): 25–66.

Kremer, William. "Is It Possible to Be a Millionaire Poet?" *BBC News*, May 31, 2014.

Lahoud, Nelly. *Jihadis' Path to Self-Destruction*. New York: Columbia University Press, 2010.

Beware of Imitators: Al-Qa'ida through the Lens of Its Confidential Secretary. West Point, NY: Combating Terrorism Center, 2012.

Lamoreaux, John C. *The Early Muslim Tradition of Dream Interpretation*. Albany: State University of New York Press, 2002.

Lane, Edward W. *Arabic-English Lexicon*. London: Williams & Norgate, n.d.

Lawrence, Bruce. *Messages to the World: The Statements of Osama Bin Laden*. London: Verso, 2005.

Leach, Edmund. *Political Systems of Highland Burma. A Study of Kachin Social Structure*. London: Bell, 1954.

Lemieux, Anthony, and Robert Nill. "The Role and Impact of Music in Promoting (and Countering) Violent Extremism." In *Countering Violent Extremism: Scientific Methods & Strategies*, edited by Laurie Fenstermacher and Todd Leventhal, 143–152. Wright-Patterson Air Force Base, OH: U.S. Air Force Research Laboratory, 2011.

Levin, Jack, and Jack Mcdevitt. *Hate Crimes Revisited: America's War on Those Who Are Different*. Boulder: Basic Books, 2002.

Li, Daryl. "Taking the Place of Martyrs: Afghans and Arabs under the Banner of Islam." *Arab Studies Journal* 20, no. 1 (2012): 12–39.

Lincoln, Bruce. *Holy Terrors: Thinking about Religion after September 11*. 2nd ed. Chicago: University of Chicago Press, 2006.

Lines, Andy. "Sick Videotape Proves Bin Laden Was the Evil Mastermind behind the Horrors of Sept 11." *The Mirror*. December 14, 2001.

Linschoten, Alex Strick van, and Felix Kuehn, eds. *Poetry of the Taliban*. London: Hurst, 2012.

Lofland, John, and Rodney Stark. "Becoming a World-Saver: A Theory of Conversion to a Deviant Perspective." *American Sociological Review* 30, no. 6 (1965): 862–875.

Lohlker, Rüdiger. *Jihadism: Online Discourses and Representations*. Vienna: V&R Unipress, 2013.

Maasri, Zeina. *Off the Wall: Political Posters of the Lebanese Civil War*. London and New York: I. B. Tauris, 2009.

Maja, Ibn. *Sunan*. Vol. 2. Beirut: Dar al-Fikr, 1988.

Mampilly, Zachariah Cherian. *Rebel Rulers: Insurgent Governance and Civilian Life during War*. Ithaca, NY: Cornell University Press, 2011.

Manzur, Ibn. "*Lisan al-'arab [The Tongue/Language of the Arabs]*." edited by Amin Muhammad 'Abd al-Wahhab and Muhammad al-Sadiq al-'Abidi, Vol. 4. Beirut: Dar Ihya' al-Turath al-'Arabi, 1999.

Matusky, Patricia, and Sooi Beng Tan. *The Music of Malaysia: The Classical, Folk and Syncretic Traditions*. Burlington, VT: Routledge, 2004.

Maynard, Richard A., ed. *Propaganda on Film: A Nation at War*. Rochelle Park, NJ: Hayden Book Co., 1975.

McCants, William. "Black Flag." *Foreign Policy*, November 7, 2011.

  The ISIS Apocalypse: The History, Strategy, and Doomsday Vision of the Islamic State. New York: St. Martin's Press, 2015.

Mekhennet, Souad. "Austrian Mohamed Mahmoud Returns to Online Jihad." *New York Times*, November 15, 2011.

Mitchell, Richard P. *The Society of the Muslim Brothers*. London: Oxford University Press, 1969.

Mittermaier, Amira. *Dreams That Matter Egyptian Landscapes of the Imagination*. Berkeley: University of California Press, 2010.

Moghadam, Assaf. "Motives for Martyrdom: Al-Qaida, Salafi Jihad, and the Spread of Suicide Attacks." *International Security* 33, no. 3 (winter 2008/2009): 46–78.

Mulder, Dirk Cornelis. "The Ritual of Recitation of the Qur'an." *Nederlands Theologisch Tijdschrift* 37, no. 3 (1983): 247–252.

Nasiri, Omar. *Inside the Jihad: My Life with Al-Qaeda*. Cambridge, MA: Perseus, 2006.

Nasr, Seyyed Hossein. "Islam and Music: The Legal and Spiritual Dimensions." In *Enchanting Powers: Music in the World's Religions*, edited by

Lawrence Eugene Sullivan, 219–235. Cambridge, MA: Harvard University Press, 1997.

'Nigeria UN Bomb: Video of 'Boko Haram Bomber' Released." *BBC News*, September 18, 2011. www.bbc.com/news/world-africa-14964554 [Accessed February 22, 2017].

O'Donnell, James J., trans. *The Confessions of Augustine (electronic Edition)*. Oxford: Oxford University Press, 1992. www.stoa.org/hippo/.

Ostovar, Afshon. *Vanguard of the Imam: Religion, Politics, and Iran's Revolutionary Guards*. Oxford: Oxford University Press, 2016.

Ostovar, Afshon, Jarret Brachman, and Lianne Kennedy Boudali. "The Islamic Imagery Project: Visual Motifs in Jihadi Internet Propaganda." Combating Terrorism Center, 2006. www.au.af.mil/au/awc/awcgate/usma/ctc_islamic_imagery_project.pdf [Accessed 16 February 2017].

Otterbeck, Jonas. "Battling over the Public Sphere: Islamic Reactions to the Music of Today." *Contemporary Islam* 2, no. 3 (November 1, 2008): 211–228.

Patel, Aniruddh H. *Music, Language, and the Brain*. Oxford: Oxford University Press, 2010.

Pelevin, Mikhail, and Matthias Weinreich. "The Songs of the Taliban: Continuity of Form and Thought in an Ever-Changing Environment." *Iran and the Caucasus* 16 (2012): 79–109.

Peskes, Esther, and Werner Ende. "Wahhābiyya." In *Encyclopedia of Islam*, edited by P. Bearman, Th. Bianquis, C. E. Bosworth, E. van Donzel, and W. P. Heinrichs, 2nd ed. Brill Online, n.d.

Petersen, Roger Dale. *Understanding Ethnic Violence: Fear, Hatred, and Resentment in Twentieth-Century Eastern Europe*. Cambridge: Cambridge University Press, 2002.

Petersen, Roger Dale, and Sarah Zukerman Daly. "Revenge or Reconciliation: Theory and Method of Emotions in the Context of Colombia's Peace Process." In *Law in Peace Negotiations*, edited by Morten Bergsmo and Pablo Kalmanovitz. Oslo: Torkel Opsahl Academic Publisher, 2010.

Philby, H. St. John. *Saudi Arabia*. London: Ernest Benn, 1955.

Philips, Abu Ameenah Bilaal. *Dream Interpretation: According to the Qur'an and Sunnah*. Kuala Lumpur: A. S. Noordeen, 2001.

Pieslak, Jonathan. *Sound Targets: American Soldiers and Music in the Iraq War*. Bloomington: Indiana University Press, 2009.

Sound Targets: American Soldiers and Music in the Iraq War. Bloomington: Indiana University Press, 2009.

Plantinga, Carl, and Greg M. Smith, eds. *Passionate Views: Film, Cognition, and Emotion*. Baltimore: Johns Hopkins University Press, 1999.

Plato. "The Republic." In *Plato: Complete Works*, edited by John M. Cooper and D. S. Hutchinson. Indianapolis: Hacket, 1997.

Plett, Barbara. "Jihadis Tap Anti-Musharraf Feeling." *BBC News Online*. July 14, 2007.

Prince, Rosa, and Gary Jones. "My Hell in Camp X-Ray." *The Mirror*. March 12, 2004.

Qabbani, Nizar. "Dafatir 'ala Hawamish Al-Naksa" [Notes on the Margins of Al-Naksa (The Day of Naksa Is in Reference to the Six-Day-War)]. In *Al-a'mal al-siyasiyya al-kamila [Complete Poetic Works]*, 4th ed. Vol. 3. Beirut: Manshurat Nizar Qabbani, 1986.

Qutayba, Ibn. *Ta'bir al-ru'ya [Interpretation of Dreams]*. Damascus: Dar al-Basha'ir, 2001.

Qutb, Sayyid. "*Al-firqa al-qawmiyya fi 'ahdiha al-jadid*" [The Nationalist Group in Its New Era]. In *Sayyid Qutb: al-mujtama' al-misri: judhuruhu wa-afaquhu [Sayyid Qutb: Egyptian Society, Its Roots and Horizons]*, edited by Alan Rossignon. Cairo: Sina li-al-Nashr, 1994.

Racy, A. J. *Making Music in the Arab World: The Culture and Artistry of Tarab*. Cambridge: Cambridge University Press, 2004.

Ramsay, Gilbert. *Jihadi Culture on the World Wide Web*. New York: Bloomsbury Academic, 2013.

Reed, Thomas Vernon. *The Art of Protest: Culture and Activism from the Civil Rights Movement to the Streets of Seattle*. Minneapolis: University of Minnesota Press, 2005.

Reid, Tim. "'Shoe-Bomber' Likely to Be Jailed for Life." *The Times*. January 30, 2003.

'Released from Prison, 'Apologetic Bandit' Writes about Life Inside." *NPR.org*, March 18, 2015.

Reuters. "Assad's Forces Seize Homs District from Rebels: Activists." *Chicago Tribune*, December 29, 2012, online edition.

Robson, James. *Tracts on Listening to Music. Being Dhamm Al-Malahi by Ibn Abi 'L-Dunya and Bawariq Al-Ila by Majd Ad-Din Al-Tusi Al-Ghazali*. London: Royal Asiatic Society, 1938.

Roggio, Bill. "US Targets Al Qaeda's Al Furqan Media Wing in Iraq." *The Long War Journal*, October 28, 2007. www.longwarjournal .org/archives/2007/10/us_targets_al_qaedas.php [Accessed February 16, 2017].

   "Shabaab Kills American Jihadist Omar Hammami and British Fighter." *The Long War Journal*, September 12, 2013. www.longwarjournal .org/archives/2013/09/shabaab_kills_americ.php [Accessed February 16, 2017].

Rohde, David, and C. J. Chivers. "A NATION CHALLENGED: Qaeda's Grocery Lists and Manuals of Killing." *The New York Times*,

March 17, 2002. Rose, Steve. "The Isis Propaganda War: A Hi-Tech Media Jihad." *The Guardian*, October 7, 2014.

Rosenau, William. "'Our Backs Are against the Wall': The Black Liberation Army and Domestic Terrorism in 1970s America." *Studies in Conflict & Terrorism* 36, no. 2 (February 2013): 176–192.

Rustomji, Nerina. *The Garden and the Fire: Heaven and Hell in Islamic Culture*. New York: Columbia University Press, 2009.

Sabbagh-Gargour, Rana. "My Marriage Was a Sham, Says Wife in Jordan Bomb Team." *The Times*, April 24, 2006.

Sa'd al-Azdi, Abu. "Ismitu fa'l-kalam li'l-abtal" [Silence! Words Are for Heroes]. *Diwan al-'izza: majmu'at qasa'id hamasiyya fi'l-jihad*, n.d. https://archive.org/details/ozaaloza_gmail_20140216 [Accessed February 22, 2017].

Sageman, Marc. *Understanding Terror Networks*. Philadelphia: University of Pennsylvania Press, 2004.

Leaderless Jihad: Terror Networks in the Twenty-First Century. Philadelphia: University of Pennsylvania Press, 2008.

"The Turn to Political Violence in the West." In *Jihadi Terrorism and the Radicalization Challenge*, edited by Rik Coolsaet, 2nd ed., 117–130. Farnham: Ashgate, 2011.

Said, Behnam. "Hymns (Nasheeds): A Contribution to the Study of the Jihadist Culture." *Studies in Conflict and Terrorism* 35, no. 12 (2012): 863–879.

Salem, Arab, Edna Reid, and Hsinchun Chen. "Multimedia Content Coding and Analysis: Unraveling the Content of Jihadi Extremist Groups' Videos." *Studies in Conflict & Terrorism* 31, no. 7 (June 24, 2008): 605–626.

Sarkissian, Margaret. "'Religion Never Had It So Good': Contemporary Nasyid and the Growth of Islamic Popular Music in Malaysia." *Yearbook for Traditional Music* 37 (2005): 124–152. See www.jstor.org/stable/20464933?seq=1#page_scan_tab_contents [Accessed February 22, 2017].

Sayigh, Yezid. *Armed Struggle and the Search for State: The Palestinian National Movement, 1949–1993*. New York: Oxford University Press, 1997.

Schucker, Werner. "The Testaments of Iranian Martyrs." In *Jihad and Martyrdom*, edited by David Cook. London: Routledge, 2010.

Seidensticker, Tilman. "Jihad Hymns (Nashīds) as a Means of Self-Motivation in the Hamburg Group." In *9/11 Handbook*, edited by Hans G. Kippenberg and Tilamn Seidensticker, 71–78. London and Oakville: Equinox Publishing, 2006.

Seidensticker, Tilman, Albrecht Fuess, Moez Khalfaoui, and Hans G. Kippenberg. "Translation of the Spiritual Manual." In *9/11 Handbook*, edited by Hans G. Kippenberg and Tilman Seidensticker. London and Oakville: Equinox Publishing, 2006.

Shekhovtsov, Anton. "European Far-Right Music and Its Enemies." In *Analysing Fascist Discourse: European Fascism in Talk and Text*, edited by Ruth Richardson and John E. Wodak, 277–296. London: Routledge, 2012.

Shiloah, Amnon. "Nashid." In *Encyclopedia of Islam*. 2nd ed. Brill Online, n.d.

    Music in the World of Islam: A Socio-Cultural Study. Detroit: Wayne State University Press, 1995.

    "Music and Religion in Islam." *Acta Musicologica* 69, no. 2 (1997): 143–155.

Sifaoui, Mohamed. *Inside Al-Qaeda: How I Infiltrated the World's Deadliest Terrorist Organization*. London: Granta Books, 2003.

Sirriyeh, Elizabeth. "Dream Narratives of Muslims' Martyrdom: Constant and Changing Roles Past and Present." *Dreaming* 21, no. 3 (2011): 168–180.

Skjoldager, Morten. *Truslen indefra: de danske terrorister*. Copenhagen: Lindhart og Ringhof, 2009.

Smith, Greg M. *Film Structure and the Emotion System*. Cambridge: Cambridge University Press, 2003.

Snoek, Jan A. M. "Defining 'Rituals'." In *Theorizing Rituals: Issues, Topics, Approaches, Concepts*, edited by Jens Kreinath, Jan Snoek, and Michael Stausberg, 3–14. Leiden: Brill, 2006.

Soriano, Manuel R. Torres. "The Road to Media Jihad: The Propaganda Actions of Al Qaeda in the Islamic Maghreb." *Terrorism and Political Violence* 23, no. 1 (December 7, 2010): 72–88.

Staniland, Paul. *Networks of Rebellion: Explaining Insurgent Cohesion and Collapse*. Ithaca, NY: Cornell University Press, 2014.

Stark, Rodney, and William Sims Bainbridge. "Networks of Faith: Interpersonal Bonds and Recruitment to Cults and Sects." *American Journal of Sociology* 85, no. 6 (1980): 1376–1395.

Stern, Jessica. "Pakistan's Jihad Culture." *Foreign Affairs* 79, no. 6 (2000): 115–126.

Sternberg, Robert J., and Karin Sternberg. *The Nature of Hate*. New York: Cambridge University Press, 2008.

'Suicide Bomber Injures Two in Saudi Capital." *Al Jazeera*, July 17, 2015.

Taarnby, Michael, and Lars Hallundbæk. "Fatah Al-Islam: Anthropological Perspectives on Jihadi Culture." Real Instituto Elcano Working Paper. Madrid: Real Instituto Elcano, 2008.

Tan, Ed S. *Emotion and the Structure of Narrative Film: Film as an Emotion Machine*. Mahwah, NJ: Lawrence Erlbaum, 1996.

Tankel, Stephen. *Storming the World Stage: The Story of Lashkar-E-Taiba*. New York: Columbia University Press, 2011.

"Tawhid and Our Duty to Our Parents." *Dabiq* 10 (July 2015): 14–17.

Thomas, T. L. "Manipulating the Mass Consciousness: Russian & Chechen 'Information War' Tactics in the Second Chechen-Russian Conflict." In *The Second Chechen War*, edited by A. C. Aldis, 112–129. Washington, DC: Conflict Studies Research Center, 2000.

Toufic, Fahd. *Artemidorus: le livre des songes*. Damascus: Institut Français de Damas, 1964.

Touma, Habib Hassan. *The Music of the Arabs*. Portland: Amadeus Press, 1996.

Trimingham, J. Spencer. *The Sufi Orders in Islam*. London: Oxford University Press, 1971.

Unknown. "Tarikh al-ma'sada" [The History of al-Ma'sada]. CTC Library, n.d.

Uthaymin, Ibn. *Fatawa al-'ulama hawla hukm al-anashid [The Legal Opinions of Scholars Concerning Anashid]*, n.d.

Vergani, Matteo, and Dennis Zuev. "Neojihadist Visual Politics: Comparing YouTube Videos of North Caucasus and Uyghur Militants." *Asian Studies Review* 39, no. 1 (January 2015): 1–22.

Weimann, Gabriel. "Terrorist Dot Com: Using the Internet for Terrorist Recruitment and Mobilization." In *The Making of a Terrorist*, edited by James J. F. Forest, 1: 53–65. Westport, CT: Praeger, 2005.

Weisburd, A. Aaron. "Comparison of Visual Motifs in Jihadi and Cholo Videos on YouTube." *Studies in Conflict & Terrorism* 32, no. 12 (November 2009): 1066–1074.

Wensinck, A. J. *Concordance et indices de la tradition musulmane*. Leyden: E. J. Brill, 1936.

Williams, Brian Glyn. *Afghanistan Declassified: A Guide to America's Longest War*. Philadelphia: University of Pennsylvania Press, 2011.

Williams, Jennifer R. "The Bureaucracy of Terror: New Secret Documents Reveal Al Qaeda's Real Challenges." *Foreign Affairs*, March 25, 2015.

Winkler, Carol K., and Cori E. Dauber, eds. *Visual Propaganda and Extremism in the Online Environment*. Carlisle: Strategic Studies Institute, 2014.

Winter, Charlie. "The Virtual 'Caliphate': Understanding Islamic State's Propaganda Strategy." London: Quilliam Foundation, July 2015.

Wood, Elisabeth J. "The Emotional Benefits of Insurgency in El Salvador." In *Passionate Politics. Emotions and Social Movements*, edited by Jeff

Goodwin, James M. Jasper, and Francesca Polletta, 267–81. Chicago: University of Chicago Press, 2001.

'Yemeni Woman's Life Gives Rare Look into Al Qaida Network." *Gulf News (online)*, February 27, 2014.

Zelin, Aaron Y. "Picture or It Didn't Happen: A Snapshot of the Islamic State's Official Media Output." *Perspectives on Terrorism* 9, no. 4 (August 21, 2015): 85–97.

Notes

Introduction

1 See, for example, Jonathan Pieslak, *Sound Targets: American Soldiers and Music in the Iraq War* (Bloomington: Indiana University Press, 2009); Iain R. Edgar, *The Dream in Islam: From Qur'anic Tradition to Jihadist Inspiration* (New York: Berghahn Books, 2011); Lianne Kennedy Boudali, Afshon Ostavar, and Jarret Brachman, *Islamic Imagery Project: Visual Motifs in Jihadi Internet Propaganda* (West Point, NY: Combating Terrorism Center, 2006).

2 Elisabeth Kendall, "Yemen's Al-Qa'ida & Poetry as a Weapon of Jihad," in *Twenty-First Century Jihad: Law, Society and Military Action*, ed. Elisabeth Kendall and Ewan Stein (London: I. B. Tauris, 2015), 247–269; Philipp Holtmann, "Casting Supernatural Spells and Fostering Communitas: Abu Yahya Al-Libi's Qasida Poetry," in *Jihadism: Online Discourses and Representations*, ed. Rüdiger Lohlker (Vienna: Vienna University Press, 2013), 103–120; Behnam Said, "Hymns (Nasheeds): A Contribution to the Study of the Jihadist Culture," *Studies in Conflict and Terrorism* 35, no. 12 (2012): 863–879; Anthony Lemieux and Robert Nill, "The Role and Impact of Music in Promoting (and Countering) Violent Extremism," in *Countering Violent Extremism: Scientific Methods & Strategies*, ed. Laurie Fenstermacher and Todd Leventhal (Wright-Patterson Air Force Base, OH: U.S. Air Force Research Laboratory, 2011), 143–152; Philipp Holtmann, "The Symbols of Online Jihad," in *Jihadism: Online Discourses and Representations*, ed. Rüdiger Lohlker (Vienna: Vienna University Press, 2013), 9–64; A. Aaron Weisburd, "Comparison of Visual Motifs in Jihadi and Cholo Videos on YouTube," *Studies in Conflict & Terrorism* 32, no. 12 (November 30, 2009): 1066–1074; James P. Farwell, "Jihadi Video in the 'War of Ideas,'" *Survival* 52 (2010): 127–150; Abdelasiem El Difraoui, *Al-Qaida par l'Image: La Prophétie du Martyre* (Paris: Presses Universitaires de France, 2013).

3 Joseph Alagha, "Jihad through 'Music': The Taliban and Hizbullah," *Performing Islam* 1, no. 2 (2013): 263–289; Joseph Alagha, "G. Banna's and A. Fadlallah's Views on Dancing," *Sociology of Islam* 2, no. 1–2

(November 21, 2014): 60–86; Mikhail Pelevin and Matthias Weinreich, "The Songs of the Taliban: Continuity of Form and Thought in an Ever-Changing Environment," *Iran and the Caucasus* 16 (2012): 79–109; Atef Alshaer, "The Poetry of Hamas," *Middle East Journal of Culture and Communication* 2, no. 2 (2009): 214–230; Atef Alshaer, "The Poetry of Hezbollah," in *The Hizbullah Phenomenon: Politics and Communication*, ed. Lina Khatib, Dina Matar, and Atef Alshaer (New York: Oxford University Press, n.d.), 119–152; Alex Strick van Linschoten and Felix Kuehn, eds., *Poetry of the Taliban* (London: Hurst, 2012).

4 Thomas Vernon Reed, *The Art of Protest: Culture and Activism from the Civil Rights Movement to the Streets of Seattle* (Minneapolis: University of Minnesota Press, 2005); Anton Shekhovtsov, "European Far-Right Music and Its Enemies," in *Analysing Fascist Discourse: European Fascism in Talk and Text*, ed. Ruth Richardson and John E. Wodak (London: Routledge, 2012), 277–296; Cheryl Herr, "Terrorist Chic: Style and Domination in Contemporary Ireland," in *On Fashion*, ed. Shari Benstock and Suzanne Ferriss (New Brunswick, NJ: Rutgers University Press, 1994), 235–266. See also Dena J. Epstein, *Sinful Tunes and Spirituals: Black Folk Music to the Civil War* (Urbana: University of Illinois Press, 2003); Pietro Castelli Gattinara and Caterina Froio, "Discourse and Practice of Violence in the Italian Extreme Right: Frames, Symbols, and Identity-Building in CasaPound Italia," *International Journal of Conflict and Violence (IJCV)* 8, no. 1 (April 16, 2014): 154–170.

5 Alagha, "G. Banna's and A. Fadlallah's Views on Dancing."

6 Philip Halldén, "Jihad, retorik och poesi i digitaliseringens tidsålder: Estetiska dimensioner i al-Qa'idas Kulturkamp," *Samlaren – Tidskrift För Litteraturvetenskaplig Forskning* 131 (2011): 330–352; Manni Crone, "Religion and Violence: Governing Muslim Militancy through Aesthetic Assemblages," *Millennium – Journal of International Studies* 43, no. 1 (2014): 291–307.

7 Claudia Dantschke, "'Pop-Jihad': History and Structure of Salafism and Jihadism in Germany," Working Paper (Berlin: Institute for the Study of Radical Movements, n.d.), www.istramo.com/index.php/publications/working-paper-series [Accessed June 29, 2014].

8 Marc Sageman, "The Turn to Political Violence in the West," in *Jihadi Terrorism and the Radicalization Challenge*, ed. Rik Coolsaet, 2nd ed. (Farnham: Ashgate, 2011), 119.

9 Ann-Sophie Hemmingsen, "The Attractions of Jihadism: An Identity Approach to Three Danish Terrorism Cases and the Gallery of Characters around Them" (Ph.D. Dissertation, University of Copenhagen, 2010), 11.

10 Maruta Herding, *Inventing the Muslim Cool: Islamic Youth Culture in Western Europe* (Bielefeld: Transcript-Verlag, 2014).

11 Jessica Stern, "Pakistan's Jihad Culture," *Foreign Affairs* 79, no. 6 (2000): 115–126; Michael Taarnby and Lars Hallundbæk, "Fatah Al-Islam: Anthropological Perspectives on Jihadi Culture," Real Instituto Elcano Working Paper (Madrid: Real Instituto Elcano, 2008).

12 Jeffrey Cozzens, "The Culture of Global Jihad: Character, Future Challenges and Recommendations," Future Action Series (London: International Centre for the Study of Radicalization, October 2008).

13 Gilbert Ramsay, *Jihadi Culture on the World Wide Web* (New York: Bloomsbury Academic, 2013).

14 The Oxford English Dictionary notes that "the sense development of the word … from the 19th cent. onwards is very complex."

15 "Culture, n.," Oxford English Dictionary (online), www.oed.com/view/Entry/45746 (Accessed July 21, 2015).

16 Edmund Leach, *Political Systems of Highland Burma. A Study of Kachin Social Structure* (London: Bell, 1954), 11.

17 Gili Cohen, "IDF Brigade Refuses to Let Soldier Read Poetry on the Radio so as Not to Ruin 'Fighter's Image'," *Haaretz.com*, June 18, 2013.

18 According to one jihadi account, the fighters "spoke about those weapons and extolled them as if they were talking about beautiful women"; Abu al-Shaqra al-Hindukushi, *"Min Kabul Ila Baghdad"* [From Kabul to Baghdad], 2007, 13, http://archive.org/details/fromcabol tobagdad [Accessed November 2, 2012] (Part 1).

19 For an interesting article on elaborate ways of killing, see Lee Ann Fujii, "The Puzzle of Extra-Lethal Violence," *Perspectives on Politics* 11, no. 2 (2013): 410–426.

20 Bruce Lawrence, *Messages to the World: The Statements of Osama Bin Laden* (London: Verso, 2005), 58–62.

21 For a treatment of beliefs in suicide missions see Jon Elster, "Motivations and Beliefs in Suicide Missions," in *Making Sense of Suicide Missions*, ed. Diego Gambetta (Oxford: Oxford University Press, 2005), 233–258. And, more generally, see Diego Gambetta, *Making Sense of Suicide Missions* (Oxford: Oxford University Press, 2005).

22 Mohamed Sifaoui, *Inside Al-Qaeda: How I Infiltrated the World's Deadliest Terrorist Organization* (London: Granta Books, 2003), 86.

23 See, particularly, Boaz Ganor, Katharina Von Knop, and Carlos Duarte, *Hypermedia Seduction for Terrorist Recruiting – Volume 25, NATO Science for Peace and Security Series: Human and Societal Dynamics* (Washington, DC: IOS Press, 2007); Thomas Hegghammer, "Can You Trust Anyone on Jihadi Internet Forums?," in *Fight, Flight, Mimic: Identity Signalling in Armed Conflicts*, ed. Diego Gambetta (Oxford: Oxford University Press, forthcoming); Ramsay, *Jihadi Culture on the World Wide Web*.

24 See notably Michael Bacharach and Diego Gambetta, "Trust in Signs," in *Trust and Society*, ed. Karen S. Cook (New York: Russell Sage Foundation, 2001), 148–184; Diego Gambetta, "Deceptive Mimicry in Humans," in *Perspectives on Imitation: From Neuroscience to Social Science*, ed. Susan Hurley and Nick Chater (Cambridge, MA: MIT Press, 2005), 221–241.

25 Hegghammer, "Can You Trust Anyone on Jihadi Internet Forums?"; Thomas Hegghammer, "The Recruiter's Dilemma: Signalling and Rebel Recruitment Tactics," *Journal of Peace Research* 50, no. 1 (2013): 3–16.

26 Reuel Marc Gerecht, "The Counterterrorist Myth," *The Atlantic*, August 2001.

27 Marc Sageman, *Leaderless Jihad: Terror Networks in the Twenty-First Century* (Philadelphia: University of Pennsylvania Press, 2008), 156–157.

28 Dantschke, "'Pop-Jihad': History and Structure of Salafism and Jihadism in Germany," 14.

29 AFGP-2002-003251 (Harmony document), Abu Hudhayfa, "*Ila al-akh al-fadil al-sheikh al-jalil Abi 'Abdallah*" [To the Dear Brother and the Reverent Sheikh Abu 'Abdallah], dated June 20, 2000, pp. 23 and 25 of the original handwritten document. The translation is Nelly Lahoud's. Another English translation of the document can be found at www.ctc.usma.edu/wp-content/uploads/2010/08/AFGP-2002-003251-Trans.pdf [Accessed November 2, 2015].

30 Anwar Al-Awlaki, "44 Ways to Support Jihad," *Authentic Tauheed*, January 2009, www.authentictauheed.com/2009/12/44-ways-of-support ing-jihad-imam-anwar.html [Accessed March 20, 2015].

31 "Yemeni Woman's Life Gives Rare Look into Al Qaida Network," *Gulf News (online)*, February 27, 2014.

32 Abu Mansuur Al-Amriiki, "The Story of an American Jihaadi – Part One," 2012, 119, https://azelin.files.wordpress.com/2012/05/omar-hammami-abc5ab-mane1b9a3c5abr-al-amrc4abkc4ab-22the-story-of-an-american-jihc481dc4ab-part-122.pdf [Accessed October 31, 2015].

33 Abu Ja'far al-Misri al-Qandahari, *Dhikrayat 'arabi afghani [Memoirs of an Afghan Arab]* (Cairo: Dar al-Shuruq, 2002), 149.

34 Diego Gambetta, *Codes of the Underworld: How Criminals Communicate* (Princeton, NJ: Princeton University Press, 2009).

35 "Released From Prison, 'Apologetic Bandit' Writes about Life Inside," *NPR.org*, March 18, 2015.

Chapter 1

1 Among the few academics who have looked at jihadi poetry in Arabic is Elisabeth Kendall, who has studied the poetry of al-Qaida in the Arabian

Peninsula; see Elisabeth Kendall, "Yemen's Al-Qa'ida & Poetry as a Weapon of Jihad," in *Twenty-First Century Jihad: Law, Society and Military Action*, ed. Elisabeth Kendall and Ewan Stein (London: I. B. Tauris, 2015), 247–69. Marc Falkoff has published a collection of poems by the Guantanamo Bay prisoners: Marc Falkoff, *Poems from Guantanamo: The Detainees Speak* (Iowa City: University of Iowa Press, 2007). On the poetry of the Taliban, see Alex Strick van Linschoten and Felix Kuehn, eds., *Poetry of the Taliban* (London: Hurst, 2012). For poetry on jihad-related themes during a much earlier period, see Hadia Dajani-Shakeel, "Jihād in Twelfth-Century Arabic Poetry: A Moral and Religious Force to Counter the Crusades," *The Muslim World* 66, no. 2 (April 1, 1976): 96–113, and Carol Hillenbrand, "Jihad Poetry in the Age of the Crusades," in *Crusades: Medieval Worlds in Conflict*, ed. Thomas F. Madden, James L. Naus, and Vincent Ryan (Farnham, Surrey, England and Burlington, VT: Ashgate, 2010), 9–24.

2 See www.jihadica.com/wp-content/uploads/2015/03/432-10-CR-019-S-4-RJD-Original.pdf see p. 13, lines 6 and 7 from the bottom [Accessed July 20, 2015].

3 Jennifer R. Williams, "The Bureaucracy of Terror: New Secret Documents Reveal Al Qaeda's Real Challenges," *Foreign Affairs*, March 25, 2015.

4 See http://archive.aawsat.com/details.asp?section=20&article=793947&issueno=13131#.VVyrJmBUOYQ and http://almasalah.com/ar/news/39872/القيــــادي-الارهــابي-أبــو-أسامة-الغريــب-ي [Accessed July 20, 2015].

5 See Souad Mekhennet, "Austrian Mohamed Mahmoud Returns to Online Jihad," *New York Times*, November 15, 2011; and "Austrian Jihadist Poses in Front of Corpses," *The Local*, November 5, 2014, www.thelocal.at/20141105/austrian-jihadist-poses-in-front-of-corpses [Accessed April 19, 2017].

6 See Abu Usama al-Gharib, *"Al-mukhtasar al-jali bi-sirat shaykhina Turki al-Bin'ali"* [The Clear Abridged Biography of Our Master Turki Al-Bin'ali], n.d., https://archive.org/details/almokhtasar.algali.high [Accessed July 20, 2015].

7 See http://justpaste.it/fursan-d-awar [Accessed July 20, 2015].

8 Ahlam al-Nasr, *Uwar al-haqq [The Blaze of Truth]* (Fursan al-Balagh li-l-I'lam, 2014). See www.youtube.com/watch?v=scBxrOZwr78 [Accessed July 20, 2015].

9 Dr. Iman Mustafa al-Bagha, *"Akhiran tharat fatati"* [At Last My Daughter Has Rebelled], Twitter, April 29, 2015, 10:31 PM. The account on which this tweet was posted has since been closed. On July 20, 2015, Iman al-Bagha posted on her Facebook page that Ahlam al-Nasr gave birth to a "terrorist" daughter in the "Land of the Caliphate."

10 al-Nasr, *Uwar al-haqq*, 26–27.

11 See Loulla-Mae Elefheriou-Smith, "Escaped Isis Wives Describe Life in the Punishing All-Female Al-Khansa Brigade Who Punish Women with 40 Lashes for Wearing Wrong Clothes," *The Independent*, September 23, 2015.

12 Ahlam al-Nasr, *Akhiran rabbuna kataba al-samaha [At Last Our Lord Has Decreed [the Caliphate] Permissible]* (al-Ghuraba' li-l-I'lam, 2014), 12–13.

13 Ibid.

14 al-Nasr, *Uwar al-haqq*, 118.

15 Qur'an 26, 224–26.

16 See www.almillion.net/ar/index.php [Accessed July 20, 2015].

17 William Kremer, "Is It Possible to Be a Millionaire Poet?" *BBC News*, May 31, 2014.

18 http://en.wikipedia.org/wiki/Hissa_Hilal [Accessed July 20, 2015].

19 Samar al Huneidi, "Prince of Poets Competitor Causes Stir," *The National*, January 26, 2011.

20 See, for instance, the following clips [Accessed July 20, 2015]: www .youtube.com/watch?v=TyCS9N_SU_U; www.youtube.com/watch?v=yz Ujgch5ky8; www.youtube.com/watch?v=Dh7p73VHPMI; www.youtube .com/watch?v=Eug4qEqej58.

21 al-Nasr, *Uwar al-haqq*, 55.

22 See www.youtube.com/watch?v=5R0XHiv_Qt0&list=PLXk54e6gWM XUY3Yr17_8fp5tgr4FjWBX8&index=2 [Accessed May 1, 2015].

23 The full poem can be found at www.saaid.net/wahat/q5.htm, and Mahmud Ghunaym's biography can be found on the Muslim Brotherhood's Wikipedia site at www.ikhwanwiki.com/index.php?title=محمود غنيــم [Accessed July 20, 2015].

24 His poems have been collected on the jihadi website *al-Minbar al-i'lami al-jihadi*. See www.mnbr.info/vb/showthread.php?p=4970 [Accessed July 20, 2015].

25 See www.muslm.org/vb/showthread.php?348495-قصـــة-مأســـدة-نصــــار and www.al-eman.com/الكتـــب/الأ-كمـــا-يرويهـــا-أميرها-أسامة-بـن-لادن-صـور %/مـا/**20%»ويـة-النـب20%السيرة«20%بـ20%المسمى20%هشام20%ابـن20%سيرة/ /قريظـة 20%وبـني20%الخنـدق 20%أمر 20%فـي20%الشـعر 20%من20%قيـل20 i109&d72778&c&p1 [Accessed July 20, 2015].

26 "*Diwan al-'izza: Majmu'at qasa'id hamasiyya fi'l-jihad*" [The Anthology of Glory: A Compilation of Zealous Poems about Armed Struggle], *Sawt Al-Jihad (Voice of Jihad)*, n.d., www.slideshare.net/AladeebShaker/ss-28041859 [Accessed July 20, 2015].

27 See www.mnbr.info/vb/showthread.php?p=4970 [Accessed July 20, 2015].

28 See www.mnbr.info/vb/showthread.php?p=4970 [Accessed July 20, 2015].

29 *Sahih Muslim, Kitab al-Iman*. See Shaykh Abdullah Ateeq Al-Harbee, "Glad Tidings to the Strangers (Ghuraba)," *Islamic Treasure*, www .islamictreasure.com/788-glad-tidings-to-the-strangers-ghuraba/ [Accessed December 3, 2015].

30 Thomas Hegghammer, "Can You Trust Anyone on Jihadi Internet Forums?" in *Fight, Flight, Mimic: Identity Signalling in Armed Conflicts*, ed. Diego Gambetta (Oxford: Oxford University Press, forthcoming).

31 See www.tawhed.ws [Accessed January 23, 2014].

32 See www.youtube.com/watch?v=QKciyCwB4bg [Accessed July 20, 2015].

33 See www.paldf.net/forum/showthread.php?t=793219 [Accessed July 20, 2015].

34 See www.youtube.com/watch?v=Rma30iJtTJ4 and www.youtube.com/ watch?v=obketceZ-M8 [Accessed July, 20 2015].

35 See, for instance, the following YouTube videos [Accessed July 20, 2015]: www.youtube.com/watch?v=N9eWmGU87u0 and www.youtube .com/watch?v=obketceZ-M8.

36 al-Nasr, *Uwar al-haqq*, 43.

37 See this at www.jihadica.com/wp-content/uploads/2014/07/القصــــيدة- البنعليـــــة.pdf [Accessed July 20, 2015].

38 To date, the most extensive treatment of Turki al-Bin‘ali's life and thought is Cole Bunzel's blog entry on Jihadica.com; see Cole Bunzel, "Bin‘ali Leaks: Revelations of the Silent Mufti," *Jihadica.com*, June 15, 2015, www.jihadica.com/binali-leaks/ [Accessed April 19, 2017].

39 Muhammad al-Zuhayri, *Wa amtara al-ghaym al-dima' [The Clouds Have Rained Blood]*, n.d., https://archive.org/details/zhiri-0–001 [Accessed November 30, 2015].

40 ‘Isa Al ‘Awshan, "*Risala ila al-la'imin*" [Epistle to the Scolders], *Diwan al-‘izza*, 11–13.

41 Andras Hamori, *On the Art of Medieval Arabic Literature* (Princeton: Princeton University Press, 1974), 40.

42 Abu Sa‘d al-Azdi, "*Ismitu fa-l-kalam li-l-abtal*" [Silence! Words Are for Heroes], *Diwan al-‘izza*, 7.

43 Usama al-Khalidi, "*Risalat shahid ila ummihi al-ghaliya*" [A Martyr's Letter to His Beloved Mother], *Diwan al-‘izza*, 10.

44 Ibid., 11.

45 Ibid., 12.

46 Sa‘d al-Azdi, "*Ismitu fa-l-kalam li-l-abtal,*" 7.

47 al-Nasr, *Akhiran rabbuna kataba*, 14–16.

48 al-Nasr, *Uwar al-haqq*, 128.

49 Ahlam al-Nasr, *Bal ata‘na Allah idh ahraqnahu ya ‘abid al-rafahiyya [We Have Obeyed God by Burning Him, Oh Slaves of Luxury]* (al-Ghuraba' li-l-I‘lam, 2015).

50 Umm Sumayyah al-Muhajira, "The Twin Halves of the Muhajirun," *Dabiq*, no. 8 (March 2015): 32–37.

51 IS has recently made the argument that while it is important not to be abusive toward one's parents, one need not obtain their permission to join the jihad. "Tawhid and Our Duty to Our Parents," *Dabiq* 10 (July 2015): 14–17. An unnamed IS ideologue, however, has made the case that it is permissible – under the doctrine of *al-wala' wa-l-bara'* ["loyalty (to Muslims) and disassociation (from non-Muslims)"] – to kill relatives deemed to be unbelievers. This opinion was published online in response to the recent attack in Saudi Arabia, during which an IS militant killed his maternal uncle (a colonel in the Ministry of the Interior) before performing a suicide bombing attack. See *Al-rumh al-thaqib li-jawaz qatl al-murtadd min al-aqarib [The Piercing Spear Allowing the Killing of the Apostate Relative]*, n.d., http://justpaste.it/mf99 [Accessed December 1, 2015]; "Suicide Bomber Injures Two in Saudi Capital," *Al Jazeera*, July 17, 2015.

52 al-Nasr, *Akhiran rabbuna kataba*, 15.

Chapter 2

I am grateful for the help I received from my colleagues Muhammad al-'Ubaydi and Nassir Abdullah in coding the *anashid* dataset, and for the meticulous copyediting of Juan Masullo. I also benefited from the feedback of the authors in this volume, especially from Thomas Hegghammer's detailed edits and suggestions. My gratitude also to the feedback I received from Alison Laywine and Stephen Menn.

1 Unknown, "Tarikh al-ma'sada" [The History of Al-Ma'sada] (CTC Library, n.d.). This is a large document that consists of scanned hand-written notes by different authors, some of which are strategic notes (with plans that require execution), others are minutes of meetings, others are translations of poetry, while others consist of budgets for items that require purchasing. The earliest notes in this document date back to February 1987 (the year is dated according to the Gregorian calendar), but it is possible that some notes were written at an earlier date but were not dated. I have also not gone through all the pages to verify if an earlier date is explicitly noted. Unless otherwise noted, translations of Arabic materials are my own.

2 Ibid. The term used for "essentials" is *daruriyyat*.

3 Ibid. The itemized list is dated April 19, 1992, the book is titled *Anashid 'ala al-darb [Anashid on the Road]*.

4 Tilman Seidensticker et al., "Translation of the Spiritual Manual," in *9/11 Handbook*, ed. Hans G. Kippenberg and Tilman Seidensticker (London and Oakville: Equinox Publishing, 2006), 19 (p. 88 for the

Arabic text). Kippenberg provides a comprehensive review of the document and surveys the literature that examined it ("Translation of the Spiritual Manual," in Kippenberg and Seidenstickler, *9/11 Handbook*, 1–9), and Seidensticker has an informative chapter on *anashid* ("Jihad Hymns [Nashīds] as a Means of Self-Motivation in the Hamburg Group," in Kippenberg and Seidensticker, *9/11 Handbook*, 71–78.).

5 Anwar Al-Awlaki, "44 Ways to Support Jihad," *Authentic Tauheed*, January 2009, www.authentictauheed.com/2009/12/44-ways-of-support ing-jihad-imam-anwar.html [Accessed March 20, 2015].

6 Ammon Shiloah, "Nashid," in *Encyclopedia of Islam*, 2nd ed. (Brill Online, n.d.). See also Henry G. Farmer, 'Ghina," in *Encyclopedia of Islam*, 2nd ed. (Brill Online, n.d.). According to Farmer, *nashid* is a type of singing (*ghina'*) that is "measured (*mizan al-shi'r*)." I am not entirely sure if all *nashids* need to follow a poetic measure; if *nashid* could be a "piece of oratory" as Shiloah remarks, it need not be.

7 Based on the collection on *Shabakat al-Mujahidin al-Iliktruniyya*, http://majahdenar.com/vb/showthread.php?t=6099 [Accessed June 1, 2011].

8 Some of Mu'assassat Ajnad's *anashid* may be accessed on this unofficial website, *Isdarat al-Dawla al-Islamiyya [Islamic States Releases]*, https://isdarat.tv/3235 [Accessed July 2, 2015]. They can also be accessed on *Ansar al-Khilafa [Supporters of the Caliphate]*, https://ansarkhilafah.wordpress.com/ajnad-media-nasheed [Accessed July 23, 2015]. Aymenn Jawad al-Tamimi identified a *nashid* that was used by the Euphrates Province of IS and that was not produced by Ajnad; see Aymenn Jawad Al-Tamimi, "'The Cheers Surge' – Nasheed Plagiarised by The Islamic State [IS]," n.d., www.aymennjawad.org/2014/11/the-cheers-surge-nasheed-plagiarised-by [Accessed February 2, 2016].

9 This chapter should be read in conjunction with the next chapter by Jonathan Pieslak, who examines *anashid* from a musicological perspective.

10 "Nashada," in Edward W. Lane, *Arabic-English Lexicon* (London: Williams & Norgate, n.d.). The lexicon can be searched online: www.tyndalearchive.com/tabs/lane/

11 Ibn Manzur, "*Lisan al-'arab*" [The Tongue/Language of the Arabs], ed. Amin Muhammad 'Abd al-Wahhab and Muhammad al-Sadiq al-'Abidi, vol. 4 (Beirut: Dar Ihya' al-Turath al-'Arabi, 1999), 138. Note that this edition of *Lisan al-'arab* is arranged alphabetically, not along the traditional arrangement of the third letter of the root).

12 Fouad Ephreim al-Bustani, *Al-shi'r al-jahili [Pre-Islamic Poetry]* (Beirut: al-Matba'a al-Kathulikiyya, 1967), 11.

13 Mustafa 'Abd al-Rahman, *Anashid laha tarikh [Anashid with a History]* (Cairo: Dar al-Sha'b, 1974), 35.

14 Ibid., 12.

15 Ibid., 11.
16 Ibid.
17 Henry G. Farmer, "Music," in *The Legacy of Islam*, ed. Sir Thomas Arnold and Alfred Guillaume (Oxford: Clarendon Press, 1931), 358.
18 al-Bustani, *Al-Shiʿr al-jahili*, 21.
19 Ibid., 14–15.
20 "Sama" in Lane, *Arabic-English Lexicon*. The lexicon can be searched online: www.tyndalearchive.com/tabs/lane/ [Accessed April 19, 2017].
21 Al-Ghazali, *Al-samaʿ waʾl-wajd [Listening (to Music and Songs)]*, trans. Anthony H. John, forthcoming. My gratitude to Tony for sharing with me his draft translation before its publication.
22 See Jonathan Pieslak's chapter in this volume.
23 Al-Ghazali, *Al-samaʿ waʾl-wajd*.
24 Ibid.
25 Ibid.
26 For a short biography of his life and work, see Muhammad Hasim Kamali, "Muhammad Abu Zahra," in *Encyclopedia of Islam*, ed. Gudrun Krämer et al., 3rd ed. (Brill Online, n.d.).
27 Cited in Muhammad Nasir al-Din al-Albani, *Tahrim alat al-tarab [(Legal Rulings) Forbidding Musical Instruments]*, 2nd ed. (al-Jubayl al-Sinaʿiyya, Saudi Arabia: Maktabat al-Dalil, 1997). Note that al-Albani is citing Abu Zahra to criticize his argument.
28 Sayyid Qutb, "*Al-firqa al-qawmiyya fi ʿahdiha al-jadid*" [The Nationalist Group in Its New Era], in *Sayyid Qutb: al-mujtamaʿ al-misri: judhuruhu wa-afaquhu [Sayyid Qutb: Egyptian Society, Its Roots and Horizons]*, ed. Alan Rossignon (Cairo: Sina li-al-Nashr, 1994), 212–215.
29 Ibid., 314.
30 Esther Peskes and Werner Ende, "Wahhābiyya," in *Encyclopedia of Islam*, ed. P. Bearman et al., 2nd ed. (Brill Online, n.d.).
31 H. St. John Philby, *Saudi Arabia* (London: Ernest Benn, c. 1955), 146.
32 I say "for the most part" because I have come across a short treatise by Muhammad b. Muhammad al-Fazazi, "*Fatawa mutasayyiba: al-Qaradawi yuhillu al-ghina*"[Negligent Legal Opinions: al-Qaradawi Makes Singing Lawful] in which he implies that he disapproves of *anashid*. Though the treatise does not focus on the subject of *anashid*, the author remarks the following: "I shall not debate Sheikh Qaradawi and his disciples about the so-called Islamic *anashid* without stringed instruments (*maʿazif*) . . . we do not believe them to be permissible in view of the legal violations therein (*lima fi dhalika min mukhalafat sharʿiyya*)." Text available on *Minbar al-Tawhid wa-al-Jihad*, www.tawhed.ws/pr?i=1061 [Accessed 26 November 2010].

33 The website *Silsilat al-'Allamatayn* has a useful collection of excerpts by leading Najdi scholars on the rules governing *anashid* under the heading "*Fatawa al-'ulama hawla hukm al-anashid*," www.3llamteen .com/index.php?option=com_content&task=view&id=249&Itemid=26 [Accessed May 29, 2011].

34 al-Albani, *Tahrim alat al-tarab*, see especially 5–7.

35 Ibn Uthaymin, *Fatawa al-'ulama hawla hukm al-anashid [The Legal Opinions of Scholars Concerning Anashid]*, n.d.

36 Muhammad al-Shafi'i, "*Jadal bayna al-usuliyyin hawla istikhdam ashritat 'al-hur al-'ayn' li-tajnid muqatilin li-'al-Qa'ida'*" [Debates between Fundamentalists Concerning the Use of [*anashid*] Tapes about Damsels to Recruit Fighters for Al-Qaida], *Al-Sharq Al-Awsat*, September 27, 2003, www.aawsat.com/details.asp?issueno=8800&article= 194981 [Accessed September 27, 2012].

37 Azifat al-Rasas, "*Hukm al-istima' ila al-anashid ma' al-daff*" [Legal Ruling Concerning Listening to *Anashid* That Include the Instrument of Tambourine], *Minbar al-Tawhid wa-al-Jihad*, www.tawhed.ws/FAQ/display_ques tion?qid=655&text=%D8%A7%D9%86%D8%A7%D8%B4%D9 %8A%D8%AF [Accessed March 23, 2011]. "*Azifat al-rasas*" literally means "bullet player"; it is obviously a penname, and in the context of the question it should be read as a metaphor combining music and militancy, with bullets taking the place of a musical instrument. To be noted, there is a *nashid* entitled "*Azf al-Rasas*" with Palestine as its dominant theme.

38 Ibid.

39 Ibid.

40 *Mu'aththirat* could be understood as "sound effects" (*mu'aththirat sawtiyya*), or it could imply emotional "effects" that might lead the hearer to act upon his or her desires. I suspect the meaning implied here refers to the former.

41 *Al-Ansar* (helpers) designates the group that invited the Prophet to Medina when he was persecuted in Mecca for preaching the monotheist creed that would become Islam; they themselves converted to Islam. Those who emigrated with the Prophet from Mecca are referred to as the *muhajirun* (émigrés).

42 Abu Usama al-Shami, "*Hukm al-istima' ila al-anashid*," *Minbar al-Tawhid wa-al-Jihad*, www.tawhed.ws/FAQ/display_question?qid=443&text= %D8%B4%D9%8A%D8%AF [Accessed September 27, 2013].

43 For background about Fadil Harun, see Nelly Lahoud, *Beware of Imitators: Al-Qa'ida through the Lens of Its Confidential Secretary* (West Point, NY: Combating Terrorism Center, 2012), chap. 1.

44 Fadil Harun, *Al-harb 'ala al-Islam [The War against Islam]*, vol. 2, 2009,
    180. The two volumes can be accessed online: www.ctc.usma
    .edu/posts/beware-of-imitators-al-qaida-through-the-lens-of-its-confiden
    tial-secretary [Accessed April 19, 2017].
45 Ibid., 2:180–181.
46 AFGP-2002-003251 (Harmony document), Abu Hudhayfa, "*ila al-akh
    al-fadil al-sheikh al-jalil Abi 'Abdallah*" [To the Dear Brother and the
    Reverent Sheikh Abu 'Abdallah], dated June 20, 2000, pp. 23 and 25 of
    the original handwritten document. This is a largely amended translation
    of the one available on the Harmony database. I am yet to ascertain the
    identity of Abu Hudhayfa.
47 Abu Amru al-Qa'idi, "A Course in the Art of Recruiting," revised 2010,
    http://archive.org/stream/ACourseInTheArtOfRecruiting-RevisedJuly2010/
    A_Course_in_the_Art_of_Recruiting_-_Revised_July2010_djvu.txt
    [Accessed April 19, 2017].
48 See *Rih al-janna [The Wind of Paradise]* (1), https://archive.org/details/
    250aoao [Accessed August 4, 2015].
49 AQ-SHPD-D-001-175, p. 34. This document can be found in the declas-
    sified documents held by the Conflict Records Research Center at the
    National Defense University in Washington, DC, under the title Security
    and Intelligence section of a larger document.
50 USA vs Usama Bin Laden, Trial Transcript Day 14, http://cryptome.org/
    usa-v-ubl-14.htm [Accessed April 19, 2017], 2028.
51 USA vs Usama Bin Laden, Trial Transcript Day 14, 2038.
52 As far I can ascertain, the release *Ma' al-khalidin* [With Those Who
    Gained Eternal Life (in Paradise)], consisting of six *anashid,* is the
    production of *al-Malahim,* the media arm of al-Qaida in the Arabian
    Peninsula (AQAP). It can be accessed on https://archive.org/details/Ma3_
    alkhaledrn [Accessed August 4, 2015].
53 Husni Afham Jarar and Ahmad al-Jada, eds., *Anashid Al-Da'wa Al-
    Islamiyya [Anashid of the Islamic Dawa]*, vol. 4 (Amman: Dar al-Diya',
    1990). I do not have access to the first three, but the Princeton University
    Library database indicates that the series began in 1984.
54 See, for instance, *Ansar al-Mujahidin*, http://as-ansar.com/vb/forumdisplay
    .php?s=9ca0b6276d2e1f1cbfae53a2f503fbc3&f=29 [Accessed September
    27, 2013].
55 See for instance al-Zawahiri's use of a poem by the Lebanese poet of
    Christian origin, Gibran Khalil Gibran in his "Missive of Hope and Joy
    to Our People in Egypt." The latter is mostly known for his book *The
    Prophet*, but he was also a painter and a poet.
56 Interview with Abu Abd al-Malik, conducted by *Sawt al-Yaman [The
    Voice of Yemen]*, available at http://ar-ar.facebook.com/note.php?note_
    id=142781859080972 [Accessed June 1, 2011].

57 *Taratil [Hymns],* see www.tarateal.com/modules.php?name=Content&
pa=showpage&pid=9 [Accessed April 27, 2011].

58 See the link to the *Bushrayat* on Abu 'Ali's website, www.abo-ali
.com/index.php?pg=nasheed&action=des&no=179 [Accessed August 4,
2015]; they can also be seen together performing it on YouTube: www
.youtube.com/watch?v=O0XRoH9VL80&feature=related [Accessed June
1, 2011].

59 See the information about *Bada'a al-Masir* on http://audio.islamweb.net/
audio/index.php?page=audioinfo&audioid=150019 [Accessed June 1,
2011].

60 Ayman al-Zawahiri, "*Al-hamla al-salibiyya tatarabbasu bi-l-sudan*"
[The Crusader Campaign Lurks in Sudan], released March 24, 2009
(tape available in the CTC collection).

61 The poem is available on al-Qaradawi's website: "*Ya ummati wajaba
al-kifah*" [O My Umma: Fighting Is Now an Obligation], http://www
.qaradawi.net/site/topics/article.asp?cu_no=2&item_no=3772&version=
1&template_id=235&parent_id=14 [Accessed March 11, 2011]; on the
website, it is dated January 5, 2005. I am assuming that if it has been
authored by someone else (a historical figure for example), al-Qaradawi
would have acknowledged it.

62 See the recruitment video, www.youtube.com/watch?v=izxbTzkr4LM
[Accessed June 1, 2011].

63 See www.tajdeed.org.uk [Accessed June 1, 2011].

64 Dawlat al-'Iraq al-Islamiyya [Islamic State of Iraq], "*Al-i'lan 'an insha'
mu'assasat al-furqan li-l-intaj al-i'lami*" [A Statement Announcing the
Founding of the Furqan Foundation] (Ana Muslim, October 31, 2006),
www.muslm.org/vb/showthread.php?184654 [Accessed March 7,
2016]. Based on preliminary research, it is possible that the Iraq-based
group's production of its own *anashid* is also part of the evolution of the
group as a distinct entity from al-Qa'ida since 2006.

65 It is important to note that one may find *anashid* produced by al-Furqan and
used by some regional jihadi groups that have not accepted IS's legitimacy.
That may be because these were produced before the declaration of the
caliphate and the public split between IS and al-Qaida. They may also
indicate that the group in question is flirting with the possibility of becoming
a province of IS. For example, the Somalia-based al-Shabab has produced a
series of videos (twelve videos at the time of going to press), beginning April
2013, entitled "*Sharrid bi-him man khalafahum*" (Q. 8: 57), using a *nashid*
by the same title produced by al-Furqan back in January 2010. It was part of
a video production entitled "*Qahir al-Bishmarka.*" Al-Sahab's latest video
in the series may be accessed on https://archive.org/details/dadaw_12HD
[Accessed July 22, 2015], while the original video produced by al-Furqan
may be accessed on https://isdarat.tv/713 [Accessed July 22, 2015].

66 Nizar Qabbani, *"Dafatir 'ala hawamish al-naksa"* [Notes on the Margins of Al-Naksa], in *Al-A'mal Al-Siyasiyya Al-Kamila [Complete Poetic Works]*, 4th ed., vol. 3 (Beirut: Manshurat Nizar Qabbani, 1986), 89. The term *al-naksa* is in reference to the 1967 Six Day War.

67 On this aspect, see Nelly Lahoud, *Jihadis' Path to Self-Destruction* (New York: Columbia University Press, 2010), Chaps. 3 and 4.

68 Based on the collection on *Shabakat al-Mujahidin al-Iliktruniyya*, http://majahdenar.com/vb/showthread.php?t=6099 [Accessed June 1, 2011].

69 It is attributed to the munshid Abu Ratib, whom I doubt is/was a jihadi.

70 It is performed by Abu Hudhayfa (Hani Muqbil) and Abu Abd al-Malak and was released as part of the album *Khayru al-Umam* on April 1, 2005.

71 The performer is Abu Usama, but it is likely that it was composed by jihadis.

72 It is performed by Abu Mus'ab and was released as part of the album *"Ushshaq al-Janna"* [Lovers of Paradise] by a Saudi-based company called *Mu'assassat Suhayl al-Yarmuk li-al-Intaj al-I'lami wa-al-Tawzi'* [Suhayl al-Yarmuk Foundation for Media Production and Distribution] on February 15, 2007.

73 It is performed by Abu Lababa al-Maqdisi; no additional information found.

74 It was performed by Abu Ali, composed by Abd al-Malik al-'Awda, and produced and distributed by *Tasjilat al-Qadisiyya bi-al-Dammam* [Qadisiyya Recordings in al-Dammam], 2004, available on *Shabakat Anashid*, www.anashed.net/anashed/ashretah/annahem.html [Accessed August 4, 2015].

75 It is performed by Abu 'Abd al-Malik, introduced by Khalid al-Rashid and was released as part of the album *Umniya*, dated 21 August 2007.

76 Plato, "The Republic," in *Plato: Complete Works*, ed. John M. Cooper and D. S. Hutchinson (Indianapolis: Hackett, 1997), 2.376e.

77 Ibid., 3.401d.

Chapter 3

1 John S. Baily, *Can You Stop the Birds Singing?: The Censorship of Music in Afghanistan* (Copenhagen: Freemuse, 2003); John S. Baily, "Music and Censorship in Afghanistan, 1973–2003," in *Music and the Play of Power in the Middle East, North Africa and Central Asia*, ed. Laudan Nooshin (Aldershot, U.K.: Ashgate Publishing, 2009), 143–163; Henry George Farmer, *A History of Arabian Music to the XIIIth Century* (London: Luzac, 1929); Lois Ibsen al Faruqi, "Music, Musicians and Muslim Law," *Asian Music* 17, no. 1 (1985): 3–36; Seyyed Hossein

Nasr, "Islam and Music: The Legal and Spiritual Dimensions," in *Enchanting Powers: Music in the World's Religions*, ed. Lawrence Eugene Sullivan (Harvard University Press, 1997), 219–235; Jonas Otterbeck, "Battling over the Public Sphere: Islamic Reactions to the Music of Today," *Contemporary Islam* 2, no. 3 (November 1, 2008): 211–228; Regula Burkhardt Qureshi, "Sounding the Word: Music in the Life of Islam," in *Enchanting Powers: Music in the World's Religions*, ed. Lawrence Eugene Sullivan (Harvard University Press, 1997), 263–298; James Robson, *Tracts on Listening to Music. Being Dhamm Al-Malahi by Ibn Abi 'L-Dunya and Bawariq Al-Ila by Majd Ad-Din Al-Tusi Al-Ghazali* (Royal Asiatic Society, 1938); Amnon Shiloah, *Music in the World of Islam: A Socio-Cultural Study* (Detroit: Wayne State University Press, 1995); Amnon Shiloah, "Music and Religion in Islam," *Acta Musicologica* 69, no. 2 (1997): 143–155; Habib Hassan Touma, *The Music of the Arabs* (Portland: Amadeus Press, 1996).

2 See, for example, the video "The West and The Dark Tunnel." This and other audiovisual material cited in this chapter are available on the book's website (www.jihadiculture.net).

3 *Tracts on Listening to Music* provides a suitable example. In this volume, Robson translates two contrasting works on the subject, *Dhamm al-malahi [The Book of Censure on the Instruments of Diversion]* by Ibn abi 'l-Dunya (823–894 C.E.), who condemns music, and *Bawariq al-ilma [Lightning Flashes on the Refutation of Those Who Declare Listening to Music to be Forbidden]* by Majd al-Din al-Tusi al-Ghazali (1061–1123/6 C.E.), who ultimately approves of it.

4 Al-Faruqi provides an otherwise satisfactory template for legitimate, controversial, and illegitimate musical forms that might guide our understanding of music across Islam. But his designations are not always in consonance with practice. The wedding and occupational songs he groups within the legitimate, "non-musiqa" category seem to have been decried as illegitimate – at times – by groups like the Taliban. John Baily's research on music in Afghanistan demonstrates this point; he cites multiple instances where the Taliban stopped the performances of such songs (Baily, *Can You Stop the Birds Singing?*, 38; Baily, "Music and Censorship in Afghanistan, 1973–2003," 162.). The Taliban, however, has not always been consistent in their censorship policies on music, at times allowing mujahideen to listen to jihad-themed *anashid* but forbidding others from so much as possessing such tapes. This further demonstrates that even hard-line groups like the Taliban do not always clearly distinguish permissible and forbidden musical genres.

5 See Shiloah, "Music and Religion in Islam," 148–153, corresponding to "the overwhelming power of music" as discussed by Muslim authors.

6 James J. O'Donnell, trans., *The Confessions of Augustine (electronic edition)* (Oxford: Oxford University Press, 1992), www.stoa.org/hippo/; www.archive.org/stream/historyscottish00macmgoog#page/n129/mode/2up.

7 Robson, *Tracts on Listening to Music*, 4.

8 Farmer, *A History of Arabian Music to the XIIIth Century*, 199; 206–207.

9 Shiloah, *Music in the World of Islam*, 4–5.

10 Ibid., 156, 74.

11 Birgit Berg, "'Authentic' Islamic Sound? Orkes Gambus Music, the Arab Idiom, and Sonic Symbols in Indonesian Islamic Musical Arts," in *Divine Inspirations: Music and Islam in Indonesia*, ed. David Harnish and Anne Rasmussen (Oxford: Oxford University Press, 2011), 222–223.

12 Farmer, *A History of Arabian Music to the XIIIth Century*, 198.

13 Patricia Matusky and Sooi Beng Tan, *The Music of Malaysia: The Classical, Folk and Syncretic Traditions* (Burlington, VT: Routledge, 2004), 262. The origins of this song may lie in religious folklore; there is no way of documenting this melody back to 622 C.E. given the almost exclusively oral tradition of Islamic musical practice. Yet it is worth noting that this *anashid* demonstrates a certain consistency of melodic structure across varying practices and geographies of Islam. Many present renditions of "*Tala'a al-Badru 'Alayna*" are based, more-or-less, on the same melody. Entirely different melodies, however, do appear.

14 Ibid., 263. Also see Margaret Sarkissian, "'Religion Never Had It So Good': Contemporary Nasyid and the Growth of Islamic Popular Music in Malaysia," *Yearbook for Traditional Music* 37 (2005).

15 Matusky and Tan, *The Music of Malaysia*, 264.

16 Touma, *The Music of the Arabs*, 14. More precisely, Touma proposes that pitch structure (the *maqam* system) is typically given priority over recurring rhythmic patterns within a piece.

17 Yezid Sayigh, *Armed Struggle and the Search for State: The Palestinian National Movement, 1949–1993* (New York: Oxford University Press, 1997), 195–196.

18 Sayigh, *Armed Struggle and the Search for State*.

19 Abu Ratib's biography on his website states, "he began to issue the albums of Islamic singing which accompanied the serious incidents which afflicted the nation (Syria) at that time (1981)"; www.aburatib .com/content/view/127/113/1/0/lang,en/ [Accessed June 4, 2011]. The website says that Abu Ratib first started singing in a group led by Abu Dujanah, but in my e-mail correspondence with him, he indicated that he first started with a different *anashid* group (he did not indicate a name) in Syria before singing with Abu Dujanah. It is not clear to me to what

extent *anashid* texts before the late 1970s and 1980s addressed political events and Muslim activist causes, but according to Abu Ratib, *anashid* texts are "mostly about the love of God, the prophet and your country and sometimes about Islamic causes." Abu Ratib, e-mail correspondence with the author, August 27, 2011. Examples of *anashid* by Abu Ratib are available on the book website (www.jihadiculture.net).

20 I would like to make the subtle but important distinction between *anashid* produced by al-Qaida and those recorded by other artists and used (perhaps without consent) by al-Qaida in its media. As Nelly Lahoud noted in Chapter 2, it is not always clear which *anashid* appearing in al-Qaida media or circulating among al-Qaida members are created by the group itself, recorded by artists who associate with or are sympathetic to al-Qaida, or are a (mis)appropriation of *anashid* by other artists. I will adopt the terms "al-Qaida *anashid*" or "jihad-themed *anashid*" to acknowledge this distinction.

21 Baily, *Can You Stop the Birds Singing?*, 151.

22 Ibid., 151–152.

23 Otterbeck, "Battling over the Public Sphere," 211–212.

24 My sample for this analysis is derived from more than 600 jihad-themed *anashid* obtained via the Internet, a collection of more than 100 Internet videos, and 146 videos circulating in Afghanistan from the approximate period 2003–2007, which were produced by various jihadi groups but mainly al-Qaida and Taliban affiliates.

25 www.maqamworld.com/maqamat.html [Accessed June 10, 2011].

26 www.maqamworld.com/maqamat/nahawand.html#farahfaza [Accessed June 13, 2011].

27 Touma, *The Music of the Arabs*, 38.

28 Matusky and Tan, *The Music of Malaysia*, 262. One problem in identifying the specific Middle Eastern rhythms that might be used in *anashid* is that there is such a wealth of possible rhythms that almost any consistent rhythmic structure fits an "authentic" rhythm. As it relates to many of the *anashid* appearing in al-Qaida media, one can observe the prevalence of a short-long rhythmic pattern that is more-or-less within a consistent pulse framework.

29 Touma, *The Music of the Arabs*, 38.

30 A. J. Racy, *Making Music in the Arab World: The Culture and Artistry of Tarab* (Cambridge: Cambridge University Press, 2004), 96. Racy's description echoes Shiloah's emphasis on the "ethical, therapeutical, and cosmological values" bound to *maqamat*. Shiloah, *Music in the World of Islam*, 120.

31 The verse-chorus form appears prominently in the recent history of *anashid*, ranging from those used by al-Qaida to the *anashid* of Abu

Ratib and others from more than 30 years ago. In my correspondence with Abu Ratib, he referred to the singing style involving a chorus and individual singer, like those described above, as "nasheed harmonie." Abu Ratib, email correspondence, August 27, 2011.

32 Touma, *The Music of the Arabs*, 162.

33 Matusky and Tan, *The Music of Malaysia*, 263.

34 Abu Ratib, e-mail correspondence, August 27, 2011.

35 See www.tawhed.net.

36 Clip available on the book website (www.jihadiculture.net).

37 The emphasis on the *Ajam* trichord appears to be a distinguish feature for labeling *maqam Farahfaza* in this excerpt over *maqam Nahawand*. Moreover, the major mode pitch structure of *Ajam* seems well-suited for the rousing call to action this *anashid* promotes.

38 http://forums.islamicawakening.com/f41/my-nasheed-rap-generosity-42309/index2.html [Accessed June 13, 2011]. Descriptions of the emotional/affective content of *maqam Nahawand* are not found in Touma, *Music of the Arabs*; Racy, *Making Music in the Arab World*; or Shiloah, *Music in the World of Islam*.

39 Clip available on the book website (www.jihadiculture.net).

40 This sample corresponds to those contained in the larger collection that Lahoud catalogs in her chapter.

41 Clip available on the book website (www.jihadiculture.net).

42 Some argue that *anashid* should qualify as illegitimate music because they potentially shift the emphasis away from the message to the quality of the singing, the melodic beauty, or other non-religious features.

43 Nelly Lahoud draws a similar conclusion in her chapter by suggesting that "jihadi leaders use *anashid* as a tool to forge bonds between jihadis and mine their emotions to produce an activist jihadi culture."

44 www.ummah.com/forum/showthread.php?60303-the-best-of-Jihadi-Nasheeds [Accessed August 21, 2011].

45 http://wup-forum.com/viewtopic.php?f=35&t=17781 [Accessed August 21, 2011]. Also, see www.unasheed.com/5-best-jihad-nasheed/ [Accessed August 23, 2011].

46 Tia DeNora, *Music in Everyday Life* (Cambridge: Cambridge University Press, 2000), 111.

47 John Lofland and Rodney Stark, "Becoming a World-Saver: A Theory of Conversion to a Deviant Perspective," *American Sociological Review* 30, no. 6 (1965): 862–875; Rodney Stark and William Sims Bainbridge, "Networks of Faith: Interpersonal Bonds and Recruitment to Cults and Sects," *American Journal of Sociology* 85, no. 6 (1980): 1376–1395; Randy Blazak, "White Boys to Terrorist Men Target Recruitment of Nazi Skinheads," *American Behavioral Scientist* 44, no. 6 (February 1,

2001): 982–1000; Marc Sageman, *Understanding Terror Networks* (Philadelphia: University of Pennsylvania Press, 2004); Paul Staniland, *Networks of Rebellion: Explaining Insurgent Cohesion and Collapse* (Ithaca, NY: Cornell University Press, 2014).

48 Stark and Bainbridge, "Networks of Faith," 1397.

49 Madeleine Gruen, "Innovative Recruitment and Indoctrination Tactics by Extremists: Video Games, Hip Hop, and the World Wide Web," in *The Making of a Terrorist*, ed. James J. F. Forest, vol. 1 (Westport, CT: Praeger, 2005), 28–46; Thomas Hegghammer, "The Recruiter's Dilemma Signalling and Rebel Recruitment Tactics," *Journal of Peace Research* 50, no. 1 (January 1, 2013): 3–16; Gabriel Weimann, "Terrorist Dot Com: Using the Internet for Terrorist Recruitment and Mobilization," in *The Making of a Terrorist*, ed. James J. F. Forest, vol. 1 (Westport, CT: Praeger, 2005), 53–65.

50 Jonathan Pieslak, *Sound Targets: American Soldiers and Music in the Iraq War* (Bloomington: Indiana University Press, 2009).

51 Video from Mohamed Sifaoui's undercover infiltration of a French-Algerian al-Qaida cell shows a scene where members of the cell listen to *anashid* as they drive. The overdubbed narration suggests that the music helps motivate their enthusiasm. My thanks to Thomas Hegghammer for bringing this video to my attention. See www.youtube.com/watch?v=pfEF_sKlgVc [Accessed June 18, 2011]. Additionally, see Marc Galanter and James J. F. Forest, "Cults, Charismatic Groups, and Social Systems: Understanding the Transformation of Terrorist Recruits," in *The Making of a Terrorist*, ed. James J. F. Forest, vol. 2 (Westport, CT: Praeger, 2005), 51–70.

52 Baily, *Can You Stop the Birds Singing?*, 152; Simon Broughton, *Breaking the Silence: Music in Afghanistan*, Documentary, (2002), 14′30″.

53 Like the hip-hop and rap intended to draw Western-exposed Islamic youth to an ideology that views Western culture and music as evil, how *anashid* function within the cultural life of al-Qaida (and conservative jihadists in general) is somewhat ironic. It is the objectionable aspects of *anashid* – its ability to eclipse the religious message – that draw the majority of listeners to it.

54 Robert J. Sternberg and Karin Sternberg, *The Nature of Hate* (New York: Cambridge University Press, 2008), 16–19; Roger Dale Petersen, *Understanding Ethnic Violence: Fear, Hatred, and Resentment in Twentieth-Century Eastern Europe* (Cambridge: Cambridge University Press, 2002), 23–29; Kathleen M. Blee, *Inside Organized Racism: Women in the Hate Movement* (Berkeley: University of California Press, 2003). Other studies of note are Donald L. Horowitz, *The Deadly Ethnic Riot* (Berkeley: University of California Press, 2003); Jack Levin and Jack

Mcdevitt, *Hate Crimes Revisited: America's War On Those Who Are Different* (Boulder: Basic Books, 2002); Roger Dale Petersen and Sarah Zukerman Daly, "Revenge or Reconciliation: Theory and Method of Emotions in the Context of Colombia's Peace Process," in *Law in Peace Negotiations*, ed. Morten Bergsmo and Pablo Kalmanovitz (Oslo: Torkel Opsahl, 2010); Elisabeth J. Wood, "The Emotional Benefits of Insurgency in El Salvador," in *Passionate Politics. Emotions and Social Movements*, ed. Jeff Goodwin, James M. Jasper, and Francesca Polletta (Chicago: University of Chicago Press, 2001), 267–281.

Emotion appears to be a strong catalyst for violence – so strong, in fact, that American society has acknowledged and nuanced the ways in which emotion plays a role in the ultimate form of violence: murder. If, for example, a man comes home to find his wife in bed with his best friend and shoots them, this will often be termed a "crime of passion," which seemingly lessens the severity of the act though the acknowledgment that intense emotional responses can bypass reason.

55 Clip available on the book website (www.jihadiculture.net).

56 Many, if not all, of the texts used in jihad-themed *anashid* would qualify as jihadi poetry with the notable distinction that – it seems – few authors of jihad-themed *anashid* have actually been involved with violent jihad. This also raises the important issue about distinguishing the author of the texts from the composer of the music from the performer. Mostly, it appears that the performer of a jihad-themed *anashid* is the poet and composer. Clip available on the book website (www.jihadiculture.net).

57 This is not to suggest that emotion stands opposite to reason in a way reminiscent of the French Enlightenment view of humanity, which resolutely emphasized reason and the individual. Rather, emotion can obfuscate our ability to critically reflect on the "reason"-able nature of our decisions and views. Emotion and reason are intertwined such that emotionally driven views can easily become rationalized through the reinforcement of propaganda. We might view this as more reflective of the British Enlightenment view of humanity, emphasizing the social side of human interaction, wherein the rationalization of the ideas expressed in violent propaganda might be seen as the product of one's need for social acceptance, or "coming to accept the opinions of one's friends."

58 See, for example, Judith Becker, *Deep Listeners: Music, Emotion, and Trancing* (Bloomington: Indiana University Press, 2004); Petr Janata, "The Neural Architecture of Music-Evoked Autobiographical Memories," *Cerebral Cortex*, January 1, 2009, 2579–2594; Aniruddh H. Patel, *Music, Language, and the Brain* (Oxford: Oxford University Press, 2010).

59 Matthias Bartsch, Matthias Gebauer, and Yassin Musharbash, "Facebook Jihad: The Radical Islamist Roots of the Frankfurt Attack," *Spiegel Online*, March 3, 2011.

60 Florian Flade, "The Double Life Of Arid U., The Frankfurt Airport Gunman," *Worldcrunch*, March 4, 2011, www.worldcrunch.com/double-life-arid-u-frankfurt-airport-gunman/world-affairs/the-double-life-of-arid-u.-the-frankfurt-airport-gunman/c1s2613/.

61 http://archive.indianexpress.com/news/osama-s-name-flows-in-our-blood-exrapper/840441/ [Accessed November 17, 2011].

62 Bartsch, Gebauer, and Musharbash, "Facebook Jihad."

63 https://ojihad.wordpress.com/2011/03/12/frankfurt-shooter-driven-by-hollywood-movie/ [Accessed February 11, 2016.]

64 Ibid. The video has since been removed from YouTube.

65 Bartsch, Gebauer, and Musharbash, "Facebook Jihad."

66 Emily Allen, "Kosovan Shot Dead Two U.S. Airmen Because He Thought Facebook Clip of Movie Showing Muslim Woman Raped by American Soldiers Was Real," *Mail Online*, September 1, 2011.

67 Ibid.

68 Ibid.

69 Another notable example of *anashid* inspiring Muslims to violence is the case of Khalid al-'Awhali, a would-be suicide bomber who happened to survive the attacks on the U.S. Embassy in Nairobi in 1998; see Lahoud's chapter in this volume.

Chapter 4

1 This is an argument convincingly made by Peter Chelkowski and Hamid Dabashi in their study of revolutionary art in Iran: *Staging a Revolution: The Art of Persuasion in the Islamic Republic of Iran* (New York: New York University Press, 1999).

2 Although still small, the body of scholarly literature on this topic is growing. See, for instance, Rudiger Lohlker, *Jihadism: Online Discourses and Representations* (Vienna: Vienna University Press, 2013); Manuel Torres Soriano, "The Road to Media Jihad: The Propaganda Actions of Al Qaeda in the Islamic Maghreb," *Terrorism and Political Violence* 23, no. 1 (2011): 72–88; P. R. Baines et al., "The Dark Side of Political Marketing: Islamist Propaganda, Reversal Theory and British Muslims," *European Journal of Marketing* 44, no. 3–4 (2010): 478–495; and Akil Awan, "Virtual Jihadist Media", *European Journal of Cultural Studies* 10, no. 3 (2007): 389–408. Also, on the strategic use of narrative and propaganda by jihadist and other violent extremist groups see Neville Bolt, *The Violent Image: Insurgent Propaganda and the New Revolutionaries* (New York: Columbia University Press, 2012).

3 For the Militant Imagery Project database: www.ctc.usma.edu/pro
grams-resources/militant-imagery-project [Accessed April 19, 2017].
Also for the precursor to this collection see Afshon Ostovar et al., *Visual
Motifs in Jihadi Internet Propaganda* (West Point, NY: Combating
Terrorism Center, 2006).

4 See, Chelkowski and Dabashi's *Staging a Revolution*, and Zeina
Maasri's work on the visual imagery used by Lebanese militias during
the civil war, *Off the Wall: Political Posters of the Lebanese Civil War*
(London: I. B. Tauris, 2009).

5 For instance, see Maasri's *Off the Wall*.

6 On the development of the IRGC's emblem see Afshon Ostovar, *Vanguard of the Imam: Religion, Politics, and Iran's Revolutionary Guards*
(New York: Oxford University Press, 2016).

7 On the politics that drive Kashmir-centric militancy in Pakistan, see
Husain Haqqani, "Ideologies of South Asian Jihadi Groups" (Washing-
ton, DC: Carnegie Endowment for International Peace, 2005). On
Lashkar-e Taiba, see Stephen Tankel, *Storming the World Stage: The
Story of Lashkar-E-Taiba* (New York: Columbia University Press, 2011).

8 The visual symbolism adopted by the Black Liberation Army, a small,
radical, criminal organization active in the 1970s is an example of this.
On the BLA's activism see William Rosenau, "Our Blacks Are against the
Wall": The Black Liberation Army and Domestic Terrorism in 1970s
America," *Studies in Conflict and Terrorism*, 36, no. 2 (2013): 176–192.
Also, for more examples of this type of leftist imagery, see Rupert
Goldsworthy, "Revolt into Style: Images of West German 'Terrorism'
from 68–77," *Aftershock Magazine*, no. 1, Winter 2006, http://aftershock
magazine.com/goldsworthy68.html [Accessed May 2012].

9 Distribution networks are particularly important in the case of al-Qaida
and the associated jihadist movement. For a discussion on jihadi internet
forums as media entities see Akil N. Anwan, "Virtual Jihadist Media:
Function, Legitimacy, and Radicalizing Efficacy," *European Journal of
Cultural Studies* 10, no. 3 (2007): 389–408. Also see Daniel Kimmage's
work on the electronic media networks of al-Qaida and Iraqi jihadist
groups: Daniel Kimmage and Kathleen Ridolfo, *Iraqi Insurgent Media:
The War of Images and Ideas*. RFE/RL Special Report, June 2007; and
Daniel Kimmage, "The Al-Qaeda Media Nexus." RFE/RL Special Report,
March 2008; Also, on media efforts more broadly see Bolt, *Violent Image*.

10 See William McCants, *The ISIS Apocalypse: The History, Strategy, and
Doomsday Vision of the Islamic State* (New York: St. Martin's Press,
2015), pp. 5–29.

11 For the historical significance of the black flag and other layers of
meaning it might have for the jihadist community see Lohlker, *Jihadism*,

pp. 43–45; see also Martin Hinds, "The Banners and Battle Cries at Siffin," *Studies in Early Islamic History 4* (Princeton: Darwin Press, 1996).

12 William McCants, "Black Flag," *Foreign Policy*, November 7, 2011, www.foreignpolicy.com/articles/2011/11/07/black_flag_al_qaeda [Accessed March 10, 2012]. Also, for AQI's original statement, see www.muslm.net/vb/showthread.php?348110 [Accessed September 2012].

13 McCants, *ISIS Apocalypse*, pp. 19–22.

14 See, for example, Ostovar et al., *Visual Motifs in Jihadi Internet Propaganda*.

15 Translation from Ahmed Ali, *Al-Qur'an: A Contemporary Translation* (Princeton: Princeton University Press, 1993).

16 See Bolt, *Violent Image*, pp. 2–50, on how tactics like terrorism attacks can play into a militant group's strategic communications.

17 On Jundallah, see Andun Kolstad Wiig, "Islamist Opposition in the Islamic Republic: Jundullah and the Spread of Extremist Deobandism in Iran," Norwegian Defence Research Establishment (FFI), July 2009.

18 Jihadist designers regularly draw from popular culture in depicting the mujahid hero. For example, popular video games such as "Call of Duty" and fantasy films such as the *Lord of the Rings* trilogy have been the inspiration for other depictions of the mujahid. See, for example, http://occident.blogspot.com/2009/12/cyber-jihadis-lord-of-rings-obsession.html [Accessed April 19, 2017].

19 On Khattab's background and activities in Chechnya see Thomas Hegghammer, *Jihad in Saudi Arabia: Violence and Pan-Islamism since 1979* (New York: Cambridge University Press, 2010), passim; Yossef Bodansky, *Chechen Jihad: Al Qaeda's Training Ground and the Next Wave of Terror* (New York: Harper, 2007); and Brian Glyn Williams, "Allah's Foot Soldiers: An Assessment of the Role of Foreign Fighters and Al-Qa'ida in the Chechen Insurgency," in *Ethno-Nationalism, Islam and the State in the Caucasus: Post-Soviet Disorder*, ed. M. Gammer (London: Routledge, 2008).

20 See, for instance, "Assad's Forces Seize Homs District from Rebels: Activists," *Reuters*, December 29, 2012, http://articles.chicagotribune.com/2012-12-29/news/sns-rt-us-syria-crisis-homsbre8bs06z-20121229_1_hama-province-homs-aleppo-province [Accessed March 2013]; see also "Details of the Death of Muhammad Qanita ..." (in Arabic), *Dam Press*, December 29, 2012, www.dampress.net/index.php?page=show_det&category_id=7&id=24552 [Accessed March 2013].

21 The image includes two different versions of the group Jama'at al-Tawhid wa'l-Jihad's emblem at left and right, along with the words "Lion of Tawhid: Abu Umar al-Maqdisi, may God be merciful (*rahmat allah*)."

22 For instance, see Assaf Moghadam, "Motives for Martyrdom: Al-Qaida, Salafi Jihad, and the Spread of Suicide Attacks." *International Security* 33, no. 3 (winter 2008/2009): 46–78.
23 See Nerina Rustomji, *The Garden and the Fire: Heaven and Hell in Islamic Culture* (New York: Columbia University Press, 2009).
24 The image is from *Inspire* no. 1, Summer 2010, p. 30.
25 Abu Muslim, *Sahih*, book 20 (*al-imara*), no. 4680.
26 For example, the group Harakat-e Ansar-e Iran has posted material to jihadist forums of much higher quality than Jundallah, whose comparably cruder designs were mostly posted to its own websites.
27 See, for example, www.as-ansar.com/vb/forumdisplay.php?f=4 [Accessed March 2012].
28 See, for example, www.as-ansar.com/vb/forumdisplay.php?f=108 [Accessed March 2012].

Chapter 5

1 The terms "jihadi film" and "jihadi video" are used interchangeably throughout this chapter. They refer to a video that is produced by, or on behalf of, a jihadi group. The term is a direct translation of the Arabic term that jihadis themselves use to describe their videos: *aflam jihadiyya*. On skepticism to moving images, see Douglas A. Boyd, "Saudi Arabian Television," *Journal of Broadcasting* 15, no. 1 (December 1, 1970): 73–78.
2 Numerous studies discuss emotional effects of films, see, for instance, Greg M. Smith, *Film Structure and the Emotion System* (Cambridge: Cambridge University Press, 2003); Ed S. Tan, *Emotion and the Structure of Narrative Film: Film as an Emotion Machine* (Mahwah, NJ: Lawrence Erlbaum, 1996); Carl Plantinga and Greg M. Smith, eds., *Passionate Views: Film, Cognition, and Emotion* (Baltimore: Johns Hopkins University Press, 1999).
3 Classical works on the "war propaganda" genre include Thomas W Bohn, *An Historical and Descriptive Analysis of the "Why We Fight" Series: With a New Introduction* (New York: Arno Press, 1977); Raymond Fielding, *The American Newsreel, 1911–1967* (Norman: University of Oklahoma Press, 1972); Winifred Josephine Johnston, *Memo on the Movies; War Propaganda, 1914–1939* (Norman: Cooperative Books, 1939); Richard A Maynard, ed., *Propaganda on Film: A Nation at War* (Rochelle Park, NJ: Hayden Book Co., 1975).
4 Key existing works on jihadi videos include Mohammed M. Hafez, "Martyrdom Mythology in Iraq: How Jihadists Frame Suicide Terrorism in Videos and Biographies," *Terrorism and Political Violence* 19, no. 1 (January 1, 2007): 95–115; Arab Salem, Edna Reid, and Hsinchun Chen,

"Multimedia Content Coding and Analysis: Unraveling the Content of Jihadi Extremist Groups' Videos," *Studies in Conflict & Terrorism* 31, no. 7 (June 24, 2008): 605–626; Maura Conway and Lisa McInerney, "Jihadi Video and Auto-Radicalisation: Evidence from an Exploratory YouTube Study," in *Intelligence and Security Informatics*, ed. Daniel Ortiz-Arroyo et al., Lecture Notes in Computer Science 5376 (Berlin: Springer, 2008), 108–118; A. Aaron Weisburd, "Comparison of Visual Motifs in Jihadi and Cholo Videos on YouTube," *Studies in Conflict & Terrorism* 32, no. 12 (November 30, 2009): 1066–1074; Asiem El Difraoui, "Al Qaida par l'Image ou la Prophétie du Martyre. Une Analyse Politique de la Propagande Audiovisuelle du Jihad Global" (Ph.D. dissertation, Science Po, 2010); Cecilie Finsnes, "What Is Audio-Visual Jihadi Propaganda? An Overview of the Content of FFI's Jihadi Video Database" (Norwegian Defence Research Establishment (FFI), March 20, 2010), www.ffi.no/no/Rapporter/10-00960.pdf [Accessed April 19, 2017]; James P. Farwell, "Jihadi Video in the 'War of Ideas,'" *Survival* 52, no. 6 (December 1, 2010): 127–150; Carol K. Winkler and Cori E. Dauber, eds., *Visual Propaganda and Extremism in the Online Environment* (Carlisle: Strategic Studies Institute, 2014); Matteo Vergani and Dennis Zuev, "Neojihadist Visual Politics: Comparing YouTube Videos of North Caucasus and Uyghur Militants," *Asian Studies Review* 39, no. 1 (January 2, 2015): 1–22.

5 Examples of audience-focused studies include Paul R. Baines et al., "Muslim Voices: The British Muslim Response to Islamic Video-Polemic – An Exploratory Study," Research Paper, Cranfield School of Management Research Paper Series (Bedford: Cranfield School of Management, 2006); Conway and McInerney, "Jihadi Video and Auto-Radicalisation."

6 Jihadi videos have been accessed via FFI's Jihadi Video Database, a collection of some 800 jihadi videos stored electronically at the Norwegian Defense Research Establishment (FFI) at Kjeller, Norway. Most of the videos referenced in this chapter are also available on the book's website (www.jihadculture.com).

7 Ali Ahmad Jalali and Lester W. Grau, *Afghan Guerrilla Warfare: In the Words of the Mujahideen Fighters* (St. Paul, MN: MBI Publishing., 2001), 108.

8 David B. Edwards, "Images from Another War in Afghanistan," *Nieman Reports* 55 (Winter 2001), 49–50.

9 Jalali and Grau, *Afghan Guerrilla Warfare*, 396.

10 Ibid., 129.

11 Izzam Diraz, *al-ansar al-'arab fi afghanistan*, FFI's Jihadi Video Database, Video No. 852.

12 Today these clips can be accessed on YouTube. See, for example, *Lovers of Martyrdom*, uploaded November 2, 2011, www.youtube.com/watch?v=-5cXADo-70Y [Accessed October 2, 2012].

13 Many of the films during the Afghan, Bosnian, and Chechen wars were made by professional filmmakers. An eyewitness account mentions one Saudi in particular, who by 1996 had made "hundreds" of films from the above mentioned areas. According to the source, "[The films] were printed in Europe and sold in the mosques after the Friday prayers." Omar Nasiri, *Inside the Jihad: My Life with Al-Qaeda* (Cambridge, MA: Perseus, 2006), 231.

14 "Abu Musa al-Almaani," *Azzam*, undated, www.azzam.com (file stored with author).

15 "Abu Musa al-Almaani" (italics in the original).

16 "Masood al-Benin," *Azzam*, undated, www.azzam.com (file stored with author).

17 *United States v. Muhamed Mubayyid and Emadeddin Z. Muntasser*, U.S. Court of Appeals, September 1, 2011.

18 *United States of America v. Hassan Abu-Jihaad*, U.S. District Court, District of Connecticut, December 7, 2007.

19 According to a court case, "in May 2000 a propaganda video was for sale at the Four Feathers mosque showing Ibn Khattab executing a Russian soldier, with all proceeds to go to support the brothers in Chechnya." http://siac.decisions.tribunals.gov.uk/Documents/QATADA_FINAL_7FEB2007.pdf [Accessed April 19, 2017].

20 *United States of America v. Babar Ahmad*, U.S. District Court, District of Connecticut, July 28, 2004. Note that Qoqaz.net was not the same web page as kavkaz.com and kavkaz.org. These were run by the Dagestani government, and Movladi Udugov's "Institute for Strategic Research," respectively. See T. L. Thomas, "Manipulating the Mass Consciousness: Russian & Chechen 'Information War' Tactics in the Second Chechen-Russian Conflict," n.d., 115–117.

21 "Biography of the Martyr: Suraqah Al-Andalusi R.A. (Battle of Tora Bora)," *Ansar al-Mujahideen* January 8, 2012, www.ansar1.info [Accessed April 18, 2012].

22 "Now on sale: The First Mujahideen Video in the English Language," Azzam.com, December 4, 2000, http://web.archive.org/web/20001204 0638/www.azzam.com/ [Accessed via *Archive*, October 15, 2012].

23 Ed Husain, *The Islamist: Why I Joined Radical Islam in Britain, What I Saw inside and Why I Left* (London; New York: Penguin, 2007), 74.

24 "Abu Zubair al-Madani," *Azzam.com* http://web.archive.org/web/2001 0211112615/http://azzam.com/html/storiesabuzubairmadani.htm [Accessed via *Archive*, September 26, 2012].

25 The video was accessed on YouTube: "*abu zubair al-madani wa abu-'abbas al-madani rahimahumma allah,*" uploaded November 29, 2008 www.youtube.com/watch?v=3HsTL6BUryI [Accessed September 26, 2012].

26 The video is stored by the author.

27 Qoqaz.net, archived on March 2, 2000, http://web.archive.org/web/20000302164055/www.qoqaz.net/ [Accessed via *Internet Archive*, October 2, 2012].

28 This assumption is based on the fact that the video was sold through Azzam publications and mentioned in several court cases against militant Islamist organizations and persons based in the West.

29 One source says that al-Sahab was founded by bin Laden and that Abu Anas al-Makki was its first leader; another source says that al-Sahab was founded by a man named Hamza al-Ghamidi (note: not the 9/11 hijacker), and that Abu Anas al-Makki was put in charge of it by bin Laden in 1999. Nasser al-Bahri and Georges Malbrunot, *Dans l'ombre de Ben Laden: Révélations de son Garde du Corps Repenti* (Paris: Michel Lafon, 2010), 117–119; Evan F. Kohlmann, "Inside As-Sahaab: The Story of Ali Al-Bahlul and the Evolution of Al-Qaida's Propaganda" (New York: NEFA Foundation, December 2008), 2.

30 Kohlmann, "Inside As-Sahaab," 2.

31 Ibid., 5.

32 The *USS Cole* video is divided into two parts: The first part bears the title *The Destruction of the American Destroyer USS Cole*, while the second part opens with the title "The Solution." FFI's Jihadi Video Database, Videos No. 647 and 648.

33 al-Bahri and Malbrunot, *Dans l'Ombre*, 117–119.

34 Al-Qaida explicitly denied responsibility for the *USS Cole* bombing in the Arab press. Thomas Hegghammer, *Dokumantasjon Om Al-Qaida: Intervjuer, Kommunikéer Og Andre Primærkilder, 1990–2002 [Documentation on Al-Qaida: Interviews, Communiqués and Other Primary Sources, 1990–2002]* (Kjeller: Norwegian Defence Research Establishment (FFI), 2002), 88.

35 Kohlmann, "Inside As-Sahaab: The Story of Ali Al-Bahlul and the Evolution of Al-Qaida's Propaganda," 4.

36 Ibid., 3.

37 Ibid., 4.

38 Ibid.

39 Ibid., 3.

40 "MBC Correspondent Says He Has Met Bin-Ladin," *MBC Television* Arabic, June 24, 2001, FBIS-translated text.

41 David Rohde and C. J. Chivers, "A NATION CHALLENGED; Qaeda's Grocery Lists and Manuals of Killing," *The New York Times*, March 17, 2002.

42 Later, the French Channel 2 was accused of distorting the clip in order to put Israeli Defence Forces (IDF) in a bad light. In 2007 a French court case ruled in support of one of one of the fiercest critics of the clip, the French media watchdog Philippe Karsenty. It was never proven that Muhammed al-Durrah had actually been shot and killed by the IDF.

43 James Fallows, "Who Shot Mohammed Al-Dura?," *The Atlantic*, June 2003.

44 *The Manhattan Raid – Pt. 1* and *The Bouchaoui Attack*, FFI's Jihadi Video Database, Videos No. 326 and 498.

45 Kohlmann, "Inside As-Sahaab: The Story of Ali Al-Bahlul and the Evolution of Al-Qaida's Propaganda," 6.

46 Al-Zarqawi's group/Al-Qaida in Iraq has had several official names: *Monotheism and Jihad*, *Al-Qaida in the Land of the Two Rivers* (or *Mesopotamia*), *The Mujahideen Shura Council*, and *The Islamic State of Iraq*. In this chapter they are all referred to as "al-Qaida in Iraq" although al-Zarqawi's group *Monotheism and Jihad* was not officially aligned with al-Qaida.

47 Finsnes, "What Is Audio-Visual Jihadi Propaganda? An Overview of the Content of FFI's Jihadi Video Database," 18–19.

48 Maura Conway, "Terrorism and the Making of the 'New Middle East': New Media Strategies of Hezbollah and Al Qaeda," in *New Media and the New Middle East*, ed. Philip Seib, Palgrave Macmillan Series in International Political Communication (New York: Palgrave Macmillan US, 2007), 235–258.

49 Rima Salihah, *Death Industry*, al-Arabiyyah Television Dubai, January 1, 2012, 19:09.

50 Abu Maysarah al-Iraqi, known as al-Zarqawi's online spokesman, praised Tsouli's efforts by writing, "Bless the terrorist, Irhaby 007. In the name of Allah, I am pleased with your presence my beloved brother. May Allah protect you." Evan F. Kohlmann, "Expert Report II: U.S. v. Amawi et al.," Expert Report (New York: NEFA Foundation, January 2008), 29.

51 Bill Roggio, "US Targets Al Qaeda's Al Furqan Media Wing in Iraq," *The Long War Journal*, October 28, 2007, www.longwarjournal.org/archives/2007/10/us_targets_al_qaedas.php [Accessed April 19, 2017].

52 Conway, "Terrorism and the Making of the 'New Middle East.'"

53 In 2005, a letter from Ayman al-Zawahiri to al-Zarqawi was found in Iraq where al-Zawahiri argues that the beheading videos give AQI

negative publicity and that they should be avoided. However, AQI stopped issuing beheading videos almost a year before the letter was written. Author's interview with Truls Tønnessen, FFI, October 4, 2012.

54 *Winds of Victory*, FFI's Jihadi Video Database, Video No. 96.
55 *Lions of the War*, FFI's Jihadi Video Database, Video No. 35.
56 Kohlmann, "Expert Report II: U.S. v. Amawi et al.," 19.
57 *The Expedition of Shaykh Umar Hadid*, FFI's Jihadi Video Database, Video No. 120.
58 *United States of America v. Tarek Mehanna*, U.S. District Court, District of Massachusetts, Cr. No. 09-00017-GAO.
59 *The Expedition of Shaykh Umar Hadid*, 59:30.
60 Ibid., 35:15.
61 Ibid., 40:35.
62 Kohlmann, "Expert Report II: U.S. v. Amawi et al.," 18.
63 *Hell of the Apostates in Somalia*, al-Shabab, 2006. Stored by the author.
64 *The Blessed Dinsur Battle*, al-Shabab, 2008. Stored by the author.
65 Omar Hammami later broke with al-Shabab and was allegedly killed by al-Shabab officials in 2013. Bill Roggio, "Shabaab Kills American Jihadist Omar Hammami and British Fighter," *The Long War Journal*, September 12, 2013, www.longwarjournal.org/archives/2013/09/shabaab_kills_americ.php.
66 *The Beginning of the End: A Response to Barack Obama*. Al-Shabab, 2009. Stored by the author.
67 *Ambush at Bardal*. Al-Shabab, 2009. Stored by the author.
68 For more elaborate studies of IS propaganda, see Charlie Winter, *The Virtual "Caliphate": Understanding Islamic State's Propaganda Strategy* (London: Quilliam Foundation, July 2015); Aaron Y. Zelin, "Picture or It Didn't Happen: A Snapshot of the Islamic State's Official Media Output," *Perspectives on Terrorism* 9, no. 4 (August 21, 2015): 85–97.
69 Olivia Becker, "ISIS Has a Really Slick and Sophisticated Media Department," *VICE*, July 12, 2014; Cori E. Dauber and Mark Robinson, "GUEST POST: ISIS and the Hollywood Visual Style," *Jihadology*, July 6, 2015, http://jihadology.net/2015/07/06/guest-post-isis-and-the-hollywood-visual-style/ [Accessed April 19, 2017]; Steve Rose, "The Isis Propaganda War: A Hi-Tech Media Jihad," *The Guardian*, October 7, 2014.
70 Zelin, "Picture or It Didn't Happen," 89.
71 Dauber and Robinson, "GUEST POST."
72 *Flames of War: Fighting Has Just Begun*, Al-Hayat, September 2014. The example is from 11:15 onwards.

Chapter 6

1 John C. Lamoreaux, *The Early Muslim Tradition of Dream Interpretation* (Albany: State University of New York Press, 2002), 84.

2 Interview by Iain Edgar with Rahimullah Yusufzai, Peshawar, April 2005.

3 Yosri Fouda and Nick Fielding, *Masterminds of Terror: The Truth behind the Most Devastating Terrorist Attack the World Has Ever Seen* (London: Mainstream Publishing, 2003), 109.

4 Robert Fisk, *The Great War for Civilization: The Conquest of the Middle East* (London: Fourth Estate, 2005), 34.

5 Iain Edgar, *The Dream in Islam: From Qur'anic Tradition to Jihadist Inspiration* (New York: Berghahn Books, 2011); Elizabeth Sirriyeh, "Dream Narratives of Muslims' Martyrdom: Constant and Changing Roles Past and Present," *Dreaming* 21, no. 3 (2011): 168–180.

6 Richard Bonney, *Jihad: From Qu'ran to Bin Laden* (Hampshire: Palgrave Macmillan, 2004); Lamoreaux, *The Early Muslim Tradition of Dream Interpretation*.

7 Edgar, *The Dream in Islam*.

8 Sirriyeh, "Dream Narratives of Muslims' Martyrdom: Constant and Changing Roles Past and Present," 168.

9 Leah Kinberg, "Literal Dreams and Prophetic 'Hadîts' in Classical Islam – A Comparison of Two Ways of Legitimation," *Der Islam* 70, no. 2 (1993): 279–281, especially fn. 2–8.

10 Iain Edgar, "A Comparison of Islamic and Western Psychological Dream Theories," in *Dreaming in Christianity and Islam Culture, Conflict, and Creativity*, ed. Kelly Bulkeley, Kate Adams, and Patricia M Davis (New Brunswick, NJ: Rutgers University Press, 2009), 188–199.

11 Lamoreaux, *The Early Muslim Tradition of Dream Interpretation*, 16.

12 Ibid., 15.

13 The Holy Qur'an, Published by King Fahd Holy Quran Printing Complex, al-Madinah al Munawarah, 1410 H (1989), Sura 8:43. All other Qur'anic quotations are from the same source.

14 Lamoreaux, *The Early Muslim Tradition of Dream Interpretation*, 116.

15 Ibid., 110–112.

16 Ibid., 112–115; Kinberg, "Literal Dreams and Prophetic 'Hadîts' in Classical Islam," 283 especially fn. 11–12.

17 Bukhari LXXXVII-112. The 1/46th part is commonly explained as pointing to a six-month period in which the Prophet received divine revelation through dreams instead of through a divine messenger.

18 Cf. Lamoreaux, *The Early Muslim Tradition of Dream Interpretation*, 118. Bukhari LXXXVII-119: "Narrated Abu Huraira: I heard Allah's

Apostle saying 'Nothing is left of prophetism except al-Mubashirat.' They asked: 'What are al-Mubashirat?' He replied: 'True, good dreams' (that convey glad tidings)." As we show later, this *hadith* became very important in the Islamic dream tradition.

19 E.g. Bukhari, LXXXVII-1:111.
20 Kinberg, "Literal Dreams and Prophetic 'Hadîts' in Classical Islam," 285–286; Cf. Edgar, *The Dream in Islam*, 7–26.
21 Later, this new means of communication with the "otherworld" expands to other dead people, which makes way for – among other things – the martyrdom tradition; David Cook, *Martyrdom in Islam* (Cambridge: Cambridge University Press, 2007), 116–134; Edgar, *The Dream in Islam*, 9ff.
22 Bukhari, LXXXVII-26:144.
23 Kinberg, "Literal Dreams and Prophetic 'Hadîts'" 291–292.
24 Lamoreaux, *The Early Muslim Tradition of Dream Interpretation*, 2–3.
25 Lamoureaux reports of an estimated compilation of 158 manuals in Arabic and 23 in Persian and Turkish. In fact, Lamoreaux concludes from this sheer number of manuals that, at the time, the interpretation of dreams must have been as important as the interpretation of the Qur'an. Cf. ibid., 4.
26 For instance, the collectors of the strongest *hadiths*, Muslim Ibn al-Hajjaj and al-Bukhari died in 875 C.E. and 870 C.E., respectively.
27 Lamoreaux, *The Early Muslim Tradition of Dream Interpretation*, 16.
28 For an overview, see ibid., 17–19.
29 Ibid., 3. He quotes Fahd, who found 158 different medieval dream manuals in Arabic and another twenty-three in Persian and Turkish; Fahd Toufic, *Artemidorus: Le Livre des songes* (Damascus: Institut Français de Damas, 1964), xxii.
30 Lamoreaux, *The Early Muslim Tradition of Dream Interpretation*, 2.
31 Ibid., 22, fn. 20.
32 Ibid., 23.
33 Ibid., 27–32.
34 Ibid., 41.
35 J. Spencer Trimingham, *The Sufi Orders in Islam* (London: Oxford University Press, 1971).
36 Iain Edgar and David Henig, "Istikhara: The Guidance and Practice of Islamic Dream Incubation through Ethnographic Comparison," *History and Anthropology* 21, no. 3 (2010): 251–262.
37 Michael Gilsenan, "Signs of Truth: Enchantment, Modernity and the Dreams of Peasant Women," *Journal of the Royal Anthropological Society* 6, no. 4 (2000): 611.

38 Andy Lines, "Sick Videotape Proves Bin Laden Was the Evil Mastermind behind the Horrors of Sept 11," *The Mirror*, December 14, 2001.

39 Iain Edgar, "The `true Dream' in Contemporary Islamic/Jihadist Dreamwork: A Case Study of the Dreams of Taliban Leader Mullah Omar," *Contemporary South Asia* 15, no. 3 (2006): 263–272; Iain Edgar, "The Inspirational Night Dream in the Motivation and Justification of Jihad," *Nova Religio* 11, no. 2 (2007): 59–76; Edgar, *The Dream in Islam*.

40 Al-Jazeera journalist Yosri Fouda interviewed Khalid Sheikh Mohammed and Ramzi bin al-Shibh in Karachi in mid-2002. Fouda has said he possesses hours of unpublished tape recordings in which the two 9/11 attack coordinators relate their dreams; Fouda and Fielding, *Masterminds of Terror*, 109.

41 Amira Mittermaier, *Dreams That Matter: Egyptian Landscapes of the Imagination* (Berkeley: University of California Press, 2010), 18–19.

42 Cf. Mittermaier, *Dreams That Matter*.

43 Edgar, "A Comparison of Islamic and Western Psychological Dream Theories."

44 According to Yusufzai, Omar trusted him because "The BBC is very powerful in Afghanistan; they [the Taliban] wanted to have good relations with the BBC, and I was the first one to reach Kandahar and report about the emerging Taliban. Mullah Omar was grateful to me; that's why he will call me up; I spoke the same language Pashto and I was a Muslim, I was a Pakistani, I was someone he could trust."

45 Edgar, *The Dream in Islam*, 83.

46 Ibid., 82.

47 Ibid., 83.

48 Katherine C Donahue, *Slave of Allah: Zacarias Moussaoui vs. the USA* (London: Pluto Press, 2007).

49 Ibid., 80–81.

50 Ibid.

51 Ibid.

52 Tim Reid, "'Shoe-Bomber' Likely to Be Jailed for Life," *The Times*, January 30, 2003.

53 Ibid., 93.

54 Leah Kinberg, "Interaction between This World and the Afterworld in Early Islamic Tradition," *Oriens* 29/30 (1986): 285–308.

55 Ibid., 297.

56 Abu Ameenah Bilaal Philips, *Dream Interpretation: According to the Qur'an and Sunnah* (Kuala Lumpur: A. S. Noordeen, 2001), 53. Quoting from Sahih al-Bukhari V-21:2–28.

57 Mohammed M. Hafez, "Martyrdom Mythology in Iraq: How Jihadists Frame Suicide Terrorism in Videos and Biographies," *Terrorism and Political Violence* 19, no. 1 (January 1, 2007): 95–115.

58 David Cook, "Suicide Attacks or 'Martyrdom Operations' in Contemporary Jihad Literature," *Nova Religio* 6, no. 1 (2002): 32–33.

59 John Cantlie, "Are You Ready to Die?," *Sunday Times*, August 5, 2012.

60 Cook, *Martyrdom in Islam*, 116–120.

61 Cook, "Suicide Attacks or 'Martyrdom Operations' in Contemporary Jihad Literature," 121.

62 Sirriyeh, "Dream Narratives of Muslims' Martyrdom: Constant and Changing Roles Past and Present," 175–177.

63 "In the Hearts of Green Birds: The Martyrs of Bosnia," Azzam Publications, www.islamicawakening.com [Accessed 18 January 2005].

64 Mariam Abou Zahab, "'I Shall Be Waiting for You at the Door of Paradise': The Pakistani Martyrs of the Lashkar-E Taiba (Army of the Pure)," in The Practice of War: Production, Reproduction and Communication of Armed Violence, ed. Aparna Rao, Michael Bollig, and Monika Böck (Oxford: Berghahn Books, 2008), 133–160.

65 Barbara Plett, "Jihadis Tap Anti-Musharraf Feeling," *BBC News Online*, July 14, 2007.

66 Ibid.

67 "Pakistan's Red Mosque: Start of Unrest: The Full Story behind the Red Mosque Crisis by Misbah Abdul-Baqi," www.onislam.net/english/politics/asia/433784.html, [Accessed 22 March 2013].

68 Edgar, *The Dream in Islam*, 73–78.

69 See Bart J. Koet, "Discussing Dreams in a Prison in Amsterdam," in *Dreaming in Christianity and Islam: Culture, Conflict, and Creativity*, ed. Kelly Bulkeley, Kate Adams, and Patricia M Davis (New Brunswick, NJ: Rutgers University Press, 2009), 226–235.

70 Khalid Ahmed, "TV Review," *Daily Times*, May 23, 2005.

71 Rosa Prince and Gary Jones, "My Hell in Camp X-Ray," *The Mirror*, March 12, 2004.

72 "Interview of Ibrahim Sen, a Turkish National Detained in Guantanamo," *Vakit*, November 10, 2006.

73 Iain Edgar, "The Dreams of Islamic State," *Perspectives on Terrorism* 9, no. 4 (July 31, 2015): 72–84.

74 Amarnath Amarasingam, "Elton 'Ibrahim' Simpson's Path to Jihad in Garland, Texas" http://warontherocks.com/2015/05/elton-ibrahim-simpsons-path-to-jihad-in-garland-texas/2/ [Accessed July 25, 2015].

75 At the time of writing, the Twitter account @Entimdrms was closed (https//twitter.com/entimdrms), but the very similar @entdrm13 was active (https://twitter.com/entdrm13).

76 Edgar, interview, North America, April 2012.
77 Shaykh Abu 'Ubaydah Mashhur bin Hasan Al Salman and Shaykh Abu Talhah 'Umar bin Ibraheem Al 'AbdurRahman, *Introductory Salafi Themes in the Interpretation of Visions and Dreams*, e-book (Salafi Manhaj, 2009), http://download.salafimanhaj.com/pdf/SalafiManhaj_Dreams.pdf [Accessed April 19, 2017].
78 Ibid., 9.
79 A Murid is a disciple of a Sufi Shaykh.
80 Jens Kreinath, "Virtual Encounters with Hızır and Other Muslim Saints: Dreaming and Healing at Local Pilgrimage Sites in Hatay, Turkey," *Anthropology of the Contemporary Middle East and Central Eurasia* 2, no. 1 (September 22, 2014): 25–66; See also Marzia Balzani, "Dreaming, Islam and the Ahmadiyya Muslims in the UK," History and Anthropology 21, no. 3 (September 1, 2010): 293–305.

Chapter 7

1 Translations are from Majid Fakhry, *The Qur'an: A Modern English Translation* (London: Garnet, 1997).
2 Ibn Kathir, *Tafsir Ibn Kathir*, vol. i (Beirut: Alam al-Kutub, n.d.), 402–406. (commentary on 3:169–170) is a major source for jihadi martyrdom mythology based in the *hadith* literature.
3 Muslim, *Sahih*, vi, p. 37; al-Tabari, *Jami'*, iv, pp. 170–171, cited in A. J. Wensinck, *Concordance et Indices de La Tradition Musulmane* (Leyden: E . J. Brill, 1936). and compare Ibn Qutayba, *Ta'bir al-ru'ya [Interpretation of Dreams]* (Damascus: Dar al-Basha'ir, 2001), 30.
4 al-Tirmidhi, *Al-Jami' Al-Sahih*, vol. 3 (Beirut: Dar al-Fikr, n.d.), 106 (no. 1712); See also Ibn Maja, *Sunan*, vol. ii (Beirut: Dar al-Fikr, 1988), 1452 (no. 4337); and al-Hindi al-Muttaqi, *Kanz al-'ummal [Treasure of the Doers]*, vol. iv (Beirut: Mu'assasat al-Risala, 1987), 397f., who cites many similar traditions from the entire *hadith* literature. The tradition is cited in Abdullah Azzam, "Martyrs: The Building Blocks of Nations" (Religioscope, n.d.), 2, www.religioscope.com/info/doc/jihad/azzam_martyrs.htm [Accessed May 11, 2011], and also in "The Will of Abdallah Azzam, who is poor unto his Lord," http://alribat.com/JTC-Part1.htm, 14 (section 8) [Accessed September 27, 2001].
5 The term "martyrology" has a double meaning. It may refer to a set of beliefs about martyrdom (as in this sentence) or to a hagiographic document describing a person's martyrdom. The two are used interchangeably throughout this chapter, but I trust that the reader will understand from context which one is intended in each case.
6 *Talqin* is a burial ritual that involves stating the *shahada* (the profession of faith) in the ear of the deceased believer in order to ward off the dread

angels Munkar and Nakir who will question him after death as to his status as a Muslim.

7 al-Bukhari, *Sahih*, vol. 3 (Beirut: Dar al-Fikr, 1991), 269 (no. 2803).

8 Interestingly echoed by Muhammad Atta, the leader of the Sept. 11, 2001, hijackers in his last will and testament: http://www.abc.net.au/ 4corners/atta/resources/documents/will1.htm [Accessed April 19, 2017] (note provisions 5, 6, 11).

9 For biographical details, see John C. Calvert, "The Striving Shaykh: Abdullah Azzam and the Revival of Jihad," *Journal of Religion and Society*, no. 2 (2007): 83–102.

10 "O youths, O sons of Islam! What will cleanse our sins? What will purify our mistakes? And what will clean our dir? It will not be washed except with the blood of martyrdom, an know that there is no path except this path." Azzam, "Martyrs: The Building Blocks of Nations," 3.

11 Ibid., 1.

12 Although there are scattered mentions of martyrs prior to 1985, it is from that date that Azzam begins to have a regular column on the subject.

13 *Al-Jihad* 80 (July–August 1991), 43–44.

14 *Al-Jihad* 99 (May–June 1993), 25 (Irfan al-Kashmiri).

15 *Al-Jihad* 102 (October 1993), 51 (previously his mother had also demanded that he get married because she wanted to have grandchildren, but said that "jihad was the most beloved to him in this world.")

16 *Al-Jihad* 110 (June–July 1994), 44.

17 "An African American Shaheed," *MyUmmah*, March 13, 2008, http:// myummah.co.za/site/2008/03/13/an-african-american-shaheed/.

18 "In the Hearts of Green Birds – Side A, Part 1," www.almansurah .com/jihaad/2003/050103i.htm [Accessed April 9, 2003], 3.

19 Rana Sabbagh-Gargour, "My Marriage Was a Sham, Says Wife in Jordan Bomb Team," *The Times*, April 24, 2006.

20 "In the Hearts of Green Birds – Side B, Part 1," www.almansurah .com/jihaad/2003/050103j.htm [Accessed April 9, 2003], 1.

21 Ibid, 3.

22 Ibid, 1–2, 4–5.

23 *Al-Jihad* 110 (June–July 1994), 43.

24 Shaykh Abdullah Azzam, *Ayat al-rahman fi jihad al-afghan [Signs of the Merciful in the Jihad of Afghanistan]* (Peshawar: Markaz al-Shahid Abdallah Azzam, 1990). English translation: Shaykh Abdullah Azzam, *The Signs of Ar-Rahman in the Jihad of Afghanistan*, ed. A. B. al-Mehri, e-book (Birmingham, UK: Maktabah), https://islamfuture.files.wordpress.com/2009/ 11/signs-of-ar-rahman-in-jihad-of-afghanistan.pdf [Accessed February 22, 2016]. The English version has no date but is probably from 2005.

25 Azzam, *Ayat al-rahman*, 15; Azzam, *The Signs of Ar-Rahman*, 32–33.

26 For example, al-Bukhari, *Sahih*, iii:264–265 (no 2787).

27 For more on martyr cemeteries, see Daryl Li, "Taking the Place of Martyrs: Afghans and Arabs under the Banner of Islam," *Arab Studies Journal* 20, no. 1 (2012): 12–39.

28 Azzam, *The Signs of Ar-Rahman*, 33–34. I could not find this story in the Arabic edition.

29 Azzam, *Ayat al-rahman*, 15–16; Azzam, *The Signs of Ar-Rahman*, 34–35.

30 Azzam, *Ayat al-rahman*, 16; Azzam, *The Signs of Ar-Rahman*, 35–36.

31 Wensinck, *Concordance et indices de la tradition musulmane*, s.v., *naisya* (many variants).

32 See Asiem El Difraoui, "Al Qaida par l'image ou la prophétie du martyre. Une analyse politique de la propagande audiovisuelle du jihad global" (Ph.D. dissertation, Sciences Po, 2010), 513–515.

33 Azzam, *Ayat al-rahman*, 17; Azzam, *The Signs of Ar-Rahman*, 41.

34 *Martyrs of Afghanistan*, www.alqimmah.net/showthread.php?t=3968 [Accessed September 28, 2009], 87.

35 Uri Rubin, "Pre-Existence and Light: Aspects of the Doctrine of *Nur Muhammad*," *Israel Oriental Studies* 5 (1975), 62–117.

36 David Cook, "The Recovery of Radical Islam in the Wake of the Defeat of the Taliban," *Terrorism and Political Violence* 15, no. 1 (2003), 31–56, at 43.

37 See Werner Schucker, "The Testaments of Iranian Martyrs," in *Jihad and Martyrdom*, ed. David Cook (London: Routledge, 2010), iv, num. 12 (trans. Steven Gilbert).

38 For example, *Hizballah: al-muqawama wa-l-tahrir [Hizbullah: Resistance and Liberation]*, vol. 2 and 3 (Beirut: al-Safir, 2006) or Wi 'ab al-Mihrawi, *Al-wa'd al-sadiq [The True Promise]* (Beirut: Dar al-Qari, 2007) on the 2006 war, which does not contain any martyrdom accounts.

39 Appearing in *Intifadat Al-Aqsa*, vol. 6 (Amman: Dar al-Jalil li-l-Nashr, 2003), 7 (of the pictures). For further analysis, see Laleh Khalili, *Heroes and Martyrs of Palestine: The Politics of National Commemoration* (Cambridge: Cambridge University Press, 2007).

40 For example Salah al-Raqab, *Al-shaykh al-shahid Ahmad Yasin: shahid al-fajr [The Martyr Shaykh Ahmad Yasin, the Dawn Martyr]* (Beirut: Dar Ru'ya, 2005); Husni Jarar, *Ma'an ila al-janna: shahid al-fajr wa-saqr filistin [Together to Paradise: The Dawn Martyr and the Falcon of Palestine]* (Amman, 2004); Mukhlis Yahya Barzuq, *Fada'il [Merits]* (London: Filistin al-Muslima, 2001); Ghassan Duw'ar, *Salah Shihata: amir al-shuhada' [Salih Shihata: The Commander of Martyrs]* (Beirut: Dar Ruy'a, 2005).

41 Barzuq, *Fada'il [Merits]*, 134–136.

42 "Virgins of Paradise" at www.youtube.com/watch?v=Qdx50q64Z-o [Accessed May 13, 2011]. This is also the case with regard to "Fatima's Fiance."

43 Tawfiq Yusuf al-Wa'i, *Mawsu'at shuhada' al-haraka al-islamiyya [Encyclopaedia of the Martyrs of the Islamic Movement]*, vol. 1 (Cairo: Dar al-Tawzi' wa-l-Nashr al-Islamiyya, 2006), 224.

44 Ibid., vol. 5, 67.

45 Ibid., vol. 5, 169. He carried out a martyrdom operation.

46 Ibid., vol. 5, 379.

47 Zarqawi followed in the footsteps of the Saudi group al-Qaida in the Arabian Peninsula, cf. their "Badr al-Riyadh," www.intelcenter .com/Badr-al-Riyadh-v1-1.pdf (February 8, 2004); however, the latter was nowhere near as well distributed as Zarqawi's videos were.

48 Abu Musa'b al-Zarqawi, "Wa-kadhalika al-rusul tubtala thumma yakun laha al-'aqiba" [In This Way the Messengers Are Tested, but the Finale Is Theirs] (January 21, 2005), in *Kalimat mudi'ya: al-kitab al-jami' li-khutab wa-kalimat al-shaykh al-mu'tazz bi-dinihi Abi Mus'ab al-Zarqawi [Enlightening Words: The Complete Speeches and Words of the One Who Made His Religion Glorious, Abu Mus`ab al-Zarqawi]* at e-prism.com, p. 160.

49 Ibid., 174–175.

50 Ibid., 212, *Wa-'ada ahfad Ibn al-'Alqami [The Descendants of Ibn al-'Alqami Have Returned]* (May 18, 2005).

51 Ibid., 268, *A-yanqus al-din [the u's should not be there] wa-ana hayy? [Will This Religion Be Diminished While I Yet Live?]* (July 7, 2005).

52 See, for example, pages 28 (Qur'an 61:10–13, Ibn Maja, on the description of heaven), 30 (Qur'an 9:38), 33 (exegesis of Qur'an 9:111, 3:169–70), 34–35, 100 (qualities of the *shahid*).

53 Ibid., 37 (Abd al-Hadi Dighlas), 143 (Abu Anas), referring to him as a *faris* (knight), also in his later description of a martyr (278).

54 Ibid., p. 60, "*Risala min Abi Mus'ab al-Zarqawi ila al-Shaykh Usama bin Ladin*" (Letter from Abu Mus'ab al-Zarqawi to Shaykh Usama bin Ladin), dated February 15, 2004.

55 See for example, Abu Mu'awiya al-Shimali in "Fatima's fiancé" at www.spike.com/video-clips/kf10td/fatimas-fiancee [Accessed May 14, 2011]. Thanks to Truls Tønnessen of FFI for the *Siyar a`lam al-shuhada' fi bilad al-rafidayn* (July 12, 2011).

56 E.g., Yusuf al-'Ayyiri's "Islamic Ruling on the Permissibility of Martyrdom Operations," at www.religioscope.com/pdf/martyrdom.pdf [Accessed October 31, 2011].

57 Note the Islamic Movement of Uzbekistan (IMU) martyrdom video featuring Abu Dujana (2004) prior to the Afghani and Pakistani videos:

www.youtube.com/watch?v=-kfDjl-xNbs [Accessed October 31, 2011]; martyrdom at 2:29.

58 See Brian Glyn Williams, *Afghanistan Declassified: A Guide to America's Longest War* (Philadelphia: University of Pennsylvania Press, 2011).

59 For example, www.youtube.com/verify_age?next_url=http%3A//www .youtube.com/watch%3Fv%3DYjCwPAn6RK4 [Accessed October 31, 2011].

60 "Lovers of the Hoor" Parts 1, 2, 3 at www.liveleak.com/view?i=a88_ 1206583743 [Accessed May 13, 2011]. Compare the treatise of Azzam, *'Ushshaq al-hur*, from which the name is derived.

61 "Nigeria UN Bomb: Video of 'Boko Haram Bomber' Released," *BBC News*, September 18, 2011, www.bbc.com/news/world-africa-14964554.

62 "Somalia's First Martyrdom Operation" Supposedly Carried Out by Adam Salad Adam (March 27, 2007) at www.liveleak.com/view?i= d2b_1175395454 [Accessed May 13, 2011].

63 E.g., Etan Kohlberg, "Bara'a in Shi'i Doctrine," *Jerusalem Studies in Arabic and Islam* 7 (1986): 139–175.

64 Dawood Azami, "Kandahar's Cemetery of 'Miracles,'" *BBC*, January 17, 2008, http://news.bbc.co.uk/2/hi/south_asia/7193579.stm.

65 Interview, Zahiruddin, associate editor of *Greater Kashmir* (Srinagar) (July 17, 2010).

Chapter 8

1 As Jan Snoek notes, "The number of definitions proposed [for the term 'ritual'] is endless, and no one seems to like the definitions proposed by anyone else." Jan A. M. Snoek, "Defining 'Rituals,'" in *Theorizing Rituals: Issues, Topics, Approaches, Concepts*, ed. Jens Kreinath, Jan Snoek, and Michael Stausberg (Leiden: Brill, 2006), 3.

2 For more on what we may call the "military bias" in the study of rebel groups, see Zachariah Cherian Mampilly, *Rebel Rulers : Insurgent Governance and Civilian Life during War* (Ithaca, NY: Cornell University Press, 2011), 6.

3 For textual content, see the online library *Minbar al-Tawhid wa'l-Jihad* (available at www.tawhed.ws or https://web.archive.org/web/201505140 60110/www.tawhed.ws/). For the content of videos, see Cecilie Finsnes, "What Is Audio-Visual Jihadi Propaganda? An Overview of the Content of FFI's Jihadi Video Database" (Norwegian Defence Research Establishment (FFI), March 20, 2010), www.ffi.no/no/Rapporter/10-00960.pdf.

4 For example, Western officials often claim that laptops confiscated from jihadis are full of pornography; see, for example, Phyllis Chesler, "Why

Are Jihadis So Obsessed with Porn?," *New York Post*, February 17, 2015. However, this alleged abundance of adult content on jihadi computers has never been documented with unclassified primary sources.

5 Nasser al-Bahri and Georges Malbrunot, *Dans l'ombre de Ben Laden: Révélations de son garde du corps repenti* (Paris: Michel Lafon, 2010), 52.

6 Aukai Collins, *My Jihad: The True Story of an American Mujahid's Amazing Journey from Usama Bin Laden's Training Camps to Counterterrorism with the FBI and CIA* (Guilford, CT: Lyons Press, 2002), 24.

7 Abdul Ghaffar El Almani, "Mein Weg nach Jannah," 2010, 86, www.scribd.com/doc/31071994/Schaheed-Abdul-Ghaffar-al-Almani-Mein-Weg-Nach-Jannah [Accessed November 20, 2012].

8 Collins, *My Jihad*, 27.

9 Abu Ja'far al-Misri al-Qandahari, *Dhikrayat 'arabi afghani [Memoirs of an Afghan Arab]* (Cairo: Dar al-Shuruq, 2002), 102.

10 Ibid., 117.

11 See, e.g., Fadil Harun, *Al-harb 'ala al-islam [The War against Islam]*, vol. 2, 2009, 169, 216, 222.

12 al-Bahri and Malbrunot, *Dans l'ombre*, 106.

13 Omar Nasiri, *Inside the Jihad: My Life with Al-Qaeda* (Cambridge, MA: Perseus, 2006), 39.

14 Harun, *Al-harb*, 2:253, 276.

15 Khaled al-Berry, *Life Is More Beautiful than Paradise: A Jihadist's Own Story* (Cairo: American University in Cairo Press, 2009), 130. See also p. 136.

16 Abu al-Shaqra al-Hindukushi, "*Min Kabul ila Baghdad*" [From Kabul to Baghdad], 2007, http://archive.org/details/fromcaboltobagdad [Accessed November 2, 2012], Part 6.

17 Harun, *Al-harb*, 2:282.

18 Abu Mansuur Al-Amriiki, "The Story of an American Jihaadi – Part One," 2012, 73, https://azelin.files.wordpress.com/2012/05/omar-hammami-abc5ab-mane1b9a3c5abr-al-amrc4abkc4ab-22the-story-of-an-american-jihc481dc4ab-part-122.pdf [Accessed October 31, 2015].

19 "*Badr al-riyadh*" [The Badr of Riyadh] (Al-Sahhab Foundation for Media Production, 2004).

20 Bruce Lincoln, *Holy Terrors: Thinking about Religion after September 11*, 2nd ed. (Chicago: University of Chicago Press, 2006), 97–102.

21 Harun, *Al-harb*, 2:255.

22 "Martyrs of Bosnia," (London: Azzam Publications, 2000), Part 8, around 1′30″

23 Harun, *Al-harb*, 2:269.

24 Mohamed Sifaoui, "Infiltration islamiste en France," in *Zone interdite* (Paris 2003), around 21′45″.

25 Ibid., around 47′40″.

26 Lincoln, *Holy Terrors: Thinking about Religion after September 11*, 97–102.

27 Harun, *Al-harb*, 2:246, 248.

28 Al-Berry, *Life Is More Beautiful*, 138.

29 See, for example, Nasiri, *Inside the Jihad*, 138.

30 Al-Qandahari, *Dhikrayat*, 151.

31 Al-Berry, *Life Is More Beautiful*, 63.

32 Omar Guendouz, *Les soldats perdus de l'Islam: les réseaux français de Ben Laden* (Paris: Editions Ramsay, 2002), 51.

33 Robert Fowler, *A Season in Hell: My 130 Days in the Sahara with Al Qaeda* (Toronto: Harper Collins, 2011), 79, 91.

34 Sifaoui, "Infiltration," around 8′35″

35 Richard Gauvain, "Ritual Weapons: Islamist Purity Practices in Cairo," *ISIM Review* 19 (2007): 40–41.

36 Harun, *Al-harb*, 2:281.

37 Collins, *My Jihad*, 16.

38 Al-Hindukushi, "*Min Kabul ila Baghdad*," Part 6.

39 Al-Qandahari, *Dhikrayat*, 182.

40 Harun, *Al-harb*, 2:162.

41 Nasiri, *Inside the Jihad*, 137, 146.

42 Al-Berry, *Life Is More Beautiful*, 35.

43 Al-Amriiki, "The Story of an American Jihaadi – Part One," 80.

44 Dirk Cornelis Mulder, "The Ritual of Recitation of the Qur'an," *Nederlands Theologisch Tijdschrift* 37, no. 3 (1983): 250–251.

45 Al-Amriiki, "The Story of an American Jihaadi – Part One," 56.

46 Nasiri, *Inside the Jihad*, 151.

47 Al-Berry, *Life Is More Beautiful*, 118–119.

48 Al-Bahri and Malbrunot, *Dans l'ombre*, 86.

49 Al-Hindukushi, "*Min Kabul Ila Baghdad*" [From Kabul to Baghdad], Part 6.

50 Al-Bahri and Malbrunot, *Dans l'ombre*, 37; al-Hindukushi, "*Min Kabul ila Baghdad*," Part 5.

51 Harun, *Al-Harb*, 2:276; al-Hindukushi, "*Min Kabul ila Baghdad*," Parts 2, 5, and 6; El Almani, "Mein Weg nach Jannah," 80; al-Bahri and Malbrunot, *Dans l'ombre*, 91.

52 See, for example, al-Berry, *Life Is More Beautiful*, 57.

53 Al-Bahri and Malbrunot, *Dans l'ombre*, 98.

54 El Almani, "Mein Weg nach Jannah," 96.

55 Al-Hindukushi, "*Min Kabul ila Baghdad*," Part 6.

56 Harun, *Al-harb*, 2:113.

57 Al-Berry, *Life Is More Beautiful*, 118. See also p. 41.

58 Harun, *Al-harb*, 2:251.

59 Al-Berry, *Life Is More Beautiful*, 65–66.

60 Al-Qandahari, *Dhikrayat*, 35. See also Sifaoui, *Infiltration*, around 13′00″.

61 Harun, *Al-harb*, 2:224.

62 Al-Amriiki, "The Story of an American Jihaadi – Part One," 82.

63 Ibid., 48.

64 Harun, *Al-harb*, 2:180.

65 Morten Skjoldager, *Truslen Indefra: De Danske Terrorister* (Copenhagen: Lindhart og Ringhof, 2009), 284.

66 "Martyrs of Bosnia," part 9, around 4′30″; Harun, *Al-Harb*, 2:275.

67 Al-Qandahari, *Dhikrayat*, 264.

68 Al-Berry, *Life Is More Beautiful*, 27.

69 Al-Bahri and Malbrunot, *Dans l'ombre*, 37.

70 Guendouz, *Les soldats perdus de l'Islam*, 64.

71 Nasiri, *Inside the Jihad*, 210–211.

72 Fowler, *A Season in Hell*, 54–55 See also p. 157.

73 Al-Hindukushi, "*Min Kabul ila Baghdad*," Part 8.

74 Nasiri, *Inside the Jihad*, 217.

75 Al-Hindukushi, "*Min Kabul ila Baghdad*", Part 1.

76 Fowler, *A Season in Hell*, 69–70; See also 140.

77 Most are night dreams. I encountered only one reference to a day vision. A Yemeni fighter in Somalia "had seen beautiful green birds … that no one else could see. … he took his visions to be a glad tiding of martyrdom"; see Al-Amriiki, "The Story of an American Jihaadi – Part One," 92.

78 Al-Qandahari, *Dhikrayat*, 200.

79 Al-Amriiki, "The Story of an American Jihaadi – Part One," 88.

80 Al-Qandahari, *Dhikrayat*, 204. See also "Martyrs of Bosnia," Part 7, around 6′30″, and Part 8 around 4′40″.

81 "Martyrs of Bosnia," Part 4, around 7′00″.

82 Al-Amriiki, "The Story of an American Jihaadi – Part One," 87.

83 Harun, *Al-Harb*, 2:267.

84 Al-Qandahari, *Dhikrayat*, 200.

85 Fowler, *A Season in Hell*, 126.

86 Al-Qandahari, *Dhikrayat*, 188.

87 "*Yawmiyat al-mujahid* [Diaries of a Mujahid]," (al-Sahab, 2011). See especially Parts 2 and 4.

88 Al-Qandahari, *Dhikrayat*, 230.

89 Robb Leech, "My Brother the Islamist" (Grace Productions [http://www.dailymotion.com/video/x2kw7bs (Accessed April 19, 2017)], 2011), around 19′00″.

90 Al-Berry, *Life Is More Beautiful*, 7.

91 Al-Hindukushi, "*Min Kabul ila Baghdad*", Part 7; Al-Amriiki, "The Story of an American Jihaadi – Part One," 56.

92 "*Yawmiyat al-mujahid*," Part 3.

93 Al-Hindukushi, "*Min Kabul ila Baghdad*", Part 8.

94 "Martyrs of Bosnia," Part 9, around 9′30″.

95 Al-Berry, *Life Is More Beautiful*, 49.

96 Leech, "My Brother the Islamist," around 31′00″.

97 Al-Berry, *Life Is More Beautiful*, 165.

98 Ibid., 53.

99 Fowler, *A Season in Hell*, 126.

100 "Martyrs of Bosnia," Part 5, around 13′40″.

101 Nasiri, *Inside the Jihad*, 125; See also al-Bahri and Malbrunot, *Dans l'ombre*, 50.

102 Al-Amriiki, "The Story of an American Jihaadi – Part One," 55, 57; al-Hindukushi, "*Min Kabul ila Baghdad*"; Nasiri, *Inside the Jihad*, 139, 222; Collins, *My Jihad*, 11; Fowler, *A Season in Hell*, 33, 45. "Martyrs of Bosnia," Part 3, around 14′30″, Part 6 around 11′30″, and Part 7 around 2′30″; Sifaoui, "Infiltration," around 7′40″.

103 "Martyrs of Bosnia," Part 8, around 0′01″.

104 Al-Berry, *Life Is More Beautiful*, 15–16.

105 Fowler, *A Season in Hell*, 78.

106 Fadil Harun, who is not one to gloss over shortcomings among jihadis, derides the notion that mujahidin take drugs; Harun, *Al-Harb*, 2:113. Recently, however, Islamic State fighters in Iraq and Syria have reportedly used Captagon, a mild amphetamine; see Peter Holley, "The tiny pill fueling Syria's war and turning fighters into superhuman soldiers," *Washington Post*, November 19, 2015.

107 Ibid., 2:78, 121, 129.

108 Richard P. Mitchell, *The Society of the Muslim Brothers* (London: Oxford University Press, 1969), 292.

109 Al-Qandahari, *Dhikrayat*, 285–286.

110 A few individual militants have had tattoos predating their recruitment. For example, a Bosnian Islamist in Denmark had a picture of Usama bin Ladin tattooed on his chest; Skjoldager, *Truslen Indefra*, 194.

111 Peter Bergen writes of 9/11 mastermind Khalid Sheikh Mohammed: "In addition to supervising the planning and preparations for the 9/11 operation, KSM worked with and eventually led Al Qaeda's media committee. But KSM states he refused to swear a formal oath of allegiance to Bin Laden, thereby retaining a last vestige of his cherished autonomy"; Peter L. Bergen, *The Osama Bin Laden I Know: An Oral History of Al Qaeda's Leader* (New York: Free Press, 2006), 301.

112 Al-Bahri and Malbrunot, *Dans l'ombre*, 158.

113 Al-Amriiki, "The Story of an American Jihaadi – Part One," 70.
114 Laleh Khalili, *Heroes and Martyrs of Palestine: The Politics of National Commemoration* (Cambridge: Cambridge University Press, 2007), 32, 124–125.
115 "B*adr al-riyadh*" (The Badr of Riyadh); "*Yawmiyat mujahid*," Part 3.
116 For details on the original quote, see Robert Ellis, *The Games People Play: Theology, Religion, and Sport* (Cambridge: Lutterworth Press, 2014), 165.

Index

a cappella singing, 46–47, 63, 69
Abbasid Revolution, 90
Abbottabad, 22–23
Abd al-Ghafur, 159
Al-Abdurrahman, Shaykh, 149
ablution, 182–183
Abraham (prophet), 131, 133
Abu Abd al-Malik, 52–53
Abu Ali, 52–53
Abu Dhabi, 27
Abu Hudhayfa, 16, 49–50
Abu al-Joud, 68
Abu Malik, 79
Abu Ratib, 68, 71
Abu Zahra, Muhammad, 45–47
al-Adani, Umar, 191–192
adhan, 64
Adobe Premiere Pro, 115
advertising industry, 82
al-Afghani, Abu Maryam, 156
Afghanistan, 32–33, 141, 167–168,
    179
Afghan-Soviet war, 109
Africa, 11, 168
afterlife, 8
Ahwaz, 33
air travel, 10–11
Ajnad, 42–43
Alagha, Joseph, 3
al-Albani, Nasir al-Din, 46–47
Algakh, Hisham, 27
Ali, Muhammad, 46
al-Almani, Abu Musa, 110
Ambush at Bardal (2009), 124
American Hell in Afghanistan and Iraq
    (2003), 116
al-Amriki, Mansoor, 123–124
anashid, 6–7, 10, 14, 18
    aspects of, 18
    Harun on, 188–189

history of, 43–45
importance of, 42
interpersonal bonding from,
    76–77
by IS, 53–54, 60–62
about jihad, 43, 58, 73–79, 113
jihadi history of, 65–69
jihadi media on, 43
on jihadi websites, 52
jihadis on, 47–48, 73–79
lawfulness of, 45–48, 65
in Malaysia, 66–67
martyrdom and, 166
musicological examination of,
    69–73, 81
production of, 51–53
from al-Qaida, 77, 81
recording of, 73
as recreational practice, 188
recruitment with, 17, 68–69
requirements for, 46–47
rhythm of, 70, 74
topics of, 55, 59
utility of, 48–51, 62
in videos, 113
Anashid al-da'wa al-islamiyya (Anashid
    of the Islamic Call), 52
Al-Andalusi, Suraqah, 111–112
Ansar al-Mujahidin, 97, 104
The Anthology of Glory (*Diwan
    al-'izza*), 36–39
anti-Mubarak protests, 91
AQAP. *See* al-Qaida in the Arabian
    Peninsula
AQI. *See* Al-Qaida in Iraq
AQIM. *See* Al-Qaida in the Islamic
    Maghreb
al-Aqsa Intifada, 116–117
Arab League, 32–33
Arab Spring, 27, 74–75, 91

The Arab Supporters in Afghanistan
   (1988), 109–110
Arabic culture, classical period, 26–27
Arab-Israeli War, 67–68
Arif, Ihsan Hammu Siddiq, 157
Asia, 11
al-Assad, Bashar, 24–25
Atef, Mohammed, 142
Augustine of Hippo, 65, 78–79
austerity, 11–12
autodidacts, 35–36
al-Awlaqi, Anwar, 16–17, 42
awliya', 164
Al Awshan, Isa bin Sa'd, 36–39
Ayat al-rahman fi jihad al-afghan
   (Azzam), 157–158
Ayyash, Yahya, 162
Azzam, Abdallah, 110, 153
   martyrology developed by, 154–160,
      169
   obituaries of, 162–163
Azzam Publications, 111
Azzam.com, 112

"Bada'a al-masiru ila al-hadaf"
   (The March to Victory Has
   Begun), 57
Badr, Qari Badruzzaman, 147–148
Badr al-Riyadh, 53, 116, 118
al-Bagha, Iman Mustafa, 24–25
al-Baghdadi, Abu Bakr, 23, 25, 32, 54,
   91, 137
al-Bahlul, Ali Hamza, 114–115
Bahrain, 34
al-Bahri, Nasir, 186, 190, 198–199
Baily, John, 68
Baluch activists, 103
Basayev, Shamil, 99
Battle of Badr, 132
Battle of Uhud, 152
The Battles of Badr in Bosnia (1995),
   112–113
bay'a (pledging of allegiance), 198–199
al-bayan, 29
beards, 195
*The Beginning of the End: A Response
   to Barack Obama* (2009), 124
beheading, 8, 61–62, 117, 120
al-Benin, Masood, 110–111
Berg, Birgit, 66

Berg, Nicholas, 120
al-Berry, Khalid, 184–186
   on beards, 195
   soccer played by, 194
   on spitting to the left, 187
   on videos, 190
Bilal, 144–145
bin Abd Allah al-Ali, 32
bin Abdullah, Sulaiman, 46
bin Ladin, Usama, 16, 49–50, 53,
   95–96, 128
   Abu Malik praises of, 79
   death of, 22–23
   dream interpretation by, 137, 139,
      142–143
   fasting of, 186–187
   homage to, 104
   poetry of, 22, 29–32
   prayer by, 180
bin Ladin, Hamza, 29–30
bin Malik, Ka'b, 29
bin al-Shibh, Ramzi, 128
al-Bin'ali, Turki, 23, 34
Black Banners Studios, 110
black flags, 87–93, 95
Blakstone, 63
The Blaze of Truth (*Uwar al-haqq*)
   (Al-Nasr), 23–25, 33
The Blessed Dinsur Battle (2008),
   123
Boko Haram, 9–11, 13, 168
Bosnia, 15, 112, 156, 184
The Bouchaoui Attack (2007), 117
Bourti, Karim, 182, 184
Breaking the Silence (2015), 76–77
Breininger, Erich, 186–187
al-Bukhari, 134–135
al-Bustani, Fouad Ephreim, 43–44

Calvin, John, 65
Care International, 111
cassettes, 67–68
Caucasus Jihad, 91–92
Chechnya, 113–114
Chechnya: Destruction of a Nation
   (1999), 113
children, 48
chivalry, 35
Christian chant, 64
cigarettes, 197–198

classical period, 26–27
CNN, 163–164
Combating Terrorism Center at West
     Point, 83
Confessions (Augustine), 65, 78–79
Cook, David, 19, 146
corpses, 157, 162
Corrie, Rachel, 162
counternarratives, 18
A Course in the Art of Recruiting
     (al-Qaʻidi), 50
court documents, 174
Cozzens, Jeffrey, 4
Creswell, Robyn, 18
Crone, Manni, 3–4

Dabiq, 40
"Dafatir ʻala Hawamish al-Naksa"
     (Qabbani), 54
dance, 10, 198
Dantshke, Claudia, 16
Day of Resurrection, 153, 161
De Looijer, Gwynned, 19
Deir al-Zor, 24
"A Denunciation of Nationality"
     (al-Binʻali), 34
Deso Dogg, 79
*The Destruction of the American
     Destroyer USS Cole*, 114–115
devotional practice, 178–188
     ablution as, 182–183
     exorcism as, 187–188
     fasting as, 186–187
     invocations, 181–182
     prayer as, 178–180
     Qurʼan recitation as, 183–185
     weeping as, 185–186
"Diary of a Mujahid," 197
Dighlas, Abu Ubayda Abd al-Hadi,
     164–165
Diraz, Izzam, 109–110
"Dirty Kuffar," 63
divine intervention, 133
*Diwan al-ʻizza (The Anthology of
     Glory)*, 36–39
Doctors without Borders, 33
doctrine, 8–9, 16
Donahue, Katherine C., 144
dream interpretation, 7–8, 19, 135, 150
     authority in, 138

by bin Ladin, 137, 139, 142–143
formal framework for, 137
Freudian theory of, 141
importance of, 128–129
by jihadis, 149–150
modern practice of, 138–139
by Muhammad, 134
by Omar, 137
propaganda from, 140
prophesy from, 138
in Qurʼan, 131–133, 143
recreational practice of, 192–193
by Reid, 144
social practice of, 142
traditions of, 135
utility of, 138
warfare guidance from, 141
dream manuals, 135–138, 148–149
dreams, 128, 149–150
     of Hammami, 193
     influence of, 143
     in IS, 148
     in Islam, 129–130
     of martyrdom, 146
     Muhammad discussion of, 129,
          133–134, 144–145
     of Omar, 141–142
     paradise imagery in, 145, 147
     prophetic wisdom from, 134
     in Qurʼan, 130–133
     in Sufism, 149
     types of, 130, 144
     utility of, 144
dress and grooming, 195, 198
al-Durrah, Mohaʻmmed, 116–117

East Africa Embassy bombings, 115
Egyptian Islamic Jihad, 9–11
elegies, 24, 32
embassy, U.S., 50–51
*Encyclopaedia of the Martyrs of the
     Islamic Movement (Mawsuʼat
     shuhadaʼ al-haraka al-Islamiyya)*,
     162–163
"Epistle to the Scolders" (Al Awshan),
     36–38
execution, 8, 114, 124
exorcism, 187–188
*The Expedition of Shaykh Umar Hadid
     (2006)*, 121–122

Farmer, Henry George, 44, 66
fasting, 186–187
Fatah al-Islam, 4, 67–68
Fatih, Bahraini Muhammad, 193
festivities, 194
"Fi kull ard li'l-Ilahi fawaris" (In Every
    Land God Has Knights), 58
al-Filistini, Abu Qatada, 111
filmmaking, 1–3, 19
Fisk, Robert, 128
flags, 86
    black, 87–93, 95
    of IS, 87–91
    of jihadi groups, 91–93
    of al-Qaida, 88
    of Saudi Arabia, 88–90
    symbolism of, 88
Flames of War: Fighting Has Just Begun
    (2014), 125
Foreign Affairs, 22–23
Fouda, Yosri, 128, 140
Four Feathers Club, 111
Fowler, Robert, 183, 191, 193, 197
Free Syrian Army, 100
Freudian theory, 141
Al-Furqan, 119–120

Gauvain, Richard, 183
Genis, Daniel, 20–21
Ghaddafi, Muammar, 74–75
Gharib, 104–105
al-Gharib, Abu Usama, 23, 30–31
al-Ghazali, Muhammad, 45–47, 185
Ghazi, Sheikh Abdul Aziz, 147
al-Ghul, Imran Umar, 162–163
Ghunaym, Mahmud, 28
Gilsenan, Michael, 139
Global Islamic Media Front, 97
Golden Age of Islam, 90
graphic design, 104–105
grief, 161
Groupe Islamique Armée, 9–10
Groupe Salafiste pour la Prédication et
    le Combat (GSPC), 117
Gruen, Madeleine, 76
GSPC. *See* Groupe Salafiste pour la
    Prédication et le Combat
Guantanamo Bay, 114–115, 147–148
guerrilla warfare, 174
guns, 7–8

Hadid, Marwan, 31
hadith, 133–134, 152, 194
Hafez, Mohammed M., 145
Hallundbæk, Lars, 4
Hamas, 6, 9, 100, 162–163
    dress of, 195
    emblem of, 87–88
    martyrdom testaments in, 117–118
    recruitment by, 68–69
Hammami, Omar, 123–124, 185
    dreams of, 193
    on pledge ceremonies, 198–199
    at training camp, 188–189
Hamori, Andras, 37
Hanif, Umar, 158
Harakat al-Shabab al-Mujahidin, 85
al-Harath, Jaram, 148
Harun, Fadil, 48, 50–51, 180
    on *anashid*, 188–189
    on exorcism, 187
    poetry by, 190
    on recitation, 183–184
    remembrance by, 181
Haykel, Bernard, 18
Hell of the Apostates in Somalia (2006),
    123
Herding, Maruta, 3–4
Herr, Cheryl, 3
Hezbollah, 9–10, 84–85, 87–88, 161
Hilal, Hissa, 27
Homer, 44
horse imagery, 95–96, 159
houris, 153, 157
Hudaybiyya, Treaty of, 132
al-Husayn, 160–161

ibn Abd al-Wahhab, Muhammad,
    46–47
ibn Abdallah, Jabir, 144–145
Ibn Abi al-Dunya, 146
Ibn Ahmad, Khalaf, 136
Ibn Baz, 46–47
Ibn Jannat Jal, 158–159
Ibn Khattab, 99–100, 114, 121
Ibn Manzur, 43
Ibn al-Musayyab, 137
Ibn al-Nahhas al-Dumyati, 153–154
Ibn Qutayba, 136–138
Ibn Sirin, 136–137
Ibn Taymiyya, 168–169

iconography, 3, 18
Id al-Fitr, 194
identity-marking practices, 177–178,
      194–195
   dress and grooming as, 195–196
   manners as, 197
   noms de guerre as, 196
   slogans as, 196
ideology, 2–3
IED. *See* Improvised Explosive Device
Ilhaq bi'l-qafila (al-Zarqawi), 164–165
Iliad (Homer), 44
immolation, 39–40
Improvised Explosive Device (IED),
      118–119
"In Every Land God Has Knights"
      (*Fi kull ard li'l-Ilahi fawaris*), 58
inshad, 43–45
insignia, 87
Inspire (magazine), 101–102
intelligence services, 15–16
intercession, 154
Internet, 11, 74–75
   AQI campaign on, 118–120
   Iraqi groups presence on, 118–119
   martyrdom videos on, 112, 164
interrogation transcripts, 174
"*Intifadat al-Aqsa*," 162
Inventing the Muslim Cool (Herding),
      3–4
invocations
   prayer difference from, 181
   remembrance as, 181
   before suicide attacks, 181
   supplication as, 181–182
Iran, 151, 161
Iran-Iraq War, 161
Iraq, 34, 165
Iraq war, 102–103, 118–122, 164
al-Iraqi, Abu Asim, 159
IS. *See* Islamic State
Ishmael, 131
Islam
   discussion forums on, 74
   dreams in, 129–130
   flags of, 92–93
   history of, 7–8
   law of, 45–46
Islamic Jihad, 162–163
Islamic Maghreb, 9–10

Islamic State (IS), 8, 10–12, 42–43
   anashid by, 53–54, 60–62
   Caliphate of, 34
   dreams in, 148
   flag of, 87–91
   military campaigns by, 28
   poetess of, 23–25
   video production of, 109,
      125–126
Isra, 132
Israel, 6, 32–33, 116–117
istishhad (martyrdom-seeking), 59–60

jahiliyya, 44
Jama'a Islamiyya, 180, 183, 194
   manners of, 197
   weeping among, 185–186
Jamaat-ud-Dawa, 86
al-Jami' al-Sahih (al-Tirmidhi), 153
Jarrah, Ziad, 117–118
Jaysh-e Muhammad, 86
al-Jazeera, 163–164
Jewish extremists, 13
jihad
   anashid about, 43, 58, 73–79, 113
   contractual basis of, 152
   defences of, 36
   poetry of, 27–29, 35
   rap about, 124
   salvational brand of, 155
al-Jihad (journal), 155
Jihad in Dagestan (1999), 113
Jihadi Culture on the World Wide Web
      (Ramsey), 4
jihadi groups, 9–13
   flags of, 91–93
   music relationship to, 63
   online lives of, 12, 31
jihadi videos
   from AQI, 120–121
   from Chechnya, 113–114
   content of, 112–114
   distribution of, 111–112
   Iraq war and, 118–122
   media cells for, 120
   origins of, 109–110
   as propaganda, 108
jihadi wedding, 16
jihadis, 31–32, 37, 75
   on *anashid*, 47–48, 73–79

dream interpretation by, 149–150
emotional life of, 200
faith of, 199–200
orthodoxy of, 200
self alienation of, 30–31
teenage, 183
jihadism
aesthetic universe of, 2
cultural dimension of, 1–2, 4–9
explanation for, 14
romance of, 35
Jihadwal training camp, 179
Jundallah, 96, 103

al-Kabili, Abu al-Zubayr, 186
Kachins, 5
Kasasbeh, Mu'az, 39
Kashmir, 86
Kata'ib Hizballah, 85
Kendall, Elisabeth, 3
al-Khallal, 136
al-Khansa' Brigades, 25, 40
Khurshid, Hammad, 189
al-Kifah Refugee Center, 111
Kinberg, Leah, 134–135, 144, 146
Koranic recitations, 72
Ku Klux Klan, 200
Kulthum, Umm, 46–47
Kuwait, 91
al-Kuwaiti, Abu Hamza, 145
al-Kuwaiti, Abu Muadh, 146, 157

Lahoud, Nelly, 18, 72
Lal Masjid, 167
Leach, Edmund, 5
Liberation Tigers of Tamil Eelam
    (LTTE), 85
lion imagery, 98–99
"The Lion's Den" (al-Ma'sada), 29
Lions of the War (2005), 121
Lisan al-'Arab (Ibn Manzur), 43
"Lovers of Hoor" (video), 168
Lovers of Martyrdom (Azzam),
    110
LTTE. *See* Liberation Tigers of Tamil
    Eelam
Luqman, Umm, 48

ma' al-shuhada', 155
al-Madani, Abu Zubayr, 112

madih al-nabawi, 71
Mahmoud, Muhammad, 23
mahraqat, 114
Maktabah al-Ansar, 111
Malaysia, 66–67
"Al-Maliki Ghada Maqhura" (Al-Maliki
    Has Been Vanquished), 61
The Manhattan Raid (2006), 117
manners, 197
maqamat, 69–72
al-Maqdisi, Abu Muhammad, 31, 40
"The March to Victory Has Begun
    (Bada'a al-Masiru ila al-Hadaf),"
    57
marriage, 154, 156, 162
The Martyr Mohammed Aldura Street,
    116–117
martyrdom, 59–60, 102, 145, 151, 160,
    165, 167–168, 193
  anashid and, 166
  Azzam development of, 154–160,
    169
  classical meaning of, 151–152
  dreams of, 146
  Hamas testaments of, 117–118
  Internet videos of, 112, 164
  material process of, 151, 169–170
  mythology of, 153, 163–164
  in Pakistan, 167–168
  in Shi'ism, 160–161
  Somalian operations of, 168
  in Sunnism, 161
  weeping and, 186
martyrdom-seeking (*istishhad*), 59–60
martyrs, 19, 98–100, 121
Martyrs of Bosnia, 111–112, 190
Martyrs of the Confrontations (2003),
    116
martyr's wedding, 6–7, 199
al-Ma'sada ("The Lion's Den"), 29
al-Masri, Abu'l-Hassan, 139
Massacres in Chechnya (1999), 113
Matusky, Patricia, 66–67, 71
*Mawsu'at shuhada' al-haraka al-
    islamiyya* (Encyclopaedia of the
    Martyrs of the Islamic Movement),
    162–163
McCants, Will, 90
Mecca, 132, 178
Mehanna, Tarek, 121

microtonal intervals, 70
Militant Imagery Project, 83
military, U.S., 49
military campaigns, 28
military life, soft dimension of, 1–2,
    4–5
Millionaire Poet (*Sha'ir al-milyun*), 27
Minbar al-tawhid wa-l-jihad
    (al-Maqdisi), 31, 47, 94
miracles, 158
Mir'aj, 132
al-Misri, Abu Hafs, 50
Mittermaier, Amira, 140
monorhyme, 23–24
Monotheism and Jihad, 118–119
"Mother, Quit Crying" (*Ummahu
    khalli al-dam'a*), 59–60
Moussaoui, Zacarias, 142–143
"MTV jihadism," 123–124
Mu'assasat al-furqan li'l-intaj al-i'lami,
    54
mu'aththirat, 47
Muhammad (Prophet), 71
    authority of, 131–132
    dream interpretation by, 134
    dreams discussed by, 129, 133–134,
        144–145
    dress of, 195
Muhammed, Khalid Sheikh, 114
Mujahidin (Afghan), 68, 93–98,
    112–113
    music of, 76–77
    Qur'an recitation by, 179
The Mujahidin Brigade, 112–113
Munkar and Nakir, 153
munshid, 44
Musharraf, Pervez, 147
music, 1–3, 10, 18
    consumption of, 67
    history of, 78
    jihadi relationship to, 63
    legal status of, 63–65
    of Mujahidin, 76–77
Music in Everyday Life (DeNora), 75
The Music of Malaysia (Matusky and
    Tan), 66
musical instruments, 46, 64, 197–198
Muslim Brotherhood, 9, 46–47, 53,
    162–163, 198
My Brother the Islamist (2011), 197

Nairobi, 50–51
Nasiri, Omar, 191–192, 196
al-Nasr, Ahlam, 23–25, 28, 33, 35,
    39–41
nation-states, 32–35
Nazi Germany, 108
neo-Nazis, 13
The News International, 141
9/11 hijacker letter, 145, 182
The Nineteen Martyrs (2002), 116
Nobel Prize in Literature, 27
noms de guerre, 196
Northern Ireland, 3
Nusra Front, 90–91, 95–96

"O My Umma: Fighting is Now an
    Obligation" (*Ya Ummati Wajaba
    al-Kifah*), 53
Omar, Mullah, 128, 137, 141–142
online discussions, 74
oral traditions, 135–136
organizational identities, 83–87
Ostovar, Afshon, 3, 19
Otterbeck, Jonas, 68–69
Ottoman Empire, 46, 100
Oxford English Dictionary, 5

Pakistan, 4, 167–168
Palestine, 116–117, 162
Palestinian Second Intifada, 162–163
paradise imagery, 101–104, 145, 147
Pattani, 33
Pearl, Daniel, 117
Philby, H. St. John, 46
Pieslak, Jonathan, 3
Plato, 62
pledging of allegiance (bay'a), 198–199
Plett, Barbara, 147
"Poet of the People" (*Sha'ir al-Milyun*),
    27
poetry, 2–4, 6–7, 18
    of bin Ladin, 22, 29–32
    by Harun, 190
    history of, 26–27
    importance of, 22
    as recreational practice, 189–190
    role of, 22
political imagery, 83–84
political posters, 84
prayer, 178–180

bin Ladin practice of, 180
  invocations difference from, 181
  weeping during, 185
prison scars, 21
propaganda, 8, 10–11, 16, 50, 126
  dream interpretation as, 140
  imagery as, 82
  on Internet, 74–75
  by IS, 125
  jihadi videos as, 108
  paradise imagery in, 102–103
  themes of, 83
  videos for, 34, 173, 190–191
Protestant Reformation, 36
The Punisher (fictional character), 97–98

Qabbani, Nizar, 54
al-Qaida, 3–4, 8–10, 34
  allegiance to, 38
  anashid from, 77, 81
  flags of, 88
  internal document of, 42
  media cells of, 120
  media from, 47
  non-participant observation of,
    171–172
  pledging of allegiance to, 198–199
  recruitment to, 75–76
Al-Qaida in Iraq (AQI)
  Internet campaign of, 118–120
  videos from, 120–121
al-Qaida in the Arabian Peninsula
  (AQAP), 87–88, 90–91
Al-Qaida in the Islamic Maghreb
  (AQIM), 183
al-Qa'idi, Abu Amru, 50
al-Qandahari, Abu Ja'far al-Masri, 20
Qanita, Muhammad Ahmad, 100–101
al-Qaradawi, Yusuf, 46–47, 53
Qariban, qariban, tarawna al-'ajiba
  (Soon, Soon, You Shall 61–62 See
  Something Wondrous)
Al-Qassam Brigade of Hamas, 100
al-Qatari, Abu Zayd, 157
Qoqaz.net, 113
Qur'an, 26, 44, 101
  combat recitation, 184
  dream interpretation in, 131–133, 143
  dreams in, 130–133
  Mujahidin recitation of, 179

  recitation of, 50, 183–185
Qusi (Shaykh), 140
Qutb, Amina, 52
Qutb, Muhammad, 47
Qutb, Sayyid, 31, 46–47, 52

Racy, Ali Jihad, 70–71
radicalization, 18
Ramadan, 180, 184, 186
Ramsey, Gilbert, 4, 12
al-Rantisi, Abd al-Aziz, 162
Raqqa, 25, 39–41
al-Rasas, Azifat, 47
Razeq, Abdul, 190, 193
rebel groups, 6
recording technology, 72–73
recreational practice, 177–178
  anashid as, 188
  dream interpretation as, 192–193
  festivities as, 194
  poetry as, 189–190
  sports as, 194
  storytelling as, 191–192
  video watching as, 190–191
recruitment, 15–16, 108
  with *anashid*, 17, 68–69
  by Hamas, 68–69
  to al-Qaida, 75–76
Red Mosque, 147
Redacted (2007), 80
Reid, Richard, 142–144
remembrance, 181
Republic (Plato), 62
ribat, 34
Rih al-janna (Winds of Paradise), 50
Rishawi, Sajida, 156
al-Riyyashi, Ra'im, 162–163
Robson, James, 65
al-Rumaysa, 144–145
rural base, 11–12, 174–177
Russian Hell in the Year 2000, 113–114,
  116, 123

safe house, 11–12, 174–177
Sageman, Marc, 16
al-Sahab, 47, 50, 53, 78, 115
  early productions of, 114–118
  goals of, 118
  innovations by, 116–117
  protagonists in, 126

sahaba, 164
al-Sa'idi, Muhannad, 119–120
Salafi-jihadism, 151, 168
salafism, 3–4, 9–12, 149, 157–158,
     169, 200–201
Salim, Mamdouh Mahmud, 115
Al-Salman, Shaykh, 149
sama', 45
Satan, 187
Saudi Arabia, 88–90
     Ministry of Information in, 52–53
     al-Qaida in, 11
     sheikhs in, 27
Sawt al-Jihad, 36
Sawt al-Yaman, 52–53
Sawyer, Diane, 27
Sayigh, Yezid, 67–68
Sayyaf, Abd Rabb al-Rasul, 109–110
scolders, 37–38
Second Chechen War, 110–111, 113
Sen, Ibrahim, 148
Sepah-e Sahabah-e Iran, 91–92
sexuality, 145, 183, 197–198
al-Shabab, 20, 87–88, 122–124
Shabakat al-Mujahidin al-Iliktruniyya
     (website), 55
Sha'ir al-Milyun ("Millionaire Poet"),
     27
al-Shami, Abu Anas, 164–165
al-Shami, Abu Usama, 47–48
Sharia Law, 141, 164
al-Sharqi, Abu Dujana, 68, 187
Shehata, Salih, 162
Shi'ism, 9, 151, 160–161
Shiloah, Amnon, 66
shoe bombs, 143–144
al-Sifaoui, Mohamed, 184
signaling theory, 14–15
Sipah-e Sahaba, 86
Sirriyeh, Elizabeth, 146
slogans, 196
soccer, 194
social media, 31
Solomon, 44
The Solution (Azzam), 110
al-Somali, Muhammad Ali, 155–156
Song of Songs (Solomon), 44
"Soon, Soon, You Shall 61–62 See
     Something Wondrous" *(Qariban,
     Qariban, Tarawna al-'Ajiba)*,

sports, 194
     hadith encouragement of, 194
     soccer, 194
state building, 43, 60–62
State of the Umma, 114–115
"Statement of the World Islamic Front
     for Jihad against Jews and
     Crusaders" (al-Qaida), 8
Stenersen, Anne, 19
Stern, Jessica, 4
storytelling, 191–192
Sudan, 32–33
Sufism, 19, 149, 157–158, 164, 169,
     185
     dreams in, 149
     influence of, 200–201
suicide attacks, 156, 167
     in Africa, 168
     behavior before, 173
     invocations before, 181
     targets of, 167–168
suicide bombers, 50–51, 121,
     126–127
Sunday Times, 145
Sunnism, 9, 151, 155, 161, 178
supplication, 181–182
Sura 37:105, 131
Surah of the Poets, 26
al-Suwaylim, Samir Salih Abdallah,
     99–100
Sykes-Picot agreement, 32
Syria, 8, 32–33
Syrian civil war, 12

Taarnby, Michael, 4
tabl khanah, 65
tahdid, 55–57
tahrid, 55–57
al-Tajdid, 53
takbir, 196
Talhah, Aboo, 144–145
Taliban, 69, 87
Tan Sooi Beng, 66–67, 71
taranas, 69
tarawih, 180
tawhid, 47
al-Tawhid wa'l-Jihad, 91–92, 100
technological change, 10–11, 119
terrorist chic, 3
theater, 198

theology, 3, 35–39
time, 10–11
al-Tirmidhi, 153
Touma, Habib, 69–70
Tracts on Listening to Music (Robson), 65
Treaty of Hudaybiyya, 132
Triumph of the Will (1935), 108
trustworthiness, 15–16
Tsouli, Yunus, 119
al-Tunsi, Mohibb al-Shaykhain, 119
al-Turki, Adib Sa'di Dhu al-Qarnayn, 156

Uighurs, 13
Uka, Arid, 79–80
Ummah.com, 74
"Ummahu khalli al-dam'a" (Mother, Quit Crying), 59–60
Unshudat al-Shuhada', 52
Urdu, 13
USS Cole video (2000), 115–117
Uthaymin, Ibn, 46–47
Uwar al-ḥaqq (*The Blaze of Truth*) (Al-Nasr), 23–25, 33

vetting, 14–15
visual culture, 19, 84, 106–107
    evolution of, 104
    horse imagery in, 95–96
    themes of, 82–83, 93–101
visual networks, 83
    casual types of, 85
    organizational identities and, 83–87

Wahhabism, 46–47
al-wala' wa'l-bara', 168–169
warfare, 141
wedding ceremonies, 49
weeping, 13–14, 19
    commonality of, 185
    among Jama'a Islamiyya, 185–186
    martyrdom and, 186
    during prayer, 185
Weimann, Gabriel, 76
The West and The Dark Tunnel (video), 72, 77
Western culture, 74–75
White House, 143
The Wills of the Heroic Martyrs of the Two Holy Cities (2003), 116
Winds of Paradise (*Rih al-Janna*), 50
The Winds of Victory (2004), 120–121
women, 25, 40, 156
World Trade Center attacks, 29
World War One, 32

Ya Ummati Wajaba al-Kifah (O My Umma: Fighting is Now an Obligation), 53
al-Yamani, Abu Mansur, 188–189
Yarmuk Magazine, 91–92
Yassin, Ahmad, 162
Youtube, 108
Yusufzai, Rahimullah, 128, 141–142

Zahab, Mariam Abou, 147
al-Zarqawi, Abu Mus'ab, 34, 118–119, 163–166
al-Zuhayri, Muhammad, 34